PHOENIX, SCOTTSDALE, SEDONA & CENTRAL ARIZONA

Great Destinations

D0030379

FIRST EDITION

PHOENIX, SCOTTSDALE, SEDONA & CENTRAL ARIZONA

Great Destinations

Christine Bailey

The Countryman Press
Woodstock, Vermont

To my sons Darrell and Nolan, may all your dreams come true.

ISBN 978-1-58157-044-1

Cover photo © Blue Agave Photography, LLC
Interior photos by the author unless otherwise specified
Book design Bodenweber Design
Page composition by Chelsea Cloeter
Maps by Mapping Specialists, Ltd., Madison, WI, © The Countryman Press

Published by The Countryman Press, P.O. Box 748, Woodstock, Vermont 05091

Distributed by W. W. Norton & Company, Inc., 500 Fifth Ave., New York, NY 10110

Printed in the United States of America

10 9 8 7 6 5 4 3 2 1

Recommended by *National Geographic Traveler* and *Travel + Leisure* magazines.

[A] CRISP AND CRITICAL APPROACH, FOR TRAVELERS WHO WANT TO LIVE LIKE LOCALS. — *USA Today*

Great Destinations™ guidebooks are known for their comprehensive, critical coverage of regions of extraordinary cultural interest and natural beauty. The authors in this series are professional travel writers who have lived for many years in the regions they describe. Each title in this series is continuously updated with each printing to insure accurate and timely information. All the books contain more than one hundred photographs and maps.

Current titles available:

THE ADIRONDACK BOOK

ATLANTA

AUSTIN, SAN ANTONIO & THE TEXAS HILL COUNTRY

THE BERKSHIRE BOOK

BIG SUR, MONTEREY BAY & GOLD COAST WINE COUNTRY

CAPE CANAVERAL, COCOA BEACH & FLORIDA'S SPACE COAST

THE CHARLESTON, SAVANNAH & COASTAL ISLANDS BOOK

THE CHESAPEAKE BAY BOOK

THE COAST OF MAINE BOOK

COLORADO'S CLASSIC MOUNTAIN TOWNS: GREAT DESTINATIONS

THE FINGER LAKES BOOK

GALVESTON, SOUTH PADRE ISLAND & THE TEXAS GULF COAST

THE HAMPTONS BOOK

HONOLULU & OAHU: GREAT DESTINATIONS HAWAII

THE HUDSON VALLEY BOOK

LOS CABOS & BAJA CALIFORNIA SUR: GREAT DESTINATIONS MEXICO

THE NANTUCKET BOOK

THE NAPA & SONOMA BOOK

PALM BEACH, MIAMI & THE FLORIDA KEYS

PHOENIX, SCOTTSDALE, SEDONA & CENTRAL ARIZONA

PLAYA DEL CARMEN, TULUM & THE RIVIERA MAYA: GREAT DESTINATIONS MEXICO

SALT LAKE CITY, PARK CITY, PROVO & UTAH'S HIGH COUNTRY RESORTS

SAN DIEGO & TIJUANA: GREAT DESTINATIONS

SAN JUAN, VIEQUES & CULEBRA: GREAT DESTINATIONS PUERTO RICO

THE SANTA FE & TAOS BOOK

THE SARASOTA, SANIBEL ISLAND & NAPLES BOOK

THE SEATTLE & VANCOUVER BOOK: INCLUDES THE OLYMPIC PENINSULA, VICTORIA & MORE

THE SHENANDOAH VALLEY BOOK

TOURING EAST COAST WINE COUNTRY

If you are traveling to, moving to, residing in, or just interested in any (or all!) of these enchanting regions, a Great Destinations guidebook is a superior companion. Honest and painstakingly critical, full of information only a local can provide, Great Destinations guidebooks give you all the practical knowledge you need to enjoy the best of each region. Why not own them all?

Acknowledgments

More than research and writing went into making this book a reality. For all of the little steps and side trips that came before this book ever came to be—I have several people to thank. My parents for their encouragement, my sister for her excitement about everything I ever wrote, my friends (old and new) for listening to my dreams, my mentors, going back as far as I can remember, for their "way to gos," my sons for inspiring me to be nothing less than my best, and my husband for saying what I needed to hear exactly when I needed to hear it, and believing in me and my dreams even when I wasn't so sure.

This book has been a collaborative effort. Thank you to all of you who shared with me your favorite pieces of the Valley and of Arizona; this is your book. I want to say a special thank-you to Linda and Mike for sharing with me their 30-plus years of exposure to all the state has to offer; some of the best places are in here because of their suggestions.

Thank you to those who took the time to share your knowledge—to Bluebird for sharing his passion for Arizona's prehistoric peoples; to Jeff H. and Jeff S. at Detours for carting me around on their tours and reminding me that I haven't seen a third of what the Valley has to offer, let alone the state. To the Piper Center at ASU and all the *amazing* people there who love books and writing as much as I do. One can never have too much inspiration. To the convention and visitor bureaus around the Valley for answering my questions, sending me information, and then sending some more. To Jana Bommersbach for an amazing magazine-writing class and for writing an excellent sidebar on Arizona's Outrageous Women—I think she's one of them! To Cori Brett for my first writer-to-writer conversation after the book deal was sealed; thank you! (Read her insightful sidebar on the great goings-on here in the Valley and take your golf experiences to a new level.)

The biggest thanks goes to Kim Grant, Jennifer Thompson, and The Countryman Press for your confidence in me, and your patience as I navigated the book-writing path; and especially to my editor, Laura Jorstad, for making my best efforts better! Writing this book was a wonderful experience, and partnering with such an incredible team made it even better. Thank you.

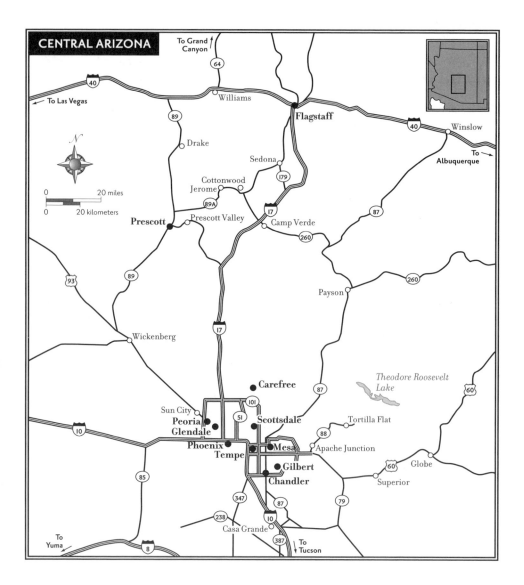

CENTRAL ARIZONA

To Grand Canyon

To Las Vegas ←

Williams

Flagstaff

Winslow

To Albuquerque →

Drake

Sedona

Cottonwood
Jerome

Prescott

Prescott Valley

Camp Verde

Payson

Wickenberg

Carefree

Theodore Roosevelt
Lake

Sun City

Peoria
Glendale

Scottsdale

Tortilla Flat

Phoenix
Tempe

Mesa

Apache Junction

Gilbert

Globe

Chandler

Superior

Casa Grande

To Yuma

To Tucson

Contents

Introduction 11

The Way This Book Works 12

I
History
Taming the Desert
14

2
Transportation
By Horse, Of Course
25

3
Phoenix
In the Valley of the Sun
42

4
Scottsdale
Fountain Hills, Paradise Valley, Cave Creek, Carefree
111

5
Tempe and the East Valley
Mesa, Gilbert, Chandler, Apache Junction and Queen Creek
139

6
Glendale and the West Valley
Surprise, Litchfield, Goodyear, Avondale, and the Sun Cities
168

7
Sedona
The Red Rock Vortex
190

8

SIDE TRIPS
Roaming the Desert
214

9

GOLF COURSES & SPAS
Relax and Play in the Desert
231

10

INFORMATION
Where, Why, When, What, and How
252

GENERAL INDEX   267

LODGING BY PRICE AND LOCATION   278

DINING BY PRICE AND LOCATION   281

DINING BY CUISINE   284

MAPS
   Central Arizona 8
   Arizona Access 26
   Central Arizona Access 27
   Valley of the Sun 28
   Phoenix 44
   Downtown Phoenix 45
   Downtown Scottsdale 112
   East Valley 140
   West Valley 170
   Sedona 192
   Side Trips 216

Introduction

If 8 years in Arizona doesn't make me a native, then the 20-plus years of listening to my father—born in Tucson in 1955 at St. Mary's Hospital—does. Less than a year old, living on a plot of land as wild as any desert you'll see today, with a swamp cooler to stave off the humid monsoon weather, he started forming the impressions that he would later pass on to his midwestern family. It would take him almost 43 years (with mere visits in between) to return for good—and in the process to bring all of us with him.

He instilled in us a sense of adventure, an excitement for exploration, and an apprecia-tion for all things Arizonan—from the snakes, spiders, and scorpions to the pungent smell of wet creosote after a summer rain. My oldest son, born in Chandler, Arizona, in 2002, already knows that while all snakes are amazing creatures, we cannot always tell which ones are poisonous and which ones aren't—and so we step around them with respect and awe. They are our neighbors.

In a state where climate is considered a commodity, it is no surprise that Arizona attracts more than 25 million visitors each year. From border to border, our state boasts one natural wonder after another—the Petrified Forest in the Painted Desert, the Grand Canyon, Organ Pipe National Forest, Kartchner Caverns, and Tonto Natural Bridge State Park, to name only a few. Even residents of Arizona—a whopping 33 percent of Ari-zona's tourists each year—travel the state on weekends searching for something new to do and see. And they are never disappointed. Art galleries, museums, historic sites, resorts, restaurants, natural parks, monuments, and shops stretch from the Arizona–Mexico border north through Tombstone, Bisbee, Tucson, Coolidge, Casa Grande, Chan-dler, Tempe, Glendale, Payson, Yuma, Prescott, Sedona, Camp Verde, Flagstaff, Winslow, Lake Havasu, and Page— and this list is but a sampling of the cities and towns and landmarks, each rich with history, culture, and geographic charm, nestled among the foothills, mountains, and deserts that cover the state.

Horny toad.

But perhaps the Valley of the Sun—home to Phoenix, the fifth largest city in the United States and the capital of Arizona—can be considered repre-sentative of all that is Arizonan. Located in the heart of the Sonoran Desert, within half a day's drive of any given point of interest, the Valley is a multifaceted jewel of emerald golf courses, sapphire skies, and the amber and ruby rays of breathtaking sunsets.

Currently more than 12,000 people flock monthly to the Phoenix metro area alone, and the famous saying of John B. L. Soule (or Horace Greeley—wherever you may have "heard" it first)—"Go west young man, and grow up with the country"—still rings true. They are the young, the old, and the active, and perhaps they, too, have found what they've been looking for. With so much to offer, Arizona might just be your little spot of happiness. So whether you're here for a romantic vacation, visiting for a 3-day conference with only a couple of hours to spare, or here to stay, we hope that you find this book full of possibility and your time here—an adventure.

THE WAY THIS BOOK WORKS

For your convenience this book has been divided into regions and cities within the Phoenix metropolitan area—known to locals as the Valley of the Sun. You will find 10 chapters: History, Transportation, Phoenix, Scottsdale, Tempe and the East Valley, Glendale and the West Valley, Sedona, Side Trips, Golf Courses & Spas, and Information, which provides important details to help you better enjoy your stay in Arizona.

While Arizona has a history that spans millennia, the Valley lay dormant between the mid–15th and the latter part of the 19th centuries. Upon the arrival of the US cavalry at Fort McDowell in the late 1800s, the Valley was once again inhabited and has grown exponentially since. Read the History chapter for a look at the evolution of Greater Phoenix and Jana Bommersbach's great sidebar on Outrageous Arizona Women; and check out the Information chapter for several books that'll tell you more about our state's past.

Most people tend to stay and visit in one particular part of the Valley. So our goal was to create an easily navigable book that provides important information about what to do, see, and visit in the particular area you've chosen. But we also wanted to highlight activities, restaurants, and sites in other parts of the Valley that you might enjoy during your stay. For instance, if you choose to spend most of your time in Scottsdale, you might also head to downtown Phoenix for the theater or a baseball game. If you're in town to see a Phoenix Cardinals game at University of Phoenix Stadium in Glendale, you'll probably choose to experience the area from the West Valley; however, you may want to check out the Phoenix Zoo and Desert Botanical Garden on the Phoenix–Tempe border. The Valley of the Sun is connected by a comprehensive highway system, making it easy to travel to any part. So feel comfortable in planning visits to other cities. You'll find information about navigating our highway systems in the Transportation chapter.

Phoenix is the largest part of the region. For this reason, you will find the most comprehensive view of the Valley in chapter 3, Phoenix. Here we'll introduce you to Greater Phoenix and all it has to offer, making it easier for you to choose where to stay and what to do. For instance, you will find that seven of the Valley's cities host spring training baseball teams. You will notice that the Phoenix Cardinals (NFL) and the Phoenix Coyotes (NHL) play in Glendale, while the Phoenix Suns (NBA) and Arizona Diamondbacks (MLB) play in downtown Phoenix. You'll discover that the area's largest university (Arizona State) is in Tempe, and that the third largest city in the state is Mesa. You'll learn where to go to find the poshest restaurants, the best nightlife, and some of the most affordable hotel prices. When you turn to the corresponding regional chapter (Scottsdale, Tempe and the East Valley, or Glendale and the West Valley), you'll find the lodging and dining options unique to that particular area. You will also find cultural, recreational, and shopping experiences.

The Sedona and Side Trips chapters feature information, maps, and best bets for exploring the rest of the state. As a top tourist destination in the country, Sedona has so many wonderful things to offer that it warranted a chapter of its own. But don't underestimate the charm and draw of the old mining towns of Jerome and Bisbee. These little communities have reinvented themselves as artist magnets, and you will find information about them in our Side Trips chapter. Since Arizona is the Grand Canyon State, we thought it important to include information about a trip to one of the world's seven natural won-

Saguaro ribs.

ders. You will also read about Prescott (home of the world's oldest rodeo), Tucson (Spanish influences abound in the Old Pueblo), and the Pima Air and Space Museum.

Arizona has some of the best golfing and spas in the country, and we thought it was important to include a separate chapter that pulls out a variety of experiences and price ranges of each in Central Arizona. Here you'll find not only some of the best courses, but some inexpensive ones, too and you'll also get a quick look at what makes them unique. Read Cori Brett's sidebar, Golf on the Cutting Edge. Some of the Valley's best spas have been included, too, and you'll get a feel for which ones will give you the experience you're looking for.

In Information, you'll find important phone numbers; an overview of our weather and surviving in it; and a bibliography of great books by Arizonans and about Arizona. If you're only here for a few days, check out the Best Bets section of this chapter for a list of must-sees and must-dos.

1

HISTORY

Taming the Desert

Arizona is defined by its landscape, its weather, its temperatures, its large beauties and little charms. From the bold and indefinable beauty of the Grand Canyon to the buttery bloom of the saguaro cactus, Arizona encompasses untold beauty and undiscovered adventures. Arizona is blue skies and layered sunsets, tall mountains and sweeping plains, saguaro cacti and pine forests, raging waterfalls and dry riverbeds, it is ski resorts and saunas, rugged climbs and poolside naps—it is both the yin and the yang.

Defined by its mild winters and hot summers, its cool redrock buttes and Sonoran Desert, Central Arizona is no different. Many visitors from big cities like Chicago, New York, and LA are surprised to learn that they can drive 20 minutes to the South Mountain Preserve and lose themselves in 26,000 acres of desert and rolling hills. Or they can just as easily use those 20 minutes to reach downtown Phoenix and hear the Phoenix Symphony Orchestra, or watch a Broadway play, or see the Diamondbacks play at Chase Field. It is amazing how much of the city you can actually see—its spectacular views quickly diminishing any urban claustrophobia. Mild winters, hot, hot summers, a beautiful jumble of luxury spas and tough mountain climbs, a place where nature is still very much a part of the environment—the Valley of the Sun won't be losing its desert charm anytime soon.

If you're here to find chic, metropolitan experiences, don't bother—locals are known to wear shorts to Symphony Hall. If you've come to find that beautiful space between urban and rural—the carefully selected best of both worlds—then welcome to Arizona. We trust that you will find what you're looking for.

HOW THE LAND CAME TO BE

The land that forms our state was once the Sea of Cortez. Over billions of years, the waters receded, and the bare granite rock gave way beneath the ferocity of wind and rain, revealing layers of geological history and forming three distinct geographic zones—Basin and Range, Mountain, and Plateau.

The largest of these geographic systems—Basin and Range—covers the southwestern and south-central region of the state and encompasses Tucson and Phoenix in the Sonoran Desert. It comprises alternating spaces of flat desert and mountaintops that reach high enough off the desert floor to support forests of ponderosa pine. The second largest system, Mountain, divides northern and southern Arizona. This higher elevation is cooler and

Photo provided courtesy of San Marcos

lusher. Here you'll find meadows and thick forests; the picturesque towns of Flagstaff, Prescott, Jerome, and Sedona; and the highest point in the state, Mount Humphreys, in the San Francisco Mountains north of Flagstaff. The third system, Plateau, extends north from the Mogollon Rim—itself a sheer cliff face that reaches heights of 2,000 feet and stretches a third of the way across the state—to cover northern Arizona. Named the Colorado Plateau, this geological region is shared by Arizona's fellow Four Corner states (Colorado, New Mexico, and Utah). It encompasses a series of vast plateaus and deep canyons, the largest and most magnificent of which is the Grand Canyon.

Geographically speaking, Arizona is all over the map, and it's the drastic changes in elevation—from 100 feet above sea level to better than 12,500—that allows for this variety. *Arizona Highways* published an article and photo essay in December 2002 called "A Land for All." It accurately matched landscape shots in Arizona with "twin scenes" in each of the other 49 states, from Vermont to Hawaii and everywhere in between. It has often been said that to drive from Phoenix to Flagstaff is the equivalent of driving from Mexico to Canada: 1,500 miles. And it can all be found within 114,000-plus square miles of what people have come to know as the "desert."

EARLY PEOPLE

The earliest settlers arrived in Arizona somewhere between 20,000 and 40,000 years ago. Back then the state was cooler and wetter, and large game like mammoth wandered the region. These paleo-Indians, as they are called, were hunters and gatherers who left behind

Lower cliff dwellings above Roosevelt Lake at Tonto National Monument.

petroglyphs and arrowheads to mark their passage. From the paleo-Indians evolved perhaps the most interesting of Central Arizona's earliest inhabitants, the Hohokam—a Pima
Indian word meaning "those who have gone."

The Hohokam (pronounced *hoho-KAM*), who settled in the Salt River Valley several hundred years BC, started out in small farming groups. Eventually the number of inhabitants
expanded into the thousands; by then the Hohokam had developed hundreds of miles of
canals to support their farms. In the early part of the 15th century, for reasons unknown,
the Hohokam and various descendants who had settled in surrounding areas—the Salado to
the east and the Sinagua to the north—mysteriously disappeared. Whether it was a long
period of drought that hampered their efforts to create life in the desert, or a series of economic and political problems, archaeologists cannot agree. But after they left the Valley
behind, their canals dusted over with age and neglect, and the area remained dormant for
the better part of 400 years.

The Hohokam's influence on the area can be seen to this day, in the Native Americans
who are considered their descendants as well as in the Salt River Valley where Phoenix and
its neighbors grow and thrive, supported by the original irrigation ditches the Hohokam
dug some 2,000 years ago.

MODERN NATIVE AMERICANS

The Hohokam, Salado, and Sinagua who had originally farmed the land were gradually
replaced by the tribes the Spaniards and Anglos met several hundred years later when they
first arrived in Central Arizona—the Apache, Yavapai, and Pima Indians.

The Apache are said to have settled into the Southwest about 1400 AD, slightly overlap-
ping the earlier Central Arizona tribes. They were hunter-gatherers who originally saw no
need for farming or irrigation. The Yavapai Indians, assumed by many to be the descendants of the earlier Sinagua people, settled in the Verde Valley, and the Pima Indians, who

consider themselves descendants of the Hohokam, farmed in the Gila River Valley south of Phoenix.

Today Native Americans represent 19 tribes on 23 reservations—27 percent of the state's 114,000 square miles. The Greater Phoenix area includes the Gila River Indian Community's 650 square miles south of the city, with 12,000 people, three casinos, the Firebird International Raceway, Wild Horse Pass Resort and Spa, and, the most recent addition, Rawhide Western Town. The Salt River Pima–Maricopa Indian Community, meantime, is surrounded by Scottsdale to the west, Fountain Hills on the north, and Mesa to the south. You'll find shops along these boundaries selling cigarettes and other goods free of state tax; the largest shopping center on Native American land in the country, the 140-acre Pavilions on Indian Bend Road west of the Loop 101; two golf courses, Cypress and Talking Stick; and two casinos at Indian Bend and McKellips Roads, both off Loop 101.

SOCIAL HISTORY

Theories abound as to how Arizona got its name, including the mispronunciation of an Indian word by Spanish explorers. The Spaniards arrived in the mid-16th century, led by Francisco Vásquez de Coronado on his infamous search for the cities of gold thought to be scattered across the region. What they found instead was desert, which some stories say they aptly named Arizona or "arid zone." For almost 300 years, the Spaniards swept through Arizona, establishing missions and forts and claiming the area for their monarchy.

While Tucson and its southern neighbors served as settlements for the European new-comers, Central Arizona remained largely untouched but for the occasional traveler. After

Majestic saguaro cacti.

almost 300 years of Spanish influence, Mexico won its independence in 1821 and quickly clashed with the Americans (in their quest to claim the continent from coast to coast). After the 2-year Mexican-American War, the Treaty of Guadalupe Hidalgo was signed, identifying the area as American territory; and in 1854 the United States expanded the territory by including what is now the southern strip of Arizona and New Mexico in the Gadsden Purchase.

In 1861, as the rest of the country was entangled in the Civil War, Tucson, the largest settlement at the time, was under constant bombardment from Apache warriors. Without the support of Union soldiers, who had been withdrawn to fight in the East, territorial residents were left to their own devices and voted to form a new territory of the Confederacy. The Confederate government agreed and quickly set up protection. For a short time the region was considered part of the South, until June 1862 when mountain man Kit Carson, along with a regiment of Union soldiers, arrived from California to reclaim the area, making the Battle at Picacho Pass the westernmost conflict of the Civil War. The acquisition led to Arizona becoming its own territory on February 24, 1863.

In response to the Apache raids upon local mines and encampments, the US Army established Fort McDowell on the Verde River, about 18 miles north of the Salt River. The fort and its soldiers needed goods, and suppliers arrived to fill those needs, including John Y. T. Smith who built the first home in the Valley after the Hohokam's disappearance, and shortly thereafter Jack Swilling, a shady character and Civil War veteran who fought on both sides of the Mason Dixon line. It was Swilling who recognized the value of the irrigation ditches left behind by the Hohokam almost 350 years before; he began cleaning the canals in 1867. Within less than a year the Swilling Irrigation and Canal Company was operational, creating a fertile oasis in the middle of the desert. As settlers arrived, they needed a name for this place they now called home. At the suggestion of self-proclaimed "Lord" Darrell Duppa from England, the Valley was dubbed *Phoenix* after the mythical bird that arose from its own ashes, just as this new town had arisen from the dust of a past.

After the first post office was established in 1869, Phoenix remained a frontier town for quite some time. At the center of the state, far from its sister cities of Tucson, Bisbee, and Tombstone to the south and Prescott and Flagstaff to the north, Phoenix existed unto itself without even a set of railroad tracks passing through. Anything the settlers needed had to be built, invented, or brought in by horse and wagon—a long and tedious journey. The desolation dictated much of life in the late 19th century, influencing everything from area architecture and construction to farming and clothing. Still, the harsh desert encouraged innovation, too.

In 1871, Phoenix was named the seat of Maricopa County; Prescott remained the capital of the territory, as it had been since 1863. As the town grew and new settlers arrived—drawn by the warm weather and the promise of hearty farmland—the canal system expanded. In 1885 the Arizona Canal Company completed the Arizona Canal. This addition became the first expansion beyond the Hohokam's original irrigation system.

In the late 1870s a transcontinental railroad passed through Maricopa, a small town 30 miles to the south of Phoenix, finally providing almost direct access to the area by rail. A stagecoach and freight wagon route carried supplies to and from the station until 1887, when the Maricopa–Phoenix line was completed and opened July 4, finally connecting Phoenix to the rest of the country.

The advent of the railroad significantly influenced Phoenix, introducing new products and creating new opportunities for growth and expansion. In 1889 Phoenix became the ter-

Roosevelt Dam was completed in 1912.

ritory's capital and home to territorial, federal, and county offices. With the influx of government agencies came a flurry of building as settlers sought to support the growing infrastructure.

While Phoenix offered great opportunity for farmers and their families, opportunities were not equal for all ethnic groups. Native Americans suffered the indignity of curfews and the opening of the Indian School to facilitate the "Americanization" of those under the employ of European landowners. Hispanics and Chinese fleeing discrimination in other regions were relegated to their own communities and religious institutions. Yet from this checkered past Phoenix has risen to host a variety of ethnic groups that celebrate their heritage and history throughout the region.

The desert offered up a number of challenges, but the flexibility and frontier attitude of those who moved to the area for a new life created opportunities. Instead of succumbing to the desert, early residents of the Valley built an infrastructure that would eventually grow to support more than a million people. The summers were hot, and a combination of floods and droughts wreaked havoc on residents and structures alike. Wrestling with Mother Nature in the same battle that the Hohokam eventually abandoned, residents fought the heat and the ebb and flow of water. Relying on their entrepreneurial fervor and desire to survive, they sought new ways to deal with age-old problems. With the creation of the Indian Bend Wash in Scottsdale and dam projects like the Roosevelt Dam at the confluence of the Salt River and Tonto Creek northeast of the city, Valley residents found ways to tame the wild floodwaters that gave the area life—while still keeping enough in reserve to outlast the droughts. Roosevelt Dam was the area's first reliable flood-control system and source of hydroelectric power. The construction of the dam created a 16,000-acre reservoir. A combination of technology and innovation created opportunities for the Valley's new residents and accomplished what the Hohokam could not: control (or at least the appearance of it) over the ebb and flow of water in the Valley—an oasis in the desert.

By the turn of the 20th century, several other agricultural and support communities had established themselves, including Mesa, Tempe, Scottsdale, Glendale, and Peoria; by the end of the first decade, 11,000 people called Phoenix home. On February 14, 1912, Arizona was admitted to the Union as the 48th state and dubbed the Valentine State.

World War I heralded an increased demand for cotton—for uniforms, tires, and airplane fabric—and the Salt River Valley's unique weather created an ideal environment. Farmers changed their fields over to cotton, which became one of the Valley's major commodities and one of Arizona's five C's (cotton, cattle, citrus, copper, and climate). Cotton, coupled with the tire-manufacturing plant in Goodyear, brought more workers; by 1920 the population had almost tripled, making Phoenix the largest city in the state. To accommodate the growing economy, the Southern Pacific Railroad expanded their route to include Phoenix in 1926. Three years later Phoenix Sky Harbor Airport opened under the ownership of Scenic Airways, only to be sold shortly thereafter as the Great

The Westward Ho, one of Phoenix's first hotels, still stands.

Depression hit. In 1935 it became the property of the City of Phoenix. As economic downfall swept the nation, the New Deal funded growth statewide, with projects like the 4,500-foot runway for Sky Harbor Airport in Phoenix and Lindley Stadium in Prescott. Such projects lessened the financial burden for many Phoenicians, and the city and its neighbors struggled forward.

Slowly this frontier town began evolving into a full-blown city. Architects designed beautiful homes, the once dusty roads were paved, and in the 1930s the Valley got its name. The Valley of the Sun, as one marketing agency or another began calling Phoenix and its surrounding cities, capitalized on its great weather to promote itself as a tourist spot. About the same time, came evaporative coolers (swamp coolers, as they are called today by Valley residents today). Gone were the days of sleeping outdoors and as life became more comfortable for residents, the decision to move to the desert became easier. In World War II the desert became a training ground for pilots and several fields around the Valley opened up, including Luke Air Force Base in the West Valley and Williams Airfield in the East Valley; the area even played host to POWs. Defense contractors—some of which are still here— arrived on the scene, bringing with them more jobs, and even more workers looking for the opportunities the West had become famous for.

By the 1950s, as air-conditioning was introduced, the area's only drawback—its oven-style summers—was suddenly negated, and growth took off. In the 1960s Phoenix acquired more land, bringing its total area to almost 200 square miles, less than half of what it would be some forty years later. As Phoenix and its neighbors expanded outward, growing faster than its highway infrastructure could bear, drives between outlying areas were long and circuitous, if not impossible. This created a fragmented existence among the cities and prompted immediate plans for expansion, as well as future plans to design and construct ample roads. The implementation of an adequate highway structure has made it easier for the thousands who move here each year. Developers have created several loops around the city, effectively decreasing drive time and connecting Valley cities with the center of Phoenix and one another. As the cities have sprawled outward, developers too often ignored the city centers; recent years, however, have seen these downtown areas return to life. Shops, boutiques, restaurants, wine bars, coffee shops, and parks have flourished, and people have returned for weekend and evening entertainment.

As the area has grown from agricultural community to metropolitan city, farmland has given way to subdivisions, but Maricopa County is still one of the largest cotton-producing

In Phoenix, converted turn-of-the-20th-century buildings vie with light-rail construction.

counties in the country. Driving on the highways, you'll see cotton fields interspersed with subdivisions. Still, on the whole, agriculture has given way to service, tourism, and high-tech manufacturing. Cotton remains one of the five C's of the economy, but tourism—precipitated by climate, another of the C's—has grown significantly. The defense support during World War II has given way to electronics companies, including Motorola, and more than one millionaire has been made. New homes sprout seemingly overnight to accommodate the influx of newcomers. Even with 30 percent of residents leaving each month, thousands more arrive, keeping city planners on their toes.

In 1995, when Jerry Colangelo (former majority owner of the Phoenix Suns, Arizona Diamondbacks, and Phoenix Mercury) won his bid to bring a baseball expansion team to Arizona, the Arizona Diamondbacks were born. Phoenix became one of the few cities to host all four major-league sports—baseball, football, basketball, and hockey. To welcome their new baseball team, the city built a new ballpark—Bank One Ballpark, renamed Chase Field in 2005 when JP Morgan Chase bought Bank One—in the downtown area, creating new opportunities for expansion and urban infill. Since then the city of Phoenix has set its sights on revitalizing the downtown, as have neighboring Tempe, Gilbert, Chandler, Glendale, Scottsdale, and Mesa.

The Valley will continue to grow as warm weather and the promise of sunshine beckon hordes of people looking for relief from the more severe weather of the East and Midwest. They're swapping bitter winters and the drenching humidity of summer for low humidity, mild winters, and cleaner air—for the most part. Some, unable to stand the heat, will return home, but others will quickly replace them. Phoenix has its share of woes when it comes to air-quality issues and increasing humidity as friends from the East and Midwest bring lawns with them, and while the summers offer triple-digit temperatures and a dryness that can make your throat ache, the mild winters make it all worthwhile. The Valley offers year-round enjoyment of the outdoors. In summer, residents have learned to set their clocks a

The Phoenix skyline from Piestewa Peak.

Outrageous Arizona Women

by Jana Bommersbach

Pioneering western women were made of stern stuff—they had to be, to face a harsh land where the saloon was the only given, snakes were everywhere, and gunslingers ruled the day. To tame this wild land demanded grit and spit.

Arizona women had these in spades—and with a special twist. Two cultures had already built lives here before the white women joined them, so old Arizona gives us heroines across the color palette.

Here's just a sampling.

There was Lozen, the Apache warrior called "America's greatest guerrilla fighter." She was a prophet, healer, and midwife who fought for her people's freedom for 40 years. She was exiled with Geronimo to a Florida detention camp in 1886 and died in confinement.

There was Pearl Hart of Globe, the only known female stagecoach robber, who pulled off the last stage heist in the Old West in 1899. Eastern media romanticized this pretty "Lady Bandit." Pearl did spend a short time in the Yuma Territorial Prison—inmate #1559—before being mysteriously paroled with a train ticket out of town.

There was Sharlot Hall, the first voice of Arizona literature, the territory's first female officeholder and the woman who helped cinch Arizona's statehood on Valentine's Day, 1912. A museum in Prescott carries her name and legacy.

There was Luisa Ronstadt Espinel of Tucson, the *first* Ronstadt superstar. This aunt of popular singer Linda Ronstadt was an acclaimed ambassador of culture in the 1920s, performing traditional Spanish and Mexican music throughout the United States and Europe.

Jana Bommersbach is a modern-day outrageous Arizona woman, an acclaimed journalist and author who stands in awe of the women who led the way.

little differently: Children bound outdoors after the sun has set, and since Arizona does not observe Daylight Saving Time, the early part of the day becomes a perfect time to run, bike, or golf before the full force of the sun takes effect. Visitors have learned to stay away between May and September, but more and more out-of-town guests have taken to braving the summer for cheaper golf games and deeply discounted resort stays.

Today, 24 towns make up the Phoenix metropolitan area. What was once a series of separate cities and townships has gradually become Greater Phoenix. And while borders may touch, each municipality has retained much of its original charm and individuality—creating a unique experience for those who live here and those who visit.

Mature palm trees line Phoenix's downtown avenues.

Transportation

By Horse, Of Course

Once a mere way station for travelers on their way to Yuma, Tucson, or California, Phoenix has become a central hub for those seeking the sun. After the Hohokam disappeared from the Salt River Valley in the mid—15th century, the area remained deserted until the late 19th century when a single soldier, astride his horse, rode into the Valley. From then until now, Phoenix has grown steadily; most recently it has grown in leaps and bounds. Cities that once took days to visit are now minutes away, their borders meeting and in some cases melding, the far reaches expanding beyond anything earlier residents ever could have imagined. Those who have lived here less than 5 years can attest to the fact that this Valley is not the same one they moved to. An intricate highway system (10 years ahead of schedule) has connected the East Valley with the West, and central Phoenix is now less than an hour's drive (in most cases less than half that) from anywhere in the Valley of the Sun.

Note that during winter and spring Arizona is on Mountain Standard Time; the rest of the year, Pacific Standard Time.

GETTING TO PHOENIX

By Car

FROM TUCSON
Travel to and from Tucson is easy and direct—simply take Interstate 10 east (if you're headed south to Tucson) or west (if you're going from Tucson to Phoenix). Depending on your starting point, your final destination in the Valley, and traffic conditions, travel time might be anywhere from 90 minutes to over 2 hours. If you're traveling from Tucson to Phoenix during the morning rush hour (6–9 AM), expect delays once you hit Pecos Rd. and Loop 202. Traffic from the East Valley headed into the city begins piling up as early as 6 AM and doesn't diminish until about 9 AM.

FROM FLAGSTAFF
This 2- to 2½-hour trip is a straight drive on I-17. The distance is just under 150 miles.

FROM SAN DIEGO
If you're traveling from San Diego, you have a couple of options depending on your final destination within the metropolitan area; in most cases, however, Interstate 8 is the quick-

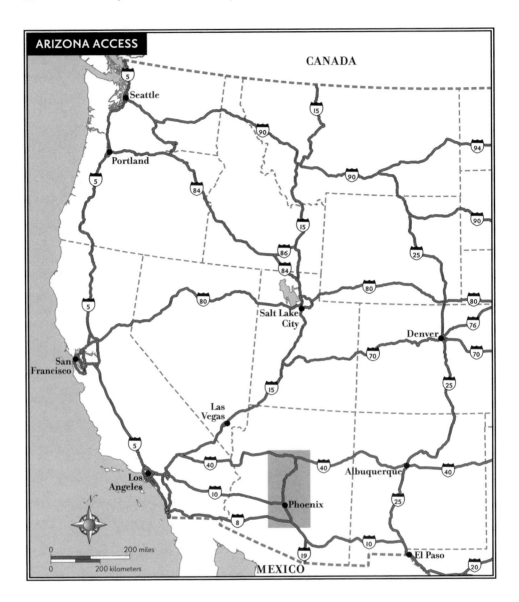

est and most direct route. You can pick up I-8 within the city limits of San Diego and take it east across the Arizona border, passing through Yuma and into Central Arizona. You have several choices once you've hit Gila Bend and AZ 85. You can take AZ 85 north to I-10 and pick it up west of Buckeye; or drive AZ 287 and then AZ 347 north through the Maricopa Ak-Chin Indian Reservation and the Gila River Indian Community, where it connects with I-10 just south of the Valley; or simply take I-8 straight west until it merges with I-10 south of Casa Grande. From there you would take I-10 north into Phoenix. Total mileage from city center to city center is 355 miles, and the trip takes between 5 and 6 hours, depending on traffic conditions, bathroom breaks, and the time change.

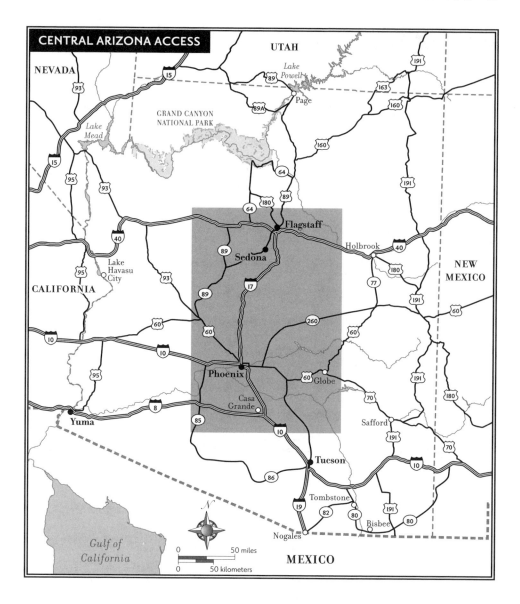

CENTRAL ARIZONA ACCESS

FROM LOS ANGELES

The drive from Los Angeles to Phoenix is only slightly farther (373 miles) than that from San Diego—though you'll be contending with LA traffic as well as Phoenix traffic as you head into the city. Travel on I-10 headed west to east is not recommended during the peak hours of 6–9 AM, when residents of the recently developed West Valley are using the fastest east–west route to central Phoenix. The same can be said for heading back to LA during peak evening hours (3–7 PM) as West Valley residents are headed home.

FROM ALBUQUERQUE

The drive from Albuquerque to Phoenix is a good 7 hours (466 miles). Take I-40 west from Albuquerque to Flagstaff, where you can pick up I-17 and head south. Once you reach the

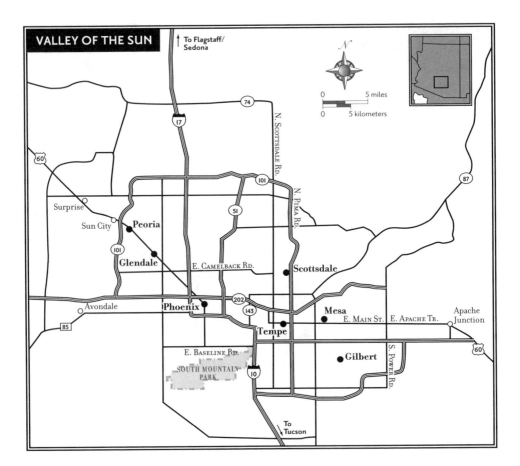

Valley, the Loop 101 can take you to East or West Valley; or you can take I-17 to central Phoenix.

FROM LAS VEGAS

Phoenix is less than 300 miles from Las Vegas, but travel is on US 93, and passage over the Hoover Dam can get gummed up depending on tourist traffic in the area. Efforts are under way to improve the highway, and the Hoover Dam Bypass Project is on its way to creating a solution. Drive carefully and watch out for construction; project completion is currently scheduled for 2010.

FROM SALT LAKE CITY

Salt Lake City is 700 miles from Phoenix and about an 11-hour drive. There are several options, but one of the shorter routes is I-15 south from Salt Lake City to UT 28, which becomes US 89; merge onto I-70 west for about 30 miles, then take the US 89 south exit (Panguitch). Here the route splits. You can continue through Utah and the Grand Staircase–Escalante National Monument, or you can take Alternate US 89 into Arizona and Kaibab National Forest. Either route will take you through Bitter Springs, Arizona, where the two routes converge. Follow US 89 south to Flagstaff, where you can take I-17 south the last 2 to 2½ hours of your journey.

FROM DENVER

Phoenix is half a day's drive from Denver (just over 900 miles), but the route is fairly simple. Take I-25 south from Denver until you connect with I-40 west. I-40 west will take you to Flagstaff, where you can pick up I-17 south and continue right into the heart of the Valley.

FROM CHICAGO

For a 1,800-mile trip, the drive from Chicago to Phoenix is pretty simple. Take I-55 south to St. Louis, where you can pick up I-44 west. Travel southwest through Missouri past the Mark Twain National Forest and into Oklahoma, then through Tulsa and into Oklahoma City, where you can pick up I-40 west to Amarillo, Texas. Travel through the panhandle of Texas into New Mexico, where you'll pass south of Santa Rosa Lake State Park halfway between the Texas border and Albuquerque. Continue through Albuquerque and the Laguna Indian Reservation before the road begins to head north to Gallup. Once you pass through Gallup, still on I-40, you'll begin heading south to the Arizona border. Over the border, you'll be on Navajo land. Next up is the Petrified Forest National Forest to either side of the interstate. Continue on through Winslow (remember the Eagles hit, "Take It Easy"?) and on into Flagstaff, where you pick up I-17 south to Phoenix. This route provides a great opportunity to see northern Arizona.

FROM NEW YORK CITY

Take I-78 west into Pennsylvania. Merge onto I-81 south to Harrisburg. Take the US 11 exit (exit 52) toward New Kingston/Middlesex/I-76/Pennsylvania Turnpike. Take the southern ramp and merge onto US 11/Harrisburg Pike. This little jaunt will take you from I-81 onto I-76 west toward Pittsburgh. Merge onto I-70 west through West Virginia, Ohio, Indiana, and Illinois to St. Louis, where I-55 south will connect you with I-44 south through Missouri and into Oklahoma. Just north of Oklahoma City, I-44 will become Turner Turnpike, which becomes John Kilpatrick Turnpike. Watch for toll roads along the way. See From Chicago (above) for details along the rest of this route—which, in short, involves taking the I-40 west exit to Amarillo, Texas, into New Mexico and then all the way to Flagstaff, where you can pick up I-17 south to Phoenix.

US 60 and the Ussery Mountains.

Mileage Chart and Maps

City	Time (hours)	Miles	City	Time (hours)	Miles
Tucson	2	116	Seattle	23	1,500
Flagstaff	2	145	Portland	20	1,335
Yuma	3	187	St. Louis	21	1,500
Las Vegas	5½	295	Oklahoma City	14	1,007
San Diego	5	355	Dallas	16	1,066
Los Angeles	5½	373	Houston	17	1,177
Albuquerque	6½	466	Chicago	26	1,800
Salt Lake City	11	701	New York City	37	2,457
Denver	13	913			

By Bus

Greyhound Lines, Inc., serves Phoenix directly; the local number is 602-389-4200. The station, located at 2115 E. Buckeye Rd., is open 24 hours daily, including holidays. There is also a station in Mesa (480-834-3360; 1423 S. Country Club Dr. Ste. 7, Mesa), open 8:30 AM until 8:30 PM daily. Fares mentioned below are for a single one-way ticket for an adult, and are provided as an approximate range. For more information about fares, discounts, and schedules, or to book travel, visit www.greyhound.com, or call the local number for your city below. Hours of operations, fares, and departures and arrivals are subject to change; many stations increase their number of departures on weekends, and fare prices fluctuate depending upon date of travel. Please verify all information, including prices, prior to making your travel arrangements.

FROM TUCSON

Greyhound has eight buses from Tucson to Phoenix that depart daily; the first leaves at 8:40 AM, and the last at 10:50 PM. Travel times range from 2 hours and 20 minutes to 1 hour and 50 minutes; midday and evening trips (after 7 PM) tend to take less time. The fare is about $30-35 one way depending upon the day. The Tucson station is located at 471 W. Congress St. For details, call 520-792-3475.

You can also take a shuttle bus from Tucson to the Phoenix airport, and fares may be less expensive than the bus. **Arizona Shuttle** picks up every hour at three locations in Tucson: Shuttles leaving from Speedway (5350 E. Speedway) depart on the hour; from University (501 N. Park Ave.) depart on the quarter hour; from Northwest (3825 W. Orange Grove Rd.) depart between 25 and 40 minutes after the hour, depending on traffic. Check-in time is 15 minutes prior to departure. At the Northwest location, check-in is 15 minutes after the hour. The shuttle drops off at Terminals 2, 3, and 4 at Phoenix Sky Harbor International Airport, and arrives at the following times: Terminal 4, 5 minutes after the hour; Terminal 3, 10 minutes after the hour; and Terminal 2, 15 minutes after the hour. Fares range from $50 for a round trip (stipulations apply) to $41 for a one-way fare, same-day departure; discounts are available for seniors, military, and groups of four or more. For more information, including departure times from Sky Harbor International Airport and the most up-to-date fares, visit their web site at www.arizonashuttle.com. To book the best-value fares, call directly 520-795-6771; outside Tucson, 800-888-2749.

FROM FLAGSTAFF
Four Greyhound buses depart for Phoenix from Flagstaff's station (928-774-4573) at 399 S. Malpais Lane between 9 AM and 8:50 PM. One-way fares run just under $30.

FROM SEDONA
The **Sedona Phoenix Shuttle** (928-282-2068 or, in Arizona, 800-448-7988; www.sedona-phoenix-shuttle.com) costs $45 one way, $85 round trip, to Sky Harbor International Airport.

FROM SAN DIEGO
Several buses leave daily from the Greyhound station located at 120 W. Broadway in San Diego. Departures begin at 7:15 AM (1:30 AM on weekends); the last bus leaves at 10:45 PM. Travel time varies greatly by time of day, fluctuating from 8 hours and 20 minutes (for the 7:15 AM bus) to 12 hours and 15 minutes (for the 7:25 and 9:55 AM buses). Additional times are available on weekends. The station is open 24 hours a day, including holidays; the local number is 619-515-1100. Fares vary depending upon travel date, but can range $45–65 one way.

FROM LOS ANGELES
Five Greyhound buses depart from Los Angeles's downtown station at 1716 E. 7th St. (213-629-8401), starting at 9 AM and ending at 11:40 PM during the week. Travel time ranges from just over 7 hours to almost 9 hours for the two midday buses. Additional times are available on weekends; prices hover around $50 one way and vary depending on travel date. Greyhound services two additional stations in the Los Angeles area.

FROM ALBUQUERQUE
Several buses depart from Albuquerque's Greyhound station (505-243-4435; 320 1st St. SW) daily. The first bus leaves at 2:35 AM, and the last departs the station at 10:45 PM. One-way fares can range $50–60 depending upon the travel date. Travel times range from just over 9 hours for the 2:35 AM bus to almost 12½ hours for the last bus of the day.

FROM SALT LAKE CITY
Two buses leave daily from the Greyhound station at 300 S. 600 W. in Salt Lake City, the first at 8:30 AM and the second at 6:30 PM. Prices are about $80 one way.

FROM DENVER
Travel by bus from Denver takes about a full day (24 hours) to traverse the almost 1,000 miles to Phoenix. Three buses leave daily—the first at 6:45 AM, the final at 7:40 PM—from the 1055 19th St. station in Denver (303-293-6555).

FROM CHICAGO
The journey from Chicago to Phoenix is about 2,000 miles and takes almost 2 full days from the downtown station at 620 W. Harrison St. (312-408-5800). Four buses leave daily; times depend upon the day, and the one-way fare can range from $110 to over $160. Greyhound services two additional stations in the Chicago area. Be aware that transfers are necessary.

FROM NEW YORK
Four Greyhound buses leave daily (additional options available on weekends) from the Port Authority Station located at 625 8th Ave. in New York City. Travel time is about 2½ days.

Transfers depend on the bus you choose. Pricing fluctuates depending on travel date and can range from $123 to more than $185 one way.

By Train

Amtrak does not directly service Phoenix, but the Amtrak Connecting Thruway bus service connects three Phoenix locations with the Maricopa Amtrak station south of Phoenix and the Amtrak station in Flagstaff. These thruway bus stations are located at the Greyhound station at 2115 E. Buckeye Rd.; the Phoenix airport at 3400 E. Sky Harbor Blvd.; and the Phoenix-Metro Transition Station at 9617 N. Metro Pkwy. in North Phoenix. For information about Amtrak's routes, schedules, and fares, visit www.amtrak.com or call 800-USA-RAIL.

TO PHOENIX VIA NORTHERN ARIZONA

The **Southwest Chief** runs daily from Chicago to Los Angeles, and services more than 30 cities along the way, including four in Arizona (Winslow, Flagstaff, Williams Junction, and Kingman). Fare depends on the city of departure and your choice of coach seats or a sleeper car option. Amtrak offers connecting Thruway service to Phoenix from the Flagstaff bus station.

TO PHOENIX VIA SOUTHERN ARIZONA

The **Texas Eagle** connects Chicago to San Antonio on its daily run and serves more than 20 cities along the way. While the Texas Eagle does not connect directly with Phoenix, travelers can pick up the Sunset Limited in San Antonio. This route serves four southern Arizona cities—Benson, Tucson, Maricopa, and Yuma—on its way to Los Angeles. The Sunset Limited typically connects the East Coast with the West; however, due to Hurricane Katrina, service east of New Orleans via Mobile and Biloxi was still suspended as of 2007.

By Plane

Phoenix is home to the sixth busiest airport for aircraft operations and the twelfth busiest for passenger traffic in the entire world. A trip that once meant months of harsh conditions now takes less than a day—and that includes moving through airport security and waiting on late arrivals. **Phoenix Sky Harbor International Airport**, which originally opened in 1935, is served by 23 domestic and international airlines, providing nonstop service to 111 cities in the United States and worldwide.

By Plane (when visiting other areas)

• ATA	• Great Lakes
• AeroMexico	• Hawaiian
• Air Canada	• JetBlue Airways
• Alaska Air	• Midwest Airlines
• American	• Northwest
• British Airways	• Southwest Airlines
• Continental	• Sun Country
• Delta	• United, TED
• Delta Connection (Skywest Airlines)	• US Airways, US Airways Express (Mesa)
• Frontier	• WestJet

Coming in for a landing at Sky Harbor International.

Located 5 miles from downtown Phoenix and easily accessible from the rest of the Valley, Sky Harbor provides low-fare services to more destinations than any other US airport. As the hub for Tempe-based US Airways (formerly America West) and an operational center for Southwest Airlines, the airport conveniently connects Phoenix and its neighbors to most major domestic cities. Sky Harbor averages almost 1,500 commercial flights a day and more than 40 million passengers annually. With an economic impact of $72 million a year, the airport moves 913 tons of cargo and over 108,000 passengers a day.

The airport is ever expanding to meet the increasing demands of the population growth and the millions of tourists who use it as a gateway to their Arizona experience. It's easily navigable, and renting a car has become simpler than ever with the opening of the airport's 140-acre Rental Car Center, which now houses all rental car companies under one roof. Shuttles are available at regular intervals—offering connections to both on- and off-site parking, the Rental Car Center, and many of the local hotels and resorts. **Super Shuttle** offers service to many locations in the Valley, and you can pick up the **Arizona Shuttle** at any of the airport's three terminals—2, 3, and 4—to Tucson.

There are a number of routes to and from the airport, depending where you're going or from which direction you're traveling. For directions to or from your part of the Valley, visit Sky Harbor International Airport online at http://phoenix.gov/skyharborairport/index.html.

Located at Butherus Dr. and N. Airport Dr. in North Scottsdale (close to Westin Kierland and Kierland Commons), **Scottsdale Airport** (480-312-2321; www.scottsdaleaz.gov/airport; 15000 N. Airport Dr., Scottsdale) capitalizes on the Valley's 300-plus clear sunny days, providing some of the best year-round flying in the country. This single-runway facility serves about 10,000 leisure and business travelers a year, and can accommodate both single-engine recreational planes and corporate jets. Originally the airport opened in 1942, and served for less than 2½ years as a training facility for Army Air Corps pilots. After World War II it changed hands a number of times before the city of Scottsdale acquired it in 1966. In 1967 the first business jet landed. By 1969 the airport housed more than 120 aircraft and

20 helicopters. By 2004 that number had jumped to 450; 200,000 takeoffs and landings that year made it the second busiest single-runway airport in the country.

Also in the area is **Williams Gateway Airport** (480-988-7600; www.flywga.org; 5835 S. Sossaman Rd., Mesa 85212). Just as Scottsdale Airport was originally built to support the training of Army Air Corp pilots during World War II, so was Williams Field, which became Williams Air Force Base and later Williams Gateway Airport. In over 52 years as a training base, more than 25,000 men and women earned their wings. Today Williams Gateway serves as relief to Phoenix Sky Harbor International Airport as well as hosting corporate, cargo, military, and general aviation aircraft. The airport has three runways and can handle single-engine planes as well as Boeing 747s.

Clear sunny days make for great flying weather, and during World War II Phoenix and its neighbors offered perfect locations to train pilots and support war efforts. Several of those sites have since become city airports. In addition to Williams Gateway, **Mesa Falcon Field** (480-644-2444; www.ci.mesa.az.us/airport) was built to train pilots in the British Royal Air Force during World War II; **Phoenix Goodyear Airport** (623-932-1200; www.phoenix .gov/goodyearairport) was originally a site to test-fly and deliver aircraft for the US Navy. Other Valley airports include **Chandler Municipal Airport** (480-782-3540; www.chandleraz.gov); **Phoenix Deer Valley Airport** (623-869-0975; www.phoenix.gov/deervalleyairport/index.html), built in the 1960s as a private airfield and purchased by the city of Phoenix in 1971; and **Glendale Municipal Airport** (623-930-2188; www.ci.glendale.az.us /airport).

Luke Air Force Base, which also opened during World War II, remains an active air force base and has trained almost 50,000 pilots since that time. It is considered the largest fighter training base in the Western world, with more than 180 aircraft, 7,000 military and reserve members, and 1,500 civilian employees. Base tours are available for organized groups between 15 and 40 people, Mon.–Fri. 8 AM–4 PM. Restrictions and conditions apply; call 623-856-5853 for more information or to schedule a tour. About 200,000 guests a year enjoy **Luke Days Air Show**, which typically takes place in late March. This 2-day show includes aerial demonstrations by the Thunderbirds, the US Air Force's Aerial Demonstration Team, ground displays including vintage aircraft, and attractions and exhibits. General admission is free, although a $5 parking fee may apply in certain areas.

GETTING AROUND THE VALLEY

By Bus

Valley Metro—the regional transportation—provides bus services to 12 communities, offering seamless, interconnected transportation throughout the Valley. All buses are wheelchair accessible (though not all buses can accommodate all types of wheelchairs—for more information, contact 602-253-5000) and equipped with bike racks. Routes range in frequency depending upon the community, route, and time of day. Sixty-three routes run morning into evening, and hours vary. Connections are fairly easy—most routes run north–south or east–west. There are 21 express routes that run Mon.–Fri. The express buses can be picked up at any of the Valley park-and-rides; they run into the city in the morning and out of the city in the evenings. Fifty-seven local routes run on Sat.; Tempe and Phoenix routes run Sun. and holidays. Fares start at $1.25 for local routes and $1.75 for express routes. Exact change is required, and currently transfers are free. In August 2007

Public transport in downtown Phoenix's Copper Square.

Valley Metro began selling a 1-day bus pass, providing riders movement between bus routes. Also available are 3-, 7-, and 31-day passes. This is an initiative in preparation for the eventual Metro Light Rail, which will commence services in December 2008. Together the bus and light rail will provide integrated, Valley-wide service.

Reduced fares are available for ages 6–18, seniors over 65, and disabled individuals. Children under 6 ride free. For more information about fares, bus routes, ticket books, and passes, you can call 602-253-5000 from 4 AM to 10 PM Mon.–Sat., and 6 AM–8 PM Sun. and holidays. Visit Valley Metro online (www.valleymetro.org) for more information, including a bus trip planner where you type in your departure or arrival time, departure and arrival locations, and date, and receive itinerary options complete with walking directions, fare, and travel time. You can also plan your return trip or find the routes that service a particular area. Valley Metro provides additional services, including Dial-a-Ride (602-253-5000), whose services vary from city to city, and a Vanpool service that provides van rentals to qualifying groups of 6–15 commuters.

With 1,345 miles of bike lanes and buses equipped with bike racks, catching a ride on the bus can quickly take riders to the far-reaching areas of the Valley. For more information about commuting via bike, visit www.azbikeped.org.

By Taxi

The Valley is most definitely a car area. Its only system of public transportation is the bus (along with the light rail, which opens late 2008). Since most Valley residents must drive to get around, taxis are not usually used; those you will find are most often either at the airport or in front of hotels ready to assist tourists. To get one, you'll need to call one of the 24-hour cab companies.

AAA Cab: 602-437-4000
Alpha Cab: 602-232-2000

Transportation in Old Town Scottsdale.

Checker Cab: 602-257-1818
Discount Cab: 602-200-2000
Tender Loving Care Taxi: 877-852-8294
Yellow Cab: 602-252-5252

Limo Services
Arizona Limousines: 602-267-7097
Desert Rose Limousine Service: 623-780-0159
Driver Provider: 602-453-0001
Scottsdale Limousine: 480-946-8446
Sky Mountain Limousine: 480-830-3944
Starlight Limousines: 480-905-1234
Valley Limousine: 602-254-1955
ExecuCar/SuperShuttle: 800-410-4444; you can also schedule a pickup online at www.execucar.com.

By Car
The Valley has a fairly comprehensive highway and interstate system that connects all regions with one another as well as downtown Phoenix. Depending on where you're going and if you're traveling during rush hour (6–9 AM and 3–7 PM), it can take you more than 1½ hours to get to the outlying areas from Phoenix or vice versa. As you might expect, drivers tend to head toward the city in the morning, and away from it during the evening commute; traffic headed in the opposite directions during this time tends to be much lighter. If you're traveling with others, on motorcycle, or have an alternate-fuel vehicle, consider driving in the HOV or high-occupancy vehicle lane (denoted by diamonds) during these peak times. Be aware that local motorists use the HOV lane to slip by slower vehicles. Speed limits within the Valley are 55 and 65, and until recently the Loop 101 through the north part of

Scottsdale sported photo radar units as an experiment for the city. Speeding decreased, so there's a good chance they will be back in use soon.

Keep in mind where your exits are: Traversing several lanes of traffic quickly can be difficult for the faint of heart. Below are some tips and descriptions about our local highways and interstates, along with the names they're most commonly known by. If you're listening to any of the local radio stations, you'll often hear names rather than numbers.

Interstate 10

Also Known As: Papago Freeway west of I-17 and Maricopa Freeway east of the I-17 interchange; "the 10."

The main thoroughfare through the heart of the Valley has an east–west orientation (since it travels most of the country this way); once it reaches the western outskirts of Tucson to the south, however, it makes a sharp turn north (note that the signage still says EAST and WEST), and travels to Phoenix in a general north–south direction as it passes Sun Lakes, Chandler, Ahwatukee, and Tempe before jogging briefly to the west at the Broadway Curve and passing south of Sky Harbor International Airport before a brief jaunt north again between 16th and 24th Sts. At the start of AZ 51 (which heads straight north), I-10 curves sharply to the west, where it passes north of downtown Phoenix, Tolleson, Avondale, Goodyear, Litchfield, and Buckeye on its way to Los Angeles.

I-10 crosses I-17 twice in central Phoenix (together they create a loop around the downtown area)—once by the airport, where I-10 jogs north, and again to the west of downtown Phoenix at the major interchange known locally as the stack, a series of interchanges about 0.5 mile south of McDowell Rd. by 23rd Ave.

If you're headed for sites north of the downtown area, I-10 is often your best bet: Getting off at 7th St. or 7th Ave. (or even the 3rd St. HOV exit when appropriate) can take you to the Phoenix Art Museum; the Heard Museum; and the Phoenix Public Library (which is actually located at Margaret T. Hance Park—Deck Park, as it's known locally—between 3rd St. and 3rd Ave. and situated over the aptly named Deck Park Tunnel.

Interstate 17

Also Known As: Black Canyon Freeway north of the I-10 Interchange, Maricopa Freeway where it converges with I-10; "the 17."

I-17 passes through south Phoenix in an east–west direction before heading north at the Durango Curve (in the area of 23rd Ave. and Durango St.) to Prescott, Sedona, and Flagstaff. If you're headed to downtown Phoenix, I-17 can often be your best route, as it passes just to the south of some of the cities major attractions, including Chase Field (home of the World Series Champion Arizona Diamondbacks), US Airways Center (Phoenix Suns and Phoenix Mercury), the newly renovated Phoenix Convention Center, Arizona Center, and the Arizona Science Center, among others.

US 60

Also Known As: Superstition Freeway; "the 60."

US 60 travels east–west and passes Apache Junction (far east of Phoenix in the Superstition Mountains), Mesa, Gilbert, and Tempe before converging with I-10 just south of the Broadway Curve and the airport exit. West of downtown Phoenix, the 60 converges with Grand

Avenue, which juts out from I-10 in a northwesterly direction (around 19th Ave.), cutting through much of the West Valley and serving as one of the most direct routes (if not the fastest in some cases) to Peoria, Sun City, Youngstown, El Mirage, Surprise, and Sun City West.

AZ 87

Also Known As: Beeline Highway.

AZ 87 connects I-10 north of Casa Grande (which is located about 50 miles south of Phoenix) with Winslow (to the northeast of the Valley). The Beeline heads straight north, passing by Sun Lakes, Chandler (where it converges with Arizona Ave.), Gilbert, and Mesa (where Arizona Ave. becomes Country Club), before intersecting with the Loop 202 and heading northwest through the Salt River Pima–Maricopa Indian Community and the Fort McDowell Yavapai Nation, passing Fountain Hills on the way. AZ 87 is one of the quickest routes to Fountain Hills, Fort McDowell Casino, and Fort McDowell Regional Park.

AZ 51

Also Known As: Squaw Peak Parkway until it was officially renamed Piestewa Peak Parkway in 2003, for Lori Piestewa, the first Native American servicewoman to die in combat.

AZ 51 passes north–south from central Phoenix (where the 10 turns west) through the central corridor of North Phoenix and Paradise Valley and connects the 10 and Loop 202 with the Loop 101 in the north. Piestewa Peak Parkway serves as a quick route to the Biltmore District (24th St. and Camelback area); get off at the Highland exit (south of Camelback Rd.), as there is no exit at Camelback.

Loop 202

Also Known As: Red Mountain Freeway.

Once it's finished, the 202 will create a horseshoe-shaped loop through the East Valley from the 10 at Pecos Rd. in Chandler, where it travels east–west through Gilbert and heads north–south just north of Williams Gateway Airport in southeast Mesa (where it connects with the 60 east of Hawes Rd. and west of Apache Junction). As of 2007 you can pick up the 202 again north of the 60 at Bush Hwy. and McDowell Rd., where it continues in an east–west orientation back to the I-10, where it connects with the 51 and heads west through central Phoenix. Eventually the 202 will provide easy accessibility to the new developments popping up on the outer edges of the East Valley. It also offers alternate access from the East Valley to Sky Harbor International Airport as well as to central Phoenix, Tempe's Mill Ave., and Tempe Town Lake as well as ASU's Main Campus (exit at Rural Rd. or Washington and follow the signs) and the COFCO Chinese Cultural Center (exit at 44th St. and head south of the 202).

AZ 143

Also Known As: Hohokam Expressway.

AZ 143 passes through Tempe and Phoenix and connects Loop 202 with I-10 and the eastern entrance to Sky Harbor International Airport.

AZ 153

Also Known As: Sky Harbor Expressway.

AZ 153 runs through Phoenix and Tempe and passes to the west of AZ 143. It serves as access to the airport and connects Washington and University Sts. with the east side of Sky Harbor.

Loop 101
Also Known As: Aqua Fria Freeway on the west side of the Valley (from west of I-17 to the north), and Pima Freeway on the east side of the Valley (from east of I-17); from south of Loop 202, Loop 101 is called Price Freeway.

Together these parts create a horseshoe that travels from the southeast Valley in a north–south direction through Tempe, the Salt River Pima–Maricopa Indian Community, and North Scottsdale before turning west at Bell Rd. and traveling through North Phoenix, where AZ 51 ends and I-17 intersects it on its way north. At 83rd Ave. the Loop 101 turns south and travels through Peoria, Glendale, and west Phoenix before ending at I-10.

Loop 303
Also Known As: Estrella Freeway.

The Loop 303 connects I-10 in Goodyear with Happy Valley and Lake Pleasant Rds. to the far north.

HOV Lanes
The HOV or high-occupancy vehicle lanes are denoted by white diamonds and are located on the left-hand sides of stretches of I-10, I-17, US 60, and Loop 202. They serve as alternate lanes for motorcycles, vehicles using alternate fuel, and motorists with passengers during rush-hour traffic (6–9 AM and 3–7 PM). These lanes are accessible to all motorists during off-peak hours and save time during rush hour; however, beware drivers using the lane to whiz around slower traffic at rush hour.

By Rented Car
Travelers arriving via plane can easily rent vehicles at the new **Airport Rental Car Center** (602-683-3741; 1805 E. Sky Harbor Circle north) at Phoenix Sky Harbor International Airport. The center, conveniently accessible by shuttle, is home to 13 car rental companies. Not all of the rental car companies have counters on site, but you can pick up their van service from the center. The multicolored **Rental Car Shuttle** picks up at the airport curb at the baggage claim level. To return your vehicle from I-10 east, use exit 148, Washington/Jefferson St. Continue south or straight along the frontage road to Sky Harbor Circle north and turn right. Follow the signs to the lot. If you're traveling from I-10 West, use exit 149, Buckeye Rd., and turn left onto Buckeye. Take this road to Sky Harbor Circle south and turn left. Follow the signs. If you're at the airport, simply follow the RENTAL CAR CENTER signs.

Airport Rental Car Center

Company	Toll-Free	Local
Advantage	800-777-5500	602-244-0450
Alamo	800-327-9633	602-244-0897
Avis	800-831-3847	602-273-3222
Beverly Hills	877-355-2555	602-258-1889
Budget	800-527-0700	602-231-0088
Dollar	800-800-4000	866-434-2226

Bicycling in North Scottsdale.

E-Z	800-277-5171	602-273-1177
Enterprise	800-736-8222	602-225-0588
Fox	800-225-4369	602-252-4399
Hertz	800-654-3131	602-267-8822
National	800-227-7368	602-275-4771
Payless	800-729-5377	602-681-9589
Thrifty	800-847-4389	602-244-0311

By Bicycle

With more than 1,345 miles of bike lanes, the Valley is a great place to tour on two wheels. For more information about bicycling here, see recreation sections in each chapter.

By Motorcycle

See Arizona by motorcycle. Rent a cycle or take a tour with **MCTours LLC** (888-BEEMER-1; international 480-970-5530; www.azride.com; 3007 N. 73rd Street, Unit B, Scottsdale). The state offers a dream vacation for all guests, and something equally as special for those on motorcycle; with over 53 national and state parks and monuments, better than 100 museums and historic sites, almost 300 ghost towns, 300-plus sunny days, over 400 events, and 2,000 miles of scenic routes, where else would you want to ride? Other options include **EagleRider Motorcycle Rentals** (480-970-0120; www.eaglerider.com), **Sonoran Motorcycle Rentals, Sales & Service** (480-844-9200); www.sonoranmotorcycles.com), and **Chester's Harley Davidson** (800-831-0404; www.chestershd.com).

On Foot

Areas in the Valley best seen on foot include downtown Phoenix, Mill Street and the ASU campus in Tempe, and Old Town in Scottsdale. Other fun walks include downtown Gilbert, downtown Chandler, Mesa's Main Street, and Historic Downtown Glendale. These downtown areas boast local boutiques and restaurants, and many have historic buildings, like the Hotel San Carlos in Phoenix and Crowne Plaza San Marcos Golf Resort in Chandler.

NEIGHBORS ALL AROUND

Phoenix is accessible via I-10, I-17, AZ 51, and Loop 101.
Scottsdale is easily accessible from the Loop 101 and Loop 202.
East Valley cities are accessible via I-10, Loop 101, Loop 202, and US 60.
West Valley cities are accessible via I-10, I-17, Loop 101, and Loop 303.
Sedona is approximately 115 miles from Phoenix and accessible from I-17 north. For more detailed information about traveling to and visiting Sedona, see chapter 7.

3

Phoenix

In the Valley of the Sun

Located in the heart of the breathtaking Sonoran Desert and the largest metropolitan area within Maricopa County's 9,000-plus square miles, Greater Phoenix encompasses 2,000 square miles of rugged, desert terrain, more than three million people, over 200 golf courses, professional sports, major sporting events, hundreds and hundreds of restaurants, shops, and boutiques, and a thriving arts and cultural scene. At an elevation of 1,117 feet, Phoenix has an average temperature of 85 degrees and an average rainfall of 7.66 inches a year; it sees more than 300 days of sun annually. It is no wonder that 13 million people visit the Valley each year.

Greater Phoenix is made up of several regions—the city of Phoenix, the East Valley, and the West Valley. Phoenix itself is broken into central Phoenix—comprising downtown, uptown, Phoenix Sky Harbor International Airport, and Papago Buttes; South Phoenix and Ahwatukee, located in the shadows of the Phoenix South Mountain Preserve; and North Phoenix, which extends north past the Loop 101 and includes Piestewa Peak, the Phoenix Mountains, North Mountain, and Shaw Butte. The city of Phoenix is the fifth largest in the United States, with more than 1.4 million people; it is roughly 515 square miles and extends from about Chandler Blvd. in Ahwatukee on its southern boundary to Jomax Rd. on the north. It shares its western borders with Glendale, Goodyear, and Avondale; its eastern with Scottsdale and Tempe. Paradise Valley is nestled in North Phoenix.

Sleeping in the Desert

In 1913 the Valley's first resort—San Marcos—opened in Chandler. Built by Dr. A. J. Chandler, this desert oasis beckoned the wealthy and famous from all over the world, among them Bing Crosby, Christian Dior, and President Herbert Hoover. As early as 1919 Phoenix was tagged the city "where winter never comes" by the Phoenix-Arizona Club, the group that most actively began promoting the city as a tourist destination. Several years later Westward Ho and Hotel San Carlos were erected in the heart of downtown some 17 miles away. About the same time Wigwam Resort—40-plus miles to the northwest in Litchfield Park—was opened to tourists. With the invention of the automobile and its growing popularity, the widely read travel magazine *Arizona Highways* joined promotional efforts in 1925, and Phoenix quickly grew as a top destination for vacationers.

Of the earliest hotels and resorts, San Marcos (now the Crowne Plaza San Marcos Golf Resort) and Wigwam Resort are still among the top choices of Valley tourists and VIPs. The

Downtown Phoenix.

San Carlos offers a unique downtown hotel option; Westward Ho still stands, but it now provides HUD housing to seniors. Since the early part of the 20th century, tourism has evolved into a major economic staple for the Valley. Today Greater Phoenix hotels and resorts are consistently ranked among the best in the nation, and several properties have been awarded AAA's Five Diamond rating consistently, including The Boulders in Carefree; The Scottsdale Fairmont Princess; and Marriott's Camelback Inn, A JW Marriott property, located in Scottsdale—a status Camelback Inn has claimed since 1977.

Tourist season lasts from October until April, when the days are warm and inviting and the nights cool and worthy of sweatshirts and fireplaces. During the height of the season, last-minute travelers have difficulty booking one of the area's 55,000 rooms. So be sure to plan ahead!

Finding Your Home Base in the Valley

You'll want to plan your stay in Phoenix around what you want to see and do while you're here. While the Valley has become more easily accessible with the recent opening of Loops 101 and 202, it still pays to stay where you plan to spend most of your time. If you're visiting ASU's Main Campus, **Tempe**, **South Scottsdale**, and the **airport area** are good choices. Not only do these areas provide inexpensive hotel rates and easy access to campus, but they are also minutes away from the Desert Botanical Garden, Phoenix Zoo, Papago Park, and Phoenix South Mountain Preserve. You are also close to downtown Phoenix and Old Town Scottsdale; combined with Mill Avenue, you have a variety of shopping, dining, and entertainment choices.

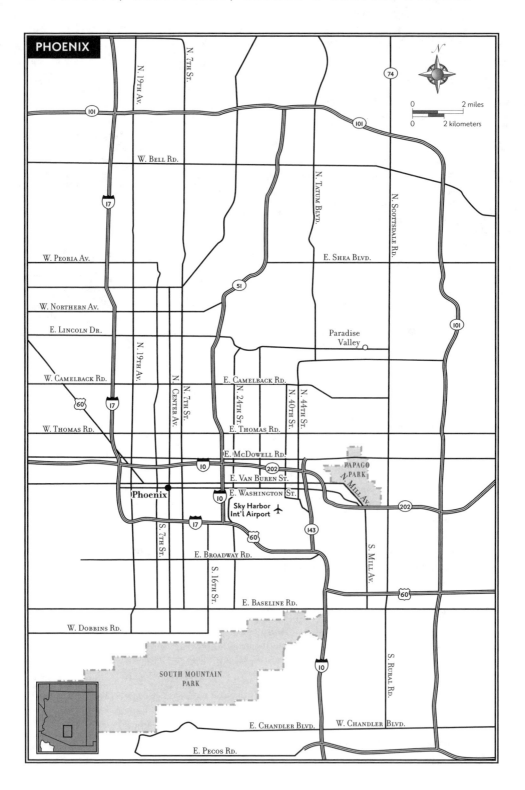

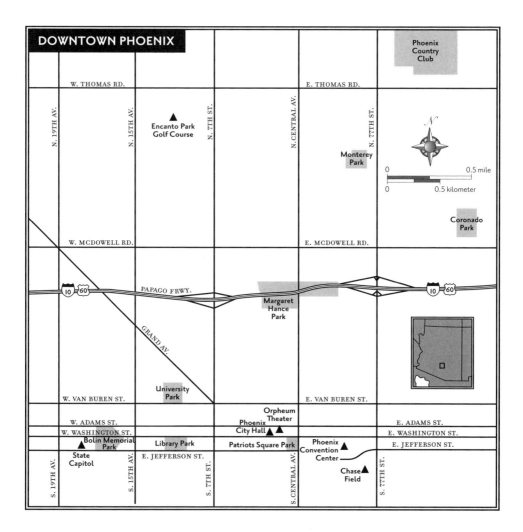

DOWNTOWN PHOENIX

Phoenix Country Club

W. THOMAS RD. E. THOMAS RD.

N. 19TH AV. N. 15TH AV. Encanto Park Golf Course N. 7TH ST. N. CENTRAL AV. Monterey Park N. 22TH ST.

0 0.5 mile
0 0.5 kilometer

Coronado Park

W. MCDOWELL RD. E. MCDOWELL RD.

PAPAGO FRWY. Margaret Hance Park

GRAND AV.

University Park

W. VAN BUREN ST. E. VAN BUREN ST.

Orpheum Theater
W. ADAMS ST. Phoenix City Hall E. ADAMS ST.
W. WASHINGTON ST. E. WASHINGTON ST.
Bolin Memorial Park Library Park Patriots Square Park Phoenix Convention Center E. JEFFERSON ST.
State Capitol E. JEFFERSON ST. Chase Field

S. 19TH AV. S. 15TH AV. S. 7TH ST. S. CENTRAL AV. S. 22TH ST.

Interested in stylish boutiques, first-class restaurants, spectacular golf, and the best spas? Try the fashionable **Biltmore District/Camelback Corridor** in Phoenix/Scottsdale. Here you'll find resorts like Camelback Inn, Arizona Biltmore, the Ritz-Carlton, The Phoenician, Montelucia, Sanctuary at Camelback, and Royal Palms Resort & Spa. In addition to the golf courses and spas, visitors enjoy hiking Camelback Mountain and Piestewa Peak or shopping at Biltmore Fashion Square. The district's close proximity to Old Town Scottsdale on the east and Piestewa Peak Parkway on the west means additional restaurant and entertainment options.

The **Gainey Ranch neighborhood** in Scottsdale is surrounded by golf courses, country clubs, spas, and boutiques. You will find the Hyatt Regency Resort and Spa at Gainey Ranch set against the breathtaking McDowell Mountains. Just north of here are the Westin Kierland and Fairmont Scottsdale Princess as well as TPC, home of the greatest show on grass: the FBR Open. Kierland Commons features a variety of shopping and dining options in an old main-street-style setting. Just north of the 101 in North Phoenix, tourists enjoy staying at one of the newest Valley resorts, the JW Marriott Desert Ridge—a resort known for Vegas-style flair, beautiful golf courses, and a pampering spa.

A stay in **Old Town Scottsdale** in March means spring training and the San Francisco Giants. If you're an art fan, Old Town features 125 art galleries, a weekly arts walk, Scottsdale Center for the Arts, and the Scottsdale Center of Contemporary Art. Old Town is home to the urban-style resorts Hotel Valley Ho and the Mondrian, but you'll also find several affordable hotel brands that give you easy access to the hundreds of shops, art galleries, restaurants, and boutiques in the area. In addition to the Main Street, Marshall Way, Old Town, and Fifth Avenue shopping and arts districts, you can visit Scottsdale Fashion Square and the Waterfront. These locales feature local shops and restaurants just north of the Old Town area.

Others may enjoy a stay in the **East Valley**, which tends to have a more relaxed atmosphere along with affordable accommodations, the historic Crowne Plaza San Marcos Resort and Golf Club, charming restaurants like the Crackers & Co. Café in Mesa or Joe's BBQ in Gilbert, and shopping at Chandler Fashion Square in Chandler and Fiesta and Superstition Springs Malls in Mesa. Golf lovers will find some spectacular courses, like the Ocotillo Golf Resort in Chandler, at great rates. Activities include hiking or horseback riding in the Ussery Mountains north of Mesa or visiting Goldfield—a touristy old mining town in the shadows of the oft-photographed Superstition Mountains—tubin' down the Salt River, or shopping Mesa's Main Street or Chandler's town square. Visitors enjoy the Mesa Contemporary Arts

The Camelback Inn is a Five Diamond property. Photo provided courtesy of Camelback Inn

Museum, and kids love the "dinosaur museum"—as local children call the Mesa Southwest Museum. RV owners might like Mesa and Apache Junction, which offer a variety of choices.

If you're here antiquing or to see the Arizona Cardinals or the Phoenix Coyotes (or for Super Bowl 2008), try the **West Valley**. Glendale's Historic Downtown is home to some of the best antiques stores and local restaurants. Enjoy the weekly arts walk, annual events like A Chocolate Affaire or the Glendale Jazz and Blues Festival, and the state-of-the-art technologically inspired shopping at WestGate at City Center adjacent to the new University of Phoenix Stadium—home of the 2008 Super Bowl. If you're looking to retire, any of the choices will do, but Sun City and Sun City West in the northwest Valley have several resort-style active adult communities, as do Goodyear and Litchfield farther south. Peoria features the Smithsonian-sponsored Challenger Space Museum and Lake Pleasant Recreational Park. Hike, camp, or horseback ride in the White Tank or Estrella Mountains; golf at the Palm Valley Golf Club in Goodyear or Raven Golf Club at Verrado in Buckeye. Shopping can be found at Arrowhead Mall in Glendale or the various shops and strip malls exploding throughout a quickly growing West Valley.

If you're here for a convention or prefer to stay in the very heart of things—**downtown Phoenix** offers everything from sports (the Diamondbacks and Phoenix Suns are within walking distance or at the very least a short drive) to arts and culture—Symphony Hall and the Herberger Theatre are mere steps away from each other, and the Dodge and Orpheum Theatres are close by, as are a variety of bars and restaurants. However, unlike many other major downtown areas throughout the country, downtown Phoenix tends to be laid back; after 5 PM on weeknights it's a quiet place unless there's a baseball or basketball game. The city of Phoenix is working hard to revitalize its downtown area, known as Copper Square. In addition to active efforts to promote existing downtown businesses and invite new ones to move in, you will also see that condos and town houses are popping up along the eastern edges, and the historic neighborhoods to the north are making a comeback.

If you're here for business, you might want to choose any of the **airport hotels** listed in this chapter. These accommodations, including the Phoenix Airport Marriott and the Airport Ramada Limited, vary in price. You'll be fairly close to Mill Avenue in Tempe and the COFCO Chinese Cultural Center. If you'd like to stay in a something other than an airport hotel, the establishments in **midtown** or **uptown Phoenix** tend to cater to busy executives. You'll be in the bustling activity of the historic Phoenix neighborhoods; you'll find plenty of restaurants and entertainment, most on Central Avenue. Plus, you won't be far from downtown Phoenix. If you have time, try the Heard Museum (Native American) or the Phoenix Art Museum on Central; or restaurants like Durant's or Macayo's. Want to unwind after a busy day? Grab a drink and an appetizer at Cheuvront's Wine Bar.

A well-chosen home base can enrich your experience, and the wonderful thing about most of these areas is that they are self-sufficient, offering a different combination of Arizona experiences. The mountains interspersed throughout the Valley mean it's but a short drive from just about anywhere to wandering paths, vigorous hikes, or escapes into the desert. Visitors can spend days exploring everything each area has to offer, from boutiques to art galleries, museums, big restaurants and little ones, theaters, mountains, golf courses, and spas.

Please note: Arizona passed a statewide law banning smoking in most public spaces; it went into effect May 2007. Some Valley cities, such as Tempe, had already banned smoking in restaurants and bars.

A Note on Valley Prices

As a tourist town, Phoenix and its neighbors tend to have some of the highest prices in the country during the season; and as more and more tourists are deciding to brave the heat for better prices, tourist prices are lingering longer and longer. However, July and August—the height of the steamy season—are still fairly quiet. That's when the best prices can be found. Many Valley hotels and resorts offer incredibly low prices and packages in high summer, and if lounging beside a pool, relaxing at the spa, or catching an early-morning golf game sounds good to you, then summer might be the right time to visit. There are often specials for families, and several area resorts have spectacular pools that border on amusement parks—check out Pointe South Mountain and Pointe Squaw Peak later in this chapter, as well as Westin Kierland in the Scottsdale chapter. Many of the Valley's favorite resorts offer both spa and golf options, making his-and-her vacations a splendid choice. See the Spas and Golf Courses chapter later in this book for tips and best bets.

LODGING

Credit Cards

The following abbreviations are used for credit card information:
AE: American Express
CB: Carte Blanche
D: Discover Card
DC: Diner's Club
MC: MasterCard
V: Visa

DOWNTOWN PHOENIX

BUDGET INN MOTEL
602-257-8331.
424 W. Van Buren St., Phoenix 85003.
Prices: $50-plus.
Credit Cards: AE, D, MC, V.
Handicapped Access: Yes.
Pets: No.

This inexpensively priced motel is fairly close to the downtown area; however, the neighborhood is questionable. The rooms offer cable, refrigerators, and microwaves. High-speed Internet access is available.

HOLIDAY INN EXPRESS HOTEL & SUITES DOWNTOWN PHOENIX
602-452-2020 or 800-HOLIDAY.
www.hiexpress.com.
620 N. 6th St., Phoenix 85004.
Prices: $119–189.
Credit Cards: AE, CB, D, DC, MC, V.
Handicapped Access: 4 rooms.
Pets: No.

Located just north of the Phoenix downtown district, this Holiday Inn Express is within walking distance of many area attractions, including Arizona Science Center, Chase Field, US Airways Center, and various theaters, attractions, restaurants, and bars. The hotel offers guests a complimentary airport shuttle, Internet access, and a continental breakfast. There is a pool and a cardio-only exercise facility.

HYATT REGENCY PHOENIX
602-252-1234 or 800-233-1234.
www.phoenix.hyatt.com.
122 N. 2nd St., Phoenix 85004.
Prices: $150–305.
Credit Cards: AE, CB, D, DC, MC, V.
Handicapped Access: 4 rooms.
Pets: No.

Located in the heart of downtown Phoenix, the Hyatt Regency offers some of the best of the city right out its front doors. Across the street lies the Phoenix Convention Center; within minutes of walking you'll find US Airways Center, Chase Field, and numerous theaters, restaurants, bars, and museums.

The Hyatt Regency sits in the heart of downtown Phoenix.

The hotel features 712 guest rooms and suites. You'll also find the state's only revolving rooftop restaurant (Compass Restaurant), as well as three additional dining options, a pool, salon, and fitness facility. Internet access and garage parking are available for a fee.

SAN CARLOS HOTEL

602-253-4121 or 866-253-4121.
www.hotelsancarlos.com.
202 N. Central Ave., Phoenix 85004.
Prices: $59–269.
Credit Cards: AE, D, DC, MC, V.
Handicapped Access: No.
Pets: No.

This 80-year-old hotel, located in the heart of downtown Phoenix, is a member of the Historic Hotels of America. Built in 1927, Hotel San Carlos was considered one of the most luxurious hotels in the Southwest; it featured air-conditioning and elevators, and beckoned some of Hollywood's most famous stars. In 1955 a swimming pool was added to the third-floor sundeck, and a recent million-dollar renovation has

brought the hotel into the 21st century, complete with complimentary wireless Internet access. The hotel offers 121 guest rooms including 12 suites (rooms are fairly small); you'll also find two restaurants, two bars, a barbershop, and a shoe shine on site.

SHERATON PHOENIX DOWNTOWN HOTEL

602-262-2500 or 800-325-3535.
www.sheraton.com.
340 N. 3rd St., Phoenix 85004.
Prices: Prices have not been set at this time.
Credit Cards: Undetermined at this time.
Handicapped Access: Undetermined at this time.
Pets: Welcome.

In response to the thousands of convention-goers that flock to downtown Phoenix every year, the Sheraton Phoenix Downtown will open in fall 2008. The hotel will feature 1,000 guest rooms, an on-site coffee bar, restaurant, and bar, as well as a 6,500-square-foot fitness center and spa, and a pool.

SPRINGHILL SUITES PHOENIX DOWNTOWN

602-307-9929.
802 E. Van Buren St., Phoenix 85006.
Prices: $69–189.
Credit Cards: AE, CB, D, DC, MC, V.
Handicapped Access: 9 rooms; 2 ADA rooms with roll-in showers.
Pets: No.

Located to the east of the downtown area, Springhill Suites Phoenix Downtown is still close enough to the downtown area to walk, or at least call a cab for a very short ride. The hotel offers all studio suite rooms with a variety of free amenities, including a complimentary airport shuttle service, on-site parking, breakfast buffet, 24-hour business center, and in-room Internet access. It also features a swimming pool, whirlpool, and exercise room.

WYNDHAM PHOENIX HOTEL

602-333-0000 or 800-359-7253.
www.wyndhamphx.com.
50 E. Adams St., Phoenix 85004.
Prices: $160–360.
Credit Cards: AE, D, DC, MC, V.
Handicapped Access: 2 rooms.
Pets: No.

The Wyndham Phoenix features 532 guest rooms and suites, complimentary Internet access, a swimming pool, and a fitness facility. It offers a full-service concierge service as well as an on-site restaurant and bar and room service.

CENTRAL PHOENIX
BEST WESTERN CENTRAL PHOENIX INN

602-252-2100 or 888-676-2100.
www.centralphoenixinn.com.
1100 N. Central Ave., Phoenix 85004.
Prices: $99–249.
Credit Cards: AE, CB, D, DC, MC, V.
Handicapped Access: 4 rooms.
Pets: No.

Located north of downtown Phoenix, the eight-story Best Western Central Phoenix Inn provides an area shuttle for a fee, and a variety of free amenities, including airport shuttle, Internet access, and free parking. It also features six luxury two-room penthouse suites; each offers views of the city's skyline, a private balcony, wet bar, and whirlpool tub. On-site bar and grill.

WINGATE INN PHOENIX

602-716-9900.
www.cmpm.net.
2520 N. Central Ave., Phoenix 85004.
Prices: $99–300.
Credit Cards: AE, D, DC, MC, V.
Handicapped Access: 6 rooms.
Pets: Yes.

Wingate offers 107 oversized rooms and suites, plus free services—airport shuttle, high-speed Internet access, continental breakfast, pool, spa and fitness center, and 24-hour business center. The Wingate brand is popular among business travelers.

MIDTOWN PHOENIX
ARTISAN HOTEL

602-265-6100.
www.artisanphoenix.com.
212 W. Osborn Rd., Phoenix 85013.
Prices: $149–349.
Credit Cards: AE, MC, V.
Handicapped Access: ADA compliant.
Pets: No.

Located at the edge of Park Central in midtown Phoenix, this recently opened boutique hotel offers 120 rooms themed after famous artists like Monet, Warhol, and Michelangelo; suites are available. The hotel provides complimentary high-speed Internet access, and features a heated pool, private cabanas, and a poolside bar and grill.

EXTENDED STAY AMERICA PHOENIX–MIDTOWN

602-279-9000 or 800-EXT-STAY.

www.extendedstaydeluxe.com.
217 W. Osborn Rd., Phoenix 85013.
Prices: $44–199.
Credit Cards: AE, CB, D, DC, MC, V.
Handicapped Access: 7 rooms.
Pets: Yes; call for details.

This 129-room extended-stay hotel located in midtown Phoenix offers a fully equipped kitchen, on-site pool and exercise facility, and free continental breakfast. It enjoys close proximity to Heard Museum and Phoenix Art Museum uptown, and Chase Field and US Airways Center downtown.

HAMPTON INN PHOENIX/MIDTOWN

602-200-0990.
www.hamptoninn.com.
160 W. Catalina Dr., Phoenix 85013.
Prices: $89–209.
Credit Cards: AE, CB, D, DC, MC, V.
Handicapped Access: 4 rooms.
Pets: No.

This centrally located hotel offers 99 rooms with complimentary Internet access and breakfast buffet, an on-site pool, and an exercise facility.

HILTON GARDEN INN PHOENIX/MIDTOWN

602-279-9811.
www.hiltongardeninn.com.
4000 N. Central Ave., Phoenix 85012.
Prices: $79–189.
Credit Cards: AE, CB, D, DC, MC, V.
Handicapped Access: Yes.
Pets: No.

The Hilton Garden Inn Phoenix/Midtown offers business-class service to its guests; complimentary Internet access and wireless is available in the lobby and meeting rooms. The hotel also features a 35,000-square-foot health club and swimming pool. On-site restaurant and bar; room service is available.

HILTON SUITES PHOENIX

602-222-1111.
www1.hilton.com.
10 E. Thomas Rd., Phoenix 85012.
Prices: $129–289.
Credit Cards: AE, CB, D, DC, MC, V.
Handicapped Access: 10 rooms, 3 with roll-in showers.
Pets: Yes, up to 60 pounds.

Tucked among the high-rises of central Phoenix, this hotel features two-room suites with microwave, refrigerator, and coffeemaker. It serves a mostly business crowd, and offers a complimentary shuttle to a number of the downtown area sites, including Dodge Theatre, the Phoenix Convention Center, and Chase Field and US Airways Center—where the Arizona Diamondbacks and Phoenix Suns play, respectively. Internet access is available for a daily fee. On-site market, restaurant, and bar.

SOUTH PHOENIX/AIRPORT

GRACE INN AT AHWATUKEE

480-893-3000 or 800-843-6010.
www.graceinn.com.
10831 S. 51st St., Phoenix 85044.
Prices: $89–165.
Credit Cards: AE, D, MC, V.
Handicapped Access: 7 rooms.
Pets: No.

Conveniently located just off of I-10 and close to the airport, Grace Inn offers an on-site restaurant, bar, and salon and day spa. This modest hotel also features a courtyard and heated pool. Amenities include an in-room refrigerator, microwave, and cable/satellite TV and movies. Room service is available.

LEGACY GOLF RESORT, THE

602-305-5500 or 888-828-FORE.
www.legacygolfresort.com.
6808 S. 32nd St., Phoenix 85042.
Prices: $249–489.
Credit Cards: AE, D, DC, MC, V.

Handicapped Access: 5 rooms.
Pets: No.

The Legacy Golf Resort, resting in the shadows of the Phoenix South Mountain Preserve, features more than 300 suites with either a kitchen or kitchenette. Amenities include an 18-hole golf course, pool, fitness center, and tennis. The on-site restaurant-lounge offers a simple menu and a beautiful view of the golf course. The rooms are attractively decorated and spacious.

POINTE SOUTH MOUNTAIN RESORT

602-438-9000 or 877-800-4888.
www.pointesouthmtn.com.
7777 S. Pointe Pkwy., Phoenix 85044.
Prices: $199–399.
Credit Cards: AE, CB, D, DC, MC, V.
Handicapped Access: 23 rooms.
Pets: No.

This award-winning resort is located at the base of the Phoenix South Mountain Preserve. The 200-acre property features six on-site restaurants, including a poolside bar and grill; spa and athletic club; and 18-hole golf course. It's close to 60 miles of hiking trails and easily accessible from I-10. The resort is child-friendly, featuring a 6-acre water park and supervised children's activities. It makes a great escape during the hotter seasons; locals love the summer packages. The 640 spacious suites are nonsmoking.

I-17/Black Canyon Freeway
in North Phoenix
This commerce corridor is located in northwest Phoenix and offers easy access to West Valley cities, including Glendale, Sun City, Peoria, and Surprise. Area attractions include University of Phoenix Cardinals Stadium, Glendale Arena, Lake Pleasant, and Arrowhead Towne Center. Note that prices at hotels in close proximity to University of Phoenix Stadium may increase due to several sporting events, including Super Bowl XLII in 2008.

BEST WESTERN BELL HOTEL

602-993-8300.
www.bestwestern.com.
17211 N. Black Canyon Hwy., Phoenix 85023.
Prices: $125–150.
Credit Cards: AE, CB, D, DC, MC, V.
Handicapped Access: No.
Pets: Yes; $10 per pet, per day, or a $30 per week nonrefundable pet fee.

This pet-friendly hotel in North Phoenix is conveniently located off I-17 and offers free high-speed wireless Internet access, free breakfast, a pool, and a hot tub. Coasters and Castles and Waterworld USA Recreational Water Park are located within 5 miles.

BEST WESTERN INNSUITES HOTEL PHOENIX

602-997-6285 or 800-752-2204.
www.bestwestern.com.
1615 E. Northern Ave., Phoenix 85020.
Prices: $69–179.
Credit Cards: AE, CB, D, DC, MC, V.
Handicapped Access: 2 rooms, based on availability.
Pets: Yes; $10 per pet, per day, or a $30 per week nonrefundable pet fee.

This Three Diamond hotel offers more than 100 suites featuring refrigerator, microwave, coffeemaker, and free high-speed Internet access. They offer a free breakfast buffet and cocktail hour.

COMFORT INN NORTH

602-866-2089.
www.comfortinn.com.
1711 W. Bell Rd., Phoenix 85023.
Prices: $79–299; call for pricing.
Credit Cards: AE, CB, D, DC, MC, V.
Handicapped Access: Yes.
Pets: Yes; ask about deposits and restrictions.

This Comfort Inn is located close to Turf Paradise horse racing track and I-17, and a mere 20 minutes from the airport. Free full

The Phoenician Resort from Camelback Mountain.

breakfast, outdoor heated pool, and hot tub. Call for pricing if you're planning to visit in early or midyear 2008; several sporting events in the West Valley may increase prices significantly.

CROWNE PLAZA PHOENIX
602-943-2341 or 888-797-9878.
www.cpphoenix.com.
2532 W. Peoria Ave., Phoenix 85029.
Prices: $89–149.
Credit Cards: AE, CB, D, DC, MC, V.
Handicapped Access: 7 rooms.
Pets: Yes, with a $25 fee.

The recently redesigned 250-room Crowne Plaza Phoenix has added elegant touches to promote a rejuvenating night of sleep—earplugs, eye mask, lavender spray, and a sleep CD. You'll also find free Internet access, a complimentary shuttle within a 5-mile radius, and express check-in and check-out. On-site restaurant and bar; room service is available.

COURTYARD PHOENIX NORTH
602-944-7373 or 800-321-2211.
www.marriott.com.
9631 N. Black Canyon Hwy., Phoenix 85021.
Prices: $249–279.
Credit Cards: AE, CB, D, DC, MC, V.
Handicapped Access: Yes.
Pets: No.

The recently renovated Courtyard Phoenix North offers free Internet access in its 134 rooms and 12 suites. A lounge and café are available on site. Recreation includes an outdoor heated pool and whirlpool, an on-site exercise room, and nearby biking, tennis, and squash. Close to Metrocenter Mall and not far from Historic Downtown Glendale.

EMBASSY SUITES HOTEL, PHOENIX–SCOTTSDALE, A GOLF RESORT
602-765-5800 or 800-EMBASSY.
www.embassysuitesaz.com.

4415 E. Paradise Village Pkwy., Phoenix 85032.
Prices: $89–259.
Credit Cards: AE, CB, D, DC, MC, V.
Handicapped Access: 9 rooms.
Pets: No.

This hotel offers more than 250 two-room suites with private balconies, as well as an 18-hole golf course. Guests can enjoy the on-site restaurant and lounge, Tatum's, and an outdoor pool, spa, and fitness facility. Close to golfing, including the Stone Creek Golf Club.

FOUR POINTS SHERATON PHOENIX METROCENTER

602-997-5900.
www.starwoodhotels.com/fourpoints.
10220 N. Metro Pkwy., Phoenix 85051.
Prices: $49–159.
Credit Cards: AE, D, DC, MC, V.
Handicapped Access: 6 rooms.
Pets: No.

This 284-room hotel is located close to the Metrocenter Mall with 250 shops and a variety of restaurant choices. It offers free wireless Internet access, pool and spa, and an on-site restaurant and bar.

JW MARRIOTT DESERT RIDGE RESORT & SPA, PHOENIX

480-293-3950 or 800-898-4527.
www.jwdesertridgeresort.com.
5350 E. Marriott Dr., Phoenix 85054.
Prices: $199–689.
Credit Cards: AE, CB, D, DC, MC, V.
Handicapped Access: 11 rooms.
Pets: No.

JW Marriott Desert Ridge Resort & Spa is a 316-acre luxury resort with 10 distinct dining experiences, championship golf, and the Revive Spa. The grounds are sprawling and majestic, the staircases sweeping and grand, and the ceilings vaulted. There are 950 guest rooms and 81 suites. The resort is close to shopping at Desert Ridge Marketplace and Kierland Commons as well as hiking at Pinnacle Peak. Check out great packages and rates; family-friendly, golf, spa, and romantic packages; activities for children.

PARK PLAZA HOTEL

602-978-2222 or 800-814-7000.
www.parkplaza.com/phoenixaz.
2641 W. Union Hills Dr., Phoenix 85027-5000.
Prices: $69–289.
Credit Cards: AE, CB, D, DC, MC, V.
Handicapped Access: 3 rooms with roll-in showers and bars.
Pets: No.

The Park Plaza Hotel Phoenix North offers complimentary Internet access, an on-site restaurant that serves breakfast and dinner, and a heated outdoor pool.

POINTE HILTON SQUAW PEAK RESORT

602-997-2626 or 800-876-4683.
www.pointehilton.com.
7677 N. 16th St., Phoenix 85020.
Prices: $89–319.
Credit Cards: AE, CB, D, DC, MC, V.
Handicapped Access: 16 rooms.
Pets: Yes; ask about their pampered pet packages.

This kid-friendly resort offers fun for the entire family. Its Hole-in-the-Wall River Ranch, on-site spa and salon services, and nearby golf, hiking, and shopping choices offer options for a variety of tastes. Conveniently located in north-central Phoenix off Piestewa Peak Pkwy. (formerly Squaw Peak Pkwy.), this Pointe Hilton resort, surrounded by beautiful mountain views, features spacious two-room suites and one- and two-bedroom casitas. Complimentary high-speed Internet access; child care services and activities. Pets are welcome. Enjoy close proximity to shopping, dining, and golf in the Camelback Corridor/Biltmore District and hiking at Piestewa Peak.

POINTE HILTON
TAPATIO CLIFFS RESORT

602-866-7500 or 800-876-4683.
www.pointehilton.com.
11111 N. 7th St., Phoenix 85020.
Prices: $89–319.
Credit Cards: AE, CB, D, DC, MC, V.
Handicapped Access: 14 rooms.
Pets: Yes.

Located farther north than the Pointe
Hilton Squaw Peak Resort, Tapatio Cliffs
offers an on-site 18-hole golf course as well
as a full-service spa and Falls Water Park—a
series of pools, waterfalls, and a 130-foot
enclosed slide. Babysitting and children's
programs are available. The resort features
two-room suites, complimentary Internet
access, and five on-site dining opportunities, including Cascade Falls—a poolside
eatery.

SHERATON CRESCENT HOTEL

602-943-8200 or 800-325-3535.
www.sheraton.com.
2620 W. Dunlap Ave., Phoenix 85021.
Prices: $149–269.
Credit Cards: AE, CB, D, DC, MC, V.
Handicapped Access: 14 rooms.
Pets: Small dogs welcome.

This hotel features 342 rooms, on-site dining options, oversized beds, and activities
like tennis, beach volleyball, squash, and
racquetball. The Olympic-sized pool sports
a waterslide, and the property has a sauna
and state-of-the-art fitness facility. Close
to the Metrocenter Mall.

PARADISE VALLEY
INTERCONTINENTAL MONTELUCIA
RESORT & SPA

602-956-9400.
www.montelucia.com.
4949 E. Lincoln Dr., Paradise Valley 85253.
Prices: $189–5,000.
Credit Cards: Call.
Handicapped Access: 10 rooms.

Pets: Call about special programs.

This resort—situated against the majestic
backdrop of Camelback Mountain—is
scheduled to open in fall 2007 and promises to offer a true luxury resort experience
with a 30,000-square-foot spa, on-site
concierge staff, and easy access to the
upscale Biltmore shopping and dining district; there are 15 golf courses within a 10-
mile radius, including the Phoenician and
Arizona Biltmore Golf Club. The Montelucia
Spa features the world-class splendor of
Andalusia.

BILTMORE DISTRICT/CAMELBACK AREA
A combination of upscale homes,
retail/office space, and incredible views,
the Biltmore District/Camelback Corridor
and surrounding areas run along Camel-
back Rd. and north between 24th and 64th
Sts. in the shadows of Camelback Mountain.
The area, which borders the west side of
Scottsdale and includes the south part of
Paradise Valley, is only minutes from Sky
Harbor International Airport and home to
some of the Valley's top resorts, including
Arizona Biltmore, Royal Palms, and Sanctu-
ary at Camelback; hotels include the Ritz-
Carlton and Embassy Suites. Biltmore
Fashion Square and the Wrigley Mansion
are two of the area's biggest attractions,
while upscale restaurants line Camelback
Rd. The corridor is close to AZ 51 or
Piestewa Peak Pkwy., which provides easy
access to Loop 202 (south), Loop 101
(north), I-10—and all the Valley has to offer.

ARIZONA BILTMORE RESORT & SPA

602-955-6600 or 800-950-2575.
www.arizonabiltmore.com.
2400 E. Missouri Ave., Phoenix 85016.
Prices: $289–1,895; call for special pricing
packages.
Credit Cards: AE, CB, D, DC, MC, V.
Handicapped Access: 17 rooms.
Pets: No.

Resting beside the pool at the Arizona Biltmore, you could dream of anything but a white Christmas; however, that's exactly what famous composer Irving Berlin did. Since its opening day on February 23, 1929, the Arizona Biltmore has been a top choice among stars, starlets, and even recent US presidents. This Frank Lloyd Wright–inspired resort sits on 39 acres of lush green lawns at the foot of the Phoenix Mountain Preserve. Pamper yourself with a German Chamomile Body Polish at the 22,000-square-foot Arizona Biltmore Spa, or enjoy 18 holes of golf at the adjacent Arizona Biltmore Golf Club. Take a shuttle (every hour on the hour) to nearby Biltmore Fashion Park; stroll among the shops or enjoy dinner at one of the many restaurants lining Camelback Rd.

COURTYARD PHOENIX CAMELBACK

602-955-5200.
www.marriott.com.
2101 E. Camelback Rd., Phoenix 85016.
Prices: $79–269.
Credit Cards: AE, CB, D, DC, MC, V.
Handicapped Access: 10 rooms.
Pets: No.

Located off AZ 51, this hotel is close to some of the Valley's best restaurants, shops, golf courses, and hikes. Both Piestewa Peak and Camelback Mountain are within a short drive; Biltmore Fashion Square is just down the street. The hotel features 12 deluxe suites in addition to its regular guest rooms, free high-speed Internet access, a pool, and an exercise facility.

EMBASSY SUITES PHOENIX BILTMORE

602-955-3992.
www.embassysuites.com.
2630 E. Camelback Rd., Phoenix 85016.
Prices: $149–409.
Credit Cards: AE, CB, D, DC, MC, V.
Handicapped Access: 4 rooms.
Pets: With a $25 deposit.

Embassy Suites features two-room suites and complimentary breakfast and cocktail hour. It's located adjacent to Biltmore Fashion Park, with shopping and dining just steps away; golfing and hiking are minutes away by car. A pool, exercise facility, on-site bar, and room service round out the hotel's amenities.

HOMEWOOD SUITES HOTEL— HIGHLAND

602-508-0937.
www.homewoodsuites.com.
2001 E. Highland Ave., Phoenix 85016.
Prices: $99–259.
Credit Cards: AE, CB, D, DC, MC, V.
Handicapped Access: 6 rooms.
Pets: With a $100 deposit.

Another suites-only hotel, Homewood on Highland features full kitchens, an on-site pool and half-court basketball, free wireless Internet access, and complimentary breakfast included with room rate; same goes for dinner Mon.–Thu.

RITZ-CARLTON PHOENIX

602-468-0700 or 800-241-3333.
2401 E. Camelback Rd., Phoenix 85016.
Prices: $199–750.
Credit Cards: AE, CB, D, DC, MC, V.
Handicapped Access: 7 rooms; ask about availability.
Pets: No.

Located in the heart of the Biltmore District, across the street from Biltmore Fashion Park and part of the Camelback Esplanade, the Ritz-Carlton Phoenix offers plenty of shopping and dining within walking distance. The hotel features a 24-hour on-site fitness facility, bistro 24 restaurant, the Esplanade Cigar Bar, and two spa treatment rooms. There are no less than 25 golf courses within a 12-mile radius.

ROYAL PALMS RESORT AND SPA

602-840-3610 or 800-672-6011.

www.royalpalmshotel.com.
5200 E. Camelback Rd., Phoenix 85018.
Prices: $389–499; call for special pricing
packages and villa pricing.
Credit Cards: AE, D, DC, MC, V.
Handicapped Access: Yes.
Pets: Yes, under 15 pounds.

Nestled against Camelback Mountain, Royal
Palms pairs its 119 casitas and guest rooms
with the original Cook Mansion built in
1929 to create this Mediterranean-inspired
resort and spa. Only 7 miles from Phoenix
Sky Harbor Airport and minutes from the
upscale Biltmore shopping district and Old
Town Scottsdale, it's a top choice among
business and leisure travelers. Enjoy complimentary valet parking, shoe shine, business services, in-room coffee, nightly
turndown, and a bowl of fresh fruit. For a
special touch for your romantic vacation,
contact the resort's very own director of
romance, Eric Sofield. Dispensing a wealth
of "love", Eric manages the details that
make the memories of a lifetime. Relax on

T. Cook's North Patio at Royal Palms Resort and Spa.
Photo provided courtesy of Royal Palms Resort and Spa

site at Alvadora Spa, dine on the quiet back
patio of T. Cook's, or unwind beneath your
private cabana poolside. They also accept
checks, debit cards, and cash.

SANCTUARY ON CAMELBACK MOUNTAIN RESORT AND SPA
480-948-2100 or 800-245-2051.
5700 E. McDonald Dr., Paradise Valley
85253.
Prices: $225–815.
Credit Cards: AE, D, DC, MC, V.
Handicapped Access: 6 rooms.
Pets: Yes.

Voted the number one resort in the United
States by *Condé Nast Traveler* readers, Sanctuary is located on Camelback Mountain
and lives up to its name, affording a relaxing escape to those who stay in one of its 98
casitas. The resort features amazing views
of the city and mountain landscape just
north of the upscale Biltmore District.
Sanctuary Spa offers both indoor and outdoor treatment rooms, a meditation garden,
and a therapeutic pool. Dine on site at well-
known elements restaurant, or relax at the
jade bar.

PHOENIX/AIRPORT LODGING
Airport hotels in the Valley are located close
to the Phoenix–Tempe border. Close proximity to I-10, Loop 202, and I-17 make the
rest of the Valley easily accessible. Like
many airport hotels around the country, the
following are located within a network of
highways, industrial parks, and office buildings; however, within a couple of miles at
most (depending on the hotel you choose),
you will find Papago Park, Desert Botanical
Garden, and the Phoenix Zoo, as well as golf
courses like Phantom Golf Club at Pointe
South Mountain Resort. Downtown Phoenix
and Mill Avenue, Tempe Town Lake, and
Arizona State University's Main Campus in
Tempe are within a 10-minute drive. The
COFCO Chinese Cultural Center is located
north of the airport on 44th St.

The jade bar at Sanctuary on Camelback. Photo provided courtesy of Sanctuary on Camelback

AIRPORT RAMADA LIMITED
602-275-5746.
www.ramada.com.
4120 E. Van Buren St., Phoenix 85008.
Prices: $60–100.
Credit Cards: AE, D, DC, MC, V.
Handicapped Access: Yes.
Pets: No.

This 47-room Ramada Limited, located just north of Phoenix Sky Harbor International Airport, features a free continental breakfast, an outdoor pool, and free wireless Internet access in guest rooms.

AIRPORT SLEEP INN BY CHOICE HOTELS
480-967-7100.
www.choicehotels.com.
2621 S. 47th Place, Phoenix 85034.
Prices: $39–109.
Credit Cards: AE, CB, D, DC, MC, V.

Handicapped Access: 8 rooms.
Pets: $25 per stay, per pet (nonrefundable); limit 1 pet per room, 50 pounds or less.

This 105-room hotel features a complimentary 24-hour airport shuttle, continental breakfast, wireless Internet access, and an outdoor heated pool and spa.

COURTYARD PHOENIX AIRPORT
480-966-4300.
www.marriott.com.
2621 S. 47th St., Phoenix 85034.
Prices: $269–309.
Credit Cards: AE, CB, DC, MC, V.
Handicapped Access: Yes.
Pets: No.

Located less than 2 miles from the airport, this Courtyard Marriott features a complimentary airport shuttle 5 AM–11 PM, free Internet access, an on-site exercise room, and Courtyard Café. There are several golf courses within 4 miles, including ASU Karsten in Tempe and Phantom Golf Club at Pointe South Mountain Resort.

CROWNE PLAZA PHOENIX—AIRPORT
602-273-7778 or 800-465-4329.
www.crowneplaza.com.
4300 E. Washington St., Phoenix 85034.
Prices: $89–179.
Credit Cards: AE, CB, D, DC, MC, V.
Handicapped Access: 6 rooms.
Pets: Small dogs.

This recently renovated Crowne Plaza is located less than a mile from the airport and offers guests a complimentary airport shuttle, Internet access, a 24-hour fitness room, and an outdoor heated pool. You will also find an on-site restaurant and lounge.

DOUBLETREE GUEST SUITES
PHOENIX—GATEWAY CENTER
602-225-0500 or 800-800-3098.
www.doubletree.com.
320 N. 44th St., Phoenix 85008.
Prices: $159–269.
Credit Cards: AE, CB, D, DC, MC, V.
Handicapped Access: 6 rooms.
Pets: No.

This modern-looking Doubletree Guest Suites, located less than 2 miles from the airport, features an on-site restaurant and bar, a courtyard pool, and a fitness center. Amenities include high-speed Internet access, microwave, refrigerator, and wet bar; the hotel offers a complimentary breakfast buffet and airport shuttle.

EMBASSY SUITES
PHOENIX AIRPORT—44TH STREET
602-244-8800 or 800-447-8483.
www.embassysuites.com.
1515 N. 44th St., Phoenix 85008.
Prices: $79–259.
Credit Cards: AE, CB, D, DC, MC, V.
Handicapped Access: 4 rooms.

Pets: No.

Located less than 2 miles from Sky Harbor International Airport, this hotel features 229 two-room suites, a full complimentary breakfast, heated pool and spa, and an on-site bar and grill. Manager's reception held nightly.

HAMPTON INN
PHOENIX AIRPORT NORTH
602-267-0606 or 877-777-3210.
601 N. 44th St., Phoenix 85008.
Prices: $89–189.
Credit Cards: AE, CB, D, DC, MC, V.
Handicapped Access: 5 roll-in showers only.
Pets: No.

This Hampton Inn, located 1 mile north of the airport, features complimentary hot breakfast, Internet access, and 24-hour airport shuttle.

HILTON GARDEN INN
PHOENIX AIRPORT
602-470-0500.
www.hilton.com.
3422 E. Elwood St., Phoenix 85040.
Prices: $69–209.
Credit Cards: AE, CB, D, DC, MC, V.
Handicapped Access: 8 rooms.
Pets: No.

Located about 3 miles east of the airport, this hotel is only minutes from downtown Tempe and offers guests a complimentary airport shuttle, on-site restaurant and lounge, pool and exercise room, and complimentary wireless Internet access.

HILTON PHOENIX AIRPORT
480-894-1600.
www.phoenixairport.hilton.com.
2435 S. 47th St., Phoenix 85034.
Prices: $89–249.
Credit Cards: AE, CB, D, DC, MC, V.
Handicapped Access: 7 rooms.
Pets: No.

Looking south from Camelback Mountain.

This Hilton is located less than 2 miles from the airport. It features an on-site restaurant and bar, pool, and exercise room; however, there's a fee per day for Internet access.

HOLIDAY INN EXPRESS
HOTEL & SUITES PHOENIX AIRPORT
602-453-9900.
www.hiexpress.com.
3401 E. University Dr., Phoenix 85034.
Prices: $69–189.
Credit Cards: AE, D, DC, MC, V.
Handicapped Access: 7 rooms.
Pets: No.

This hotel features 114 rooms and suites (each suite has a kitchenette), and offers complimentary airport shuttle, happy hour, and wireless Internet access.

PHOENIX AIRPORT MARRIOTT
602-273-7373.
www.marriott.com.

1101 N. 44th St., Phoenix 85008.
Prices: $149–239.
Credit Cards: AE, D, DC, MC, V.
Handicapped Access: 18 rooms.
Pets: No.

This 347-room hotel is located just north of the Loop 202 and COFCO Chinese Cultural Center and less than 2 miles from the airport. You will find an on-site bistro and lounge, as well as a complimentary airport shuttle. In-room amenities include Internet browser/web TV and wired high-speed Internet access (wireless is available throughout public areas of the hotel).

RADISSON HOTEL
PHOENIX AIRPORT NORTH
602-220-4400.
www.radisson.com.
427 N. 44th St., Phoenix 85008.
Prices: $89–174.
Credit Cards: AE, CB, D, DC, MC, V.

Handicapped Access: 6 rooms.
Pets: No.

At this 210-room hotel you will find an on-site café serving breakfast, lunch, and dinner; daily happy-hour specials in the bar; free Internet access; and an airport shuttle service. Located only 2.5 miles from the airport. On-site amenities include a pool and fitness center.

RESIDENCE INN PHOENIX AIRPORT
602-273-9220.
801 N. 44th St., Phoenix 85008.
Prices: $109–209.
Credit Cards: AE, D, DC, MC, V.
Handicapped Access: 7 rooms.
Pets: Yes, with $100 nonrefundable sanitary deposit.

This 200-suite hotel offers complimentary wireless Internet access, hot breakfast buffet, and social hour Mon.–Thu., and features an outdoor pool and an exercise room. All rooms are studio or two-bedroom suites with a full kitchen.

PETS

THE PAWS CONCIERGE
602-588-7833.
www.pawsconcierge.com.
2734 W. Bell Rd., Suite 1390, Phoenix 85083.

More than just a concierge service for your pet, it's a first-class pampering service. Paws Resort and Spa provides a full-service vacation experience for your companion. With all the bells and whistles they have to offer, expect your pet to beg to return here.

DINING

Credit Cards
The following abbreviations are used for credit card information:

AE: American Express
CB: Carte Blanche
D: Discover Card
DC: Diner's Club
MC: MasterCard
V: Visa

DOWNTOWN PHOENIX
ALICE COOPERSTOWN
602-253-7337.
www.alicecooperstown.com.
101 E. Jackson St., Phoenix.
Open: Daily for lunch and dinner; closed major holidays.
Prices: Moderate.
Cuisine: BBQ and home-style.
Credit Cards: AE, DC, MC, V.
Reservations: Recommended, except on game nights.
Special Features: Indoor and outdoor bar, mezzanine, 2 patios, spacious courtyard.

The slogan at Alice Cooperstown—"Where rock and jock meet"—captures the essence of the legendary musician's gastronomic tribute to music and sports. The restaurant is decorated with authentic sports and music memorabilia. Whether you're a fan of sports, music, or Alice Cooper, you'll enjoy a visit to this fun and raucous restaurant where good food shares equal time with live musical entertainment and the latest sports flashes across the mounted TV screens. Located just a short walk from Chase Field and US Airways Center, this is a good place to grab a bite before or after a baseball or basketball game. The wait on game days can be long; arrive early.

CITY BAKERY AT BENTLEY PROJECTS
602-253-7200.
www.citybakeryaz.com.
215 E. Grant St., Phoenix.
Open: Mon.–Fri. 11 AM–3 PM; closed weekends.
Prices: Inexpensive.
Cuisine: Gourmet sandwiches and salads.
Credit Cards: AE, MC, V.

Owner Carolyn Ellis has succeeded in creating another delicious culinary experience in the very heart of downtown Phoenix. Sharing space with Bentley Projects—a commercial art gallery with a revolving display of works by internationally recognized artists—City Bakery is located just south of US Airways Center in a somewhat iffy part of town. Sit beneath the shade on the patio or cool off inside at a table for two. Take a few minutes to wander through the art gallery. For lunch, try the turkey club (a tasty combination of smoked turkey, applewood-smoked bacon, avocado, tomatoes, and lettuce on focaccia) or the caprese (organic tomatoes, roasted artichokes, fresh mozzarella, basil, and arugula with pesto dressing), but the truth is, everything's good. And don't forget to save room for dessert—these larger-than-life delicacies are perfect to share with a companion, or even the table next to you! Or you can take it home for later—try the individual chocolate raspberry cake served with fresh raspberry sauce.

COACH AND WILLIE'S

602-254-5272.
www.coachandwillies.com.
412 S. 3rd St., Suite 104, Phoenix.
Open: Daily at 11 AM for lunch and dinner.
Prices: Moderate.
Cuisine: Pasta, wood-fired pizza, sandwiches.
Credit Cards: AE, D, MC, V.
Special Features: Outdoor patio, sunken mahogany bar, water fountain.

Located a short walk from both Chase Field and US Airways Center, Coach and Willie's offers an excellent opportunity to enjoy the Arizona weather before a big game.

COMPASS RESTAURANT, THE

602-440-3166.
www.phoenix.hyatt.com.
122 N. 2nd St., Hyatt Regency Phoenix.

Open: Dinner Sun.–Wed. 5:30–10 PM, Thu.–Sat. 5–10 PM; lounge Mon.–Sun. 5:30 PM–midnight; champagne brunch Sun. 10 AM–2 PM.
Prices: Expensive.
Cuisine: Contemporary American cuisine.
Credit Cards: AE, D, DC, MC, V.
Reservations: Yes.
Special Features: Revolving rooftop restaurant, lounge.
Dress Code: Business/business casual.

Enjoy a 360-degree view of Phoenix from one of the best seats in town—atop Arizona's only revolving rooftop restaurant. Executive chef Troy Knapp incorporates local ingredients like butternut squash and jalapeño peppers into creations that leave guests in awe. Park in one of the surrounding parking garages or snag a rare spot on the street. Parking is validated for 2 hours at the Regency Garage (valet) only.

FRIDAY'S FRONT ROW SPORTS GRILL

602-462-3503.
www.frontrowphoenix.myfridays.com.
401 E. Jefferson St., Phoenix.
Open: Daily 11 AM–9 PM for lunch and dinner; closed Thanksgiving and Christmas.
Prices: Moderate.
Cuisine: American.
Credit Cards: AE, D, MC, V.

Friday's Front Row Sports Grill is located at Chase Field overlooking left field and third base. Good food, good drinks, and a *great* view. Ask about patio seating even if there's not a game going on—sometimes you can catch the Arizona Diamondbacks at batting practice. What a relaxing way to spend a spring afternoon!

On game days, you can reserve a table outside on the patio. A table for four runs $260; you get a $130 credit to spend on food or beverage throughout the game. A 20 percent gratuity added to your tab; any remaining credit cannot be used to pay the gratuity. To reserve a table, call 602-462-3503. Tick-

Dining alfresco is standard in the Valley.

ets go on sale the first of the month for the next month's games. Tickets for July, for instance, would go on sale June 1.

The entrance is located on the north side of Bank One Ballpark on Jefferson St., between 4th & 5th Sts., Gate L.

HARD ROCK CAFE

602-261-7625.
www.hardrockcafe.com.
3 S. 2nd St., Suite 117, Phoenix.
Open: Lunch and dinner Sun.–Thu. 11 AM–11 PM, Fri.–Sat. 11 AM–midnight; bar Mon.–Sun. 11 AM–1 AM.
Prices: Moderate.
Cuisine: American.
Credit Cards: AE, D, MC, V.

What started out as a joke between two American proprietors of a little-known restaurant called the Hard Rock Cafe across the pond in London—and a very well-known Eric Clapton and his guitar—has expanded into a 138-restaurant, hotel, and casino dynamo with more than 70,000 pieces of hard-rock memorabilia crowding space in 42 countries around the world. And there's one here in Phoenix. If you're a fan of rock 'n' roll, then you will be awed by Elton John's cactus suit, Tom Petty's autographed jacket, Prince's purple stage costume, a Stones' two-piece suit from the early '70s, and Judas Priest's handwritten lyrics for "Breaking the Law" and "Another Thing Coming." And if you're not, the good food, loud music, and proximity to Chase Field and US Airways Center make it a great stop for a game-day meal.

PIZZERIA BIANCO

602-258-8300.
www.pizzeriabianco.com.
623 E. Adams St., Phoenix.
Open: Dinner Tue.–Sat. 5–10 PM.
Prices: Moderate.
Cuisine: Pizza.
Credit Cards: AE, MC, V.

Chris Bianco—Bronx native, winner of the James Beard Best Chef: Southwest award, and Phoenix proprietor of not one, not two, but three local favorites—makes his own mozzarella, and each pizza is baked in a wood-fired brick oven from the Old Country at this eatery in downtown Phoenix. The lines are long, and reservations are taken for groups of 6–10 only. No take-out, so the only way to experience this very popular pizza place is to wait. And it's worth it!

It's located at Heritage and Science Park off 7th St. between Monroe and Jefferson. Your best bet for parking is the garage at 5th St. and Monroe. Note that Monroe is one way headed north.

BAR BIANCO
602-528-3699.
www.pizzeriabianco.com.
609 E. Adams St., Phoenix.
Open: Tue.–Sat. 4–11 PM.

Prices: Moderate.
Cuisine: Appetizers.
Credit Cards: AE, MC, V.

If you prefer to have a drink and hearth-baked bread while you wait for space to open up next door, sidle up to Bar Bianco. This historic home has been converted into charming little bar, making it a great place to wait out the crowds or cap off the evening.

SAM'S CAFÉ
602-252-3545.
www.canyoncafe.com.
455 N. 3rd St., Suite 114, Phoenix.
Open: Lunch and dinner Sun.–Wed. 11 AM–9 PM, Thu.–Sat. 11 AM–10 PM.
Prices: Moderate to expensive.
Cuisine: Southwestern.
Credit Cards: AE, D, MC, V.

The urban landscape in downtown Phoenix.

Other Locations: Biltmore Fashion Park on 24th St. and Camelback (602-954-7100).

This upscale chain restaurant is worth mentioning. Its two locations in the Valley serve Nuevo Southwestern fare that is simply delicious. Traditional dishes like meat loaf, pasta, and mashed potatoes have been infused with a mixture of Mexican, Native American, and western US flavors, creating dishes like pasta with a jalapeño cream sauce; meat loaf stuffed with peppers, bacon, and onions, topped with roasted tomato BBQ sauce; and mashed potatoes blended with green chiles. They also serve chimichangas, fajitas, and enchiladas. Their margaritas are top notch—try the Grand Canyon. This house margarita is a mixture of cranberry, lime, and orange juices; tequila; and juice from the prickly pear cactus native to the Sonoran Desert. Ask for it on the rocks with salt.

STOUDEMIRE'S DOWNTOWN

602-307-5825.
www.stoudemiresdowntown.com.
3 S. 2nd St., Suite 113, Phoenix.
Open: Lunch Mon.–Fri. 11 AM–2 PM; happy hour Mon.–Fri. 4:30–7 PM; dinner Mon.–Tue. 4–9 PM (when there's a Suns game or event at US Airways Center), Wed.–Sat. 4–9 PM.
Prices: Moderate to expensive.
Cuisine: American.
Credit Cards: AE, MC, V.

Local celebrity chef Eddie Matney has designed tasty meals for sports fans, and on game nights this well-placed restaurant (across the street from US Airways Center and down the street from Chase Field) is teeming with enthusiastic ball fans and sports celebs. Catch dinner before the game or simply watch it here on one of the two bar's 34 television screens. Or relax outside on the patio. Non–game days, the place is quiet and relaxed.

UPTOWN/MIDTOWN PHOENIX
BARRIO CAFÉ

602-636-0240.
www.barriocafe.com.
2814 N. 16th St., Phoenix.
Open: Lunch Tue.–Fri. 11 AM–2:30 PM; dinner Tue.–Thu. 5–10 PM, Fri.–Sat. 5–10:30 PM, Sun. 3–9 PM; Sunday brunch 11 AM–3 PM.
Prices: Expensive.
Cuisine: Gourmet Mexican.
Credit Cards: Call.
Reservations: No.

At the Barrio—named Best Mexican Restaurant 5 years running by the *Arizona Republic*—chef Silvana Salcido Esparza takes your palate south of any Mexican cuisine you might normally find in the Valley. While the menu might look familiar—tacos, enchiladas, tortas—these gourmet dishes are a cornucopia of ingredients that set your senses into overdrive. Try the chiles en Nogado, a mixture of pears, apricots, apples, pecans, garlic, onions, and chicken stuffed into roasted poblano peppers and topped with pomegranate and a tasty almond sauce. The dessert menu includes traditional flan as well as goat's milk caramel stuffed crêpes; fritters and vanilla ice cream; and a mouthwatering chocolate cake stuffed with Oaxacan chocolate and almond sauce. Located south of Thomas Rd. next to La Vacqueria de la Ropa and the discoteca, this storefront restaurant presents a medley of traditional Mexican decor (devotion candles dot the tables) and Mexican art by local artists; fans spin lazily above and waiters make guacamole tableside while festive music blends with the laughter and voices in its crowded little rooms.

CORONADO CAFÉ

602-258-5149.
www.coronadocafe.com.
2201 N. 7th St., Phoenix.
Open: Lunch Mon.–Sat. 11 AM–2:30 PM; dinner Tue.–Thu. 5–9 PM, Fri.–Sat. 5–10

The friendly staff at Coronado Café in the Coronado District.

PM; closed Sun. Saturday brunch is served.
Prices: Inexpensive to expensive.
Cuisine: Gourmet comfort foods with a
twist.
Credit Cards: Call.
Reservations: Yes.
Special Features: Full bar.

Located in the historic Coronado District in
central Phoenix, this neighborhood favorite
is a 1915 Craftsman-style bungalow refurbished into a cozy and inviting dining experience. The Coronado Café offers soups,
salads, and sandwiches for lunch along with
a daily special such as chicken enchiladas or
baked salmon. The dinner menu includes
appetizers, soups, salads, and sandwiches
as well as featured entrées—Bing cherry
barbecued chicken or oven-roasted Alaskan
halibut. Once a BYOB establishment, the
café's full-service bar now includes cocktails, specialty drinks, wines by the glass or
bottle, and international and regional beer.

COUP DES TARTES

602-212-1082.
www.nicetartes.com.
4626 N. 16th St., Phoenix.
Open: Dinner Tue.–Sat. 5:30 PM–close.
Prices: Expensive.
Cuisine: French.
Credit Cards: AE, MC, V.

An ambience of candlelight, bare wooden
floors, and French-bistro cuisine has
transformed this 1930s farmhouse into a
cozy little French restaurant with only 14
tables. Celebrating 10 years in 2007, Coup
des Tartes is the brainchild of chef-owner
Natascha Ovando-Karadsheh after she
graduated from the French Culinary Insti-
tute in New York City in 1996. This little
BYOB encourages you to bring your favorite
bottle of wine ($8 corkage fees on regular-
sized bottles) to complement their ever-
changing menu. You will find appetizers
like Canadian Cove mussels from Prince

Edward Island, an exquisite plate of creamy cheeses, nuts, and fruit both fried and fresh, and the house favorite Brie Brule (warm Brie topped with caramelized apples and served with toast and fruit). Salad options might include a mixture of endives, oranges, walnuts, and dates drizzled with creamy tarragon vinaigrette. Entrées feature filet mignon, lobster, Chilean sea bass, and vegetarian fare crafted into culinary masterpieces. Tarts are baked fresh every day; these mouthwatering once-in-a-life-time treats are made with real butter. Reservations recommended on Friday and Saturday nights—though cancellations do occur to accommodate those spur-of-the-moment dinner decisions.

DURANT'S
602-264-5967.
www.durantsfinefoods.com.
2611 N. Central Ave., Phoenix.
Open: Cocktails, lunch, and dinner.
Prices: Moderate to expensive.
Cuisine: American.
Credit Cards: AE, MC, V.
Reservations: Yes.
Special Features: Full bar.

You have to enter through the kitchen, unless you want to be pegged as a tourist; in fact, most locals can't even tell you where the front entrance is! Founded by Jack Durant, this restaurant, located at the corner of Central and Virginia in central Phoenix, continues to boast red velvet and black vinyl decor—the interior is dark and "smoky." You can almost imagine the air thick with cigar smoke, raucous laughter, and big dealings of the 1950s. The food is delicious, the staff friendly, and the clientele respectful of the restaurant's desire to keep itself firmly entrenched in the past. Cell phones are not allowed—in fact, if you stop to chat you may be asked to leave. Enjoy this treat and take a step into the Old West when John Wayne might have visited.

The prices are a bit high, but the journey back makes it worth it!

FRY BREAD HOUSE
602-351-2345.
4140 N. 7th Ave., Phoenix.
Open: Mon.–Thu. 10 AM–7 PM, Fri.–Sat. 10 AM–6 PM.
Prices: Inexpensive.
Cuisine: Native American.
Credit Cards: D, MC, V.

A must-do while you're in Phoenix, this is an authentic Arizona experience. A Native American staple throughout the Southwest, fried bread—or fry bread—is just as delicious as it sounds. Similar to the elephant ears of the midwestern carnival or Mexican sopapillas, it can be eaten plain, salted, or with honey; it's also used like tortillas to make Indian tacos.

PANE BIANCO
602-234-2100.
4404 N. Central Ave., Phoenix.
Open: Lunch (take-out only) Tue.–Sat. 11 AM–3 PM.
Prices: Inexpensive.
Cuisine: Sandwiches.
Credit Cards: AE, MC, V.

Another Bianco success, it offers a limited but delicious selection of panini sandwiches and salads. Located next the energetic and popular Lux Coffee Bar.

BILTMORE/CAMELBACK CORRIDOR
BISTRO 24 (AT THE RITZ-CARLTON)
602-952-2424.
2401 E. Camelback Rd., Phoenix.
Open: Daily; breakfast Sun.–Sat. 6:30–11 AM; lunch Mon.–Sat. 11 AM–2:30 PM; dinner Tue.–Fri. 5:30–9:30 PM, Sat.–Sun. 5:30–10 PM; Sunday brunch 11 AM–2 PM.
Prices: Expensive.
Cuisine: French.
Credit Cards: AE, D, MC, V.

This American-style bistro, befitting the elegance and sophistication of the Ritz-Carlton, serves a seasonal menu steeped in chef Robert Graham's classical French training and influenced by his exposure to international cuisine.

DONOVAN'S STEAK AND CHOP HOUSE

602-955-3666.
www.donovanssteakhouse.com.
3101 E. Camelback Rd., Phoenix.
Open: Dinner Mon.–Thu. 5–10 PM,
Fri.–Sat. 5–11 PM; closed Sun.
Prices: Expensive to very expensive.
Cuisine: Steak house.
Credit Cards: AE, CB, DC, MC, V.
Reservations: Yes.
Special Features: Handicapped accessible, cigar room, over 700 wines, nonsmoking restaurant, smoking area, private room/banquet area, take-out.

Donovan's is an upscale and elegant steak house; enjoy pork chops or seafood as an excellent alternative.

EL CHORRO RESTAURANT AND LODGE

480-948-5170.
www.elchorrolodge.com.
5550 E. Lincoln Dr., Paradise Valley.
Open: Mon.–Fri. 11 AM–2 PM, Mon.–Sat.
5:30–10 PM, Sun. brunch 9 AM–2 PM and dinner 5:30–9 PM; lounge open nightly,
Sun.–Thu. until midnight, Fri.–Sat. 1 AM.
Piano bar open for happy hour Mon.–Fri
3–6:30 PM.
Prices: Expensive to very expensive.
Cuisine: American.
Credit Cards: AE, D, MC, V.
Reservations: Suggested.
Special Features: Outdoor patio, fireplace, 22 acres.

Originally built in 1934 by John C. Lincoln (you may have seen the hospital named after him) as the Judson School for Girls, the property was purchased 3 years later by Jan and Mark Gruber, who turned it into a lodge and dining room. Over the next 30-plus years, the Grubers built the lodge into a favorite stop for locals and celebrities alike, and hired as bartender that man who would later become the owner with his wife. In 1973, after 25 years as key elements of the lodge and its reputation for hospitality, Joe and Evie Miller purchased the property from the Grubers. Since then, the restaurant has expanded to seat a total of 165 diners, while the Grubers' original sticky bun recipe still delights guests. Over the decades the lodge has continued to grow in popularity as regulars have introduced its charms to friends and family, and newcomers have been drawn to its warmth.

HAVANA CAFÉ

602-952-1991.
www.havanacafe-az.com.
4225 E. Camelback Rd., Phoenix.
Open: Lunch and dinner Mon.–Thu. 11
AM–9:30 PM, Fri.–Sat. 11 AM–10 PM; dinner
Sun. 4–9:30 PM.
Prices: Moderate to expensive.
Cuisine: Cuban.
Credit Cards: AE, D, MC, V.

A Valley institution, Havana Café has been pleasing guests since 1989. Adapted from traditional Cuban foods and influenced by Spanish and Latin American cuisine, this menu—developed by chef-owner B. J. Hernandez—has created a following of loyal patrons, facilitating the opening of two additional restaurants in Scottsdale and Ahwatukee. B. J. and her husband, Gilbert, have been racking up the awards and rave reviews . . . Best Flan, Best Tapas Bar, Best Black Bean Soup. You'll find combinations of sweet peppers, garlic, and tomatoes; plantains, tropical fruit, and veggies; and traditional Cuban recipes like the Emperadado Cubano. Stop by and try these delectable dishes for yourself.

Morning Glory Café at the Farm at South Mountain.

AIRPORT

STOCKYARDS RESTAURANT & 1889 SALOON

602-273-7378.
www.stockyardsrestaurant.com.
5009 E. Washington St., Suite 115, Phoenix.
Open: Lunch Mon.–Fri. 11 AM–2 PM; dinner
Mon.–Sat. 5–9 PM, Sun. 4–8 PM; happy hour
Mon.–Fri. 3–6:30 PM.
Prices: Expensive.
Cuisine: Steaks.
Credit Cards: AE, D, MC, V.
Special Features: Full bar.

The Stockyards is Arizona's original steak
house, and has served the Valley for more
than 50 years. Originally part of the Tovrea
Cattle Ranch, the restaurant serves prime
rib, hand-cut steaks, and fresh seafood.
Steeped in the area's rich, ranching culture,
the 1889 Saloon features a massive hand-
carved cherry-and-mahogany bar and a
cut-glass chandelier.

SOUTH PHOENIX

FARM AT SOUTH MOUNTAIN, THE

602-243-9081.
www.thefarmatsouthmountain.com.
6106 S. 32nd St., Phoenix.

A 10-acre pecan grove boasting three
restaurants in three distinct settings; stalls
selling handmade goods, herbs, and plants;
and a farmers' market on Saturdays that
sells great breads from some of the Valley's
best bakeries.

QUIESSENCE

602-276-0601.
Open: Dinner Tue.–Sat. 5–9 PM.
Prices: Expensive to very expensive.
Cuisine: New American
Credit Cards: AE, MC, V.

This charming little restaurant does its best
to support local growers like Queen Creek
Olive Mill and Schnepf Farms, and in the
process creates an ever-changing and

delightful mix of native flavors. Starters include house-made charcuterie, vegetable crudités, or red onion and sherry soup. Meals are served à la carte—try entrées like wood-grilled diver scallops or Arizona-raised beef casserole with a side of roasted baby carrots or turnips. Desserts are simply sinful—the plates of artisan cheeses, nuts, and dried fruits, homemade desserts like farm cheesecake with red pears and dried cranberries with caramel sauce, and after-dinner drinks like Hartley & Gibsons Valdespino sherry will make it simply impossible to decide on a final treat. Take your time, enjoy the experience; dinner is a meal to be savored here.

To reach the restaurant, pull into the Farm at South Mountain's rock parking lot and follow the tree-lined drive to another parking lot. Park here; you'll see the lights of the restaurants peeking from among the plants and trees. Follow the footpath through the gardens to the back of the property, where you'll see a sign marking your way.

MORNING GLORY CAFÉ

602-276-8804.
Open: Breakfast Tue.–Fri. 8 AM–noon, Sat.–Sun. 8 AM–1 PM.
Prices: Moderate.
Cuisine: New American.
Credit Cards: AE, MC, V.

Also located at the Farm at South Mountain adjacent to Quiessence, the Morning Glory Café offers a wonderful outdoor dining experience. Sit on the garden patio beneath the mesquite and palo verde trees, and relax for a wonderful breakfast of fresh muffins, scones, freshly squeezed orange juice or just-brewed coffee; the omelets and breakfast burrito include veggies from the garden. Weekends usually mean a wait, but you can browse the fresh breads, plants, herbs, and handmade goods at the assortment of outdoor stalls.

FARM KITCHEN, THE

602-276-7288.
Open: Breakfast and lunch Tue.–Sun. 8 AM–4 PM.
Prices: Inexpensive.
Cuisine: American.
Credit Cards: AE, MC, V.

Sister restaurant to the Morning Glory Café, The Farm Kitchen is located at the front of the Farm at South Mountain's property and serves breakfast pastries and lunch cafeteria-style. Order from the menu inside and relax outside on one of the many picnic tables. You'll find tasty sandwiches, wraps, and salads as well as freshly baked cookies, muffins, scones, pies, and cakes. Call to order in advance.

Cafés

DUCK AND DECANTER

602-266-6637.
www.duckanddecanter.com.
1 N. Central Ave., Phoenix.
Open: Breakfast and lunch Mon.–Fri. 7 AM–4 PM and special events; closed weekends.
Prices: Inexpensive.
Cuisine: Deli.
Credit Cards: Call.
Other Locations: Camelback Arboleda, 1651 E. Camelback Rd., Phoenix (602-274-5429); open Sat.–Wed. 9 AM–7 PM, Thu.–Fri. 9 AM–9 PM. North Central, 3111 N. Central Ave., Phoenix (602-234-3656); open Mon.–Fri. 7:30 AM–3 PM.

This Valley staple (local distributor of the famous Fairytale Brownies) has fed area residents since 1972. On offer are specialty sandwiches, soups, salads, and other goodies including specialty wines, beers, cheeses, coffees, and teas. The Duck (as it is affectionately called by locals) has some of the best and most inventive sandwiches around, including signature creations like Where's the Beef?—a vegetarian concoction packed with so many tasty ingredients, you forget to ask where the beef is; and The Duckling—smoked breast of duck, smoked turkey, cream cheese, cranberry walnut relish, and watercress on walnut raisin country bread, a meal that confounds your taste buds into a state of stunned joy. The Duck's three locations are favorites of the city's lunchtime crowd, so expect to wait in line for a lunch that's worth it. You can call ahead or order online for faster pickup.

MACALPINE'S SODA FOUNTAIN

602-262-5545.
www.macalpinessodafountain.com.
2303 N. 7th St., Phoenix.

MacAlpine's, originally established in 1928, now serves up home-style cookin' to area residents. With space for 45 diners, the restaurant is reminiscent of a 1950s-style soda fountain with old-fashioned malts, phosphates, and the same counter that was here when this was a drugstore. Modern fare like their black bean vegetarian burger joins home-style favorites like the chicken cheese melt and French onion soup.

LA GRANDE ORANGE

602-840-7777.
www.lagrandeorangegrocery.com.
40th St. and Camelback, Phoenix.
Open: Daily for all 3 meals, Mon.–Sat. 6:30 AM–6:30 PM, Sun. 6:30 AM–8 PM.
Prices: Inexpensive to moderate.
Cuisine: New American.
Credit Cards: MC, V.

Set in an older Phoenix neighborhood, this very popular restaurant is hopping no matter how early you arrive. Park in front or in the back, where you enter through the kitchen. Patio seating beneath a canopy of trees or beside the floor-to-ceiling windows embraces the desert setting of this local favorite; Camelback Mountain looms blocks away. The food is great, and the bustling atmosphere is enough to pump you up for an early-morning mountain climb; better yet, it can be your treat afterward!

MY FLORIST CAFÉ

602-254-0333.
www.floristcafe.com.
534 W. McDowell, Phoenix.
Open: Daily for breakfast, lunch, and dinner 7 AM–midnight.
Prices: Inexpensive to moderate.
Cuisine: New American.
Credit Cards: AE, MC, V.

Located at the corner of 7th Avenue and McDowell right in the middle of the Phoenix historic districts, this is a popular choice for breakfast, lunch, dinner, or even a late-evening meal. My Florist Café (named as such because that's what the big sign above it says, and the city of Phoenix would not allow a new one to replace it) is adjacent to the Willo Baking Company. Together they make the delicious sandwiches, French toast, and bread baskets that the locals find so tasty. Other breakfast choices include a yogurt and granola parfait, breakfast burrito, and salmon plate. Lunch and dinner include a variety of gourmet sandwiches (The Portabello—roasted portobello, eggplant, red pepper, and more on a rosemary focaccia bread) and salads like the Brie Salad (Brie, chicken, fresh berries, roasted almonds…). The dinner menu adds an array of appetizers, and the bar serves mixed drinks and wine, including several choices by the glass. Enjoy live piano music (Nicole Pesce on the concert grand Steinway) Wed. through Sun. from 7:30pm until midnight.

WEST PHOENIX

GARCIA'S LAS AVENIDAS

602-272-5584.
www.theoriginalgarcias.com.
2212 N. 35th Ave., Phoenix.
Open: Daily for lunch and dinner.
Prices: Moderate.
Cuisine: Mexican.
Credit Cards: AE, MC, V.

Shopping at the Downtown Phoenix Public Market.

Garcia's Mexican Restaurants, founded by Julio and Olivia Garcia in West Phoenix back in 1956, went on to become a nationally recognized chain; this restaurant, however, remains within the family that started it all. Good, traditional, inexpensive Mexican foods have kept this a local favorite.

MI COCINA, MI PAIS

602-548-7900.
4221 W. Bell Rd., Phoenix.
Open: Tue.–Sun. for lunch and dinner.
Prices: Inexpensive.
Cuisine: Latin American.
Credit Cards: AE, MC, V.

Tucked away in a nondescript strip mall, this little restaurant might not look like much on the outside, but inside its owner-chef—Ecuador-born Rosa Rosas—serves up delicious and inexpensive Central and South American fare.

Wine Bars

CHEUVRONT WINE AND CHEESE CAFÉ

602-307-0022.
www.cheuvronts.com.
1326 N. Central Ave., Phoenix.
Open: Lunch and dinner Mon.–Wed. 11 AM–10 PM, Thu. 11 AM–11 PM, Fri. 11 AM–midnight; dinner Sat. 4 PM–midnight, Sun. 4–9 PM.
Prices: Expensive.
Cuisine: Eclectic.
Credit Cards: AE, D, MC, V.

Cheuvront, on Central Ave. in the north end of downtown Phoenix, is a city favorite and has been recognized on the national stage by *Bon Appétit* as one of the 50 best restaurants in the United States. The menu offers an array of dishes to choose from, including entrées like the maple bourbon glazed pork chop and pan-seared Alaskan halibut. Cheuvront rounds out their menu with eclectic pizzas, tasty gourmet salads, and a variety of cheese plates designed to delight the senses. Enjoy the added element of suggested wine pairings on your menu, or ask your server to assist you in making a choice that will heighten your dining experience. If you're new to wine . . . sit at the bar and the bartender can point out excellent choices based on your novice tastes; hungry . . . ask him or her to pair your wine with a tasty cheese plate. Oh, and they make an excellent mojito—perfect for a hot summer afternoon!

Cheuvront can also ship custom wine and cheese baskets anywhere in the state. Baskets include a bottle of wine, three cheeses, a fig cake from Spain, a box of Arizona's Star Ridge crackers, and an assortment of gourmet chocolates. You can choose from their collection of domestic and international wines as well as from an assortment of farmstead cheeses from around the world. Baskets may be shipped out of state, without the wine (per Arizona law). They start at $60, plus shipping.

Farmers' Markets

DOWNTOWN PHOENIX PUBLIC MARKET
www.phoenixpublicmarket.com.
721 N. Central Ave. (SE corner Central and McKinley, 2 blocks south of Roosevelt).
Open: Every Sat., year-round.

Arizona agriculture, cooking, and creativity are represented here as vendors from across the state bring their best to Phoenix. You will find handmade noodles; olive oil from the Valley's own Queen Creek Olive Mill; delicious hummus and pita chips by Dr. Hummus; wines from Granite Creek Vineyards in Chino Valley north of Phoenix; fresh eggs, vegetables, and herbs from local growers; and handmade crafts. Listen to live music and wander among the shaded stalls on this once empty lot. Parking is free.

Caterers
A number of the restaurants mentioned in this book cater local weddings and events, from Arcadia Farms to Joe's BBQ to Santa Barbara Catering, which is affiliated with the Farm at South Mountain. In addition, several fantastic chefs in town cater exclusively, including Valley favorites Maria and Martin Osete of **Mi Catering** (623-748-4547; www.micatering.com; 17423 N. 25th Ave., Phoenix) and Robert Richter of **Robert's Catering** (480-963-4040; www.robertscatering.net; 46 E. Galveston, Chandler).

The terms *passionate*, *meticulous*, and *inventive* best describe Maria and Martin's love of food, attention to detail, and creative culinary styles. Their menus are a mixture of European and Old World Mexican cuisine, influenced by the training and experiences of this husband and wife duo.

After more than 20 years in the Valley, Robert's Catering continues to create memorable culinary experiences for his clients and their guests. First-class service, gourmet menus, and mouthwatering wedding cakes are his signature; his staff are helpful and friendly. Both catering companies work with clients to design menus that reflect the style and substance of the event, its guests, and its host and hostess.

Deli/Gourmet Shops

AJ'S FINE FOODS (CENTRAL AND CAMELBACK)
602-230-7015 or 800-280-7105.
www.ajsfinefoods.com.
5017 N. Central Ave., Phoenix.
Open: Daily 6 AM—9 PM.
Other Locations: 13226 N. 7th St., Phoenix (602-863-3500 or 877-841-4118); 4430 E. Camelback, Phoenix (602-522-0956).

AJ's is an upscale market selling gourmet products, including made-to-order sushi, high-quality meats, fish, cheeses, and ready-made meals. You will also find an extensive selection of fine wines and liquors. Staff are wonderfully helpful in picking the right items for a special meal or the perfect wine to complement dinner. AJ's also features a selection of some of the best desserts in the Valley. Stop by for a quick lunch or pick up a gourmet meal ready to go.

Health Food Stores

SPROUTS FARMERS MARKET
602-553-3131.
www.sprouts.com.
2824 E. Indian School Rd., Phoenix.
Open: Daily 8 AM–10 PM.
Other Locations: 18040 N. 19th Ave., Phoenix (602-864-6130); 2824 E. Indian School Rd., Phoenix (602-553-3131); 12415 N. Tatum Blvd., Phoenix (602-971-4177).

Arizona is the home of Sprouts Farmers Markets. This quickly growing retail chain features farm-fresh produce, often from local growers, as well as natural meats, cheeses, vitamins, and supplements, all at reasonable prices. In the West Valley, Sprouts can also be found in Surprise, Avondale, and Peoria.

HI-HEALTH
602-279-5200.
www.hihealth.com.
3121 N. 3rd Ave. (Central & Thomas—Park Central Mall), Phoenix.

Hi-Health features quality health foods and nutritional supplements. There are 15 more stores located throughout the city of Phoenix and an additional 35 throughout the rest of the Valley.

Wines & Liquors

SPORTSMAN'S FINE WINE & SPIRITS
602-955-WINE.
www.sportsmans4wine.com.
3205 E. Camelback Rd., Phoenix.
Other Locations: Arrowhead Towne Center, Glendale; Scottsdale Rd. north of Shea Blvd., North Scottsdale.

This well-known liquor store has been in the Valley (under one owner or another) since the 1950s; the current owners have been at the helm since 1987 and have transformed its focus from somewhere to buy a six-pack to the place where you can purchase fine wine and spirits. You'll find single-malt scotch, whiskey, rum, and other spirits, sparkling and still wines, and a collection of beers—all from various points on the globe—as well as a wine bar, tastings, and events ranging from a classic malt seminar to Irish beer tastings. The wine bar serves appetizers, a comprehensive list of cheeses, sandwiches, and salads for lunch and dinner. Check out the lengthy menu of wines by the glass. Staff are very helpful and full of all sorts of great info. They can help you find the perfect wine for a special meal or assist you in discovering a new favorite.

CULTURE

Architecture
Originally touted as a paradise for lungers (slang for individuals suffering from tuberculosis), 19th-century Phoenix saw an influx of settlers with health problems. As area boosters realized that this might not be the healthiest population with which to build a city, they began advertising the area as a year-round playground for the healthy and wealthy.

In either case, however, the city has been a place to come and begin anew rather than hold on to the past. More recently, as the city realizes the value of its own history, Phoenicians are marrying the best of the past and a hope for the future. Many city neighborhoods remain well-preserved remnants from its early days. More than the Old West movies and ambling cowboys, the very homes that lined its canopied streets were worth keeping and restoring.

Vernacular Era: 1867–1900

Housing in early Phoenix was driven by the availability of materials, and the need for materials that provided relief from the desert's harsh weather. Adobe (hand-packed brick made of clay-based mud and hay binders, dried in the sun) was clearly the best option for keeping interiors cool in summer and warm in winter. Early homes were simple, functional, one story, and made of local materials, especially adobe. The floor plan was usually rectangular or square with a horizontal emphasis, a low- to medium-pitch roof with wood shingles, a wide front porch, exposed adobe walls, and little or no ornamentation. Small and economically built, these are the homes you'll find in photographs taken prior to 1878—when the railroad finally made its way to Phoenix, bringing with it bricks, oak and glass.

Lasting examples of this style in the Valley include the Jones and Montgomery Homes (on Buckeye and 7th Avenue respectively), with their deep porches supported by wooden columns that provided relief from the heat and the sun.

Victorian Era: 1885–1905

The Victorian era produced significant changes in building styles. While earlier homes were rudimentary and symmetrical, Victorian homes were asymmetrical and highly ornamental. The homes were either one or two stories with irregular floor plans, towers, turrets, porches, bay windows, and polygonal wings, and modeled after historic British architecture. Windows were tall; front porches and verandas dominated the structures. The visual movement, varied color, and fancy stone or brick lintels made the homes fancier and prettier than Vernacular homes, and Phoenix grew much more pleasing to look at. The Evans House, which still stands at 1100 W. Washington, is an example of Eclectic Victorian with its custom-designed architecture that combines disparate elements, free-flowing space, and ornamentation used with abandon. Other examples include the Judge Tweed House (1611 W. Filmore), circa 1887, which is the only surviving French Second Empire–style home in the city; and the Smurthwaite House (1735 W. Jefferson), an example of the new England-influenced Shingle-style architecture.

In the late 19th century the railways connected Phoenix to the West Coast and to northern and southern Arizona, establishing this as a major crossroads in the Southwest. Post-1880 homes boasted imported glass, fired brick, stone, and even redwood. Professionally trained architects made their mark as well, including Fred Heinlein and James Miller Creighton, a well-known resident of Phoenix from the late 19th century into the 1940s and builder of the 1892 Niels Peterson House (it still stands in Tempe, at the northwest corner of Southern and Priest). These influences combined to visually transform Phoenix from dusty settlement into thriving, attractive urban center.

Fewer than 50 buildings representing the Victorian era remain today.

Phoenix Architecture Today

The Victorian era was followed by the Bungalow (1905–1925); Period Revival (1914–1940); and Ranch (1935–1960). There are 35 neighborhoods in Phoenix representing various combinations of these home styles. Representative of the rise, fall, and revitalization of these neighborhoods is the F. Q. Story Historic District, which runs from McDowell Rd.

south to Roosevelt St. and from 7th Ave. west to Grand. The area is named after Francis Quarles Story, who purchased the acreage in 1887 as a speculative investment. Though Story never lived here, he was instrumental in several projects that make the Phoenix area what it is today, including Grand Avenue, which creates the western boundary of the district. The 600-plus homes that make up this historic neighborhood were built between the 1920s and 1940s and include Spanish Colonial Revival, English Tudor, Craftsman, and ranch homes. The neighborhood, as with many of the historic districts in central Phoenix fell into disarray as families moved out of the area and purchased homes farther from the city center in the 1950s and '60s. By the late 1970s and early '80s, however, residents began recognizing the value of these historic homes; in 1984 F. Q. Story residents founded a nonprofit historic preservation association, as did many other districts.

Since then, the value of these neighborhoods has increased 10-fold; homes are coveted by those who enjoy the urban lifestyle. Some of the neighborhoods offer annual tours, including the Willo and Encanto Districts. Several neighborhoods are still in redevelopment, including the Coronado and Roosevelt Districts. For more information about the F. Q. Story Historic District, visit their web site at www.fqstory.org. You can also find information about historic districts in Phoenix at www.phoenix.gov/NBHDPGMS/histpres.html or www.ci.phoenix.az.us/HISTORIC/residents.html; for information on homes for sale in these areas, visit www.historicphoenix.com.

Cinema

CINEMA LATINO DE PHOENIX
888-588-CINE (2463).
www.cinemalatino.com.
7611 W. Thomas Rd., Phoenix (at the Encanto Blvd. entrance to the Desert Sky Mall, between 75th and 79th Aves.).
Admission: $7.25 adults, $6 matinee, $6 students and seniors over 65, $5 children.

This theater shows new movies, dubbed or with Spanish subtitles.

WHITEMAN HALL AT THE PHOENIX ART MUSEUM
602-257-1222 (24-hour information available) or 602-257-1880.
www.phxart.org.
1625 N. Central Ave., Phoenix.
Open: Visit online for show times.
Admission: Museum admission runs $10 adults, $8 seniors and full-time students with ID, $4 ages 6–17; free for museum members and children under age 6, plus free to all Tue. 3–9 PM!

Whiteman Hall, located within the Phoenix Art Museum, hosts independent and classic movies and documentaries about art, artists, and the various works on display in the museum. Movies are free with museum admission, and seating is first come, first served.

Gardens

DESERT BOTANICAL GARDEN
480-941-1225.
www.dbg.org.
1201 N. Galvin Pkwy., Phoenix.

Open: Daily; Oct.–Apr., 8 AM–8 PM; May–Sep., 7 AM–8 PM. Closed July 4, Thanksgiving Day, and December 25; note that some trails are closed during evening hours.
Admission: $10 adults, $9 seniors, $5 students (ages 13–18 and college with ID), $4 ages 3–12; under 3 free.

An absolute must for Valley visitors, the Desert Botanical Garden is home to 50,000 arid-land plants (including 39 species that are endangered, rare, or threatened) from deserts all over the world. Situated among the red-hued rocks of Papago Park on the Phoenix–Tempe border, the garden boasts five thematic trails representing conservation, living in the desert, Sonoran Desert plants and people, and desert wildflowers. Several seasonal events, including the annual butterfly and wildflower exhibits, reveal just how colorful the desert can be in spring. The site also features a garden shop (open daily 9 AM–5 PM; 480-481-8113) and library (open Mon.–Fri. noon–4 PM as a reading room; 480-481-8133). Enjoy live jazz in fall and spring at the Patio Café (open daily 8 AM–4 PM; 480-941-1225). Guided tours are available daily Oct.–May; bird walks occur weekly year-round; and to enjoy the garden in summer, partake in a sunrise or flashlight tour.

Historic Places

HISTORIC HERITAGE SQUARE/HERITAGE & SCIENCE PARK
602-262-5071.
www.phoenix.gov/PARKS/heritage.html.
115 N. 6th St., Phoenix.
Open: Tue.–Sat. 10 AM–4 PM, Sun. noon–4 PM.

Located on the original town site of the city of Phoenix and listed on the National Register of Historic Places, Heritage Square comprises several historic homes, restaurants, and shops, including the Victorian Rosson House museum built in 1895. The square shares space with the Arizona Science Center and Phoenix History Museum to create Heritage & Science Park. Several events take place here throughout the year, including auto shows, holiday and cultural events. Visit online for a calendar of events.

The best place to park is in the garage at the southeast corner of 5th and Monroe; obtain a discount by getting your ticket validated at any one of the park sites. Enter the garage's north entrance from Monroe St.; its west entrance, from 5th Street. Note that 5th Street is one way headed north. To access it, take Washington St. (also one way). Exit the garage from the west side only. On event days parking is harder to find; try the dirt lot on the northeast corner of 7th and Van Buren.

ROSSON HOUSE MUSEUM
602-262-5070; recorded information 602-262-5029.
Open: Wed.–Sat. 10 AM-4 PM; Sun. noon–4 PM; last tour of the day begins at 3:30 PM. Closed Mon.–Tue.; Easter Sunday; and mid-Aug.–Labor Day.
Admission: $4 adults; $3 seniors, AAA members, and groups; $1 ages 6–12.

Named after the original owner, Dr. Roland Lee Rosson, the Rosson House was built in 1895, when he was mayor of Phoenix. However, Dr. Rosson resigned after only a year due to a disagreement with the city council; in 1897 he and his family sold their home and moved to LA. Today the Rosson House Museum has been restored to its original splendor and depicts life in the late 19th and early 20th centuries when Phoenix was still a territory. The home is almost 3,000 square feet with 10 rooms and five fireplaces—large even by today's standards.

ARIZONA DOLL & TOY MUSEUM

602-253-9337.
602 E. Adams St., Phoenix.
Open: Tue.–Sun.; closed Aug.
Admission: $3 adults, $1 children.

Located in the Stevens House at Heritage Square, this museum boasts a collection of dolls, dollhouses, and all things miniature. Gift shop on site.

ORPHEUM THEATRE

602-534-5600.
www.phoenix.gov/STAGES/facility.html.
203 W. Adams St., Phoenix (at 2nd Ave.).
Open: Times vary by performance.
Admission: Pricing depends upon performance.

The Spanish Baroque Revival–style Orpheum Theatre was originally opened in 1929 and took two years and $750,000 to build. The city's only remaining historic theater, the Orpheum outlived both the Fox and Rialto. It has seen the rise and fall of downtown Phoenix and itself has been both vaudeville stage and movie house. In 1968 it was purchased, renamed Palace West, and brought Broadway favorites like *Annie*, *Cabaret*, and *The Best Little Whorehouse in Texas* to Phoenix until the early 1980s. At that point it was saved from the fate of its contemporaries by the joint efforts of then mayor Terry Goddard and the Junior League of Phoenix; it was added to the National Register of Historic Places. After a 12-year, $14 million renovation, the Orpheum reopened its 1,364 seats in 1997 to Carol Channing in *Hello Dolly!* Joined by the smaller and more intimate Herberger Theater and the much larger Symphony Hall and Dodge Theatre, the Orpheum contributes to a once again growing downtown theater district.

The Orpheum Theatre is owned by the city of Phoenix and managed by Phoenix Stages, as is Symphony Hall. For more information, including event dates and times, visit online. Tickets can be ordered at the Phoenix Convention Center Ticket Office, located at 100 N. 3rd St. The office is open Mon.–Fri. 10 AM–4 PM. You can also order online at www.ticket-master.com for most events. Tickets for performances by the Phoenix Symphony Orchestra, Arizona Opera, or Ballet Arizona should be ordered directly through those companies; see their separate entries in this chapter.

WRIGLEY MANSION CLUB, THE

602-955-4079.
www.wrigleymansionclub.com.
2501 E. Telawa Trail, Phoenix.
Open: 1-hour tours Wed.–Sat. 10 AM–3 PM; lounge Fri.–Sat. 4–11 PM; happy hour 4–7 PM (light complimentary appetizers).
Admission: $11 per person; reservations requested.

Built in 1932 by William Wrigley Jr. (of the chewing gum conglomerate) for his wife, Ada, Wrigley Mansion, named La Colina Solana or "sunny hill," was one of the family's five homes and served as a winter cottage. While the 16,850-square-foot home with 24 rooms and 12 bathrooms embodies more splendor and opulence than you might associate with a "cottage," it was the smallest of the Wrigley homes and used two months out of the year at most. Wrigley Mansion remained in the family for 40 years, and was once part of a portfolio of property owned by Tally Industries that included the Arizona Biltmore Resort and Golf Club, which rests below the 100-foot hill the mansion calls home.

The Wrigley Mansion Club, as it is now called, is technically a private club due to restrictions and regulations imposed upon it in 1982 when then owner Western Savings made it a private club and corporate retreat. In 1992 the mansion once again changed hands and found itself owned by another well-known family—Geordie Hormel of the meatpacking Hormels. Hormel lowered club membership to just $10 per household, making it an affordable opportunity for just about anyone in the Valley, and 100 percent of the proceeds go to children's charities throughout the state. The club is open for tours, and Geordie's Lounge is open Friday and Saturday nights. The club serves an amazing Sunday brunch. Mr. Hormel recently passed away, but has left a legacy here in the Valley.

Historic Tours

In the late 1970s several older neighborhoods in the city of Phoenix decided to preserve their little pieces of history, when they lobbied for the inclusion on the National Register of Historic Places. Since then a total of 35 neighborhoods in central Phoenix have been designated historic. Homeowners have taken great pride in restoring their homes to their previous splendor, and every year many of them open their homes to tours. Don't be discouraged if you miss the tours—a drive through these neighborhoods is an enjoyable experience for any lover of history or period homes. Some of these neighborhoods have been completely restored, while others are still in the process. The palm-lined avenues in the Encanto Park or the Willo District, west of Central Ave., offer some of the most visually pleasing drives. For more information about Phoenix's historic districts, visit www.ci.phoenix.az.us /HISTORIC/residents.html or www.phoenix.gov/NBHDPGMS/histpres.html.

ENCANTO PALMCROFT HOME TOUR

www.encantopalmcroft.org.
Open: Usually mid- to late March, 10 AM–4 PM.
Admission: About $18 per person.

The Encanto Palmcroft Historic District is located between 7th and 15th Aves. north of McDowell Rd. Festivities take place on 9th Ave. and Monte Vista; you'll find live music, food, and vendor booths at this street fair, as well as a ticket window and information about the homes on tour. With your map in hand, you can wander off and take a look at what these proud owners have done to restore and preserve their little piece of Phoenix history. Tickets can be purchased online via PayPal. Discounts apply if you order before the event date. Simply bring your printed receipt to the ticket booth. Parking can be found at Phoenix College on the northeast corner of 15th Ave. and Thomas Rd. You can pick up a shuttle there to take you to the festivities.

WILLO HOME TOUR

www.willohistoricdistrict.com.
Open: Usually the Sunday before Valentine's Day.
Admission: About $18 each.

The Willo Historic District is just west of Central Ave. between Thomas and McDowell Rds., from 1st to 7th Aves. The annual Willo Home Tour provides Valley residents and visitors the opportunity to see firsthand what residents have done to restore their homes to their original splendor. Built in the 1920s, '30s, and '40s, these historic homes comprise bungalow-style as well as Tudor Revival, Greek Revival, American Colonial Revival, Spanish Colonial Revival, and Pueblo Revival. Homes built in the late 1930s are representative of French Provincial and Monterey styles; some homes are similar in architectural design to the modern-day ranch home. In the 1980s Willo residents lobbied to have their neighborhood preserved as a historic district. Between 12 and 14 neighborhood homes open their doors to the public for this event.

Tickets are available online after December 1 of the previous year for a discount. You can also purchase tickets the day of at Walden Park at 3rd Ave. and Holly. During the tour, guests can walk from home to home or take the available trolley cars. For more information, visit the tour online at www.willohistoricdistrict.com.

Walking Tours

PHOENIX FIRST FRIDAY ART WALK DOWNTOWN
602-256-7539.
www.artlinkphoenix.com.
Admission: Free.

Downtown Phoenix has hosted the very popular art walk since 1994. The event now includes more than 90 art venues, street performers, and sidewalk vendors. First Friday is held on, well, the first Friday of each month, 6–10 PM. We suggest you start at the Phoenix Public Library, 1221 N. Central Ave. There you can pick up a First Friday brochure with information about the event and the locations of the galleries in downtown Phoenix. You can also pick up one of the four shuttle buses, which run every 20 minutes. It's an excellent alternative to navigating the downtown area with its construction and crowded streets. Be prepared to catch the last bus by 9:30 for a ride back to your car; however, your walk may be fairly short, and a cab ride is only about $5.

Stops along the way are a combination of eclectic art galleries like Avenue 10 Studio and Gallery; renovated buildings such as First Studio, built in 1949 to house Phoenix's first television station, now home to a display of art that changes monthly; ethnic centers like the Irish Culture Center and Japanese Friendship Garden Ro Ho En; and restaurants like Coach and Willie's near Chase Field. First Fridays bring together all of the cultural, artistic, and sports-oriented elements of downtown Phoenix and showcase the many restaurants, galleries, boutiques, and museums that dot this historic area. Detailed information is available online, including descriptions of each stop and a great map of the entire district. Be prepared to come back next month—the choices are endless, and many of the displays change from month to month.

Libraries

PHOENIX PUBLIC LIBRARY
General information and reference 602-262-4636; TDD 602-254-8205.
www.phoenixpubliclibrary.org.
1221 N. Central Ave., Phoenix.
Open: Mon.–Thu. 10 AM–9 PM, Fri.–Sat. 10 AM–6 PM, Sun. noon–6 PM.

The main library, known as the Burton Barr Central Library, is located south of McDowell Rd. on Central Ave., at the edge of Margaret T. Hance "Deck" Park. A fun choice on a hot summer day, this five-story library boasts an innovative design inspired by the Monument Valley and a 10,000-square-foot children's section with its own story room.

Museums

HEARD MUSEUM

602-252-8848.
www.heard.org.
2301 N. Central Ave., Phoenix.
Open: 9:30 AM–5 PM.
Admission: $10 adults, $9 seniors (65-plus), $5 for students with a valid student ID, $3 ages 6–12; children under 6, Heard Museum members, and Native Americans are free.
Credit Cards: AE, MC, V.
Handicapped Access: Yes.

The Heard Museum was founded in 1929 by Dwight B. and Maie Bartlett Heard to house their personal collection of cultural and fine art. It is now a private, nonprofit museum dedicated to preservation,

At the Annual World Championship Hoop Dance Contest. Photo provided courtesy of Heard Museum

awareness, and education of Native American culture and art, specifically of the Southwest. The museum includes about 35,000 objects; displays within the 10 exhibit halls and out-door courtyards change from season to season, providing ample display time for all of the pieces over time. Visit the museum online for information about live performances, like the Annual World Championship Hoop Dance Contest, and annual art shows and festivals. There are free public guided tours (45 minutes) daily at noon, 1:30, and 3 PM.

PHOENIX ART MUSEUM

602-257-1222 (24-hour information available) or 602-257-1880.
www.phxart.org.
1625 N. Central Ave., Phoenix.
Open: Tue., 10 AM–9 PM, Wed.–Sun. 10 AM–5 PM; closed Mon. and major holidays.
Admission: $10 adults, $8 seniors and full-time students with ID, $4 ages 6–17; free for museum members and children under age 6, plus free to all Tue. 3–9 PM!

In 2006 the Phoenix Art Museum completed a $50 million expansion. In addition to a new entrance off Central Ave. and a four-level gallery, the 2006 expansion included a new sculpture garden with 40,000 square feet of relaxing outdoor space in the heart of Phoenix and an expanded museum store. More than 17,000 works of modern, contemporary, and western American art and fashion design from across the globe make Phoenix Art Museum worth more than one trip. Opened in 1959, the original space has been expanded to incorporate 203,000 square feet. The museum's collection includes works from such greats as Monet, Picasso, and Georgia O'Keeffe. Changing exhibits have included Rembrandt and the Golden Age of Dutch Art, and Curves of Steel: Streamlined Automobile Design; these are often specially ticketed events. Additional features include an interactive ArtWorks Gallery and Art Museum Café by Arcadia Farms. Museum-trained volunteer docents give daily 1-hour tours, included with museum general admission; the Featured Exhibition Tour takes place at 1 PM, the Museum Masterworks Tour at 2 PM (Sat., 11 AM and 2 PM), and both are repeated Tue. at 6 PM.

PUEBLO GRANDE MUSEUM

602-495-0901 or 877-706-4408.
www.pueblogrande.org.
4619 E. Washington, Phoenix (just east of 44th St. on the south side of Washington).
Open: Mon.–Sat. 9 AM–4:45 PM, Sun. 1–4:45 PM.
Admission: $3; free on Sun.

Pueblo Grande Museum features the remains of the Hohokam culture including a partially excavated platform mound and a ball court along the Ruin Trail. The museum has rebuilt Hohokam houses on site based on archaeological data.

PHOENIX HISTORY MUSEUM

602-253-2734, ext. 221.
www.pmoh.org.
Heritage and Science Park, 105 N. 5th St., Phoenix.
Open: Tue.–Sat. 10 AM–5 PM; closed Sun.–Mon.
Admission: $6 adults; $4.50 AAA; $4 students, seniors, and military; $3 ages 7–12; ages 6 and under free. Group rates available.

Part of Heritage & Science Square, adjacent to the Arizona Science Center and the Rosson House, the Phoenix History Museum is dedicated to preserving and sharing the rich culture and history of those who have influenced Phoenix and the Salt River Valley. With light-rail construction clogging downtown traffic, your best bet for reaching the museum is to take Monroe St. off 7th St. (head west to 5th St.), or take 7th St. to Washington St. and turn right onto 5th; there is a parking garage on the east side of the street. Remember to get your parking ticket validated.

ARIZONA SCIENCE CENTER

602-716-2000.
www.azscience.org.
600 E. Washington St., Phoenix.
Open: Daily 9 AM–7 PM, closed Thanksgiving and Christmas.
Admission: Nonmembers: $9 adults, $7 ages 3–12 and 62-plus; members free. Planetarium admission for nonmembers runs $5 and $4.

Located at Heritage & Science Square (see the directions for the Phoenix History Museum, above), Arizona Science Center provides fun for children of all ages, including grown-ups.

At the Arizona Science Center.

Beware the sneezing nose and find out how well your paper airplane can fly at these fun, interactive exhibits that engage the entire family. The center also hosts special exhibits that have included the popular Animal Grossology and the controversial Body Worlds exhibits. Features include the interactive Waterworks, Dorrance Planetarium, and IMAX Theater. Special exhibits require tickets.

Note: If you and your family are avid museum-goers, consider purchasing an annual membership, which gains you access to 250 science and technology museums nationwide among other perks.

Music
See Celebrity, Dodge, Herberger, and Orpheum theaters in this chapter for additional music venues.

CRICKET PAVILION
Box office 602-254-7200, ext. 223.
www.livenation.com/venue/getVenue/venueId/113.
2121 N. 83rd Ave., Phoenix.
Open: Depending on show times.
Admission: Varies.

An easily accessible outdoor concert venue (north of I-10 between 75th and 83rd Aves.)—visit online for a schedule of upcoming acts. Parking is usually included in the price of your ticket. Parking lots open 2 hours prior to the stated showtime; premier parking is also available at $20 per car and $40 per bus, limo, or RV (available for purchase through the web site). The premier lot is off the 79th Ave. entrance.

Nightlife

Downtown Phoenix is slowly creating an urban nightlife. What exists today centers on sports (US Airways Center and Chase Field) or on theaters like Dodge, Herberger, and the Orpheum. A growing number of renowned restaurants and bars are making Copper Square home, though, and downtown Phoenix is starting to shake loose and rise again. First Fridays have gone a long way toward introducing Phoenicians and their neighbors to the multitude of venues that downtown has to offer.

You will also find several bars and lounges. **Majerle's Sports Grill** (602-253-0118; 24 N. 2nd St., Phoenix) is located in the oldest commercial building in downtown Phoenix. Majerle's (it's pronounced *mar-LEES*, and named after owner and former Phoenix Suns player Dan Majerle) has been a popular spot before and after Suns and Mercury (WNBA) games at US Airways Center just one block away for more than 13 years. **Volume/Club 245** (602-254-5303; 245 E. Jackson St., Phoenix) pumps out high-energy music Fri. and Sat. nights. There's also **Chop Shop** (602-258-7880; 1 E. Jackson St., Phoenix); and **Jackson's on Third** (602-254-5303; 245 E. Jackson St., Phoenix)—a great indoor-outdoor bar mere

Jackson's on Third makes a great stop before, during, or after the game.

yards from Chase Field and US Airways Center, and an excellent place to grab last-minute tickets to one of the games. **Bar Bianco** (602-528-3699; 609 E. Adams St., Phoenix) in Heritage & Science Park is a great place to have a drink while you wait for a table to open up at Pizzeria Bianco next door.

Travel back to a time when couples when out for "dinner and dancing" at **Johnny's Uptown Restaurant & Music Club** (602-277-5999) at Camelback and Central in Phoenix.

Stage

ACTORS THEATRE OF PHOENIX AT HERBERGER THEATER
602-253-6701, ext. 110.
www.atphoenix.org.
222 E. Monroe Ave., Phoenix.
Open: Visit online for shows, times, and tickets.
Admission: Varies by performance.

This 21-year old nonprofit theater company produces professional renditions of contemporary performances, musicals, and the classics. Located in the heart of downtown, Actors Theatre of Phoenix may be one of the Valley's best-kept secrets, and it's a favorite of those familiar with the downtown theater scene.

Most productions are held in Stage West, a 300-seat theater, except for their annual production of *A Christmas Carol*, which is performed in a larger 750-seat venue. Parking can typically be found along Monroe and Second Sts. as well as at nearby public parking facilities; however, with the light-rail construction, surface street parking is difficult and streets tend to be one way. Metered parking is free on weekdays after 5 PM and on weekends. Nearby public parking facilities include the former Bank One (now Chase) Garage (enter from 1st or 2nd St. between Monroe and Van Buren), Civic Plaza Garage (enter east of 3rd St. on Monroe), The Arizona Center (enter from 3rd St. heading south from Filmore), the Arizona Republic Parking garage (enter north of Van Buren on 2nd St.), and the Hyatt Regency Garage (enter off 2nd St. just north of Adams and south of Monroe). The box office is located on the southeast corner of the complex. It's open Mon.–Fri. 10 AM–5 PM and 1 hour before showtime daily. For more information about performances and the company itself, visit online at www.atphoenix.org.

ARIZONA OPERA COMPANY
877-639-0188.
www.azopera.org.
Open: Varies by performance.
Admission: Varies by performance.

Originally founded in Tucson in 1971, this company is the only producer of professional grand opera in all of Arizona, with a five-opera season that includes three performance dates in Tucson at the Tucson Convention Center Music Hall and four performances at Symphony Hall in Phoenix, on the corner of Washington and 2nd St. (behind the construction on the new Phoenix Convention Center.) The entrance can be found on the west side of the building, which is located on 2nd Street and Adams, half a block north of Washington. Light-rail and convention center construction mean you'll want to leave earlier to account for additional travel time through the downtown area. Check the Arizona Opera Company's

Public art at the Herberger Theater.

web site for current street closures and an interactive map of area parking lots—click on the Company tab and choose Directions and Parking. The site can also tell you how to best experience the opera, as well as performance dates and times.

ARIZONA THEATRE COMPANY
602-256-6995.
www.arizonatheatre.org.
502 W. Roosevelt St., Phoenix.

A 40-year old tradition in the Valley of the Sun, the Arizona Theatre Company is the state's leading professional theater company, and presents six performances per season at the Temple of Music and Art in Tucson and the Herberger Theater in Phoenix, as well as individual performances at the Mesa Arts Center in Mesa. For information about the company, its shows, and times, visit online at www.arizonatheatre.org.

BALLET ARIZONA
602-381-0184, ext. 526.
www.balletaz.org.
3645 E. Indian School Rd., Phoenix.
Open: Varies by show.
Admission: Varies by show.

Ballet Arizona, known as the Southwest's premier professional ballet company, was created in 1986 with the consolidation of three struggling ballet companies throughout the state. In

2000 the company hired Ib Andersen, principal dancer with the New York City Ballet for 10 years, as artistic director. Under his direction, Ballet Arizona has enhanced its level of performance and its national stature. Ballet Arizona performs at the Orpheum Theatre and Symphony Hall in downtown Phoenix. For more information about tickets and performances, visit their web site and click on At the Show.

CELEBRITY THEATRE

602-267-1600.
www.celebritytheatre.com.
440 N. 32nd St., Phoenix.
Open: Event times vary.
Admission/Fee: Ticket prices vary by event.

Known locally as the Valley's favorite theater, this venue boasts seating for over 2,500 with a revolving center stage and no seat more than 75 feet away. Originally designed in 1963 as a multiuse conference center, the theater hosts a variety of performances, including comedic entertainment, concerts, and special events. Box office hours are 10 AM–6 PM Mon.–Fri., Sat. 10 AM–1 PM; open Sun. for special on-sale events and event days.

The theater is located off of 32nd St. between Van Buren Ave. and the Loop 202. You can purchase tickets online, via phone (602-267-1600, ext. 1), or at the box office located on 32nd St., four blocks south of the 202 Loop in Phoenix. Five acres of parking lots are patrolled by security. There is a $5 fee for parking. Off-site parking is available but not secured.

DODGE THEATRE

602-379-2802.
www.dodgetheatre.com.
400 W. Washington St., Phoenix.
Open: Event times vary.
Admission/Fee: Ticket prices vary by event.

Dodge Theatre hosts a variety of entertaining performances, including Broadway and family stage shows and concerts for groups of 1,900–5,000 guests. Box-office hours are Mon.–Fri. 10 AM–5 PM, Sat.–Sun. for sales and events. Summer hours are shortened to Mon.–Thu. 10 AM–5 PM and Fri. 10 AM–noon unless an event is scheduled. Tickets can be purchased on site and at a variety of Ticketmaster locations, including Tower Records, Macy's, and Fry's Marketplace. Tickets can also be purchased by calling 480-784-4444 or 520-321-1000 or online at www.ticketmaster.com, best accessed from the Dodge Theatre web site via the Ticketing link. Visa, MasterCard, American Express, and Discover are accepted at ticket sales locations and online.

HERBERGER THEATER CENTER

602-252-8497 or 602-254-7399.
www.herbergertheater.org.
222 E. Monroe St., Phoenix.
Open: Event times vary.
Admission/Fee: Ticket prices depend upon the event.

Symphony Hall in downtown Phoenix.

The Herberger Theater Center, home of the Actors Theatre of Phoenix and host to a variety of performance groups including the Arizona Theatre Company, was built in 1989 in support of the growing performance arts presence in Phoenix.

The theater is located between Van Buren and Monroe Sts. and 2nd and 3rd Sts. Visitors from the East Valley can take 1-10 to I-17 west to 7th St., and head north on 7th to Monroe and west to 3rd St. Those from the West Valley can take I-10 east to 7th Ave., then head south to Van Buren and continue on Van Buren east to 2nd St. Please be aware that convention center and light-rail construction may affect traffic and parking. Visit www.copper square.com for up-to-date information on street conditions and closures.

Box-office hours are Mon.–Fri. 10 AM–5 PM, Sat.–Sun. noon–5 PM, and evenings 1 hour prior to performances. Tickets can be purchased there or by calling 602-252-8947, as well as through Ticketmaster (480-784-4444; www.ticketmaster.com). Metered parking is available on Monroe and 2nd Sts. It's free after 5 PM on weekdays and all day on weekends. Public parking facilities in the area include the Bank One (now Chase) Garage (enter from 1st or 2nd St. between Monroe and Van Buren), Civic Plaza Garage (enter east of 3rd St. on Monroe), The Arizona Center (enter from 3rd St. heading south from Filmore), the Arizona Republic Parking garage (enter north of Van Buren on 2nd Street), and the Hyatt Regency Garage (enter off 2nd Street just north of Adams and south of Monroe). Cost of parking depends upon garage and area events; it can range from a $5–7 flat fee to an hourly rate.

ORPHEUM THEATRE
See Historic Places—Heritage Square, above.

THE PHOENIX SYMPHONY
602-495-1117; box office 800-776-9080; local 602-495-1999.
www.phoenixsymphony.org.
75 N. 2nd St., Phoenix.
Open: The season lasts Sep.–May.
Admission: Ticket prices depend upon the program.

Founded in 1947, this is Arizona's only full-time professional orchestra and serves not only the Phoenix metropolitan area but also Central Arizona and the southwestern United States with 275 concerts and presentations a year. The season features a regular series of classics, symphony pops, chamber orchestra, and family performances at Symphony Hall, Orpheum Theatre, Scottsdale Center for the Arts, and Mesa Arts Center. The 75-member Phoenix Symphony also performs for special community events and holidays. Visit online for programs, times, locations, and tickets.

PHOENIX THEATRE
602-889-5284.
www.phoenixtheatre.com.
100 E. McDowell Rd., Phoenix.
Open: Show times vary for the season schedule.
Admission: Ticket prices vary.

Phoenix Theatre, the oldest theater company in Arizona, was founded in 1920 as the Phoenix Players, and is one of the oldest continuously operating arts groups in the United States. In 1923 the Phoenix Little Theatre, as it was called, found a permanent home at 100 E. McDowell in the stables of the Heard family homestead. In 1950, when the Heard family donated part of their land to Phoenix, the city agreed to keep Phoenix (Little) Theatre in place. In 1950 the current MainStage was completed and the Phoenix Theatre grew into the professional company it is today. It's known for encouraging appreciation for theater and performs musicals, comedies, and drama, as well as productions just for kids through the 25-year-old Cookie Company Theatre for Young Audiences. Hollywood greats Nick Nolte and Steven Spielberg launched their careers from the Phoenix Theatre's MainStage, and the company continues to encourage new talent with their Artist-in-Residence Program.

For tickets, click on the Box Office link from their web site; call 602-254-2151; or visit the box office, which is open Mon.–Fri. 10 AM–5 PM, Sat.–Sun. noon–showtime. Weekday hours are extended until showtime on show days.

Phoenix Theatre shares a building with the Phoenix Art Museum; it's found on the northeast corner of Central and McDowell Aves. Parking is to the north of the complex on Coronado, which is one block north of McDowell.

VALLEY YOUTH THEATRE
602-253-8188.
www.vyt.com.
525 N. 1st St., Phoenix.
Open: Show times and dates depend upon the production.
Admission: Single-event tickets run $18 ($2 service charge for phone orders made with a credit card); for performances held at Herberger Theater Center, $16.50, $19.50, and $22.50 (plus $3 Herberger box-office fees). Season-ticket information is available online.

Valley Youth Theatre (VYT) was founded in 1989 as a way to encourage and foster an appreciation for the performing arts among the community's children. Participation in VYT is fee-free. Professional directors, choreographers and technicians are hired to train the cast and crew for each of the seven annual productions.

Tickets can be purchased by calling 602-253-8188, ext. 2, Mon.–Fri. 10 AM–3 PM, or on site at the theater box office 1 hour prior to performance. For tickets to VYT events held at the Herberger Theater Center, call 602-252-8497 Mon.–Fri. 10 AM–5 PM, Sat. noon–5 PM; you can also buy these at the Herberger box office an hour before showtime. We suggest that you call in advance, as shows may be sold out.

Zoos & Wildlife

PHOENIX ZOO
602-273-1341.
www.phoenixzoo.org.
455 N. Galvin Pkwy., Phoenix.
Open: Jan.–May, 9 AM–5 PM; June–Sep., 7 AM–2 PM; Oct.–mid-Nov. 9 AM–5 PM; winter holidays 9 AM–4 PM and 6–10 PM (for Zoolights).
Prices: $14 adults, $9 seniors (ages 60-plus), $6 ages 3–12; ages 2 and under are free.
Credit Cards: AE, MC, V.
Handicapped Access: Yes.

Voted one of the top five zoos in the nation for kids, the Phoenix Zoo is home to over 1,000 animals and more than 200 species—including fish, mammals, birds, and lizards. The park covers 25 acres, and four separate trails combine to make up about 2.5 miles of walking trails. The Africa, Tropic, Arizona, and Children's Trails take between 30 and 60 minutes to walk. Set aside a good 2 or 3 hours to visit all the animals, and don't forget to peek over the sides of the bridge as you cross from the parking lot onto park grounds: You might see turtles basking in the sun. Wheels of some types are welcome at the zoo—wend your way along the paths on bike, in a stroller or wheelchair, or on in-line skates. No scooters or skateboards. And as always, watch out for pedestrians! No smoking is allowed on the property, and shoes must be worn at all times. Bring your own cooler of food and lunch at the available picnic tables. There are several food vendors along the way, but it's a pricey option—and the zoo is known for feeding animals, not people.

RECREATION

Ballooning
Sunny days and clear skies make for perfect ballooning weather, and the Phoenix metropolitan area offers tourists several options. The best time of year to go ballooning is between November and May, when weather is optimal. Morning trips leave just before sunrise; some companies also offer trips during the hotter months (June–Oct.) 2 hours prior to sunset. Consider **Over the Rainbow** (602-225-5666; www.letsgoballooning.com); **Zephyr Balloon** (888-991-4260 or 480-991-4260; www.azballoon.com); and **Adventures Out West** (800-755-0935; www.adventuresoutwest.com). Dress comfortably, wear sturdy shoes, and—as with any Arizona adventure—wear layers. While it might be chilly when you leave, it could be quite warm upon your return.

Multiuse Trails: Biking, Hiking, Walking, and Running

Just about all of the trails and paths that snake their way through the Phoenix metropolitan area—along canals and roads and among the foothills and mountains—can be navigated by bikers, hikers, walkers, and runners.

Canals maintained by SRP (Salt River Project, a statewide utility) are popular choices. With almost 150 miles of trail, most of which are unhindered by vehicles, outdoor enthusiasts can pick a spot on just about any of the paths and enjoy a wonderful Arizona experience. As far back as the early 20th century, residents and tourists alike enjoyed (and even celebrated) the water that has made desert living so comfortable. The existing canal system is almost 100 years old, and many of them were built on the centuries-old irrigation ditches dug by the Valley's original residents—the Hohokam Indians.

Several canals run through the Valley, providing excellent biking, running, and walking paths. Almost 40 miles long, the **Arizona Canal** runs from Salt River Pima—Maricopa Indian Community to Northwest Valley. The **Grand Canal** travels just over 22 miles from east-central Phoenix to Peoria. Also look for the **Consolidated Canal** (almost 19 miles) from northwest Mesa to Chandler; the **Eastern Canal** from northwest Mesa to Gilbert (14.7 miles); the almost 10-mile **South Canal** that runs from south Scottsdale to SRPMIC; the **Tempe Canal** (almost 10 miles) from Tempe into northwest Mesa; the **West Canal** (more than 13 miles) along Baseline Rd. from Price Rd. in Tempe to Dobbins Ave. in south-central Phoenix; and the **Crosscut Canal**, a jaunt of a little over 3 miles just south of Camelback Mountain.

For more information about the canals, including distances and entry points, visit www.srpnet.com/water/canals/distances.aspx. You can download a map online. In addition, the Maricopa Association of Governments (MAG) includes the canals on their Valley-wide bike map (www.mag.maricopa.gov/detail.cms?item=4644). Or you may want to call 602-254-6300 to order a free print copy of the map, because it's quite large and detailed, and includes more than just the canal bike paths. To learn more about biking and busing through the Valley, see chapter 2, Transportation.

A canal at Papago Park.

There are also several bike paths that parallel surface streets. **Indian Bend Wash** is one of the most popular. Located in Scottsdale, this 10-mile paved path parallels Hayden Rd. from Shea Blvd. to the northern end of Tempe. The route is accessible at any point off Hayden, and there are several parking lots, including one at the northwest corner of Indian School and Hayden Rds. The path is shared by every type of wheels, including bikes, in-line skates, and baby strollers.

Tempe boasts more than 150 miles of dedicated bikeway—not to mention the Silver Level Bicycle Friendly Community Award, given by the League of American Bicyclists to only 13 other communities in the United States. Bikeways connect various sections of town including Arizona State University's Main Campus, Tempe Town Lake, and Papago Park in Phoenix. Surrounding Tempe Town Lake are 5 miles of paths for bicycling, jogging, or in-line skating. The paths connect to the historic **Tempe Beach Park**. Originally built in 1931, this 25-acre park was completely renovated in 1999 as part of the construction of the Town Lake.

Biking

The Valley offers a number of biking-specific trails for serious road racers as well as parents looking to wander paved paths with their little ones. The city has hundreds of miles of on- and off-street bike paths, including two major paths that follow the city's canals. There are also several mountain preserves and parks with a variety of technical trails for mountain biking enthusiasts.

The best way to access more information about bicycling in the Valley, is to visit the city of Phoenix web site at http://phoenix.gov/DISCOVER/AROUND/BICYCLING. This web page addresses biking in general and has links to several popular resources, some of which are discussed above. Depending on your particular needs, any one of the sites or a combination will provide you with the details and maps you need to begin your biking adventure.

There are several excellent choices for **mountain biking** in the Valley. Beginners can try Papago Park (Galvin Pkwy. and Van Buren—where the Phoenix Zoo and Desert Botanical Garden are located): The paths are wide, and the scenery is beautiful. For die-hard mountain biking, try the National Trail at Phoenix South Mountain Preserve (enter off of Baseline and 48th St.). South Mountain offers easier trails such as the Desert Classic. Be aware that paths through the parks are also used by walkers, runners, and even those on horseback. North Mountain Preserve (7th St. between Dunlap and Thunderbird) offers good trails for intermediate riders.

AOA ADVENTURES

480-945-2881; fax 480-970-1825; toll-free 866-455-1601.
www.azoutbackadventures.com.
16447 N. 91st St., Suite 101, Scottsdale

Arizona and Whistler Outback Adventures (they operate in Whistler, British Columbia, too) offers guided hiking and biking day tours, as well as multiday adventure tours and bike rentals of all kinds, including mountain bikes, road bikes, tandem bikes, and bikes for little tykes, as well as trailers and tag-alongs if your children are too young to ride. Reservations are honored; you can call 602-935-7566 or go online to fill out a reservation form. The shop offers additional services including repairs, tune-ups, replacement parts, and accessories, as well as used-bike sales.

TEMPE BICYCLE

480-966-6896.

www.tempebicycle.com.

330 W. University Dr., Tempe.

Voted the best bike store in Phoenix (again) in 2006, Tempe Bicycle, located west of Mill Ave. on University Dr., has served Valley residents and tourists for more than 30 years. Owners Bud and Yvonne Morrison are passionate bicyclists. Together with their well-trained staff, they can help you find a new bike and accessories, or rent a road bike or mountain bike. Bikes are available for half- and full-day rental, or for several days at a time. There is also the option to purchase your rental bike.

Hiking

To hike in these parts you don't need to go far, no matter what part of the Valley you're in. All of the biking paths mentioned above double as hiking trails, including Papago Park and Phoenix South Mountain Preserve (www.phoenix.gov/PARKS/hiksogud.html).

Papago Park is a popular site located on the border of Phoenix and Tempe. The park is home to the Phoenix Zoo and Desert Botanical Garden. Its central location and easy paths with little or no elevation change make it a popular hiking and biking choice. To hike around Papago Buttes, park on W. Park Dr., and to explore the famous Hole in the Rock—a natural opening in the redrock butte—park just past the zoo at the information center. Be aware that light-rail construction has bound up some of Washington Ave. south of the Papago Park borders; use Van Buren instead. The park's trails range from 0.1 mile (Hole-in-the-Rock Trail) to 4 miles (West Park Loop Trail). For more information, visit http://phoenix.gov/PARKS/hikpagud.html.

Some of the best hiking trails can be found at the **Phoenix South Mountain Preserve**. With incredible views and easy accessibility, you would think that the preserve would be overrun with hiking, biking, and horseback-riding enthusiasts; however, 58 trails on 16,000 acres leaves plenty of room to roam. While paths close to the entrances tend to be busy, the crowds thin out as you head farther from the trailheads. **Mormon Trail** (24th St. and Valley View Ave. south of Baseline Rd.) is 1.1 miles at an elevation of about 1,000 feet. **Beverly Canyon Trail** (8800 S. 46th St. south of Baseline Rd.) is a 1.5-mile-long, moderate hike with some steep sections. **Javelina Canyon Trail** (Beverly Canyon parking lot at 46th St.) is an easy to moderate hike at 1.7 miles long. **Pima Canyon** is located at 9904 S. 48th St. and Guadalupe Rd. (Guadalupe cannot be accessed off I-10; instead take the Elliot Rd. exit, take Elliot to 48th St., and head north to the park road, which is set somewhat off the street on the west side). Hikers at Pima Canyon can choose several trails including the aforementioned Beverly Canyon Trail, the 14.3-mile **National Trail**, and the 9-mile **Desert Classic Trail**. Both of the latter trails are moderate to difficult.

From Desert Foothills Pkwy. just north of Chandler Blvd. (head west of 48th St. on Chandler until you reach Desert Foothills Pkwy., then go north to 6th St.), access **Telegraph Pass Trailhead**. The first 0.5 mile of the trail is paved. While there are some steep sections toward the top, the 1.5-mile trail is easy to moderate. The **Holbert Trailhead**, accessible from Central, is located at the Activity Complex (the first left turn immediately after entering the park off Central). This 2.5-mile trail is difficult and fairly steep; it passes near Mystery Castle. Also accessible from the Central Ave. entrance is **Kiwanis Trail**—turn left at the dip in the road and go straight at the next intersection. Follow the road to the gravel parking

Hiking the trail up Piestewa Peak.

area. This short, moderate hike is only a mile long and gets steeper toward the top. **Ranger Trail** and **Bajada Trail** (shorter, moderate hikes) and **Alta Trail** (a very difficult 4.5-mile route not recommended for bikes or horses) are also accessible off the Central Ave. entrance; follow the main road to the parking lot that serves the trailhead. Be aware of when the parking lot closes and plan your trip accordingly.

Two of the most popular places to hike in Phoenix are Camelback Mountain and Piestewa Peak. **Camelback Mountain**, aptly named for its striking resemblance to a reclining camel, is located north of Camelback Rd. between 44th and 64th Sts. Two hikes to the summit—Summit Trail and Cholla Trail—provide hikers with a steep climb (1,200-foot elevation change) and incredible views along the way. At the top is a panoramic vista of the Valley. The hikes are both long and difficult and recommended for experienced hikers only. There are several easier hikes and opportunities to explore along the base of the mountain from the Echo Canyon entrance. Parking for the Summit Trail is in Echo Canyon. On weekends during the cooler months there is actually a line to park here (east of Tatum off McDonald Dr.). Cholla Trail begins at Cholla Lane off 64th St./Invergordon. There is no parking lot; however, limited parking is available on Invergordon/64th St. near Cholla Lane. Please note that dropping off hikers on Cholla Lane is prohibited.

Piestewa Peak's Summit Trailhead—part of Phoenix Mountains Park and Recreation Area/Dreamy Draw Park (602-262-7901)—is located on Squaw Peak Dr. off Lincoln Dr. between 22nd and 24th Sts. This trail is a 2.5-mile round-trip hike that gains more than 1,200 feet in elevation. Its views, which almost rival those of Camelback Mountain, provide hikers with a different perspective of the Valley. The trail offers an intense but short hike. Other hiking trails are accessible from the various lots in the park and recreation area and from Dreamy Draw Park.

Pinnacle Peak Park (480-312-0990; www.scottsdale.gov/parks/pinnacle) is located in Scottsdale, north of the 101 where it curves west. Take the Pima Rd. exit, head north to Happy Valley Rd., and continue east to Alma School Rd. past the Four Seasons Resort. Turn left at the PINNACLE PEAK PATIO RESTAURANT sign. This hike is about 3.5 miles round trip and climbs 1,300 feet above North Scottsdale, offering an amazing view of the surrounding landscape and some of the Valley's most expensive homes. Horseback riding is allowed at the 150-acre park, but dogs and bicycles are not permitted.

Boating

Despite the fact that Phoenix sits in the middle of the desert, it is surrounded by no less than seven lakes—all within a 2-hour drive (six of them are within 75 minutes), including Lake Pleasant in the Northwest Valley, and Bartlett Reservoir and Horseshoe Lake north of Carefree and Cave Creek, respectively. Canyon, Saguaro, Apache, and Theodore Roosevelt Lakes, which formed along the Salt River after the Theodore Roosevelt Dam was built in 1911, are located east of the Valley in Tonto National Forest and the Superstition Mountains. The Valley also has many urban lakes, including Tempe Town Lake (located at the north end of Mill Avenue) and Encanto Lake, in Encanto Park in central Phoenix and Kiwanis Park in Tempe. With so many opportunities to enjoy the water, it is not surprising (or maybe it is) that Arizona has one of the highest number of boats per capita of any state. At least this is what Arizonans like to claim—it actually ranked 30th according to the US Coast Guard in 2004. Given that this *is* the desert, however, it's still a noteworthy feat.

All motorized watercraft in Arizona must be registered with the Arizona Game and Fish Department. A life jacket is required for each individual on board; children 12 and under must wear a US Coast Guard approved life jacket. If you're planning to bring a boat (sailboards, large boats, and jet bikes included) and it's registered in another state, review the department's web site for exceptions to registering in Arizona. Consider reading *The Boater's Guide of Arizona*, published by the Arizona Game and Fish Department. The entire guide is available and navigable online at http://boat-ed.com/az/handbook/index.htm, or via a downloadable PDF version. You may also want to take a formal boating education class, available through the Arizona Game and Fish Department, the US Coast Guard Auxiliary, or the US Power Squadrons. For more information, visit azgfd.gov or call 602-789-3235.

Camping

The **Maricopa County Parks System** (602-506-2930; www.maricopa.gov/parks) includes 10 parks offering a variety of camping conditions from developed sites like Cave Creek, McDowell Mountain, and Lake Pleasant Regional Parks—which offer electrical/water hookups, dump stations, restrooms, picnic tables, and grills—to primitive sites at Buckeye Regional Park as well as Lake Pleasant and McDowell Mountain Regional Parks, with no amenities at all. Before camping, it is important to familiarize yourself with the parks and their rules, especially those related to fire safety. Maricopa County limits stays to 14 consecutive days and often closes during the very hot summer months of June, July, and August. The parks are located far enough away from the city that you can enjoy the outdoors, and many offer beautiful examples of the Sonoran Desert, including the colorful sunrises and sunsets that are a must for any visitor. Camping fees are per day, nonrefundable, and must be paid in advance. Tent and RV rates are $18 for developed sites (electrical/water hookups, dump station, restrooms, picnic tables, and grills), $10 for semi-developed sites (restrooms, picnic tables, and grills—available at White Tank and

Lake Pleasant only), and $5 for shoreline camping, which offers no amenities and is available at Lake Pleasant. Sites are available on a first-come, first-served basis.

The **Cave Creek Regional Park** (653-465-0431) campground (1.5 miles north of Carefree Highway off 32nd St.) provides campers with 38 individual "developed" sites and space for a large group, each with a parking area that can accommodate an RV up to 45 feet long, and a fire ring, in addition to the standard developed site amenities. The park provides restrooms with flush toilets and hot showers. Large groups can reserve (for a fee) the 2-acre group campground, which includes restrooms, ramadas with picnic tables, a fire ring, and an activity area. A six-unit commitment is necessary to use the facility for dry camping. The park also has 11 miles of trail and a horse staging area. For more information, see Horseback Riding later in this chapter.

Lake Pleasant Regional Park, located in the northwest Valley approximately 15 miles north of Sun City, offers developed campsites with electrical and water hookups, dump station, restrooms, picnic tables, and grills. In addition to camping, the park offers boating, fishing, swimming, and hiking trails. Call 928-501-1710 for more information and to obtain permits. Also in the northwest is the **White Tank Mountain Regional Park** (15 miles west of Peoria off Olive Ave.), whose 40 sites are considered semi-primitive; there are no electrical or water hookups, although grills, picnic tables, and comfort stations with showers are available.

McDowell Mountain Regional Park is located 4 miles north of Fountain Hills in the northeast part of the Valley; it offers a total of 76 camping sites with a nightly rate of $18. This includes water and electrical hookups, and showers are available. Located in the Verde Basin, the McDowell Mountain Regional Park has an elevation ranging from 1,500 feet to just over 3,000 feet, along with some of the most beautiful views in the area. For more information, call 480-471-0173.

The **Ussery Mountain Recreation Area** (480-984-0032), in the southeast part of the Valley, is 12 miles northeast of Mesa and offers 73 developed sites for $18 per night including hookups. There are numerous hiking and horseback-riding trails, as well as an archery range. Some of the spaces at the Buckhorn Family Campground are handicapped accessible.

Lost Dutchman State Park in the Superstition Mountains is north of Apache Junction and has 35 sites for campers. There are showers, but no hookups. For more information, visit www.pr.state.az.us/Parks/parkhtml/dutchman.html or call 480-982-4485.

Further options include **Saguaro Lake Ranch, Inc.** (480-984-2194; www.saguarolakeranch.com; 13020 Bush Hwy., Mesa); **Apache Lake Marina** (928-467-2511; www.apachelake.com; AZ 88, Roosevelt); and **Canyon Lake Marina and Campground** (602-944-6504; www.canyonlakemarina.com; 16802 NE AZ 88, Tortilla Flat).

Casinos

Harrah's Ak-Chin Casino Resort (480-802-5000 or 800-HARRAHS; 15406 Maricopa Rd., Maricopa). **Casino Arizona** (480-850-7777 or 602-850-7777; 524 N. 92nd St., Scottsdale), located at Loop 101 and Indian Bend. **Fort McDowell** (480-837-1424; AZ 87 and Fort McDowell Rd., Fountain Hills). **Casino Arizona** (480-362-1357; 8900 E. Chaparral Rd., Scottsdale).

Fitness Centers/Indoor Gyms

The Valley is home to numerous fitness centers, including national and local chains. The best known of them are **LA Fitness** (949-255-7200; www.lafitness.com), **Pure Fitness** (888-894-PURE; www.purefitnessclubs.com), **24 Hour Fitness** (800-432-6348; www.24hourfitness.com), **Lifetime Fitness** (www.lifetimefitness.com), which doubles as a private country club, and local chain **Fitness Works** (480-325-4641; www.fitnessworks .com) in the East Valley, as well as many smaller gyms and training centers. In addition to the traditional centers where free weights, Nautilus machines, and lap pools abound, Phoenix also boasts rock-climbing gyms, such as Phoenix Rock Gym and AZ on the Rocks.

PHOENIX ROCK GYM
480-921-8322.
www.phoenixrockgym.com.
1353 E. University Dr., Tempe.
Open: Weekdays 3 PM–10 PM, weekends 10 AM–7 PM.
Fees: $10 for a day pass; $5 for equipment (shoes, harness & carabiner); discounts for children under 12.

Phoenix Rock Gym, located in Tempe, offers an indoor rock-climbing experience for beginners as well as intermediate- and lead-level climbers. With 30-foot walls and 15,000 square feet of climbing space (including a bouldering area), it's a fun and invigorating experience. Show up and sign a waiver; you can rent equipment or bring your own. If you're new to climbing, don't worry: You get a quick but thorough review first. Staff are helpful; always check and recheck your equipment, and enjoy the experience.

AZ ON THE ROCKS
www.azontherocks.com.
480-502-9777.
16447 N. 91st St., Scottsdale.
Open: Mon.–Fri. 3 PM–10 PM, Sat.–Sun. 9 AM–7 PM
Fees: $15 for a day pass; $5 for equipment (shoes and harness); discounts for children, students, and government employees.

AZ on the Rocks is the largest indoor rock-climbing gym in the state. With 14,000 square feet of climbing terrain, an additional 2,800 square feet of bouldering space, and incredibly helpful staff, this gym promises hours of indoor fun for all ages—whether you're honing your skills or climbing for the first time.

For Kids
The Valley offers its share of fun for the kids. With cool and inexpensive choices like the **Alltel Ice Den** (480-585-7465; www.coyoteice.com), the official training center for the Phoenix Coyotes in Scottsdale; **Arcadia Ice** (602-957-9966; www.arcadiaice.com), a full-service skating facility in central Phoenix; and **Oceanside Ice Arena** in Tempe (480-941-0944; www.iskateaz.com), anyone can brave 110 degrees. The ice rinks offer skating programs and lessons, public skating sessions, and a cool reprieve from Phoenix's hot weather. Temperatures hover around 50 degrees, so wear (or bring, depending on the weather) appropriate clothing.

The 70-year-old, family-owned **Cerreta Candy Company** in historic downtown Glendale opens its doors 8 AM–6 PM Mon.–Sat. Come in at any time during retail hours to watch the candy being made and watch a video about the process, or visit between 10 AM and 1 PM

Mon.–Fri., when Cerreta shares the magic of candy making during 30-minute guided tours. Sampling is expected, and a full line of items is available for purchase.

Tempe Beach Park provides an excellent outdoor adventure during the hotter months. Children of all ages can enjoy Splash Playground. This free 1-acre playground teaches children and parents alike about how water cycles through the desert—beginning as raindrops and ending in the city's water supply or the ocean. First comes a light mist from a metal circle of clouds; thunder and lightning herald the rainstorm, and water rushes through the falls and into the canals. Children can play in the rain, the waterfalls, and the "canals." Slides, showers, and rubberized padding make this a fun place for toddlers and older children, too.

Perhaps the summer heat combined with children out of school has made this a prime area for indoor "parks" for kids. The Valley offers numerous opportunities to run the energy out of your children no matter the age. These indoor amusement parks are typically geared toward children 12 and younger, but some—like **Amazing Jake's** (480-926-PIZZA; www.amazingjakes.com) in Mesa with its bumper cars, LaserTag, and rock-climbing walls, and **Makutu's Island** (877-MAKUTUS; www.makutusisland.com) in Chandler with ceiling-high tree houses, tunnels, and a 35-foot banana slide—can inspire energy in parents, too. Most locations offer softer and shorter options for preschoolers and toddlers, making these suitable for the entire family. These indoor playgrounds are filled with the cacophony of excitement, energy, and noise as little bodies jockey for their space in the crowd. Some offer pizza buffets like Amazing Jake's, **Chuck E. Cheese** (www.chuckecheese.com), and **Peter Piper Pizza** (www.peterpiperpizza.com); others a standard kid-friendly menu, including Makutu's Island and **Jeepers** in Mesa (480-820-8300; www.jeepers.com). Most, if not all, host birthday parties and group events.

Indoor–outdoor options include **Kiwanis Park Recreation Center** (480-350-5201— then press 0; www.tempe.gov/kiwanis) in Tempe, **Cracker Jax** (480-998-2800; www.crackerjax.com) in Scottsdale, **Golfland** (480-834-8319; http://mesa.golfland.com)

Mystery Castle is an amazing feat of architecture and imagination.

in Mesa, and **Fiddlesticks** (www.zumafuncenters.com) in Tempe and Scottsdale. Cracker Jax, Golfland, and Fiddlesticks offer video games, miniature golf, go-carts, LaserTag, bumper boats, driving ranges, food, and more. Kiwanis provides a number of choices for fun, including an indoor wave pool and spiral slide, batting ranges, tennis courts, sand volleyball courts, outdoor picnic areas, and playgrounds. Kiwanis Park also offers a wonderful outdoor dinner and a movie option for families. Beginning in April and extending into May, the city of Tempe hosts a Free Family Film Series on Saturday nights. Families are encouraged to bring a picnic dinner and a blanket and stretch out for a relaxing evening. Movies begin at dusk around 7 PM and are shown by the fire pit on the west side of Kiwanis Lake. The city of Tempe also hosts a fall film series at the 6th Street Park at 6th St. and Mill Ave. Visit www.tempe.gov/recreation/movies for the schedule of movies. You can enter Kiwanis Park off Baseline or Guadalupe between Mill and Hardy in Tempe.

Arizona offers its share of unique attractions, and **Mystery Castle** (602-268-1581) is one you won't find anywhere else in the world. In the 1930s and '40s Boyce Gulley spent 15 years building a castle fit for a princess—his only daughter, Mary Lou. Today Mary Lou still lives in the house her daddy built, and conducts tours Thu.–Sun. 11 AM–4 PM. Children under 6 are free, ages 6–15 are $2, adults are $5, and seniors are $4. There are almost 20 rooms, 13 fireplaces, and plenty of nooks and crannies even a grown-up can get lost in. Mystery Castle is on the Historic Register, and it's an amazing feat of architecture and imagination. To get there, take 7th St. south of Baseline until you reach a roundabout where 7th runs into the Phoenix South Mountain Preserve. Take a left—you'll see a MYSTERY CASTLE sign with an arrow. You'll find out what the mystery is all about!

A trip to Arizona is not complete without the signature "western experience." Kids will enjoy a trip to **Rawhide** (480-502-5600 or 800-527-1880; www.rawhide.com), now located southwest of Phoenix at Wild Horse Pass. Take the Wild Horse Pass exit off I-10 and head south on 48th St. past N. Loop Rd. Parking is available off 48th St. Rawhide re-creates an 1880s western town, complete with midafternoon shoot-outs, stunt shows, train and stagecoach rides, rock climbing, and gold panning. Shops and other attractions (including a jail—don't get arrested, the town sheriff regularly rounds up scoundrels) line the main drag.

Dine at the Rawhide Steakhouse or Wagon Wheel Cafe. Hours vary depending upon the season; admission to Rawhide is free, as is parking. Rides and shows require tickets. Purchase a full-day pass for $12 per person, or tickets to individual attractions for $4 each. Special Sundown Cookouts take place Saturday nights usually from February until June, and October through November. Enjoy country music, line dancing, stunt shows, and a marshmallow roast and grilled steaks or BBQ chicken the old-fashioned way—under the stars in the desert. A mule-drawn hay wagon takes guests to the cookout site. Call 480-502-5600 for more information or to make your reservations.

Kids love **McCormick-Stillman Railroad Park** (480-312-2312; www.therailroadpark .com) in Scottsdale at the southeast corner of Indian Bend and Scottsdale Rds. Admission to the park is free; a ride on the Paradise and Pacific Railroad costs $1 (children under 3 are free with a paying adult). The train is an exact replica (to scale—5 inches equals 1 foot) of a Colorado narrow-gauge railroad. In addition the park has shops, picnic ramadas, a carousel, exhibits, and a railroad museum. If you or your little ones like trains, you can also visit **The Arizona Railway Museum** (480-821-1108; www.azrymuseum.org) in Chandler (330 E. Ryan Rd.—south of Germann, east of Arizona Ave.). The museum specializes in acquiring, preserving, and displaying trains and related paraphernalia from the Southwest's railways, past and present. The main building is a replica of an original depot located in Chandler. The museum is open Labor Day through Memorial Day, Sat.–Sun. noon–4 PM.

Awesome Atom's Science Store (602-716-2085; 600 E. Washington St., Phoenix). Open daily 10 AM–5:30 PM. This store—part of the Arizona Science Center facility—provides science- and nature-related educational toys and books for children of all ages.

Sandy's Dream Dolls (623-931-1579; 7154 N. 58th Dr., Glendale). Open Mon.–Sat. 10 AM–4 PM. Enter the enchanting world of dolls; there is a collection of antique, artist, and modern dolls and bears and gift items. Sandy's offers classes where you can make a gift for yourself or someone special.

Golf
See chapter 9, Golf Courses & Spas.

Horseback Riding
The various preserves and parks throughout the metropolitan area provide ample opportunity for horseback riding. As mentioned in this chapter, **Maricopa County parks** offer horseback-riding trails and staging areas for horses. The White Tank Mountain and Cave Creek Parks have horse stables that offer guided tours.

White Tank Riding Stables offers guided riding tours Nov.–Apr. One-hour rides start at $33 per person; private rides are available for $60 per hour, and children 7 and under can ride a pony for 15 minutes ($15 per child). Moonlight rides and wagon rides are available. The stables are located at 20300 W. Olive Ave. in Waddell. Call 623-935-7455 or visit www.whitetanksriding.com for more information.

Cave Creek Trailrides offers guided horseback riding tours at Cave Creek Regional Park. One-hour rides start at $33 per person. Two- and 3-hour rides and sunset rides are available. Children under 6 receive complimentary pony rides; ages 6–12 get a $5 discount. The Cave Creek Recreation Area can be reached by taking 32nd St. north from Carefree Highway, which is located halfway between I-17 and Scottsdale Rd. There is a $5 fee to enter the park; once you're inside, follow the horse signs to the stables. For more information, call 623-742-6700 or visit www.cavecreektrailrides.com.

Located at the Phoenix South Mountain Preserve, **Ponderosa Stables** offers a variety of rides, including guided tour rides, a breakfast ride, and a fun sunset dinner ride that ends up at the T-Bone Steakhouse. They also offer wagon rides and riding lessons. Ponderosa Stables is located on Central Ave. Head south on Central past Dobbins. Before you reach the entrance to the South Mountain Preserve, you'll see Ponderosa Stables on the mountain side of the road. If you pass Scorpion Gulch, you've gone too far. Rides start at $25 per person for an hour ride. There is a two-rider minimum for tours over an hour. For rides 2 hours or longer, they recommend morning—the sun gets hotter later in the day, which can be hard on the horses.

You can also take a ride along the trails at **Saguaro Lake Ranch** (480-984-0335; www.saguarolaketrailrides.com). If you're riding on your own, remember to stay on designated trails, bring plenty of water, and always tell someone your planned route.

Hunting and Fishing
Depending upon the season and Arizona's habitats that year, hunters might be on the prowl for black bear, buffalo, mule deer, mountain lions, and turkeys, to name a few of the big-game animals. Central Arizona regions include Pinetop (Region I), Mesa (Region VI, which

includes the entire Phoenix metropolitan area, the Verde Valley, Payson, Pine, and Casa Grande), and the southern part of Flagstaff (Region II). Smaller game includes migratory birds like duck, geese, and common snipe as well as pheasant and quail, tree squirrels, and cottontail rabbits. Those fishing in Central Arizona might catch bass, trout, crappie, walleye, sunfish, and catfish.

In order to hunt or fish in Arizona, a valid license is required. Residents and nonresidents 14 and older must have a license to hunt wildlife other than big game in the state. Individuals younger than 14 may hunt wildlife other than big game if accompanied by a properly licensed individual 18 or older. No more than two unlicensed children may accompany any licensed individual. No one under 10 years old may take big game; those between 10 and 14 must first complete a hunter education course. For more information about hunting in Arizona, review the Arizona Hunting Regulations document available online at www.azgfd.gov/h_f/hunting_rules.shtml. To obtain hunting and fishing licenses, Arizona residents must have lived in the state for 6 months prior to their application date (members of the armed forces stationed in Arizona must be here for 30 days before applying). All other individuals must purchase a nonresident license. You can obtain a license via phone (800-705-4165), online (https://www.wildlifelicense.com/az/start.php), or from a license dealer, such as Wal-Mart, most sporting goods stores, some grocery stores in smaller towns, and at the Game and Fish Offices at 2222 W. Greenway Rd., Phoenix, or 7200 E. University, Mesa.

For a complete list, visit www.azgfd.gov/eservices/documents/AGFDLicenseDealerList 061121.pdf.

General fishing licenses cover fishing in the state of Arizona; as of spring 2007 annual licenses cost $23.25 for residents and $70.25 for nonresidents. Nonresidents also have the option of purchasing single-day ($17.25), 5-day ($32), and 4-month licenses ($39.75). Urban fishing licenses are $18.25 for residents and nonresidents and gain you access to urban lakes and canals in Chandler, Gilbert, Mesa, Peoria, Phoenix, Scottsdale, and Tempe. There are 15 urban lakes and ponds (less than 3 acres). For a complete list of fishing locations in the metropolitan area, including directions, maps, rules, limits, and handicapped accessibility, download the Urban Fishing Booklet from www.azgfd.gov/h_f/fishing_rules .shtml.

For more information on fishing in Arizona, including where to fish, read Arizona Fishing Requirements available online at www.azgfd.gov/h_f/fishing_rules.shtml.

Special stamps are required for hunting waterfowl and migratory fowl, or fishing for trout. You can also purchase a combination hunting and fishing license ($54 for residents and $225 for nonresidents). Visit online for more information or call the Arizona Game and Fish Department to find out about discounts and additional options.

To replace a lost or destroyed license, visit any license dealer. An application for a duplicate license and fee are required.

Guides and Outfitters

Both **360 Adventures** and **Arizona Climbing and Adventure School** offer guided adventures. Companies like **Detours—Off the Beaten Path** and **Open Road Tours** offer tours that are just as exciting for those interested in getting an up-close and personal, but less vigorous, experience. Knowledgeable guides narrate the journey, often providing a mix of historical and geological information about what you're seeing. Both companies offer a variety of tours, including single-day and multiday tours to Flagstaff, the Grand Canyon, and

Sedona. They also offer signature tours—such as Open Road Tours' Scottsdale Shop and Play and Evening Dine and Play (enjoy Scottsdale's downtown/waterfront district and/or Tempe's Mill Avenue and Tempe Town Lake), and Detours' High Spirits tour to Arizona's only distillery (in Flagstaff) and their Tony Hillerman tour—and can schedule other tours, such as a helicopter ride over the red rocks of Sedona or the Grand Canyon, while you're visiting. Open Road also offers tours to Nogales, Mexico, and a Best of Tucson Tour. Call 800-766-7117 for availability and prices; visit www.openroadtours.com for more information. See the sidebar for more about touring in Arizona and about Detours' (866-438-6877; www.detoursaz.com) critically acclaimed specialized tours.

Rock Climbing

Arizona's landscape welcomes rock climbers and bouldering buffs to explore the desert terrain. One of the most popular rock-climbing sites—**Praying Monk**—is located at Camelback Mountain and accessible from the Echo Canyon entrance. This 80-foot tower is between a 5.4 and a 5.6 and offers a sheer angle with incredible views of the Valley and permanent bolts along its route. Another top spot for experienced climbers with the appropriate gear is **Pinnacle Peak Park**. Pinnacle Peak affords climbers three separate climbing areas of varying degrees of difficulty. If you're a novice to rock climbing, or if you prefer to work with knowledgeable guides, several tour companies specialize in outdoor adventures, including **360 Adventures** (480-722-0360; www.360-adventures.com) and **Arizona Climbing and Adventure School (ACAS)** (480-363-2390; www.climbingschool.com). Both offer hiking/backpacking and rock-climbing trips. 360 Adventures also offers mountain biking, canyoneering (described as "hiking, wading, swimming, scrambling & rappelling" in a canyon), and single- and multiday tours. They specialize in the Phoenix metropolitan area, Sedona, and the Grand Canyon. Climbing trips start at $235/person for half-day trips, including gear, water, snacks, transportation, if necessary, and meals (for full to multiday trips). In addition to climbing and hiking, Arizona Climbing and Adventure School offers climbing and development courses as well as kayaking adventures and single- and multiday climbing trips. ACAS prices start at $215 for a half-day session; however, there are additional fees for transportation outside Maricopa County, food, lodging or camping equipment, and permits.

Sports Complexes

SNEDIGAR SPORTSPLEX
480-782-2727 or 480-782-2640.
4500 S. Basha Rd., Chandler.

Chandler features this top-rated skate park. With 35,000 square feet of space, this free facility includes concrete bowls, decks, blocks, and metal rails for all skill levels. Baseball, softball, and soccer fields; playground equipment; a dog park; and picnic pavilions round out amenities. Open daily; hours vary seasonally.

TUMBLEWEED TENNIS COMPLEX
480-963-5265.
2200 S. McQueen Rd., Chandler.

This 12-acre facility features 15 lighted courts; lessons, leagues, and tournaments; a pro shop; and locker rooms with showers. Open daily; hours vary seasonally.

DESERT BREEZE PARK

660 N. Desert Breeze Blvd. East, Chandler.

The Hummingbird Habitat at Desert Breeze Park demonstrates the beauty and value of southwestern plants. You will also find ball fields, a lake, a walking trail, picnic pavilions, a playground, and tennis courts.

Rafting, Canoeing, Kayaking

One of the most unusual features in Tempe is **Tempe Town Lake**. Located just north of the Mill Avenue District and Arizona State University (ASU), this is a 220-acre urban lake, the largest in the United States. It's a great spot for boating, kayaking, and fishing. Visitors can rent boats and kayaks at the marina on the lake or try something a little more wild—tubin' down the Salt River. Contact **Salt River Tubing & Recreation, Inc.** (480-984-3305; www .saltrivertubing.com), or **Desert Voyagers Guided Raft Trips** (480-998-7238; www.desert voyagers.com) for more information about this favorite local summer activity.

Urban Parks & Lakes

See Desert Botanical Garden in Culture—Gardens.

Water Parks

Big Surf (480-947-7873; 1500 N. McClintock Dr., Tempe), America's original water park, is 20 acres of white-water slides, speed slides, tubes, play areas, and volleyball courts. You can body-surf in the largest oceanlike wave pool and enjoy over 15 waterslides, including a 300-footer. Special boogieboarding sessions are also available.

The **Surprise Aquatic Center** (623-266-4644; 15831 N. Bullard, Surprise) features a zero-depth area with water play features, flume slide, tunnel slide, vortex whirlpool, eight-lane competition pool, and diving well with two 1-meter boards. Call for more information. Surprise resident youth 17 and under pay 50 cents; those 18 and over, $1.50. Please provide proof of residency; the nonresident fee is $5 per person.

SHOPPING

Shopping Centers

BILTMORE FASHION PARK

602-955-8400.
www.shopbiltmore.com.
2502 E. Camelback Rd., Phoenix.
Open: Mon.–Wed. 10 AM–7 PM, Thu.–Fri. 10 AM–8 PM, Sat. 10 AM–6 PM, Sun. noon–6 PM.
Handicapped Access: Yes.

At the corner of 24th St. and Camelback Rd., in the luxurious Biltmore District, sits "nirvana for the passionate shopper." More than 60 boutiques and restaurants line the courtyard garden, creating the perfect outdoor shopping experience. Pottery Barn and Saks Fifth Avenue share space with specialty stores like Lilies and Ladybugs, a delightful shop providing fanciful art and accessories for your outdoor garden, and Amy Inc., the "Chic Boutique," offering the latest fashions from European and American designers. Take a break at Christopher's Fermier Brasserie & Paola's Wine Bar; take a trip across Camelback to lunch at the Ritz-Carlton; or try any one of the many restaurants located at the Camelback Esplanade (a combination of restaurants, retail and office space, and a theater).

Biltmore Fashion Park offers a collection of upscale options like Gucci, Tommy Bahama's, Ann Taylor, and Escada; department stores Macy's and Saks Fifth Avenue; as well as Borders Books and Music, Häagen-Dazs, and Godiva Chocolate. Find top-notch gadgets at The Sharper Image and unique gifts at Brookstone; gourmet cookware at Williams-Sonoma; one-of-a-kind fixtures at Restoration Hardware; designer accessories and clothing at Betsey Johnson, Cole-Haan, or Gucci; lotions and candles at L'Occitane en Provence; handblown glassware at BeDazzled; high-quality clothing, books, and toys for newborns to 14-year-olds at This Little Piggy Wears Cotton; and gourmet doggy treats at Three Dog Bakery.

But Biltmore Fashion Park offers more than a unique shopping experience—you can meet for coffee at Coffee Plantation, lunch at The Cheesecake Factory (anticipate a wait) or California Pizza Kitchen, dine on oysters and sushi at Steamer's Genuine Seafood, or thoroughly pamper yourself at Elizabeth Arden Red Door Spas.

CAMELBACK COLONNADE
602-274-7642.
www.shopurbanvillages.com/camelback.html.
18th St. and Camelback Rd., Phoenix.

The Colonnade is a mixture of large retail stores, including Old Navy, Mervyn's, PetsMart, Ulta, Bed, Bath and Beyond, and Michael's, to name a few. Popular choices are E & J's Designer Shoes, with designer shoes and accessories for great prices, and Nordstrom's Last Chance Bargain Shoes and Apparel—this last stop for returned, reconditioned, or refurbished items from Nordstrom department stores can sometimes cough up great buys or bad ones in disguise. The Colonnade also has a good selection of food choices, including Fuddruckers (for great build-'em-yourself burgers and milk shakes) and Miracle Mile Deli (for cafeteria-style dining—try the Straw—yum!). The Colonnade is located within a busy office district, and restaurants in the area draw lunchtime crowds during the week.

COFCO CHINESE CULTURAL CENTER
602-275-8578.
www.phxchinatown.com/index.html.
668 N. 44th St., Phoenix.

Phoenix's Chinatown—the COFCO Chinese Cultural Center—offers a unique combination of Asian restaurants and shops. The Super L Ranch Market, a grocery store, sells traditional Asian foods, items imported from Asia, fresh produce, and baked goods. They boast the freshest seafood in Phoenix. Asian restaurants at the center include the Golden Buddha (Cantonese and Mandarin), Lao Ching Hing (Shanghai-style), Szechwan Palace (spicy Szechuan), and Asian Seafood Buffet. Together, shops like Asian Video/Audio (5,000 CDs, DVDs, VCDs, and cassettes in Chinese make it one of the largest stores of its kind in the nation); Oriental Factory Direct, which offers imported goods from Hong Kong, Thailand, and other Asian locales at bargain prices; the Chinese Herbal Shop; and Golden Gifts (bonsai trees, bamboo, and vases) create a unique shopping experience. Stroll through the energy-balanced landscape of The Gardens, designed by famous garden architect Madame Ye. Ye used both feng shui and yin-yang principles in her designs and created a harmonious atmosphere for guests as they wander among the carefully sculpted grounds.

Outdoor shopping at the Desert Ridge Marketplace in North Phoenix.

DESERT RIDGE MARKETPLACE

480-513-7586.
www.shopdesertridge.com.
21001 N. Tatum Blvd. at Tatum & Loop 101, Phoenix.
Open: Daily; call for hours.

Energetic, fast paced, and *huge* are the three terms that best describe one of the Valley's newest malls. This 1.3-million-square-foot entertainment complex is the ultimate master-planned community. With several gated communities, golf courses, five separate shopping districts, and plenty of restaurants, a stay at the Marriott here gives the term *vacation package* a whole new meaning. Desert Ridge features a beautifully landscaped open-air marketplace with an 18-screen cinema, rock-climbing wall, bowling alley, dozens of nationally recognized shops, and a couple of local favorites like As You Wish (paint your own pottery) to choose from, and 30 dining experiences that offer a mixture of national favorites, with a few local specialties like Malee's Thai Bistro thrown in. AMC Fountain and District Stage host local talent and events (Firefighter Bachelor Auction at Rock Bottom Brewery).

ARIZONA CENTER

This two-story open-air marketplace features shops, restaurants like Sam's Café, Mi Amigos, and Hooters, and a 24-theater AMC Cineplex in the heart of downtown Phoenix. The urban setting, meandering paths, towering palm trees, and a fantastic waterfall and fountain all make for a great outdoor shopping and dining experience.
Flag World (602-254-6265 or 800-584-7535; 455 N. 3rd St., lower level, Phoenix). Open

Mon.–Thu. 10 AM–9 PM, Fri.–Sat. 10 AM–10 PM, Sun. noon–6 PM. The world's largest selection of flags and flag-related items.

Outwest Gifts (602-371-8087; 455 N. 3rd St., Suite 162, Phoenix). This tourist shop features jewelry, collectibles, pottery, and home decor from more than 400 artists and 19 Native tribes.

Oak Creek (480-368-1874; 455 N. 3rd St., Suite 128, Phoenix). Open: Mon.–Sat. 10 AM–9 PM, Sun. noon–6 PM. Unique gifts, many by local artists, with a southwestern orientation. Free shipping (purchases over $25) limited to continental United States.

Jayne's Marketplace (602-253-2410; 455 N. 3rd St., Suite 130, Phoenix). Open: Mon.–Thu. 10 AM–9 PM, Fri.–Sat. 10 AM–10 PM, Sun. 11 AM–6 PM. Located in downtown Phoenix, this specialty shop features one-of-a-kind Southwest gifts and apparel, salsas, Mexican glassware, pottery, chiles, and more.

Sportsfan (602-261-7852; 455 N. 3rd St., Suite 124, Phoenix). Open: Mon.–Thu. 10 AM–9 PM. Sportsfan is your headquarters for licensed sports apparel and gifts. There's a huge selection of teams from across the leagues. Great selection of products and competitive prices.

Specialty Stores

Teamshops—Chase Field (602-462-6701; 401 E. Jefferson St., Phoenix). Open Mon.–Fri. 10 AM–5 PM, Sat. 10 AM–3 PM, game days 10 AM–2 PM. Where else could you buy authentic Arizona Diamondbacks merchandise? This shop, located at Chase Field in downtown Phoenix, offers hats, T-shirts, jerseys, and other baseball paraphernalia.

Teamshops—US Airways Center (602-514-8321; 201 E. Jefferson St., Phoenix). Open Mon.–Fri. 10 AM–5 PM, Sat. 10 AM–3 PM, game days 10 AM–2 PM. Suit up for Phoenix Suns, Arizona Rattlers, or Phoenix Mercury games on site at US Airways Center.

John & Kathy's Smoke Shop (602-258-4859; 21 W. Jefferson St., Phoenix). Open Mon.–Fri. 7 AM–5 PM. This convenience store located in downtown Phoenix features sandwiches, cards, US Postal Service, dry cleaning, photo service, and the Arizona lottery.

Heritage Square Emporium (602-261-8063; 113 N. 6th St., Phoenix). A combination of specialty stores, restaurants, and attractions make up Heritage Square, including Pizzeria Bianco. The emporium offers Victorian-inspired cards and gifts.

Cowtown Boot Co., Inc. (602-548-3009; 2710 W. Thunderbird Rd., Phoenix). Arizona's largest western-wear store, featuring handmade leather boots—crocodile, ostrich, snake, lizard, and shark. Open daily. There's an additional location in Tempe (480-968-4748; 1001 N. Scottsdale Rd., Tempe).

Outlet Shopping

Outlets at Anthem (623-465-9500 or 888-482-5834; 4250 W. Anthem Way, Phoenix). More than 80 brand-name stores, 10 eateries, and luxurious restrooms.

Antiques

Along McDowell Ave. between 17th and Central Aves., in the historic Willo and Encanto Districts, antiques lovers can find a series of shops. **Garden Party Vintage and More** (602-604-1831; 4302 N. 7th Ave.) specializes in midcentury vintage furniture and collectible. **Antique Market** (602-255-0212; 1601 N. 7th Ave.), features Fiestaware and rare books, among other treasures. You'll also find **MacAlpine's Vintage Treasures** (602-253-9613) not far away at 2302 N. 7th St., Phoenix. And in other parts of the city, try **Those Were the**

Days (480-967-4729; 516 S. Mill Ave., Tempe), which specializes in antique and out-of-the-ordinary books; **Antique Treasure Trove** (480-947-6074; 2020 N. Scottsdale Rd., Scottsdale)—a series of stalls specializing in antique goods; and **Antique Outpost** (602-943-9594; 10012 N. Cave Creek Rd.), mom-and-pop-run since 1967, and stuffed to the gills with goodies. For more antiquing, check out the Glendale and the West Valley chapter.

Arizona Specialty Shops

Heard Museum Shop (2301 N. Central Ave., Phoenix). Located at the Heard Museum, the shop features authentic artworks by Native Americans, as well as books and information on Arizona and its Native American cultures.

Arizona Highways Magazine (602-712-2045 or 800-543-5432; www.arizonahighways.com; 2039 W. Lewis Ave., Phoenix). What better place to purchase an Arizona treasure than from *Arizona Highways* magazine? *Arizona Highways* publishes those award-winning coffee-table books that you find around the country. You can also purchase maps, trail guides, clothing, and jewelry.

SPECTATOR SPORTS

Phoenix is one of the few cities with four major-league sports teams: the Phoenix Coyotes (NHL), Arizona Cardinals (NFL), Phoenix Suns (NBA), and Arizona Diamondbacks (MLB). In addition, the city hosts other major teams, including the Phoenix Mercury (WNBA), as well as several major sporting events, including the FBR Open, two NASCAR events, spring training, and Arizona State University Division I sports. In 2008 the Valley hosts Super Bowl XLII at University of Phoenix Stadium in Glendale. The Valley also offers thoroughbred racing, arena football, and the Indy Racing League.

Professional Sports/Sporting Events

The **Arizona Cardinals** play Sep.–Dec. After sharing ASU's Sun Devil Stadium for years, the Cardinals have finally moved into University of Phoenix Stadium (1 Cardinals Dr., Glendale). For game schedules and ticket information, visit www.azcardinals.com or call 602-379-0102. The **Phoenix Coyotes** play at Glendale Arena. For game dates and ticket information, call 623-850-PUCK or visit www.phoenixcoyotes.com. The NBA **Phoenix Suns** (602-379-SUNS; www.phoenixsuns.com) play Oct.–Apr., and the WNBA **Phoenix Mercury** (602-379-7878; www.phoenixmercury.com) play May–Aug. at US Airways Center in downtown Phoenix. The **Arizona Diamondbacks** play Apr.–Oct. at Chase Field in downtown Phoenix. For more information call 602-514-8400 or visit www.azdiamondbacks.com. **Indy Racing League** in March and **NASCAR** events in April and November take place at Phoenix International Raceway (602-252-2227; www.phoenixintlraceway.com). **ASU Athletics** Pac-10 sports take place between August and May (480-965-2381; www.asu.edu). The Insight Bowl, an NCAA football game, occurs in December (480-350-0911; www.insightbowl.com), and the Fiesta Bowl (480-350-0911; www.tostitosfiestabowl.com), now at University of Phoenix Stadium in Glendale, typically falls in late December or early January. See the West Valley chapter for more information about University of Phoenix Stadium.

Horse Racing

For information on thoroughbred horse racing Oct.–May, call 602-375-6478 or visit www.turfparadise.com. **Turf Paradise**—set against the mountains in northern Phoenix—

features seating options for everyone. Cheer on the horse of your choice as these magnificent beasts thunder across the finish line.

FBR Open

The FBR Open, a PGA Tour event, annually draws more than 500,000 spectators. First held in 1932, the Phoenix Open, as it was originally called, failed after only three years. Under the vision and direction of Bob Goldwater Sr. and with the help of his fellow Thunderbirds, the Phoenix Open thrived again, and "the greatest show on grass" was born. This championship—one of the Valley's signature events—has raised almost $50 million for Arizona charities.

The FBR Open is held in late January at TPC of Scottsdale. This stadium course was designed to host the Open, and can accommodate the hundreds of thousands of people who attend. It does not sell out. Daily ticket admissions run about $25 per person, and prices increase to provide additional perks and advantages like access to lounges and special seating to skyboxes on the most coveted holes. This event lasts 6 days, with the PGA Tour the final 3—Friday, Saturday, and Sunday. The Thunderbirds do an excellent job coordinating parking; access to the parking lots is convenient, and the cost of the shuttle from the parking lots to just outside the golf course is included in your ticket price. For more information, visit www.phoenixopen.com. Some of the area's resorts offer great golf and accommodation packages this time of year. For accommodations close by, check this book's sites in North Scottsdale.

Cactus League

Spring training in Arizona calls out over a million baseball fans each year. It is not uncommon for local residents to skip out of work on a Friday afternoon to catch a game—or for avid sports fans to follow their teams to Arizona for the duration of spring training. The Cactus League hosts 12 teams at nine stadiums in the Valley and Tucson. For more informa-

Chase Field at 7th and Jefferson.

Game Day at US Airways Center.

tion about spring training in Arizona, visit www.cactus-league.com, or see each team's individual site. Ticket prices start at $5 and are available online from each team's site, on site, or by phone. Please note that most stadiums do not allow food, beverage, large bags, or coolers to be brought in. To find out more about where your favorite team plays, visit the appropriate city chapter. The Anaheim Angels play in Tempe; Chicago Cubs, Mesa; Kansas City Royals and Texas Rangers, Surprise; Milwaukee Brewers, northwest Phoenix; Oakland A's, central Phoenix; Seattle Mariners and San Diego Padres, Peoria; and San Francisco Giants, Old Town Scottsdale. Tucson hosts the Arizona Diamondbacks, Colorado Rockies, and the Chicago White Sox at two parks.

MILWAUKEE BREWERS
623-245-5500
milwaukee.brewers.mlb.com
Maryvale Baseball Park, 3600 N. 51st Ave., Phoenix
Directions: I-10 to 51st Ave., then head north to Thomas Rd. The parking lot is located on 51st Ave. between Thomas and Indian School Rds.

OAKLAND A'S
602-392-0217
www.oaklandathletics.com
Phoenix Municipal Stadium, 5999 E. Van Buren, Phoenix
Directions: Take the Loop 202 to Priest exit. Go north on Priest; Phoenix Municipal Stadium will be approximately 1 mile up from the highway.

Old Town Scottsdale.

4

Scottsdale

Fountain Hills, Paradise Valley, Cave Creek, Carefree

The self-proclaimed "West's Most Western Town" was founded by US Army chaplain Winfield Scott in the late 19th century and, after a brief stint as Orangedale, was renamed Scottsdale in 1894. The land for which Scott originally paid $2.50 an acre is now the place where homes run about $250 a square foot and up. Scottsdale has since grown to more than 225,000 people and 184 square miles. With an average elevation of 1,260 feet, Scottsdale is slightly higher than Phoenix and has a tad lower average temperature: 84.6 degrees Fahrenheit. Scottsdale is home to a quarter of the Valley's 200-plus golf courses and better than 70 resorts and hotels, accounting for 25 percent of the Valley's 55,000 guest rooms. It hosts more than seven million visitors a year; over six million people drop in for a day. Located off the Loop 101 and just north of both the Loop 202 and US 60, Scottsdale is easily accessible from anywhere in the Valley. Only minutes from Phoenix Sky Harbor International Airport, it also features the second busiest single-runway airport in the country—Scottsdale Municipal Airport, which handles about 200,000 takeoffs a year.

Host to more than 125 art galleries and 60 public artworks, Scottsdale is the sophisticated sister to the rest of the Valley. The city features hundreds of upscale restaurants, boutiques, and shops, and boasts a number of the Valley's top resorts, golf courses, and spas. Nestled between both Camelback and Mummy Mountains and set against the magnificent McDowell Mountains, it is home to four of the Valley's five Five Diamond resorts. Take a seat at one of its many pools and you will find yourself in an oasis of palm trees, blue skies, and mountain backdrops. Enjoy a plethora of dining options; there are more than 600—from the landmark Pink Pony Steakhouse to the controversial Pink Taco restaurant. Rub shoulders with sports stars, movie stars, famous authors, and celebrities of all kinds; many of the Valley's VIPs have made this beautiful city home. Experience the greatest show on grass—the FBR Open at TPC in North Scottsdale—or the famous Barrett-Jackson Auto Show. Shop at any number of unique outdoor malls, including Shops at Gainey Ranch, el Pedregal, or the Waterfront, or spend hours wandering the sidewalks of Old Town Scottsdale's shopping and arts districts, visiting the numerous art galleries, cafés, restaurants, shops, and boutiques selling everything from high-priced original art to Native American handiwork to locally designed apparel and accessories.

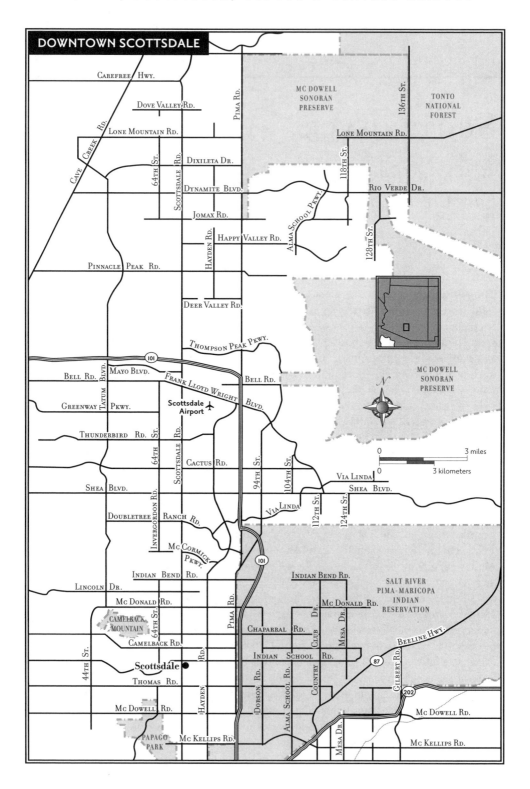

Destination Weddings in Arizona

By Suzy R. Siegel

If you find the bride in your life is enchanted by the Sonoran Desert, and has decided that the Valley is the place for her fairytale wedding, rest assured there are plenty of locations that can host family and friends for an out of town wedding. With no less than 5 five-diamond resorts in the Valley, you're bound to find the perfect site. Many of the Valley's top resorts, like The Phoenician, Arizona Biltmore, Fairmont Scottsdale Princess and Sheraton Wild Horse Pass Resort & Spa can plan the wedding from the rehearsal dinner to the day-after-the-wedding brunch. Not only can these sites take care of every last wedding detail, but you'll also find plenty of opportunities to pamper the bride and groom, and their guests. His and hers spa treatments, golf games for the groom and his party, a spa day for the bride and her bridesmaids. The best part . . . with backdrops like Camelback Mountain or the McDowell Mountains, the wedding pictures can't be anything less than amazing!

Suzy R. Siegel is the publisher of Arizona's Finest Wedding Sites *magazine and the site www.arizonas finestweddings.com; she is an active member of the Association for Bridal Consultants.*

Fountain Hills

Fountain Hills—a small community to the east of North Scottsdale—is located on the eastern slope of the McDowell Mountains. It is accessible by Shea Boulevard on the west and Beeline Highway (AZ 87) to the south. At about 1,700 feet in elevation, it offers some amazing views of the Valley. It's home to the Eagle Mountain and Copperwynd Resorts, as well as the famous fountain that shoots 560 feet into the desert air. This man-made fountain was developed as a landmark for this community in the early 1970s, and uses recycled and reclaimed water from the 28-acre lake surrounding it. It's located in Fountain Park at the heart of the community; the uniquely designed nozzle weighs 2,000 pounds and can conduct 375 pounds of water per square inch—at a rate of 7,000 gallons a minute—to heights unmatched throughout the world. At present the fountain operates 15 times a day as weather and wind velocity permit. For 10 minutes every hour on the hour 10 AM–9 PM daily, this is an amazing sight to behold.

Cave Creek

Hark back to the earlier days of the Valley in Cave Creek. Located just north of Carefree Highway or AZ 74 on Cave Creek Road, this little community encompasses about 30 square miles and is home to just over 4,000 people. It's had its share of gold mining, dude ranching, and such since its inception in 1874, though it didn't become a city until 1986. Tourists like to wander through Frontier Town—a collection of saloons and western-style shops.

Carefree

Established in the late 1950s as a master-planned community, Carefree is home to only a few thousand people. The town has an artistic element including several galleries, and tourists enjoy the charming bed & breakfasts and restaurants. The huge boulders you see are the geographic inspiration for the name of the Boulders Resort. Carefree Highway (AZ 74), which connects the town of Carefree with I-17, inspired Gordon Lightfoot's song of the same name.

Early Sunday morning at Scottsdale's Waterfont outdoor mall.

LODGING

Credit Cards

The following abbreviations are used for credit card information:

AE: American Express
CB: Carte Blanche
D: Discover Card
DC: Diner's Club
MC: MasterCard
V: Visa

FOUNTAIN HILLS
COMFORT INN

480-837-5343.
17105 E. Shea Blvd., Fountain Hills 85268.
Prices: $300–400.
Credit Cards: AE, CB, D, DC, MC, V.
Handicapped Access: Yes.
Pets: No.

This Comfort Inn hotel is close to several area attractions including Fort McDowell Casino, Saguaro Lake, WestWorld of Scottsdale, and TPC—home of the FBR Open. And it's only 2 miles from the world-famous Fountain Hills fountain. Amenities include free Internet access and an outdoor heated pool.

COPPERWYND RESORT AND CLUB

480-333-1848 or 877-707-7760.
www.copperwynd.com.
13225 N. Eagle Ridge Dr., Fountain Hills 85268.
Prices: Call for rates.
Credit Cards: AE, D, MC, V.
Handicapped Access: Yes.
Pets: No.

Named a Four Diamond resort by AAA, this small luxury resort features breathtaking views from its 32 mountainside guest rooms; in-room amenities include gas-burning fireplace, wireless Internet access, and private balcony. The resort's 10 villas range in size from 1,900 to 2,700 square feet and have beautifully appointed living space, two or three bedrooms, gourmet kitchens, laundry equipment, and a private garage unit. Several award-winning golf courses are close by, and the Spa at Copperwynd offers an array of European-influenced services and treatments. Alchemy, the on-site restaurant, features delicious cuisine and incredible views of the Sonoran Desert.

HOLIDAY INN HOTEL & SUITES AT FOUNTAIN HILLS

480-837-6565.
www.holidayinn.com/fountainhills.
12800 N. Saguaro Blvd., Fountain Hills 85268.
Prices: $145–199.
Credit Cards: AE, CB, D, DC, MC, V.
Handicapped Access: 8 rooms.
Pets: Yes.

Located adjacent to the famous fountain of Fountain Hills, this Holiday Inn Hotel and Suites features more than 100 guest rooms with 26 suites.

INN AT EAGLE MOUNTAIN

480-816-3000 or 800-992-8083.
9800 N. Summer Hill Blvd., Fountain Hills 85268.
Prices: $245–295.
Credit Cards: AE, D, DC, MC, V.
Handicapped Access: Yes.
Pets: No.

This Santa Fe–style property set in the Sonoran Desert is located above the 18th green of the prestigious Golf Club at Eagle Mountain, and features 42 mini suites with fireplace, private deck, and whirlpool tub for two. The resort offers golf packages.

SCOTTSDALE
CAMELBACK INN, A JW MARRIOTT RESORT AND SPA

480-948-1700 or 800-582-2169.
www.camelbackspa.com.
5402 E. Lincoln Dr., Scottsdale 85253.
Prices: $159–529.
Credit Cards: AE, MC, V.
Handicapped Access: 17 rooms.
Pets: Small dogs permitted.

Named a Five Diamond resort by AAA 30 times over, Camelback Inn features more than 450 casita guest rooms and suites with private entrances (a couple even have private pools). The 125-acre resort, overlooking Camelback Mountain, boasts 36 holes of championship golf, six tennis courts, an award-winning spa, three pools, and seven distinct dining experiences. The views are stunning and the service, impeccable—a true opportunity to pamper yourself.

CHAPARRAL SUITES RESORT SCOTTSDALE

480-949-1414.
www.chaparralsuites.com.
5001 N. Scottsdale Rd., Scottsdale 85250.
Prices: Call for rates.
Credit Cards: AE, D, DC, MC, V.
Handicapped Access: Yes.
Pets: Small dogs under 50 pounds.

Chaparral Suites features more than 300 two-room suites. Room rates include a full breakfast for two, airport transportation, and a 2-hour nightly reception. On-site amenities include two outdoor heated pools, free high-speed and wireless Internet access, and a fitness center. The resort is conveniently located close to the downtown Scottsdale area, putting it only minutes away from hundreds of shops, restaurants, and entertainment venues, including Scottsdale Fashion Square.

COMFORT SUITES OF OLD TOWN SCOTTSDALE

480-946-1111.
www.comfortsuites.com.
3275 Drinkwater Blvd., Scottsdale 85251-6405.
Prices: $299–309.
Credit Cards: AE, CB, D, DC, MC, V.
Handicapped Access: Yes.
Pets: Yes.

The proximity to Old Town Scottsdale makes this Comfort Suites a convenient choice. The hotel features a deluxe continental breakfast, indoor pool and spa, and free Internet access.

COURTYARD BY MARRIOTT SCOTTSDALE MAYO CLINIC

480-860-4000.
www.marriott.com.
13444 E. Shea Blvd., Scottsdale 85259.
Prices: $219–279.
Credit Cards: AE, CB, D, DC, MC, V.
Handicapped Access: Yes.
Pets: No.

Located within walking distance of the Mayo Clinic in North Scottsdale, this Marriott features an on-site restaurant, free Internet access, and fitness center, as well as in-room refrigerator and coffeemaker.

DAYS INN SCOTTSDALE

480-947-5411.
www.scottsdaledaysinn.com.
4710 N. Scottsdale Rd., Scottsdale 85251-7608.
Prices: $150–199.
Credit Cards: AE, D, DC, MC, V.
Handicapped Access: Yes.
Pets: No.

Adjacent to Fashion Square Mall and close to downtown Scottsdale, this Days Inn features free Internet access, in-room refrigerator and coffeemaker, outdoor pool and spa, and complimentary deluxe continental breakfast.

DOUBLETREE PARADISE VALLEY RESORT

480-947-5400 or 877-445-6677.
www.hilton.com.
5401 N. Scottsdale Rd., Scottsdale 85250.
Prices: $339–359.
Credit Cards: AE, CB, D, DC, MC, V.
Handicapped Access: Yes.
Pets: Yes.

This resort features 378 rooms, a pool, tennis courts, and a putting green; its location in central Scottsdale offers close proximity to the charms of Old Town as well as the golf and shopping in North Scottsdale.

EXTENDED STAY DELUXE PHOENIX–SCOTTSDALE

480-483-1333.
www.extendedstayhotels.com.
10660 N. 69th St., Scottsdale 85254.
Prices: $125–130.
Credit Cards: AE, D, DC, MC, V.
Handicapped Access: Yes.
Pets: 1 per room; fees apply.

This 105-room Extended Stay offers open studio suites, living space, and fully equipped kitchens; on-site amenities include fitness facility and outdoor pool. Wireless Internet access is available for a fee.

FAIRMONT SCOTTSDALE PRINCESS

480-585-4848 or 800-344-4758.
www.fairmont.com/scottsdale.
7575 E. Princess Dr., Scottsdale 85255.
Prices: $539–649 and up.
Credit Cards: AE, CB, DC, MC, V.
Handicapped Access: Yes.
Pets: Call for information.

A Five Diamond resort in North Scottsdale, close to the Loop 101 and Kierland Commons, this desert oasis provides a wonderful escape from the rest of the world. Relax beside one of several pools with beverage service. It's located adjacent to TPC of Scottsdale, with an on-site spa that brings the full Scottsdale experience to you.

FOUR SEASONS RESORT SCOTTSDALE AT TROON NORTH

480-515-5700 or 888-207-9696.
www.fourseasons.com/scottsdale.
10600 E. Crescent Moon Dr., Scottsdale 85262.
Prices: $545 and up.
Credit Cards: AE, CB, D, DC, MC, V.
Handicapped Access: Yes.
Pets: No.

In the shadows of Pinnacle Peak, high above North Scottsdale, lies this desert oasis with

The desert appeal of the Four Seasons Resort Scottsdale at Troon North.

enchanting city views, a restaurant and bar, poolside service, on-site tennis, horseback riding, hiking, golf, and spa; guest suites and casitas are available with high-speed Internet access. This is a Four Seasons experience set in the rugged Sonoran Desert.

HOTEL VALLEY HO

480-248-2000 or 866-882-4484.
www.hotelvalleyho.com.
6850 E. Main St., Scottsdale 85251.
Prices: Promotional packages available; call for information.
Credit Cards: AE, D, DC, MC, V.
Handicapped Access: Call for information.
Pets: Yes.

Originally built in 1956, Hotel Valley Ho has been renovated into an urban oasis with 194 rooms and a unique style. Amenities include complimentary wireless Internet access, morning espresso, tea and coffee,

on-site fitness room, and a courtyard pool where you can get a foot massage. Find out more about the VH Spa in the Golf Courses & Spas chapter. Proximity to Old Town Scottsdale means restaurants, bars, and entertainment are only minutes away.

HYATT REGENCY SCOTTSDALE RESORT & SPA AT GAINEY RANCH

480-444-1234 or 800-483-1234.
www.scottsdale.hyatt.com.
7500 E. Doubletree Ranch Rd., Scottsdale 85258.
Prices: $159–625.
Credit Cards: AE, CB, D, DC, MC, V.
Handicapped Access: 14 rooms.
Pets: No.

Elegant southwestern style is the essence of the Hyatt Regency Scottsdale Resort at Gainey Ranch. World-class spa, world-class golf, and world-class service meet you upon check-in. Located close to the Shops at

Gainey Ranch, as well as shopping, dining, and entertainment in North Scottsdale.

MILLENNIUM RESORT—SCOTTSDALE MCCORMICK RANCH

480-948-5050 or 800-243-1332.
7401 N. Scottsdale Rd., Scottsdale 85253.
Prices: $120–299.
Credit Cards: AE, CB, D, DC, MC, V.
Handicapped Access: 2 rooms.
Pets: Yes.

This resort features 125 rooms and 51 villas. Combined with magnificent views, a lakefront location, and award-winning golf, it's a top choice for Scottsdale visitors.

PHOENICIAN, THE

480-941-8200 or 800-888-8234.
6000 E. Camelback Rd., Scottsdale 85251.
Prices: $195–725.
Credit Cards: AE, D, DC, MC, V.
Handicapped Access: 150 rooms.
Pets: Small dogs.

Located at the base of Camelback Mountain, the AAA Five Diamond Phoenician offers a lush resort setting close to shopping, dining, and golf. You'll also find award-winning French cuisine at Mary Elaine's.

RADISSON FORT MCDOWELL RESORT & CASINO

480-789-5300 or 800-715-0328.
10438 N. Fort McDowell Rd., Scottsdale 85264.
Prices: $269–279.
Credit Cards: AE, CB, D, DC, MC, V.
Handicapped Access: Yes.
Pets: Yes.

Golf at We-Ko-Pa and gamble in the casino. This resort and casino—tucked behind the McDowell Mountains—features 248 guest rooms and suites, and offers high-speed Internet access, a pool, and a fitness facility. The on-site Anhala Restaurant and Lounge features dishes made with locally grown citrus, pecans, herbs, and mesquite from the Fort McDowell Yavapai Farm.

The desert is prominent in North Scottsdale.

SCOTTSDALE PLAZA RESORT

480-948-5000 or 800-832-2025.
www.scottsdaleplaza.com.
7200 N. Scottsdale Rd., Scottsdale 85253.
Prices: $85–249.
Credit Cards: AE, D, DC, MC, V.
Handicapped Access: 20 rooms.
Pets: Yes; minimal fees apply.

This 400-plus-room hotel features accommodations of varying sizes, from traditional guest rooms to two-story villas that have been recently renovated. Conveniently located between North Scottsdale and Old Town, it offers five pools, a fitness center, tennis, and award-winning dining at Remington's—a favorite among locals.

SCOTTSDALE RESORT
& CONFERENCE CENTER

480-991-9000 or 800-540-0727.
www.thescottsdaleresort.com.
7700 E. McCormick Pkwy., Scottsdale 85258.
Prices: $99–800.
Credit Cards: AE, D, DC, MC, V.
Pets: No.
Handicapped Access: 12 rooms.

This hacienda-inspired resort is close to golf, shopping, and dining and offers 300-plus guest rooms, casitas, and suites. Amansala Spa and Salon provides a great pampering experience; enjoy the full-service salon, tennis courts, or one of two pools. The Palm Court Restaurant serves award-winning cuisine.

WESTIN KIERLAND RESORT & SPA

480-624-1000 or 800-WESTIN-1.
www.kierlandresort.com.
6902 E. Greenway Pkwy., Scottsdale 85254.
Prices: $289–549.
Credit Cards: AE, CB, D, DC, MC, V.
Handicapped Access: 27 rooms.
Pets: Yes.

Located in the bustling hub that is North Scottsdale, Westin Kierland offers an on-site spa and salon, three 9-hole golf courses, and a complimentary fitness center, as well as a teen club, kids' club, and 8,000-square-foot pool, complete with a zero-entry sandy beach, a 110-foot waterslide, and a flowing river ride. To top it off, the Westin Kierland is adjacent to the 38-acre Kierland Commons shopping and dining extravaganza. The 732-room resort features 55 suites and 32 casita units, along with nine dining experiences, including deseo, which serves Latin-influenced cuisine under the direction of award-winning chef Douglas Rodriguez.

CAREFREE

BOULDERS RESORT
& GOLDEN DOOR SPA, THE

480-488-9009 or 800-553-1717.
www.theboulders.com.
34631 N. Tom Darlington Dr., Carefree 85377.
Prices: $279–649.
Credit Cards: AE, D, DC, MC, V.
Handicapped Access: 3 rooms.
Pets: Yes.

The Boulders Resort and Golden Door Spa has been named America's Top Resort 14 consecutive years, earning it a top spot among Valley visitors. An award-winning spa, two championship golf courses designed by Jay Moorish, eight tennis courts, five dining experiences, and one bar—not to mention incredible views of the Sonoran Desert—make it a true destination resort. To top it off, they offer excellent golf, spa, and summer packages. The resort features 160 casitas and one-, two-, and three-bedroom villas. See more about the Golden Door Spa in chapter 9.

CAREFREE RESORT & VILLAS

480-488-5300 or 800-949-1994.
www.carefree-resort.com.
37220 Mule Train Rd., Carefree 85377.
Prices: $95–240.

Credit Cards: AE, D, DC, MC, V.
Handicapped Access: 9 rooms.
Pets: Yes.

Located in the foothills of the Continental Mountains, just north of Scottsdale, Carefree Resort & Villas embodies western-style charm and hospitality. Twenty-six acres of Sonoran Desert, golf at nearby Legend Trails, and the new Spa at Carefree Resort & Villas all make for a relaxing experience in a lovely setting. The resort features 360 beautifully appointed guest rooms, suites, and one- and two-bedroom villas; three swimming pools; and several dining options, including a great little coffee bar called the Roadrunner Café and the Red Horse Saloon (styled after a turn-of-the-20th-century saloon with a billiards table and dartboards), which serves up burgers, pizza, and cold beer and margaritas. The Lariat Grill serves steaks, seafood, and thin-crust pizzas.

PARADISE VALLEY
HERMOSA INN
602-955-8614 or 800-241-1210.
www.hermosainn.com.
5532 N. Palo Cristi Rd., Scottsdale 85253.
Prices: $500-plus; ask about packages.
Credit Cards: AE, CB, D, DC, MC, V.
Handicapped Access: Call for more information.
Pets: Yes; $50 fee per reservation.

Hand built by cowboy artist Lon Megargee as his home and studio, the Hermosa Inn is a historic, boutique luxury hotel set against Camelback Mountain. The 35 hotel accommodations make for an intimate experience. Amenities include an outdoor pool, two spas, in-room massage service, and the award-winning restaurant LON's at the Hermosa.

RVs

SCOTTSDALE TRAILER CORRAL
480-947-8532.
3202 N. Scottsdale Rd., Space 11, Scottsdale 85251-6412.

Located only a couple of blocks from Old Town Scottsdale and Scottsdale Baseball Stadium, where the Giants play their spring training games, Scottsdale Trailer Corral offers nightly, weekly, or monthly spaces; there are also one- and two-bedroom units available for rent. The site offers laundry and bathroom facilities.

DINING

Credit Cards
The following abbreviations are used for credit card information:
AE: American Express
CB: Carte Blanche
D: Discover Card
DC: Diner's Club
MC: MasterCard
V: Visa

ARCADIA FARMS
480-941-5665.
www.arcadiafarmscafe.com.
7014 E. 1st Ave., Scottsdale.
Open: Daily for lunch 11 AM–3 PM.
Prices: Moderate.
Cuisine: American Southwest.
Credit Cards: AE, MC, V.

If the food here is spectacular, then the desserts are absolutely magnificent. They are sized to share, though it might be hard to do after you've had your first bite. The tuxedo and chocolate raspberry baby cakes are layered with chocolate mousse and covered in ganache; raspberry sauce joins the chocolate mousse in the latter—and the truth is, you won't be able to decide which is your favorite. Add the coconut baby cake, key lime tart, and warm fruit crisp with vanilla ice cream (there is fresh fruit for those strong enough to be good) to the dessert menu, and you'll need to order lunch accordingly. That being said, owner Carolyn Ellis has created a delightful dining

Scottsdale street scene.

experience in this charming little downtown café; lunch is meant to be savored. The salads are wonderful medleys of fruits, greens, nuts, cheeses, and veggies drizzled with vinaigrette dressings; the delicious sandwiches are built for two; and house specialties include wild mushroom, spinach, and goat cheese tart, and fresh lump crabcakes. If you have the chance try one of her other successes—each featuring a unique menu and a different kind of experience—check out Arcadia Farms locations at the Phoenix Art Museum, Heard Museum on Central, and City Bakery at Bentley Projects in downtown Phoenix. Reservations are suggested at this North Scottsdale location, which is located one block south of Indian School Rd., between Goldwater Blvd. and Scottsdale Rd.

CAFÉ CARUMBA

480-947-8777.
www.cafecarumba.com.

7303 E. Indian School Rd., Scottsdale.
Open: Daily for breakfast 7 AM–2 PM, lunch 10 AM–3 PM; happy hour Tue.–Sat. 3–6 PM; dinner Tue.–Thu. 5–10 PM, Fri.–Sat. 5 PM–midnight.
Prices: Moderate.
Cuisine: American Southwest.
Credit Cards: AE, MC, V.

Located on the corner of Indian School Rd. and Brown Ave., just east of Scottsdale Rd., is Café Carumba—an all-day café with a neighborhood feel. Two outdoor patios and a spacious indoors make for plenty of seating on busy weekend mornings. For breakfast, try the eggs and corned beef hash, citrus-infused French toast, or Santa Fe Breakfast Burrito; at lunch you might like the saguaro grilled cheese with Pepper Jack, bacon, tomato, and avocado, a gourmet burger, or a salad. For dinner they will dazzle your taste buds with dishes like habanero braised ribs or the Scottsdale

Old Town Scottsdale.

Burger: half a pound of sirloin topped with portobello mushrooms, pancetta, and Brie. Try one of the house margaritas with dinner—these specialty drinks are top shelf, and Patron Silver is the house tequila. Start your evening early with their happy hour 3–6 PM, when all drinks, beer, and wine are half price.

CARLSBAD TAVERN & RESTAURANT

480-970-8164.
www.carlsbadtavern.com.
3313 N. Hayden Rd., Scottsdale.
Open: Daily for lunch and dinner 11 AM–2 AM; happy hour 3–6 PM.
Prices: Moderate.
Cuisine: New Mexican.
Credit Cards: AE, D, MC, V.

When the menu comes with a heat chart, you know they're serious about spicy. You'll find New Mexican cuisine with lots of chiles—both green and red—in this out-of-the-way restaurant off Hayden Rd. Sit inside or outside on the patio, where you'll often hear live acoustical music. They have a late-night menu, so stop by anytime before 2 AM. House specialties include Carlsbad Pasta, chipotle BBQ baby back ribs, and pecanwood-grilled fish; steaks and burgers and enchiladas, too. Everything has pizzazz, so just ask them to dial up or down according to your tastes. Located in a mostly residential neighborhood—you'll miss it if you're not looking for it on the east side of the road, south of Osborn between Thomas and Indian School Rds.

COWBOY CIAO

480-WINE-111.
www.cowboyciao.com
7133 E. Stetson Dr., Scottsdale.
Open: Daily for lunch 11:30 AM–2:30 PM; dinner Sun.–Thu. 5–10 PM, Fri.–Sat. 5–11 PM.
Prices: Expensive to very expensive.
Cuisine: Modern American with global influences.
Credit Cards: Call.

Think out of the box and you have Cowboy Ciao—an eclectic mix of personality, panache, and amazing food in an environment as bold as its flavors. One visit will having you begging for more—more food, more fun, and more of whatever it is they're putting in the wine. Sister hot spots and neighbors Sea Saw and Kazimierz World Wine Bar are located close by, and any combination will provide a fun, relaxing, and satiating experience of excellent food paired with great spirits and, well...the company you share is up to you.

DON & CHARLIE'S RESTAURANT

480-990-0900.
www.donandcharlies.com.
7501 E. Camelback Rd., Scottsdale 85251-3510.
Open: Daily for dinner, Sun. 5 PM–9 PM, Mon.–Thu. 5–9:30 PM, Fri.–Sat. 5–10 PM.
Prices: Expensive.
Cuisine: Steak house.
Credit Cards: AE, D, DC, MC, V.

Considered home of the best ribs in town, Don & Charlie's has been serving hearty meals for almost 30 years. Owner Don Carson is a Chicago native whose passion for great barbecue and beef have made his restaurant a top pick among locals and drawn praise from several media outlets in town. You'll find just about every cut and type of meat here, from lamb chops, pork chops, skirt steaks, and filet mignon to sautéed calf's liver, ribs, chicken, and even seafood; there's also kids' meals, soups, salads, pasta, and burgers. The sports paraphernalia and huge meals make it a top spot for male bonding.

EDDIE V'S EDGEWATER GRILLE

480-538-8468.
www.eddiev.com.
20715 N. Pima Rd., Scottsdale.

Open: Daily for dinner, Mon.–Sat. 5–11 PM, Sun. 5–10 PM; happy hour 4:30–7 PM.
Cuisine: Seafood.
Prices: Very expensive.
Credit Cards: AE, DC, D, MC, V.

From the makers of Southwest success Z'Tejas, Larry "Eddie" Foles and Guy "Mr. V" Villavaso have brought the best of Boston, San Francisco, and New Orleans inland—better yet, they've brought it to the desert. One of only three Southwest locations, Eddie V's has married sophistication and elegance with fresh-from-the-boat seafood—sautéed New Zealand grouper with fresh Jonah crab and Chilean sea bass, roasted crisp; you'll also find steaks and chops on this à la carte menu. Complement your entrée with potato and Gruyère fritters or crab-fried rice with scallions and mushrooms. Save room for dessert: Their menu of freshly baked pastries includes cinnamon raisin bread pudding soufflé with hot bourbon sauce, and hot dark chocolate Godiva cake with vanilla bean ice cream. Happy hour at the adjacent V Lounge runs 4:30–7 PM; enjoy 50-cent oysters and live music nightly.

FRANK AND LUPE'S
480-990-9844.
4121 N. Marshall Way, Scottsdale.
Open: Daily, 11 AM–10 PM.
Prices: Inexpensive to moderate.
Cuisine: Mexican.
Credit Cards: AE, MC, V.

This family-owned, neighborhood-favorite restaurant is the offspring of Frank and Lupe's in Socorro, New Mexico. Owned and operated by their sons Eddie and Ted Bernal, it's been featured in *Bon Appétit* and *Gourmet* magazines. The laid-back atmosphere and colorful decor invite an appetizing experience of delicious New Mexican fare and wonderful margaritas. The chips and guacamole make an excellent appetizer; however, they have plenty of choices, including tamales, burritos, chiles rellenos, and enchiladas, all spiced with varying degrees of heat for those looking for a full meal.

FUSION RESTAURANT & LOUNGE
480-423-9043.
www.azeats.com/fusion.
4441 N. Buckboard Trail, Scottsdale.
Open: Lunch Tue.–Fri. 11 AM–2:30 PM, dinner Tue.–Sat. 5 PM, happy hour Tue.–Fri. 5–7 PM; closed Sun.–Mon.
Prices: Moderate to expensive.
Cuisine: New American.
Credit Cards: AE, DC, D, MC, V.

From executive chef at Biltmore seafood restaurant Steamers to owner of Fusion with wife Jen Lyn, Matt Long has leapt from the frying pan into the fire with great success. The menu here introduces an eclectic mix of delightful flavors in dishes like fruit and goat cheese salad drizzled with mint lime vinaigrette; Kobe beef burger layered with caramelized jalapeño peppers and red onions; and a maple and coffee glazed salmon partnered with Parmesan-stuffed butternut squash. For dessert try the homemade fudge and ice cream. Note that reaching the restaurant may be complicated during construction of the W Hotel, when some streets may be one way. Your best bet is to take Brown Ave. south from Camelback Rd., turn left onto Shoeman Lane, and then take the next left, which is Buckboard Lane.

HANDLEBARJ RESTAURANT & SALOON
480-948-0110.
www.handlebarj.com.
7116 E. Becker Lane, Scottsdale.
Open: Daily at 11 AM for lunch and dinner.
Prices: Moderate to expensive.
Cuisine: Steak house.
Credit Cards: AE, D, MC, V.

A Scottsdale landmark, HandlebarJ has been providing locals and tourists alike with a wild, western time since 1966.

Steaks, BBQ ribs, homemade biscuits, and corn-on-the cob combined with live country music and country dance lessons make it an authentic "out west" experience. Wed.–Sun. the Herndon Brothers Band plays starting at 8:30 PM; live music Mon.–Tue.; free country dance lessons Wed., Thu., and Sun. starting at 7 PM.

KYOTO JAPANESE RESTAURANT

480-990-9374.
7170 E. Stetson Dr., Scottsdale.
Open: Lunch Mon.–Fri. 11:30 AM–2:30 PM; dinner Mon.–Thu. 5:30–10 PM, Fri.–Sat. 5:30–11 PM.
Prices: Moderate to expensive.
Cuisine: Japanese.
Credit Cards: AE, D, MC, V.

Teppanyaki-style dining and sushi bar, serving unique delicacies such as sea urchin, green mussels, and octopus sashimi as well as New York steaks.

LON'S AT THE HERMOSA

800-241-1210.
www.lons.com.

5532 N. Palo Cristi, Paradise Valley.
Open: Brunch, lunch, and dinner, 11:30 AM–2PM and 5:30–10 PM.
Prices: Expensive to very expensive.
Cuisine: New American.
Credit Cards: AE, D, MC, V.

Just as cowboy artist Alonzo (Lon) Megargee lassoed the beauty of the Southwest and spread it out on canvas for others to enjoy, executive chef Michael Rusconi has captured successfully the tastes of the West and artistically arranges their flavors with flair for his guests' enjoyment. Since 2005 Rusconi has garnered local and national acclaim for his artistry. Enjoy dishes like roast Fulton Valley free-range chicken or maple and cinnamon lacquered natural breast of duck on the beautiful patio beneath the mesquite trees in the radiating warmth of the outdoor fireplace. The restaurant is located in the shadows of Camelback Mountain as part of the Hermosa Inn compound. In keeping with the artistic image of Lon Megargee, the restaurant hosts an artist-in-residence series. Past guests have included author Aaron Elkins, musician Tito Puente Jr., and

Old Town Scottsdale.

artists David L. Bradley and Victor Ostrovsky. Guests can purchase tickets ($125 per person, plus tax and gratuity) to attend the events hosted for these inspiring artists. For reservations, call 602-955-7878.

MALEE'S ON MAIN THAI BISTRO

480-947-6042.
www.maleesonmain.com.
7131 E. Main St., Scottsdale.
Open: Lunch and dinner Mon.–Wed. 11:30 AM–2 PM and 5–9 PM, Thu.–Fri. 11:30 AM–10 PM, Sat. noon–10 PM, Sun. 5–9 PM; closed major holidays.
Prices: Moderate.
Cuisine: Thai.
Credit Cards: AE, MC, V.
Other Locations: Desert Ridge Marketplace at Loop 101 and Tatum Blvd., North Phoenix (480-342-9220).

Malee's on Main is nestled among the art galleries and shops of Old Town Scottsdale in a 1921 building that has been a tea house, a French restaurant, and an Italian eatery. Today it's a Thai bistro serving an array of exotic dishes and sushi. Keep in mind that Thai spicy is not the same as salsa spicy, so when you tell them, *No problem, I can handle it*, you may want to think twice. Their mild spicy is *hot*; anything more and you may need to use your napkin to mop your brow. Delicious Thai cuisine with a kick.

PASTA BRIONI'S

480-994-0028.
www.azeats.com/PastaBrioni.
4416 N. Miller Rd., Scottsdale.
Open: Daily, lunch Mon.–Fri 11:30 AM–2 PM; dinner Sun.–Fri. 5–10 PM, Sat. 5–11 PM; bar opens at 4:30 PM daily.
Prices: Moderate.
Cuisine: Italian.
Credit Cards: AE, MC, V.

The famous Pink Pony Steakhouse.

Tasty Italian fare makes up the regular menu—but forget that and listen to the whiteboard specials, where you'll find delish dishes like Chicken Martini (chicken breast sautéed with Parmesan, lemon, and white wine, topped off with asparagus) or tilapia piccata (tilapia in a white wine piccata sauce). Staff are delightful, and the restaurant has a great "old Italian neighborhood" feel. Great happy-hour specials Sun.–Wed., when you sit at the bar 4:30–10 PM: half off the menu, house wines, "well drinks," and domestic beers.

PINK PONY STEAKHOUSE

480-945-6697.
3831 N. Scottsdale Rd., Scottsdale.
Open: Daily for lunch and dinner, Mon.–Fri. 10 AM–10:30 PM, Sat.–Sun. 4–10:30 PM; bar open late.
Prices: Expensive.
Cuisine: Steak house.
Credit Cards: AE, D, DC, MC, V.

Just the steak and potatoes, ma'am—you won't find any frills at this Old Town steak house, but they do it so well that, after the first bite, you won't notice. Juicy steaks and huge baked potatoes with the works crowd out the cracker basket and the iceberg lettuce salad—the Pink Pony is a Scottsdale institution. You'll find photos and memorabilia of the famous folks who've wined and dined here since it opened in 1950; including Gene Autry, Joe DiMaggio, and Ty Cobb. *Sports Illustrated* featured it in an article, and in 2004 the city of Scottsdale named it a historic landmark. Located next to Bandera, which offers gourmet, upscale cowboy cuisine, but you can't miss it—it's painted pink!

REATA PASS STEAKHOUSE/ GREASEWOOD FLAT

480-585-7277.
www.reatapass.com.
27500 N. Alma School Pkwy., Scottsdale.
Open: Lunch and dinner Wed.–Thu. 11 AM–9 PM, Fri.–Sat. 11 AM–10 PM; closed Sun.–Tue.
Prices: Moderate.
Cuisine: Steak house.
Credit Cards: AE, D, DC, MC, V.

Chow down on burgers and steaks cowboy-style at this 120-year-old bunkhouse-turned-restaurant. Located at Reata Pass—a stagecoach stop between Fort McDowell and Phoenix back when Phoenix was a long and dusty 30-mile ride away—it's a steak house and saloon (Greasewood Flat) where the tables are picnic and the steaks are grilled to perfection.

SALT CELLAR

480-947-1963.
www.savvydiner.com/details.php?r=649.
550 N. Hayden Rd., Scottsdale.
Open: Dinner Sun.–Thu. 5–11 PM, Fri.–Sat. 5 PM–midnight
Prices: Expensive.
Cuisine: Seafood.
Credit Cards: All major credit cards.

Literally, this restaurant is nothing to look at. When you drive up, you'll wonder how the tiny shack could serve perhaps the best seafood in town. But looks can be deceiving. What you see is simply the entrance; the rest of the Salt Cellar is three flights underground. While the dress is casual, the food is anything but. Delicious seafood is flown in fresh daily from places like Georges Bank, Chesapeake Bay, and the Gulf of Mexico: the freshest trout, lobster, ahi, sea bass, scallops, king crab, and the list goes on. They also serve sumptuous steaks—filet mignon, beef Wellington. White tablecloths, fantastic servers, and elegant dishes share space in this enchanting little restaurant. Reservations are highly recommended. Should you arrive early, enjoy a drink at the full bar; on weekends space is tight.

Cafés

The Breakfast Club (480-222-2582; www.breakfastbar.com; 4400 N. Scottsdale Rd.) features a great little barista bar (they make best café mochas in town), and a Southwest-infused breakfast and lunch menu.

Orange Table Café (480-424-6819; www.dress4dinner.com; 7373 Scottsdale Mall, Suite 6) has been featured in *The New York Times* and *USA Today* as well as local media outlets like *Sonoran Living* and *Desert Living* and serves breakfast, lunch, and dinner.

Blu Burger Grille (www.bluburger.com; 15425 N. Scottsdale Rd., 480-948-3443; and 10428 E. Jomax Rd., Suite 101, 480-585-0454) puts a whole new kind of spin on the traditional fast-food burger experience—in fact, they've elevated it past fast food altogether. Choose your cow, the way it's cooked, and all the toppings. With what a fast-food meal costs these days, the prices aren't bad, and you might not need to eat your next meal!

Sugar Bowl Ice Cream Parlor & Restaurant (480-946-0051; 4005 N. Scottsdale Rd.) has been keeping the heat at bay for Valley residents since 1958 with its delicious assortment of cold treats; they also serve old-fashioned American fare.

Qwik Chinese (480-991-6400; 7353 N. Via Paseo Del Sur, Suite 490). This eatery, located in the Paseo Village Shopping Center, has been serving Scottsdale residents—both part time and full time—for 20 years. Owner Gary Xie serves up fast and delicious meals. Expect a bit of a wait during the busy tourist season as part-time residents line up to order their favorites.

Wine Bars

Scottsdale is a haven for wine lovers with such choices as **Tapino Kitchen & Wine Bar** (480-991-6887; www.tapino.com; 7000 E. Shea Blvd., Suite 1010) and **Uncorked! The Unpretentious Wine Bar** (480-629-9230; www.uncorkedwinebar.com; 16427 N. Scottsdale Rd., Suite 130). Of course **Kazimierz World Wine Bar** (480-946-3004; www.kazbar.net; 7137 E. Stetson Dr.) has a wine list the size of a novel, as well as great appetizers and cheese plates; so hip you can't find it unless someone shows you the secret entrance, which is in the back of the building. To get there, head south on Scottsdale Rd., take the first right-hand turn south of Camelback Rd. (this is Stetson), and find a parking spot on Stetson. You'll see the faux stained-glass windows on your left and two black columns next to them; head down the outdoor corridor (the sign above it says STETSON PLAZA), turn left, and you'll see a door with a sign reading THE TRUTH IS INSIDE. You've made it. Also check out **Su Vino Winery** (480-994-VINO; www.suvinowineryaz.com; 7035 E. Main St., Suite 110, Scottsdale). Founded in Grapevine, Texas, this new award-winning winery is located in the arts district of Old Town Scottsdale.

Cooking Schools

If you're in town for a while, try your hand at one of the Valley's cooking schools, such as **Sweet Basil Gourmetware & Cooking School** (480-596-5628; www.sweetbasilgourmet .com; 10749 N. Scottsdale Rd., Suite 101); **AndyFood** (480-951-2400; www.andyfood.com; 7000 E. Shea Blvd., Suite 1740), a culinary studio; or **The Epicurean Palette** (480-488-4955; www.epicureanpalette.com; 6137 E. Cave Creek Rd., Cave Creek).

CULTURE

Cinema

FARRELLI'S CINEMA SUPPER CLUB

480-905-7200.
www.cinemasupperclub.com.
14202 N. Scottsdale Rd., #14, Scottsdale.
Open: Call for show times.
Admission: Show tickets are $7 each and added to the final bill with your meal and drinks.

Reminiscent of the movie-palace days of the 1940s, Farrelli's Cinema Supper Club serves dinner and a movie in one of its two tiered restaurants. Twelve-foot screens show movies toward the end of their first runs as guests enjoy a meal from an extensive menu of contemporary American cuisine and a full bar. Reservations are suggested on weekends.

SCOTTSDALE 6 DRIVE-IN

480-949-9451.
8101 E. McKellips, Scottsdale.

Located at the corner of Hayden and McKellips, the Scottsdale 6 is open year-round and offers movies on six screens. Call for shows and times.

Historic/Walking Tours

SCOTTSDALE ARTWALK

Open: Every Thu. year-round, 7–9 PM

Take a stroll through downtown Scottsdale on any given Thursday and partake in a 30-year-old tradition. Home to more than 100 galleries, Scottsdale encourages visual arts of all types, from Southwest landscapes and Native American subjects to cutting-edge contemporary. Local galleries stay open late to show off the works of various artists. Special exhibits, artists' receptions, and live music often coincide with this weekly event.

Scottsdale is home to more galleries per capita than almost any other city in the United States. The city's zest for art is mirrored by residents' votes to allocate a portion of city taxes toward the funding of public art, and has made Scottsdale a prominent arts hub in the Southwest. Downtown Scottsdale is made up of five districts that meld and flow into one another, but each with a distinct personality: The 5th Avenue shopping district, world-renowned Marshall Way contemporary arts district, Main Street arts and antiques district, Old Town (the city's origins), and the Brown & Stetson business districts. These areas are easily navigated on foot and are peppered with specialty shops, bars, restaurants, and art galleries.

Try an early dinner at one of the area's many restaurants—perhaps Malee's on Main St. for Thai or Bandera on Scottsdale Rd. for gourmet western cuisine—then take a walk through the winding avenues that make up the heart of "the West's Most Western Town."

HISTORIC OLD TOWN SCOTTSDALE

Scottsdale Convention and Visitors Bureau: www.scottsdalecvb.com

Old Town Scottsdale encompasses much of the 40 original acres subdivided by Rhode

Island transplant Albert G. Utley in 1894. He named the city after US Army chaplain Winfield Scott, who played a monumental role in encouraging the first settlers to make this their new home. The 60-minute self-guided walking tour begins at the "Little Red Schoolhouse" built in 1909, now home of the Scottsdale Historical Museum; it ends with the Scottsdale Public Library (Civic Center Branch). A total of 15 stops along the way paint a picture of this once small farming town's past, including the Rusty Spur Saloon, originally built in 1921 as the Farmer's State Bank of Scottsdale, as well as nationally known landmarks like the Pink Pony Steakhouse on Scottsdale Rd. For more information on this walk, including a map and descriptions of each of the sites, visit www.scottsdalecvb.com and click on the Maps link.

Library

SCOTTSDALE PUBLIC LIBRARY

480-312-2474; TDD 480-312-7670.
http://library.scottsdaleaz.gov.
3839 N. Drinkwater Blvd., Scottsdale.
Open: Mon.–Thu. 9 AM–9 PM, Fri.–Sat. 10 AM–6 PM, Sun. 1–5 PM. Holiday hours may apply; check online for specifics.

The main library branch is located on the northeast side of 2nd St. and N. Drinkwater Blvd., two blocks south of Indian School Rd. and three blocks east of Scottsdale Rd. There's a great medieval-style children's library.

Museums & Galleries

CATTLETRACK STUDIOS AND STABLES GALLERIA

480-991-6994 or 800-774-5020.

Cattletrack Compound Gallery, known locally as Cattletrack, is an artists' compound home to a variety of artists, including photographers, painters, and sculptors. It's hidden in a maze of dead-end streets in Scottsdale south of the Gainey Ranch neighborhoods—though once you find it, it's easy to find again. Off Scottsdale Rd., take Lincoln Dr. (between McDonald and Indian Bend) east. You'll come to an L in the road; head south on Cattletrack (also known as Miller throughout the rest of Scottsdale). Before you reach McDonald Rd., you will see an obscure entrance on the east side of the road, complete with mesquite trees and wooden fences. Pull into the drive, which is nothing more than a dirt road, and park.

FRANK LLOYD WRIGHT'S TALIESIN WEST

480-860-2700.
www.franklloydwright.org.
12621 N. Frank Lloyd Wright Blvd., Scottsdale.

A living monument to the life and work of architect Frank Lloyd Wright, Taliesin West (pronounced *tally-ES-in*) is the western counterpart to Wright's home and studio Taliesin in Spring Green, Wisconsin. Today Taliesin West serves as an architectural school for Wright enthusiasts. Tours are available at different times in summer–fall and winter–spring; ranging from 1 to 3 hours, they highlight different aspects of the property and Wright's work.

HEARD MUSEUM NORTH SCOTTSDALE
480-488-9817.
www.heard.org.
34505 N. Scottsdale Rd., Scottsdale.

The North Scottsdale branch of the original Heard Museum in central Phoenix has featured such artists as Allan Houser—a renowned Native American painter and sculptor.

SCOTTSDALE HISTORICAL SOCIETY
480-945-4499.
www.scottsdalemuseum.com.
7333 Scottsdale Mall, Scottsdale.
Open: Wed.–Sun.; Sep., 10 AM–2 PM; Oct.–Apr., 10 AM–5 PM; May, 10 AM–2 PM.

Get a taste of Scottsdale's history, including information about its founder Winfield Scott, art created by some of its earliest artists, and bits and pieces of Scottsdale's younger days. The gift shop has a collection of unique Arizona children's books for sale.

SCOTTSDALE MUSEUM OF CONTEMPORARY ART
480-874-4666.
www.smoca.org.
7380 E. 2nd St., Scottsdale.
Open: Tue.–Sat. 10 AM–5 PM, Thu. 10 AM–9 PM, Sun. noon–5 PM. There are shorter summer hours June–Sep.: Wed. noon–5 PM, Thu. 10 AM–8 PM, Fri.–Sat. 10 AM–5 PM, Sun. noon–5 PM; closed Mon.–Tue.
Admission: $7 adults, $5 students; free to museum members and children 15 and under.

Scottsdale Museum of Contemporary Art (SMoCA) was founded in 1999 as the city's only museum devoted to contemporary art, architecture, and design. The museum, originally a movie theater, was designed by award-winning architect Will Bruder; it features five galleries and a combination of permanent and changing exhibits and works. SMoCA offers the community and visitors educational programs and special events, lectures, docent-led tours, workshops, and classes.

SCOTTSDALE GALLERY ASSOCIATION
480-990-3939.
www.scottsdalegalleries.com.
P.O. Box 2810, Scottsdale 85250.

Created to promote the many fine-art galleries in Scottsdale, this association offers a comprehensive schedule of member galleries' schedules and individual events. The weekly Scottsdale ArtWalk (see above) is the signature event.

Nightlife

If there is a place to see and be seen in the Valley, Scottsdale is probably that place. You will find stretch Hummers pulling up to some of these night spots; Hollywood and sports celebrities are known to party here. In Old Town top spots like **e4** (480-970-3325; 4282 N. Drinkwater Blvd., Scottsdale)—an award-winning venue—and **Myst and the Ballroom**

(480-429-6000; 7340 E. Shoeman Lane, Scottsdale) let you rub elbows with celebrities as you sip cocktails.

In the North Scottsdale/Phoenix area, locals like to frequent **Barcelona North Scottsdale** (480-603-0370; 15440 Greenway-Hayden Loop, Scottsdale), a restaurant with live music and a vibrant night scene. **Desert Ridge Marketplace** (480-513-7586; www.shop desertridge.com; 21001 N. Tatum Blvd., Phoenix) hosts live, local musicians in its two free outdoor venues—District Stage and AMC Fountain—on Fri.–Sat. beginning at 7 PM.

AXIS/RADIUS
480-970-1112.
www.axis-radius.com.
7340 E. Indian Plaza, Scottsdale.
Open: Thu.–Sat. 9 PM–2 PM.

Joined by a glass catwalk, Axis/Radius brings you two clubs for the price of one. Dance to the high-energy beat of Radius or relax to a more mellow mix of '70s, '80s, and '90s music at Axis. Both inspire a see-and-be-seen crowd including celebrity-status VIPs. While jeans are allowed, anything less might get you a head shake at the door. There's a cover charge of $10; free to ladies on Thu.

BLUE WASABI—DC RANCH
480-538-5161.
www.azeats.com/bluewasabi.
20715 N. Pima Rd., Scottsdale (Market St. at DC Ranch).
Open: Daily 5 PM–midnight.
Other Locations: Hilton Village, 6137 N. Scottsdale Rd., Scottsdale (480-315-9800).

Blue Wasabi is an energetic, stylish bar that merges modern sushi and fabulous cocktails.

COMEDY SPOT, THE
480-945-4422.
www.thecomedyspot.net.
7117 E. 3rd St.
Open: Showtimes Fri.–Sat. 8 and 10 PM, Sun. 8 PM.

The Comedy Spot in Scottsdale is a small and intimate comedy shop where you'll see your ticket taker opening on stage. You'll find locally and nationally known comics and have a hilariously good time. Want to brave the stage yourself? Try out for open-mike night on Sunday or sign up for their comedy classes on Sunday afternoons. Reservations are recommended; call and leave your name, number, and the number of tickets you'll need, and you'll be set.

CROWN ROOM
480-423-0117.
7419 E. Indian Plaza.
Open: 8 PM–2 AM; closed Mon.

If quiet and relaxing is what you have in mind for your night out, you might want to head over to the Crown Room for a martini and a little Frank Sinatra music filtering through the speakers.

FURIO
480-945-6600.
www.furio.tv.
7210 E. 2nd St.
Open: Mon.–Thu. 5–10 PM, Fri.–Sat. 5–11 PM (late-night menu 11 PM–1 AM), Sun. 6–10 PM; happy hour Mon.–Fri. 4–7 PM.

This chic restaurant and lounge serves Italian cuisine and unique specialty drinks you'll find only here. Monday nights, ladies love the martini and a manicure for $10.

SUEDE EURO-ASIAN RESTAURANT & LOUNGE
480-970-6969.
www.suedeaz.com.
7333 E. Indian Plaza.
Open: Wed.–Sat. 7 PM–2 AM, Sun. 9 PM–2 AM.

Located just across the street from Axis/Radius is its sexy sister Suede. This sophisticated lounge and restaurant has a sleigh bed, a flaming fountain, and a selective admissions policy. Late-night menu available; reservations are a must.

SUGAR DADDY'S BLUES
480-970-6556.
www.sugardaddysaz.com.
3102 N. Scottsdale Rd., Scottsdale.
Open: 11 AM–2 AM.

Enjoy acoustic and amplified live music every night of the week at this Scottsdale favorite. On the patio 5–8 PM you'll find acoustical artists like local guitarist Bob Dutcher. After 9:30 music moves inside to the dance floor and rocks the house until 2 AM. They serve lunch and dinner, and their menu is available 11 AM–2 AM; Sunday brunch 10 AM–4 PM.

Stage

SCOTTSDALE CENTER FOR THE ARTS
480-994-ARTS; TDD 480-874-4694.

The Scottsdale Center for the Arts features a wide variety of cultural and arts programs, including musical performances by the likes of Joan Baez, Grammy Award winner and jazz performer Sonny Rollins, and the Glenn Miller Orchestra. You might also enjoy dance performances by groups like Urban Tap and Les Grands Ballets Canadiens de Montreal; stage productions such as the Valley's longest-running play, *Late Nite Catechism*, or *Fired! Tales of Jobs Gone Bad*; comedic performances by commentator-author David Sedaris and the political satire group Capitol Steps; and global performances by performers like the South American instrumental and vocal group Inti-Illimani.

Event times, prices, and locations vary. Events take place in Old Town Scottsdale at the Scottsdale Center for the Performing Arts Virginia G. Piper Theater and Stage 2, located at 7380 E. 2nd St.; Theater 4301, at the Galleria Corporate Center, on the corner of Drinkwater Blvd. and 5th Ave. one block east of Scottsdale Rd.; and the Amphitheater at 75th and Main Sts.

SCOTTSDALE DESERT STAGES THEATRE

480-483-1664.
www.desertstages.com.
4720 N. Scottsdale Rd., Scottsdale.

Enjoy dinner and a play at this local theater in Scottsdale. Family-friendly productions such as *Oliver!* and *Footloose* share the stage with programs performed by the Children's Theatre (actors ages 3–19) like *Cinderella* and *Charlotte's Web*. Dinner is provided by one of several local restaurants; simply make your reservations through the box office. Prices start at about $65 per person and do not include gratuities.

SHOPPING

Shopping Centers and Districts

There are so many upscale shopping centers and strip malls in Scottsdale—not to mention the Old Town arts and shopping districts—that it will take you several return trips to catch them all. And each one offers its own shopping and dining experience.

Scottsdale Pavilions (480-991-6007; www.scottsdalepavilions.com; 8969 E. Indian Bend Rd., Scottsdale). The Pavilions offers a wide variety of chains including Target, Toys R Us, Ross Dress for Less, Best Buy, and Bookstar/Barnes and Noble. Shops are located on both the north and south sides of Indian Bend Rd., just off the 101 in Scottsdale.

Kierland Commons (480-348-1577; www.westcor.com; 15044 N. Scottsdale Rd., Scottsdale). Kierland Commons is a unique, upscale main-street-style experience that blends shopping, dining, and entertainment into a relaxing full day of entertainment.

The Borgata (480-994-8048; www.westcor.com; 6166 N. Scottsdale Rd., Scottsdale). An upscale experience of local and national specialty shops and restaurants.

Promenade Shopping Center (480-385-2820; www.pedersonic.com; 16427 N. Scottsdale Rd., Scottsdale). The Promenade, located at one of Scottsdale's most prominent intersections, offers a variety of shops and restaurants.

Scottsdale Fashion Square (480-994-8048; www.westcor.com; 7014 E. Camelback Rd., Scottsdale). One of the most popular shopping experiences in Scottsdale, Fashion Square features novelty shops and upscale national brands like Crate and Barrel.

The Shops at Gainey Village (www.theshopsgaineyvillage.com; 8787 N. Scottsdale Rd., Scottsdale). Upscale boutiques and restaurants.

Scottsdale Waterfront (480-247-8071; www.scottsdalewaterfront.com; 7135 E. Camelback Rd., Scottsdale). This 1.1-million-square-foot project in downtown Scottsdale includes retail, office, and high-rise residential buildings.

el Pedregal Shops & Dining at The Boulders Resort and Golden Door Spa (480-488-1072; www.elpedregal.com; 34505 N. Scottsdale Rd., Scottsdale). This bi-level outdoor courtyard and its shops embody Scottsdale sophistication. Located in the shadows of the boulders, el Pedregal features the northern site of the Heard Museum, a full-service salon, boutiques, and fine and casual dining.

OLD TOWN SCOTTSDALE

Scottsdale Rd. between Indian School and Camelback Rds.

Experience the flavor of the Old West where Scottsdale began more than 100 years ago.

Scottsdale's Fashion Square.

What locals and tourists alike think of as Old Town is actually made up of several distinct districts. The Fifth Avenue Shops and Boutiques offer choices from salons and art galleries to nightlife and dining. The Scottsdale Arts District is home of the Thursday-night Art Walk; this district features a mix of art from traditional to contemporary, along with craft and jewelry venues; taken together it represents one of the largest concentrations of galleries in the United States. The Entertainment District is just that, a combination of nightclubs and restaurants. The Brown and Stetson Businesses comprise a number of established businesses, hotels, restaurants, and shops. The Old Town District embodies the Old West spirit of Scottsdale with historic buildings, western-wear shops and galleries, and jewelry, craft, and bookstores highlighting the Southwest. The Civic Center Mall features most prominently the library, Scottsdale Center for the Arts, and the Giants' spring training compound. Combined, the area offers 300-plus shops and 90 restaurants.

Here's just a sampling of the shops on offer in downtown Scottsdale:

American Leather Company of Arizona, Inc. (480-421-2166; www.americanleatheraz .com; 7236 E. 1st Ave.). Custom handmade boots, belts, and leather accessories.

American Sky Hats (480-990-9058; 4260 N. Scottsdale Rd.). A complete selection of hats, boots, gifts, and jewelry.

Atkinson's Indian Trading Post (480-949-9750; 3957 N. Brown Ave.). Hand-painted Southwest-design pottery, statues, and accent pieces.

Barbwire Western Couture (480-443-9473; 15425 N. Scottsdale Rd., Suite 230).

Chief Dodge Indian Jewelry & Fine Arts (480-970-1133; www.chiefdodge.com; 1332 N. Scottsdale Rd.). Direct from Native American jewelry artists.

Conservatory, The (480-946-1300; 4167 N. Marshall Way). The Conservatory is located in the heart of Old Scottsdale's arts district.

Cornelis Hollander (480-423-5000; www.cornelishollander.com; 4151 N. Marshall Way). Cornelis Hollander is one of the most awarded jewelry designers in the nation; check out his unique creations here.

Estilo Boutique (480-664-0365; www.estiloboutique.com; 7135 E. Camelback Rd., #185). Original designers and the latest Hollywood trends in clothing, purses, shoes, accessories, and jewelry.

FeriArte (602-309-0558; 7101 E. Stetson Dr.). FeriArte specializes in antique Spanish ironwork from the late 1400s to the early 1900s, including crosses, swords, candleholders, andirons, and kitchen implements.

Jewelry by Gauthier (480-941-1707; www.jewelrybygauthier.com; 4211 N. Marshall Way). Elegant handcrafted jewelry.

The Jewish Collection (480-368-0001; www.thejewishcollection.com; 10701 N. Scottsdale Rd., Suite 105). This store specializes in unique Southwest Judaica.

Kactus Jock (480-946-7566; www.kactusjock.com; 7121 E. 5th Ave.). This unique shop in downtown Scottsdale offers a variety of gifts and active wear, including golf wear.

Miranda Jewelry (480-425-1200; www.mirandajewelry.com; 7231 E. 1st Ave.). Third-generation jeweler Alex Miranda infuses his work with elegance and simplicity.

Natural Fashions (480-941-6908; www.naturalfashions.com; 7121 E. 5th Ave., Studios 3 and 4). A unique ladies' boutique.

Open Range Gallery (480-946-0044;7077 E. Main St.). Open Range Gallery features a wide variety of hand-tied and -woven rugs, both Oriental and southwestern-style.

Saba's Western Store (480-949-7404; www.sabaswesternwear.com; 7254 Main St.). Saba's has been serving Arizona for more than 75 years and features a large collection of western wear for the whole family; styles range from exotic to practical. Also in Chandler.

Bookstores

Many of the area's local bookstores offer both used and new books and feature best-selling author events and book signings.

Barnes and Noble (www.bn.com) and **Borders Bookstores** (www.borders.com) locations are scattered throughout the Valley; several offer workshops and author events.

Poisoned Pen, A Mystery Bookstore (480-947-2974 or 888-560-9919; fax 480-945-1023; www.poisonedpen.com; 4014 N. Goldwater Blvd., Suite 101, Scottsdale). Mystery book lovers cannot spend too much time at the Poisoned Pen. Check the web site for a schedule of author events and book signings. The Poisoned Pen has featured such mystery greats as Dennis Lehane, Robert B. Parker, and Edna Buchanan. These events fill up quickly, so early arrival provides a better chance at a seat; book signings typically follow. Events tend to be conversational with time for questions. It's an excellent opportunity to learn about the writer behind your favorite mystery characters.

Specialty Stores

Edible Arrangements (480-840-0300; www.ediblearrangements.com; 4320 N. Miller Rd., Suite 102, Scottsdale). A unique spin-off of the traditional bouquet of flowers: Edible Arrangements designs come in fresh fruit.

Little Blue Choo Choo (480-994-5888; www.littlebluechoochoo.com; 7120 E. Indian School Rd., Scottsdale). This toy store in downtown Scottsdale features Thomas the Train, educational toys, and books for infants through preteens.

Sewell's Indian Arts (480-945-0962; www.buyindianarts.com; 7087 E. 5th Ave., Scottsdale). Since 1932 Sewell's has offered handcrafted Native American jewelry, and specializes in Hopi kachina dolls, Pueblo pottery, and storytellers.

Scottsdale Museum of Contemporary Art. The museum store at SMoCA (see Museums, above) features classic design objects and furnishings, contemporary jewelry, art and architecture books, and imaginative gifts for all occasions. Open during regular museum hours.

Tourneau (480-429-2304; www.tourneau.com; 7014 E. Camelback Rd., #1055, Fashion Square). The world's largest watch store, featuring 8,000 styles and more than 100 renowned brands.

SPECTATOR SPORTS

Cactus League Spring Training

SAN FRANCISCO GIANTS
480-990-7972 or 800-225-2277.
www.sfgiants.com.
Scottsdale Stadium, 7408 E. Osborn, Scottsdale.

Located in Old Town Scottsdale, Scottsdale Stadium is home to the San Francisco Giants. Accessible from both Scottsdale and Indian School Rds., the stadium is located on the northeast corner of Drinkwater Blvd. and Osborn across the street from Scottsdale Health-care—Osborn. From the highway, take the 101 north or south to Indian School Rd. Turn west onto Indian School, continue to Drinkwater Blvd., and turn right or head north until you see the stadium.

Strolling ASU's Main Campus in Tempe.

5

TEMPE AND THE EAST VALLEY

Mesa, Gilbert, Chandler, Apache Junction, and Queen Creek

The East Valley is a thriving mecca for both retirees and young families just starting out. Here you'll find that each of the cities carries a distinct personality and individual appeal. From the smart little shops in downtown Chandler to the wild, eclectic nightlife of Tempe's Mill Avenue, from the quiet old-town feel of Gilbert's main drag to spring training for the Cubs in Arizona's fourth-largest city, Mesa, visitors flock to the fun in the sun that each of these towns offers—relaxing resorts, great golf, attractive restaurants, and beautiful weather.

Tempe (pronounced *tem-PEE*) was established about 1870 when Charles Trumbull Hayden settled on the banks of the Salt River and quickly built a flour mill, store, and what came to be called Hayden's Ferry to help newly settled residents traverse the waters. In 1879 Lord Darrell Duppa—the same man to suggest *Phoenix* as the name for another Valley city— stated that the area reminded him of the Vale of Tempe in Greece, and so the name was changed. In 1885 the Arizona legislature chose Tempe as the site of the Territorial Normal School. For the most part it remained a small agriculturally based community until after World War II; then the farms began to disappear, replaced by homes, businesses, and the ever-expanding Normal School, which became Arizona State University in 1958. Today Tempe is home to 165,000 people. As the geographic center of the Valley of the Sun and bordered on all sides by the Valley's extensive highway system, it is offers its residents prime real estate and easy accessibility to the rest of the Greater Phoenix.

LODGING

The Priest Drive–Broadway Road area in Tempe is home to several hotels, extended stays, and resorts. It's close to I-10, US 60, Loop 202, and the Sky Harbor International Airport, providing easy access to Arizona State University's Main Campus, downtown and uptown Phoenix, Chase Field, US Airways Center, and the Phoenix Convention Center, as well as Scottsdale and both the east and west parts of the Valley. The hotels here range from the Holiday Inn Express just south of Baseline on Priest to the Buttes, A Marriott Resort, located just off Broadway in Tempe. Also located in this area are extended stays, like

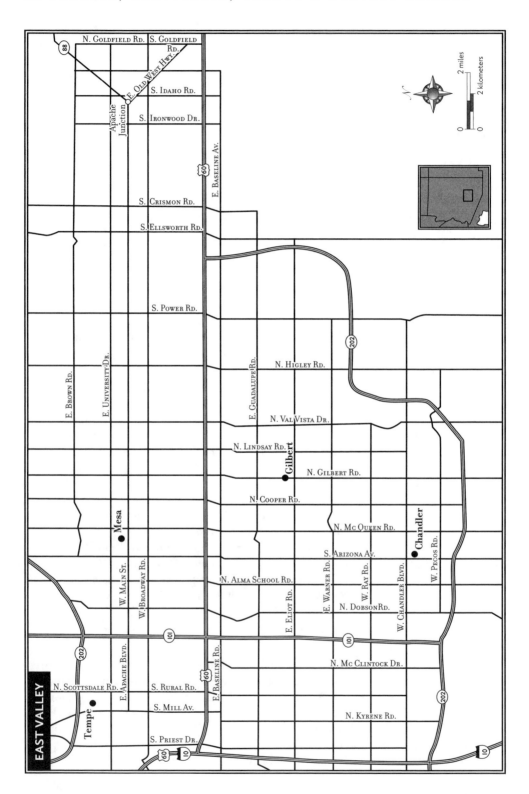

Springhill Suites Tempe. More lodgings exist in the downtown and around ASU's Main Campus.

Credit Cards

The following abbreviations are used for credit card information:
AE: American Express
CB: Carte Blanche
D: Discover Card
DC: Diner's Club
MC: MasterCard
V: Visa

BEST WESTERN TEMPE BY THE MALL

480-820-7500 or 800-822-4334.
www.bestwesterntempe.com.
5300 S. Priest Dr., Tempe 85283.
Prices: $109–129.
Credit Cards: AE, CB, D, DC, MC, V.
Handicapped Access: 2 rooms.
Pets: Yes, with $25-per-night fee.

This Best Western features 158 rooms, a full continental breakfast, and high-speed Internet access; it's located close to Arizona Mills Mall, and only 5 miles from Arizona State University and Sun Devil Stadium.

THE BUTTES, A MARRIOTT RESORT

602-225-9000 or 888-867-7492.
www.marriott.com.
2000 Westcourt Way, Tempe 85282.
Prices: $199–430.
Credit Cards: AE, CB, D, DC, MC, V.
Handicapped Access: 8 rooms.
Pets: No.

The Buttes, built into Tempe Twin Butte, offers 350-plus rooms, with two swimming pools, a spa, a fitness facility, three dining options, and room service. With beautiful views and a lush setting, it's conveniently located close to Arizona State University.

COMFORT INN & SUITES AT ASU

480-966-7202.
www.choicehotels.com.

1031 E. Apache Blvd., Tempe 85281.
Prices: $170–200.
Credit Cards: AE, CB, D, DC, MC, V.
Handicapped Access: Yes.
Pets: No.

Conveniently located within walking distance of Arizona State University, Comfort Inn & Suites at ASU offers a free continental breakfast and high-speed Internet access. The site features a pool, whirlpool, sauna, and exercise room. Close proximity to ASU Karsten, Mill Avenue shopping and dining, and Tempe Town Lake.

COURTYARD TEMPE DOWNTOWN

480-966-2800.
www.marriott.com.
601 S. Ash Ave., Tempe 85281.
Prices: $289–329.
Credit Cards: AE, CB, D, DC, MC, V.
Handicapped Access: Yes.
Pets: No.

This hotel is conveniently located in downtown Tempe and just west of the shops, dining, and entertainment on Mill Avenue; close by you will find Tempe Town Lake and ASU Karsten Golf Course. The 155 rooms offer high-speed Internet access and cable television. There is a pool and café on site.

ECONO LODGE
AT AZ STATE UNIVERSITY

480-966-5832.
www.choicehotels.com.
2101 E. Apache Blvd., Tempe.
Prices: $90–100.
Credit Cards: AE, CB, D, DC, MC, V.
Handicapped Access: Yes.
Pets: $15 per night, per pet of 20 pounds or less.

The Econo Lodge is located 1.5 miles from Casino Arizona and 2 miles from Mill Avenue and ASU's Main Campus; there are three separate malls—Arizona Mills, Fiesta Mall, and Chandler Fashion Center—within close proximity. Amenities include an outdoor pool and free continental breakfast.

EMBASSY SUITES PHOENIX/TEMPE
480-897-7444.
www.embassysuites.com.
4400 S. Rural Rd., Tempe 85282.
Prices: $99–229.
Credit Cards: AE, CB, D, DC, MC, V.
Handicapped Access: 4 rooms.
Pets: $15 per night, per pet of 20 pounds or less.

Located just off US 60 in Tempe, Embassy Suites offers 224 two-room suites, wireless Internet access propertywide, and a courtyard and pool. There is a Garcia's Mexican restaurant on site. This hotel is only a few miles from ASU's Main Campus, Tempe Town Lake, and Mill Avenue shopping, dining, and entertainment.

FIESTA INN RESORT
480-967-1441 or 800-528-6481.
www.fiestainnresort.com.
2100 S. Priest Dr., Tempe 85282.
Prices: $99–209.
Credit Cards: AE, D, DC, MC, V.
Handicapped Access: 2 rooms.
Pets: No.

Located on Tempe's west side, close to I-10, this resort sits on 10 lushly landscaped acres with a heated pool, Jacuzzi, and poolside beverage service. The recently renovated 270-room property features complimentary high-speed Internet access, an on-site restaurant and lounge with a happy hour, and complimentary hors d'oeuvres.

INNSUITES HOTEL TEMPE/PHOENIX AIRPORT
480-897-7900 or 800-841-4242.
www.innsuites.com.
1651 W. Baseline Rd., Tempe 85283.
Prices: $65–149.
Credit Cards: AE, D, DC, MC, V.

Handicapped Access: 1 room.
Pets: With $25 deposit.

This hotel is located across the street from Arizona Mills and adjacent to I-10, providing easy access to shopping and dining as well as Arizona State University and Phoenix South Mountain Preserve.

TEMPE MISSION PALMS HOTEL & CONFERENCE CENTER
480-894-1400 or 800-547-8705.
60 E. 5th St., Tempe 85281.
www.missionpalms.com.
Prices: $179–309.
Credit Cards: AE, CB, D, DC, MC, V.
Handicapped Access: 10 rooms.
Pets: Small dogs welcome.

This beautiful hotel is located at the north end of Mill Avenue, providing immediate access to more than 170 restaurants, shops, and entertainment options. A hike up "A" Mountain can start right out the front doors, and Tempe Town Lake and Tempe Beach Park are a short walk away. The hotel features a lush courtyard setting, fitness center, rooftop outdoor heated swimming pool, tennis court, and basketball hoop. Dine at Mission Grille or have a drink at Harry's Place. The 300-plus rooms offer high-speed Internet access.

TWIN PALMS HOTEL
800-367-0835.
www.twinpalmshotel.com.
225 Apache Blvd., Tempe 85281.
Prices: Call.
Credit Cards: Call.
Handicapped Access: Call.
Pets: $200 deposit.

This seven-story high-rise hotel is located adjacent to Arizona State University's Main Campus. The 139 rooms feature sliding glass doors, satellite TV, and 24-hour room service. An International House of Pancakes is located on the property. Complimentary access to ASU's Recreation Complex and its three Olympic-sized pools, fitness equipment, and aerobics classes.

TEMPE/AIRPORT LODGING

COMFORT SUITES AIRPORT

480-446-9500.
1625 S. 52nd St., Tempe 85281.
Prices: $125–140.
Credit Cards: AE, CB, D, DC, MC, V.
Handicapped Access: Yes.
Pets: No.

You will find complimentary airport shuttle service, deluxe continental breakfast, and wireless Internet access. The hotel features an outdoor pool and whirlpool, as well as exercise room.

QUALITY INN AIRPORT

480-967-3000.
www.choicehotels.com.
1550 S. 52nd St., Tempe 85281.
Prices: $135–155.
Credit Cards: AE, CB, D, DC, MC, V.
Handicapped Access: Yes.
Pets: $25 per stay.

This hotel is located on the west side of Tempe closer to I-10 and Phoenix Sky Harbor International Airport, and features complimentary Internet access, deluxe continental breakfast with waffles, and 24-hour airport shuttle.

APACHE JUNCTION

GOLD CANYON GOLF RESORT

480-671-5546 or 800-624-6445.
www.gcgr.com.
6100 S. Kings Ranch Rd., Gold Canyon 85218.
Prices: $99–185.
Credit Cards: AE, DI, MC, V.
Handicapped Access: Call for details.
Pets: Yes, with a $75 nonrefundable deposit per pet.

Gold Canyon Golf Resort at the foot of the Superstition Mountains offers guests

casitas, championship golf, a fitness center, and a full-service spa. There are three on-site dining options and Internet access. Golf packages available.

MESA

The city of Mesa is thriving and dynamic. Visitors can choose from more than 60 hotels, motels, and resorts varying in amenities from first-class, full-service properties to cozy inns.

ARIZONA GOLF RESORT AND CONFERENCE CENTER

480-832-3202 or 800-528-8282.
www.azgolfresort.com.
425 S. Power Rd., Mesa 85206.
Prices: $99–209.
Credit Cards: AE, D, MC, V.
Handicapped Access: 6 rooms, 2 with roll-in showers.
Pets: Yes.

This 187-room resort and conference center offers on-site golf, fitness center, swimming pool, three restaurants, and seasonal entertainment in its lounge. Some of the suites have full kitchen. The 150-acre property is 25 miles from Sky Harbor International Airport, and located at Superstition Springs, with a variety of shopping options.

BEST WESTERN DOBSON RANCH INN & RESORT

480-831-7000 or 800-528-1356.
www.dobsonranchinn.com.
1666 S. Dobson Rd., Mesa 85202.
Prices: $65–180.
Credit Cards: D, MC, V.
Handicapped Access: Yes.
Pets: Yes.

Centrally located in Mesa, Best Western Dobson Ranch Inn and Resort features 200-plus rooms on 10 acres in the west part of Mesa; the resort offers a complimentary American breakfast buffet, on-site pool and exercise facility, and free Internet access.

BEST WESTERN MEZONA INN

480-834-9233; 800-528-8299.
www.mezonainn.com.
250 W. Main St., Mesa 85201.
Prices: $119–134.
Credit Cards: AE, CB, DC, C, MC, V.
Handicapped Access: Call.
Pets: Yes, under 50 pounds.

The moderately priced Mezona Inn features 132 rooms and a pool. Close to downtown Mesa, antiques shops, dining, and golf are close by.

BEST WESTERN SUPERSTITION SPRINGS INN & SUITES

480-641-1164.
www.bestwesternarizona.com.
1342 S. Power Rd., Mesa 85206.
Prices: $119–134.
Credit Cards: AE, CB, DC, C, MC, V.
Handicapped Access: 4 rooms.
Pets: Yes, with $10-per-day fee.

Located next to Superstition Springs Mall, this modest hotel provides easy access to 175 shops and restaurants, 10 different golf courses, and hiking in the nearby Superstition Mountains. Find a pool, fitness center, Internet access, and free breakfast.

COURTYARD BY MARRIOTT PHOENIX MESA

480-461-3000.
www.marriott.com.
1221 S. Westwood, Mesa 85210.
Prices: $239–259.
Credit Cards: AE, CB, D, DC, MC, V.
Handicapped Access: Yes.
Pets: No.

This Courtyard features 137 rooms and 12 suites, complimentary high-speed Internet access, and a balcony in most rooms. There is a free shuttle service within a 5-mile radius Mon.–Fri. 7 AM–8 PM. The hotel is conveniently located close to Fiesta Mall; various restaurants and shops lie in and around the mall, including a recently opened branch of Oregano's Pizza on Dobson and just north of Southern Ave.

DAYS INN—EAST MESA

480-981-8111.
www.daysinn.com.
5531 E. Main St., Mesa 85205.
Prices: $77–115.
Credit Cards: AE, D, DC, MC, V.
Handicapped Access: Yes.
Pets: Yes; fees apply.

This hotel offers free breakfast, high-speed Internet access, and an on-site pool. All rooms have a microwave and refrigerator.

HILTON PHOENIX EAST/MESA

480-833-5555 or 800-544-5866.
www.hiltonphoenixeast.com.
1011 W. Holmes Ave., Mesa 85210.
Prices: $155–280.
Credit Cards: AE, CB, D, DC, MC, V.
Handicapped Access: 6 newly renovated rooms.
Pets: No.

This recently renovated Hilton features 260 guest rooms and suites; an on-site outdoor heated pool and spa, fitness center, and restaurant and bar round out the amenities. It is conveniently located just off US 60 and less than 20 minutes from the airport. Fiesta Mall and surrounding areas offer plenty of shopping and dining options.

HOLIDAY INN HOTEL AND SUITES

480-964-7000.
www.holidayinn.com.
1600 S. Country Club Dr., Mesa 85210.
Prices: $85–159.
Credit Cards: AE, CB, D, DC, MC, V.
Handicapped Access: 10 rooms, 3 with roll-in showers.
Pets: Yes, $20 per pet.

This 246-room hotel offers 83 suites, in-room microwave and refrigerator, high-

Tempe Town Lake.

speed Internet access, and a charming courtyard with a heated pool, spa, and waterfall. Just off US 60, the hotel is afford-able and conveniently located.

LA QUINTA INN & SUITES PHOENIX MESA EAST

480-654-1970 or 800-531-5900.
www.lq.com.
6530 E. Superstition Springs Blvd., Mesa 85206.
Prices: $169–199.
Credit Cards: AE, CB, D, DC, MC, V.
Handicapped Access: Yes.
Pets: Yes.

Located on the east side of Mesa, closer to the Superstition Mountains, this hotel offers an outdoor pool, fitness center, free continental breakfast, and free parking. There are more than 100 rooms and 6 suites with in-room amenities such as cof-feemaker and cable. Internet access is available in some rooms.

LA QUINTA INN & SUITES PHOENIX MESA WEST

480-844-8747 or 800-531-5900.
www.lq.com.
902 W. Grove Ave., Mesa 85210.
Prices: $129–159.
Credit Cards: AE, CB, D, DC, MC, V.
Handicapped Access: Yes.
Pets: Yes.

Located on the west side of Mesa, closer to the Tempe border, this hotel is within walk-ing distance of Fiesta Lakes Golf Course, and minutes away from Fiesta Mall. Seven floors and 117 rooms, the hotel features an outdoor heated pool and spa, complimen-tary continental breakfast, and free Internet access. A local shuttle is available.

PHOENIX MARRIOTT MESA

480-898-8300.
www.marriott.com.
200 N. Centennial Way, Mesa.

Prices: $279–299.
Credit Cards: AE, CB, D, DC, MC, V.
Handicapped Access: 4 rooms.
Pets: No.

Adjacent to the Mesa Convention Center and within walking distance of the Mesa Public Library, the recently renovated Phoenix Marriott Mesa offers 275 rooms, a heated pool, a spa, and a fitness center. Downtown Mesa (with several museums, including the fabulous Mesa Art Center) and Hohokam Stadium (where the Cubs play their spring training games) are only minutes away.

RESIDENCE INN BY MARRIOTT
480-610-0100 or 800-331-3131.
www.marriott.com.
941 W. Grove Ave., Mesa 85210.
Prices: $189–229.
Credit Cards: AE, CB, D, DC, MC, V.
Handicapped Access: Yes.
Pets: Yes, with nonrefundable sanitation fee of $100; call for details.

The Residence Inn in Mesa is a 117-suite hotel offering separate living and sleeping areas, fully equipped kitchens, complimentary breakfast buffet, and free Internet access.

TRAVELODGE SUITES
480-832-5961 or 800-515-2785.
www.travelodge.com.
4244 E. Main St., Mesa 85205.
Prices: $129–139.
Credit Cards: AE, D, DC, MC, V.
Handicapped Access: Yes.
Pets: Yes, with nonrefundable sanitation fee of $100; call for details.

This modest motel offers an on-site pool, wireless high-speed Internet access, and large guest rooms and mini suites.

WINDEMERE HOTEL AND CONFERENCE CENTER
480-985-3600 or 800-888-3561.

www.resortmesa.com.
5750 E. Main St., Mesa 85205.
Prices: $59–109.
Credit Cards: AE, DC, MC, V.
Handicapped Access: 2 rooms.
Pets: Yes.

Located at Superstition Springs and only 30 minutes from Sky Harbor International Airport, the Windemere features 114 guest rooms and suites, a heated swimming pool, and a fitness center. Complimentary gourmet breakfast buffet daily, plus two complimentary evening cocktails at the on-site sports lounge.

CHANDLER
COMFORT INN
480-705-8882 or 800-4-CHOICE.
www.comfortinn.com.
255 N. Kyrene Rd., Chandler 85226.
Prices: $99–129.
Credit Cards: AE, CB, D, DC, MC, V.
Handicapped Access: Yes.
Pets: Yes, $10 per night.

Featuring 70 rooms, a heated pool, and a free, full hot breakfast, this Comfort Inn is within a mile of Chandler Fashion Center, restaurants, and shopping.

CROWNE PLAZA SAN MARCOS RESORT AND CONFERENCE CENTER
480-812-0900 or 800-528-8071.
www.sanmarcosresort.com.
1 San Marcos Place, Chandler 85225.
Prices: $229–289.
Credit Cards: AE, CB, D, DC, MC, V.
Handicapped Access: 3 rooms; however, elevator access to the upper floors of the main building is tucked out of the way.
Pets: Yes, up to 50 pounds; $50 deposit.

The Valley's first resort, the Crowne Plaza San Marcos boasts 295 rooms, an 18-hole golf course, tennis courts, two heated pools, two Jacuzzis, a fitness center, two restaurants, and a lounge. This resort has recently been renovated and is situated in the heart

The lobby of the Crowne Plaza San Marcos Resort. Photo provided courtesy of San Marcos

of Chandler's downtown shopping and dining district. Walk out the front doors to a number of entertaining local restaurants, from 98 South Wine Bar and Restaurant to Cupid's Diner.

FAIRFIELD INN

480-940-0099.
7425 W. Chandler Blvd., Chandler 85226.
Prices: $209–219.
Credit Cards: AE, CB, D, DC, MC, V.
Handicapped Access: Yes.
Pets: No.

This hotel features 66 rooms, heated pool and Jacuzzi, extended continental breakfast, in-room coffeepot, hair dryer, and pay-per-view movies.

HAWTHORN SUITES

480-705-8881 or 800-527-1133.
www.hawthorn.com.
5858 W. Chandler Blvd., Chandler 85226.
Prices: $125–145.
Credit Cards: AE, CB, D, DC, MC, V.
Handicapped Access: Yes.
Pets: Yes; $125 nonrefundable fee at check-in.

Hawthorn Suites offers 100 one- and two-bedroom suites, a heated pool and spa, a fitness center, a daily hot breakfast buffet, and an on-site guest laundry. Each room features a fully equipped kitchen and bedroom with separate living space.

HOLIDAY INN AT OCOTILLO

480-203-2121 or 800-887-5096.

www.holiday-inn.com.
1200 W. Ocotillo Rd., Chandler 85248.
Prices: $126–259.
Credit Cards: AE, CB, D, DC, MC, V.
Handicapped Access: 9 rooms.
Pets: No.

This Holiday Inn features 106 rooms, including two-room Jacuzzi suites. Each has refrigerator, microwave, coffeemaker, hair dryer, iron and ironing board, and high-speed Internet. The site offers a pool and whirlpool, restaurant, lounge, on-site fitness center, and 24-hour business center.

RADISSON HOTEL PHOENIX/CHANDLER

480-961-4444 or 800-814-7000.
www.radisson.com.
7475 W. Chandler Blvd., Chandler 85226.
Prices: $79–119.
Credit Cards: AE, CB, D, DC, MC, V.
Handicapped Access: Yes.
Pets: Yes.

This recently renovated Radisson features 159 rooms, a heated pool and Jacuzzi, fitness room, full-service restaurant, lounge, and in-room high-speed Internet access.

SHERATON WILD HORSE PASS RESORT & SPA

602-225-0100 or 888-218-8989.
5594 W. Wild Horse Pass Blvd., Chandler 85226.
Prices: $89–540.
Credit Cards: AE, D, MC, V.
Handicapped Access: 23 rooms.
Pets: Small dogs accepted.

The Sheraton Wild Horse Pass & Spa is a Native American–owned luxury resort featuring 500 culturally themed rooms, 36 holes of Troon Golf, the Aji Spa, Koli, an on-site equestrian center, and three restaurants. Additional amenities include high-speed Internet access, private balcony or patio, and mountain, pool, river, or golf

course views. Rawhide Western Town is now located on site, as is the Bird Golf Academy; the Bob Bondurant School of High Performance Driving is a mile away. See more about the resort's award-winning spa, Aji, in chapter 9.

WINDMILL INN SUITES

480-812-9600 or 800-547-4747.
www.windmillinns.com/cha.htm.
3535 W. Chandler Blvd., Chandler 85226.
Prices: $166–184.
Credit Cards: AE, D, DC, MC, V.
Handicapped Access: Yes.
Pets: Yes; notify upon reservation.

Adjacent to Chandler Fashion Center, the Windmill Inn Suites provides guests with a free extended continental breakfast, a heated pool and whirlpool, and a fitness room. Each suite features a microwave, refrigerator, hair dryer, iron and full-sized ironing board, dataport, and voice mail. Access the free business center 24 hours a day.

RVs

The East Valley offers RV drivers a variety of options, including **Canyon Vistas RV Resort** (480-288-8844; 6601 E. US 60) in Gold Canyon; **Aztec RV Resort** (480-832-2700 or 800-848-6176; www.mesacvb.com; 4220 E. Main St.), **Carriage Manor RV Resort** (480-984-1111 or 800-637-5510; 7750 E. Broadway), and **Desert Vista RV Resort** (480-663-3383; 124 S. 54th St.) in Mesa; **Eagle View RV Resort** (480-836-5310; 9605 N. Fort McDowell Rd.) in Fort McDowell; **Gold Canyon RV & Golf Resort** (480-982-5800 or 866-787-2754; 7151 E. US 60) and **Weaver's Needle Travel Trailer Resort** (480-982-3683; 250 S. Tomahawk Rd.) in Apache Junction; and **Apache Palms RV Park** (480-966-7399; www.apachepalmsrvpark.com; 1836 E. Apache Blvd.) in Tempe.

DINING

Credit Cards

The following abbreviations are used for credit card information:

AE: American Express
CB: Carte Blanche
D: Discover Card
DC: Diner's Club
MC: MasterCard
V: Visa

56 EAST BAR & KITCHEN

480-705-5602.
www.56east.com.
7131 W. Ray Rd., Chandler.
Open: Lunch Mon.–Sat. 11:30 AM–2 PM; dinner Mon.–Thu. 5 PM–at least 9 PM, Fri.–Sat. 5 PM–at least 11 PM; closed Sun.
Prices: Moderate to expensive.
Cuisine: American.
Credit Cards: AE, D, MC, V.

This East Valley bar and restaurant—sibling to downtown Chandler's 98 South Wine Bar and Kitchen—includes some of the best elements of dining in the desert: an indoor–outdoor bar, fire pit on the patio, and live music. Weekday drink specials, happy hour 4:30–6:30 PM daily, ever-changing wine-by-the-glass offerings, and a satisfying menu. Reservations recommended.

98 SOUTH WINE BAR & KITCHEN

480-814-9800.
www.98South.com.
98 S. San Marcos Place, Chandler.
Open: Lunch and dinner Mon.–Thu. 11:30 AM–at least 10 PM, Fri.–Sat. 11:30 AM–at least 11 PM; closed Sun.
Prices: Moderate to expensive.
Cuisine: American.
Credit Cards: AE, D, MC, V.

Live music, delicious food, and a great selection of wines make this an excellent choice in downtown Chandler. Relax in the comfy lounge furniture beside the bar in back with an appetizer and a glass of wine, or enjoy dinner at one of the cozy tables up front. Happy hour 2–6:30 PM daily. Reservations recommended.

AJ'S

480-857-4422.
1 San Marcos Place, Crowne Plaza San Marcos Golf Resort, Chandler.
Open: Breakfast 6–11 AM, lunch 11 AM–2 PM, dinner 5–9 PM; Sunday brunch served.
Prices: Expensive.
Cuisine: American.
Credit Cards: AE, D, MC, V.

AJ's Café, located in the historic Crowne Plaza San Marcos Golf Resort in downtown Chandler, offers a casual dining experience. Seating is available inside and out. There's an excellent Sunday brunch and Saturday-night prime rib dinner buffet. Locals love the weekly lunch buffet that's entirely too inexpensive. Try the famous grilled banana bread—a definite treat.

BISTRO @ KOKOPELLI WINERY

480-792-6927.
www.kokopelliwinery.com.
35 W. Boston St., Chandler.
Open: Lunch and dinner Mon.–Wed. 11:30 AM–6 PM, Thu.–Sat. 11:30 AM–10 PM, Sun. 11 AM–5 PM.
Prices: Moderate.
Cuisine: European.
Credit Cards: AE, D, MC, V.

Wine and good food are an enjoyable combination at this quiet little winery, located on the south side of the downtown Chandler square.

BISON WITCHES

480-894-9104.
www.bisonwitches.com.
21 E. 6th St., #146, Tempe.
Open: Daily for lunch and dinner; kitchen 11 AM–10 PM, bar 11 AM–2 AM.

Pizza in the Desert

Pizza and *desert* may not be the first connection you'd make, but the Valley is a haven for transplants from New York City and Chicago—and they brought with them their love of pizza. The Valley has a number of well-known ('round these parts anyway) pizza parlors.

The Valley institutions include **Nello's** (480-897-2060; www.nellosscottsdale.com; 1806 E. Southern Ave., Tempe), where great salads complement their pizzas. **Organ Stop Pizza** (480-813-5700; www.organstoppizza.com; 1149 E. Southern Ave., Mesa) is home to one of the world's largest Wurlitzer theater organs. **Rosati's** (480-820-4444; www.rosatispizza.com; 1730 E. Warner Rd., Tempe) cooks up perhaps the best Chicago-style thin-crust pizza in town. And **Grimaldi's Coal Brick-Oven Pizzeria** (480-994-1100; www.patsygrimaldis.com; 4000 N. Scottsdale Rd.) is a Scottsdale favorite.

Each of these spots has its faithful followers—after all, each turns out first-class pizza. Still, they just don't seem to invite the explosion of excitement generated by the Valley's two top contenders—Pizzeria Bianco (a single shop) and Oregano's Pizza Bistro (which has expanded across the Valley and halfway to Mexico). The only thing these two restaurants have in common is that they both serve pizza. From there they diverge into two wildly different culinary experiences.

Pizzeria Bianco (602-258-8300; www.pizzeriabianco.com; 623 E. Adams St., Phoenix) is perhaps the most famous of chef Chris Bianco's triumvirate of eateries (Bar Bianco and a sandwich shop, Pane Bianco, round out the trio). It can be found at Heritage and Science Park in downtown Phoenix.

Prices: Inexpensive.
Cuisine: Deli.
Credit Cards: AE, D, MC, V.

Instead of a bar and grill, you'll find a bar and deli at this little neighborhood hangout featuring domestic, imported, and micro-brew beers as well as sandwiches, soups, and salads.

BYBLOS RESTAURANT
480-894-1945.
www.byblostempe.com.
3332 S. Mill Avenue, Tempe.
Open: Lunch 11 AM–2:30 PM, dinner 5–10 PM, Sunday 4–9:30 PM; closed Mon.
Prices: Inexpensive to moderate.
Cuisine: Middle Eastern and Mediterranean.
Credit Cards: Call.

Voted the number one Middle Eastern restaurant in town by both *Arizona Republic* and *Tempe Magazine*, this local favorite has been in the Tempe for 30 years serving authentic Mideast and Mediterranean fare in a warm and welcoming atmosphere. Staff are attentive and helpful as you choose a meal from their standard menu and selection of daily specials. And for dessert, try the tiramisu. Yum!

CAFE LALIBELA
480-829-1939.
www.cafelalibela.com.
849 W. University Dr., Tempe.
Open: Lunch and dinner Tue.–Thu. 11 AM–9 PM, Fri.–Sat. 11 AM–10 PM, Sun. noon–9 PM; closed Mon.
Prices: Inexpensive to moderate.
Cuisine: Ethiopian.
Credit Cards: AE, D, MC, V.

This little storefront café serves up Ethiopian fare. You won't find any forks here; instead, large platters of wat (a stew-like sauce made with vegetables or meat), Yekik Alicha (split peas with turmeric, herbs, and onion), and Tikil Gomen (a mixture of carrots, cabbage, and potatoes)

Just follow the line! On game nights you'll find impatient guests queued up outside this hip little garage-turned-restaurant (complete with old grease spots on the floor). Bianco, a Bronx native, serves his world-renowned pizza the only way . . . for New Yorkers . . . straight from the brick oven. Winner of the James Beard Best Chef: Southwest award, Bianco has made perfecting the pizza his lifework, and it has not gone unnoticed by locals, tourists, or the world of international foodies. These pies present such ingredients as pistachios and house-made mozzarella or salami, making pizza an art form.

While Pizzeria Bianco embodies the spirit of its chef, **Oregano's Pizza Bistro** (480-858-0501; www.oreganos.com; 523 W. University, Tempe) embodies the spirit of its "founder," Lawrence of Oregano. Though Lawrence never saw the pizzeria that bears his nickname, his essence has infused the restaurant with the ingredients that keep folks coming back again and again—Chicago-style pizzas, family, and fun. Be prepared for a wait—over an hour is not unheard of and, depending on day and time, often the norm. Still, with big-band music, drinks from the bar, and the occasional garlic bread treat making the rounds, this place makes waiting fun. And the pizza is delish! Known for deep-dish pizzas, Oregano's offers myriad toppings as well as gourmet thin-crust pizzas, traditional spaghetti (loved by many), and a stack of other choices, including sandwiches and salads so big you'll need to share with your neighbors the next table over. And despite the pizza, great frozen Bellinis (sparkling wine and peach puree), and appetizers, you need to save room for dessert—a *huge* chocolate or macadamia nut cookie topped with vanilla ice cream. It might be the best dessert in town!

arrive on injera, a crêpelike sourdough bread that you tear into pieces and use to scoop up your food. The food is flavorful and spicy, and the restaurant is welcoming and full of chatter. Vegetarians and meat lovers alike can find plenty of choices here.

CAFFE BOA
480-968-9112.
www.cafeboa.com.
398 S. Mill Ave., Tempe.
Open: Lunch and dinner Mon.–Wed. 11 AM–10 PM, Thu.–Sat. 11 AM–11 PM.
Prices: Moderate to expensive.
Cuisine: Italian.
Credit Cards: AE, D, MC, V.

Since opening their Italian restaurant in 1994, husband-and-wife team Jay and Christine Wisniewski have received numerous awards and accolades. Flavorful dishes, an extensive wine list including 50 wines-by-the-glass, and award-winning desserts make it a local favorite. Live jazz several nights a week.

CRACKERS & CO. CAFÉ
480-898-1717.
www.crackersandcompanycafe.com.
535 W. Iron Ave., Mesa.
Open: Daily for breakfast and lunch 7 AM–2:30 PM.
Prices: Inexpensive.
Cuisine: American.
Credit Cards: MC, V.
Other Locations: 1325 N. Greenfield Rd., Suite 101 (480-924-9977).

For more than 20 years, this local favorite has been serving burgers, sandwiches, and salads for lunch and a huge breakfast menu that will have you bouncing back and forth between choices. Their array of pastries is delicious; staff are friendly, too.

D'VINE WINE BAR & BISTRO
480-654-4171.
www.dvinewine101.com.
2837 N. Power Rd., Mesa.
Open: Daily for lunch and dinner; kitchen Mon.–Thu. 11 AM–10 PM, Fri.–Sat. 11

AM–10:30 PM, Sun. 4–10 PM; bar open till
everyone goes home.
Prices: Moderate.
Cuisine: New American.
Credit Cards: AE, D, MC, V.

One of the few restaurants of this caliber in
East Mesa. Guests can enjoy entrées of pan-
seared duck, pan-roasted salmon, or slow-
braised confit of rabbit leg. The extensive
wine list includes 40 by-the-glass choices.
Staff are helpful and delighted to recom-
mend new wines and help you expand your
palate. Wine tasting Tue. 5:30–7:30 PM.

EL ZOCALO MEXICAN GRILLE

480-722-0303.
28 S. San Marcos Place, Chandler.
Open: Mon.–Sat. for lunch and dinner.
Prices: Inexpensive to moderate.
Cuisine: Mexican.
Credit Cards: AE, MC, V.

Tasty Mexican meals and live Mexican
music make this a fun, spirited location on
weekends. Dine in the lush courtyard with
twinkle lights aglow from surrounding
trees; here the energetic music can sweep
you away. If you stay inside, you can still
catch the beat. Enjoy a cool margarita on the
rocks and partake of the Sonoran fare.

FARM HOUSE RESTAURANT

480-926-0676.
228 N. Gilbert Rd., Gilbert.
Open: Breakfast and lunch Mon.–Sat. 6
AM–2 PM, Sun. 8 AM–2 PM.
Prices: Inexpensive.
Cuisine: American.
Credit Cards: MC, V.

North of Elliot on Gilbert Rd., this restaurant serves up good old-fashioned breakfast
fare—eggs, bacon, biscuits and gravy.
There's usually a wait outside on weekends;
inside you'll find a hodgepodge of mis-
matched tables and chairs, and silverware,
too. But it doesn't detract from the meal,

especially the baked goods—try the cinnamon buns.

FOUR PEAKS BREWING COMPANY

480-303-9967.
www.fourpeaks.com.
1340 E. 8th St., Tempe.
Open: Lunch and dinner Mon.–Sat. 11 AM–2
AM, Sun. 10 AM for brunch; happy hour 3–7
PM and 10 PM–close.
Prices: Inexpensive.
Cuisine: American.
Credit Cards: AE, D, MC, V.

Winner of several national and international awards for their microbrew efforts,
this bar and restaurant is tucked away in
one of the neighborhoods around ASU's
Main Campus. You'll find seasonal brews,
handcrafted ales, and standard bar fare
including burgers, sandwiches, and pizzas
(the menu lists recommended beer pairings). The local press has touted this as best
beer pub, best brewpub, and even best bar
food. Four Peaks beers can be found in grocery stores and convenience marts, and
served on tap and by the bottle at a number
of restaurants and resorts throughout the
state.

GUEDO'S TACO SHOP

480-899-7841.
71 E. Chandler Blvd., Chandler.
Open: Tue.–Sat. 11 AM–9 PM; closed
Sun.–Mon.
Prices: Inexpensive.
Cuisine: Mexican.
Credit Cards: Cash only.

Traditional Mexican fare is served border-
style at this little taco shop in downtown
Chandler. Try the pork-stuffed cheese
crisp. On hot summer afternoons, enjoy
one of nine types of ice-cold Mexican beers
or a margarita on the rocks.

GOLD BAR ESPRESSO

480-839-3082.

www.goldbarespresso.com.
3141 S. McClintock Dr., Tempe.
Open: Daily 6 AM–11 PM.
Prices: Inexpensive.
Cuisine: Coffee bar.
Credit Cards: AE, D, MC, V.

This locally owned coffee bar thrives in Tempe. It's a quiet place to read, relax, and listen to the live jazz band (Jazz Alliance) Fri.–Sat. 7:30–11 PM, or classical guitarist Scott Anderson and the Arizona Guitar Trio 9–11 AM Sun. Food and beverage encompass coffees, teas, hot chocolate, Italian sodas, and fresh-baked goods from local bakeries, including Karsh's Bakery in central Phoenix. Free wireless Internet access available. Sit outside on the patio or inside at one of the tables.

HOUSE OF TRICKS RESTAURANT
480-968-1114.
www.houseoftricks.com.

114 E. 7th St., Tempe.
Open: Lunch and dinner Mon.–Sat. 11 AM–10 PM; closed Sun.
Prices: Expensive.
Cuisine: New American, southwestern.
Credit Cards: AE, D, MC, V.

Nestled on a little side street off Mill Ave. and north of the ASU campus, House of Tricks occupies a 1920s cottage and 1900s adobe brick home in historic downtown Tempe. An outdoor patio and bar, several fireplaces, twinkle lights in the mature trees, and a white picket fence complete this charming space. After almost 20 years owners Robin and Robert Trick continue to offer—through an ever-changing menu—a delightful culinary experience of New American cuisine with a twist of Southwest in entrées like seared ahi tuna on masa tortillas with avocado and grapefruit chipotle relish; Korean braised Cedar River short ribs; or coriander crusted opah with grilled

Gold Bar Espresso coffee bar in Tempe.

Locals line up at Joe's BBQ in Gilbert.

pineapple stuffing, macadamia nut mole, and fire-roasted pepper salad. Patio dining is romantic, and tables inside offer a cozy experience.

JOE'S REAL BBQ

480-503-3805.
301 N. Gilbert Rd., Gilbert.
Open: Daily for lunch and dinner; closed Thanksgiving, Christmas, Easter.
Prices: Inexpensive.
Cuisine: BBQ.
Credit Cards: AE, D, MC, V.

Even those who claim not to be barbecue fans can't get enough of Joe's one-of-a-kind BBQ sauces. This restaurant serves its barbecued goods cafeteria-style. Get in line, order from the big menu board, and grab your food. You'll find old-fashioned sodas (like 7Up in a bottle!) and Joe's own homemade root beer; barbecued chicken, pork, ribs, and beef; the biggest potatoes you've ever seen (get them heaped with everything

you can think of, including meat); and homemade desserts including cookies, cakes, and brownies. They also have an old-fashioned candy counter. There are booths and tables inside and picnic tables out the side door; you can also order to go from an outdoor window. The decor is reminiscent of Gilbert's agricultural heritage.

KAI RESTAURANT

602-225-0100 or 888-218-8989.
www.wildhorsepassresort.com.
5549 W. Wild Horse Pass Blvd., Chandler.
Open: Dinner Tue.–Sat.
Prices: Very expensive.
Cuisine: Native American, New American.
Credit Cards: AE, D, MC, V.

Kai offers fine dining infused with Native American flair and Southwest hospitality. Each dish is an incredible culinary experience. For a less pricey taste of what Wild Horse Pass has to offer, try Kai's younger brother, Ko'sin, which means "kitchen" in the Pima Indian language. Ko'sin serves breakfast, lunch, and dinner; the menu is considered moderate to expensive.

MARCELLO'S PASTA GRILL

480-831-0800.
www.marcellospastagrill.com.
1701 E. Warner Rd., Tempe.
Open: Lunch and dinner Mon.–Sat.; closed Sun. and holidays.
Prices: Moderate.
Cuisine: Italian.
Credit Cards: AE, MC. V.

On the south side of Warner Rd., west of McClintock. Always a delicious and relaxing dining experience, this little neighborhood restaurant is family-friendly—kids eat free on Mon. and Tue. The bread they bring out is delicious, and their dishes are delightful; try the chicken and homemade sausage in a white wine, garlic, and pepperoncini sauce, or the fettuccine Alfredo made with white cream, butter, fresh Parmesan, and mascarpone cheese—it is decadent.

MINT THAI CAFÉ

480-497-5366.
www.mintthaicafe.com.
1111 N. Gilbert Rd., Suite 103, Gilbert.
Open: Lunch Mon.–Fri 11 AM–3 PM, Sat. noon–3 PM; dinner Mon.–Thu. 5–9 PM, Fri.–Sat. 5–9:30 PM.
Prices: Inexpensive.
Cuisine: New American.
Credit Cards: MC, V.

Authentic, home-style Thai. These entrées can be made with beef, pork, chicken, or tofu—or even squid, shrimp, or scallops—and spiced to your liking. For dessert you'll find an assortment of treats: Thai custard, homemade coconut ice cream, and the highly recommended sticky rice and mango when in season.

MONTI'S LA CASA VIEJA

480-967-7594.
www.montis.com.
100 S. Mill Ave., Tempe.
Open: Daily for lunch and dinner, Sun.–Thu. 11 AM–10 PM, Fri.–Sat. 11 AM–11 PM.
Prices: Moderate to expensive.
Cuisine: Steak house.
Credit Cards: Major credit cards accepted.

Monti's La Casa Vieja is a Tempe institution for more than one reason—the restaurant is not only the oldest continuously occupied structure in the Valley, but also the birthplace of Carl Hayden, who served in the US Senate and Congress for 57 years, and is an Arizona institution in his own right. Built in 1871 by Hayden's father, Charles Trumbull Hayden, "the Old House"—as the Hayden family called the original adobe structure—was purchased in 1954 by Leonard F. Monti Sr. as a restaurant. Since then Monti's has dazzled locals and visitors alike with its steaks, seafood, and homemade desserts, and serves half a million meals a year. The restaurant is a hodgepodge of additions; making your way among the various rooms is like wandering through a maze. If you get lost on your way to the bathroom, just ask one of the friendly wait staff to lead you back. This family-friendly restaurant is a must.

PAPARAZZINI'S

480-345-6560.
www.paparazzinis.netfirms.com.
1825 E. Guadalupe Rd., F110, Tempe.
Open: Lunch and dinner Tue.–Sun.
Prices: Inexpensive to moderate.
Cuisine: Italian.
Credit Cards: AE, D, MC, V.

This great little Italian eatery may be the best-kept secret in south Tempe. Its unassuming decor and location in a busy strip mall might give you second thoughts, but once you taste the homemade bruschetta served in a bowl salsa-style with fresh-sliced baguettes, you'll know you've found a treasure. Staff are friendly and helpful if you're looking for recommendations. Frank Sinatra–style music plays in the background, and you might hear Aldo "Papa" Razzini belt out an Italian tune. Salad, pasta, or entrée—you won't be disappointed. For lunch try any of the panini served with beer-battered fries. For dessert the tiramisu is mouthwatering, and the chocolate cannoli is pretty darn good.

PHOENICIA GRILL

480-967-8009.
www.phoeniciagrill.com.
616 Forest Ave., Tempe.
Open: Lunch and dinner 11 AM–9 PM.
Prices: Inexpensive.
Cuisine: Mediterranean and Greek.
Credit Cards: AE, MC, V.
Other Locations: 1150 S. Gilbert Rd., #104, Gilbert (480-503-GYRO).

This modest restaurant—located just a block off of ASU's Main Campus—is a favorite among professors and students. Flavorful Greek and Mediterranean pita sandwiches, shish kebabs, gyros, falafel, baba ghanouj, and hummus are the mainstays. Patio seating available.

RIAZZI'S ITALIAN GARDEN

480-731-9464.
www.riazzis.com.
2700 S. Mill Ave., Tempe.
Open: Daily; Lunch and dinner Mon.–Thu. 11 AM–9:30 PM, Fri. 11 AM–10 PM; dinner only Sat. 5–10 PM, Sun. 4–9:30 PM.
Prices: Inexpensive to moderate.
Cuisine: Italian
Credit Cards: AE, CB, D, DC, MC, V.

An institution since 1947, the Riazzi family's restaurant has had several homes around the Valley before it settled in Tempe. Twinkle lights and a courtyard are what you'll see on the corner of Mill Avenue just south of Broadway. Their menu is quite extensive; locals love the sauces and pasta. The main part of the restaurant is large and open. The courtyard offers outdoor seating, and the bar features cozy tables in front of the fireplace.

RINALDI'S ON THIRD

480-921-9344.
51 W. 3rd St., Suite 108, Tempe.
Open: Breakfast and lunch Mon.–Fri. 8 AM–4 PM, Sat. 9 AM–3 PM; closed Sun.
Prices: Inexpensive.
Cuisine: Deli.
Credit Cards: MC, V.

This New York–style deli is around the corner from Mill Ave. on 3rd St. Sandwiches are made with Boar's Head meats and cheeses.

ROMEO'S EURO CAFÉ

480-962-4224.
www.eurocafe.com.
207 N. Gilbert Rd., Gilbert.
Open: Lunch and dinner Mon.–Thu. 11 AM–11 PM, Fri.–Sat. 11 AM–midnight, Sun. 11 AM–10 PM.
Prices: Moderate.
Cuisine: Mediterranean.
Credit Cards: AE, D, MC, V.

Located in downtown Gilbert, Euro Café wows locals and visitors alike with its eclectic and extensive menu of Greek-inspired entrées, salads, pita sandwiches, pastas, and homemade desserts. Try the adjacent coffee shop, Undici Undici, or the gift shop next store.

RULA BULA IRISH PUB & RESTAURANT

480-929-9500.
www.rulabula.com.
401 S. Mill Ave., Tempe.
Open: Daily for lunch and dinner, Sun.–Thu. 11 AM–1 AM, Fri.–Sat. 11 AM–2 AM.
Prices: Inexpensive to moderate.
Cuisine: Irish.
Credit Cards: AE, MC, V.

Located on the south end of Mill Ave., the aptly named Rula Bula—taken from a Gaelic saying meaning "uproar and commotion"—provides a rowdy good time; just what the owners were aiming for. It's been named best Irish pub in town by several local media outlets. You'll find live Irish entertainment and an excellent Irish menu with so many delicious options; you will have a hard time choosing. But the dishes are large enough to share, so keep that in mind when you're deciding between the best fish-and-chips in town, the incredible shepherd's pie, and one of several mouthwatering salads—and that's *if* you haven't already stuffed yourself on the Irish soda bread they bring to your table and that glass of Guinness you ordered first.

CULTURE

Cinema

Pollack Tempe Cinemas (480-345-6461; www.pollacktempecinemas.com; 1825 E. Elliot, Tempe). Located in the strip mall on the southeast corner of McClintock and Elliot, Pollack Tempe Cinemas offers a moviegoing experience at a discount—showing those movies already on their way to the rental store. Visit online for discounts, movies, and showtimes, or call for more information.

See the Phoenix chapter for movie theaters.

Education

ARIZONA STATE UNIVERSITY
480-965-9011.
www.asu.edu.
Main Campus, University Dr. and Mill Ave.

Arizona State University has expanded incredibly since its start as the Arizona Normal School in Tempe in 1885. With only 20 women and 13 men in its first graduating class, ASU has grown to a major university offering 87 undergraduate degrees, 95 master's degrees, 48 doctoral and terminal programs, and a law degree program to almost 60,000 students on four campuses throughout the Valley: the 700-acre Main Campus in downtown Tempe, ASU West at 47th Ave. and Thunderbird in the West Valley, ASU East in Mesa, and the newest—ASU Extended Campus in downtown Phoenix. ASU offers a variety of credit, noncredit, evening, weekend, and alternative-delivery-style courses to accommodate working students, as well as traditional-style classes for full-time learners. It also offers a variety of events, programs, and resources that are open to the public, including events at Gammage Auditorium (see Stage, below), exhibits at Nelson Fine Arts Center (see Galleries, also below), the ASU Planetarium, and a 3.2-million-volume library system, to name a few.

ARIZONA STATE UNIVERSITY'S
VIRGINIA G. PIPER CENTER FOR CREATIVE WRITING
480-965-6018.
www.asu.edu/clas/pipercwcenter/index.html.
PO Box 875002, Arizona State University, Tempe 85287-5002.
Open: Thu. 10 AM–4:30 PM.

Made possible by local philanthropist Virginia G. Piper, the center offers some free programs and events, and workshops to the public, including ASU's annual Desert Nights, Rising Stars Writers Conference, the Distinguished Writers Series, and the Piper Writer's Studio—fall and spring writing workshops led by experienced writers within the community. Note that while the Piper Writers House is open for center business and for use by students and faculty involved with ASU's MFA creative writing program Mon.–Thu. 10 AM–4:30 PM, the living room and Resource Center Library are open to the public Thu. 10 AM–4:30 PM; tours are given at 10 AM (call 480-965-6018 to schedule one).

ART STUDIOS AT MESA ARTS CENTER
Administration 480-644-6501; TeleTrac 480-644-4449.
www.mesaartscenter.com.
1 E. Main St., Mesa.
Open: Mon.–Fri. 8:30 AM–10 PM, Sat. 8:30 AM–5 PM during class sessions.

Art Studios offers more than 750 classes, workshops, and lectures for youth and adults at all skill levels. Courses in a wide variety of areas—including acting, ceramics, dance, drama, drawing, glass, jewelry, metals, music, painting, photography, printmaking, and sculpture—are offered intermittently and led by recognized local, regional, and national visual and performing artists. Art Studios holds three sessions each year, usually in fall, winter–spring, and summer; classes vary in length from a few weeks to 16 weeks. For more information, visit www.mesaartscenter.com/ArtStudios.aspx.

Libraries
Chandler Public Library, Downtown Branch (480-782-2800; www.chandlerlibrary.org; 22 S. Delaware St., Chandler). Open Mon.–Thu. 9 AM–9 PM, Fri.–Sat. 9 AM–6 PM, Sun. 1–5 PM.
Mesa Public Library, Main Branch (480-644-2207; www.mesalibrary.org; 64 E. 1st St., Mesa). Open Mon.–Thu. 10 AM–9 PM, Fri.–Sat. 10 AM–5 PM, Sun. 1–5 PM.
Tempe Public Library (voice 480-350-5500; TDD 480-350-5050; www.tempe.gov/library; 3500 S. Rural Rd., Tempe). Located at the southwest corner of Southern and Rural Rds.; enter off either one. Open Mon.–Thu. 9–9, Fri.–Sat. 9–5:30, Sun. noon–5:30. Free wireless Internet access available. Enjoy a good book and great company at Tempe Connections Café, which is open during regular business hours and serves beverages and pastries until an hour before closing.

Museums

ARIZONA STATE UNIVERSITY ART MUSEUM
AT NELSON FINE ARTS CENTER
480-965-2787.
http://asuartmuseum.asu.edu.
ASU Main Campus, Mill Ave. and 10th St., Tempe.
Open: Tue. 10 AM–9 PM, Wed.–Sat. 10 AM–5 PM, Sun. 1–5 PM.
Admission: Free.

As a division of the Katherine K. Herberger College of the Arts at Arizona State University, this art museum features an eclectic collection of contemporary work from a diverse group of artists, including those using new and unique methods of presentation, contemporary

Latin American pieces, and art of the Southwest. Named "the single most impressive venue for contemporary art in Arizona" by *Art in America* magazine, the museum holds more than 10,000 pieces, with almost 50,000 square feet of space in five galleries. It's found on the east side of Mill Ave., just north of Gammage Auditorium.

ARIZONA WING COMMEMORATIVE AIR FORCE MUSEUM

480-924-1940.
www.arizonawingcaf.com.
2017 N. Greenfield Rd., Mesa.
Open: Oct. 15–May 14, daily 10 AM–4 PM; closed Thanksgiving & Christmas.
Admission: $7 ages 14–adult, $3 ages 6–13; ages 5 and under are free.

This aircraft museum is dedicated to preserving aviation history and wartime memorabilia and primarily focuses on maintaining and operating aircraft from World War II to Vietnam. Planes on display have included the F4F Wildcat, PV2 Lockheed Harpoon, and MiG-15 UTI "Midget" Trainer. It's located at Falcon Field Airport at the intersection of Greenfield and McDowell Rds.

CHANDLER MUSEUM

480-782-2717.
www.chandlermuseum.org.
178 E. Commonwealth Ave., Chandler.
Open: Mon.–Sat. 11 AM–4 PM; closed Sun. and holidays.
Admission: Free.

Students stroll through ASU's main campus in Tempe.

Find artifacts of prehistoric southwestern Native Americans, photographs, and a replica of Chandler's first store in this tribute to Chandler and Central Arizona. Find it at Arizona Ave. and Buffalo St., a block south of Chandler Blvd. or a block north of Boston St.

MESA CONTEMPORARY ARTS AT MESA ARTS CENTER
Box office 480-644-6500; administration 480-644-6501.
www.mesaartscenter.com.
1 E. Main St., Mesa.
Open: Tue.–Wed. 10 AM–5 PM, Thu.–Sat. 10 AM–8 PM, Sun. noon–5 PM.
Admission: $3.50; free for ages 7 and under, and free to all Thu.

A part of the Mesa art scene since 1976, Mesa Contemporary Arts has presented juried and curated exhibits of art by both emerging and internationally recognized contemporary artists. Its varying exhibits and works make up the five-gallery, subterranean visual arts compound within the 212,755-square-foot Mesa Arts Center (found at the southeast corner of Main and Center Sts.). Public tours are available Wed. noon for an additional $3.50 per person; private tours can be arranged for an additional $5-per-person fee. To schedule one, call the Volunteer & Tours Hotline at 480-644-6626. Leave a voice-mail message; messages are checked regularly.

MESA SOUTHWEST MUSEUM
480-644-2230.
www.cityofmesa.org/swmuseum.
53 N. Macdonald, Mesa.
Open: Tue.–Fri. 10 AM–5 PM, Sat. 11 AM–5 PM, Sun. 1–5 PM; closed Mon. and holidays.
Admission: $8 adults, $7 seniors 65-plus, $6 students 13-plus with ID, $4 ages 3–12; children 2 and younger are free.

A mere 3,000 square feet when in opened in 1977, the Mesa Southwest Museum has expanded to an 80,000-square-foot facility that features a variety of exhibits illustrating southwestern natural and cultural history. Often called "the dinosaur museum" by local children, Mesa Southwest features the largest collection of dinosaur bones in the state. It includes a noncirculating research library that specializes in Southwest natural and cultural history; open Tue.–Fri. 1–4 PM, and other times are available by appointment (call 480-644-2277 to schedule).
    The museum is sited one block north of Main St. in downtown Mesa. Take US 60 or 202 to Country Club Dr., go to Main St., and proceed 0.5 mile east to Macdonald.

PETERSON HOUSE MUSEUM
480-350-5151.
www.tempe.gov/museum/aphm.htm.
1414 W. Southern Ave., Tempe.
Open: Tue.–Thu. 10 AM–2 PM, Sat. 10 AM–2 PM.
Admission: Free, but a $1 donation is recommended.

One of the few remaining historic homes in the Valley representing the Victorian architectural era, the Peterson House was built in 1892. It was the home of Niels Peterson, a businessman, community leader, and rancher who arrived in Tempe in 1871. His sprawling

Public art in downtown Mesa.

160-acre ranch stretched from what is now Southern Avenue north to Alameda Street, and from I-10 east to Priest Drive. The Peterson House, donated in 1979 to the city of Tempe, stands at the northwest corner of Priest and Southern. The home, with its 12-foot ceilings, gables, porches, balconies, and restored period furnishings, continues to be an excellent reflection of period architecture.

TEMPE HISTORICAL MUSEUM
480-350-5100; TDD 480-350-5050.
www.tempe.gov/museum.
809 E. Southern Ave., Tempe.
Open: Mon.–Thu. 10 AM–5 PM, Sat. 10 AM–5 PM, Sun. 1–5 PM; closed Fri. and holidays.
Admission: Free.

Take a stroll through this tribute to Tempe's history. Learn about the development of water as a major resource for the desert town, and catch a glimpse of what life was like for Tempe's early residents as you view artifacts from daily life. Enjoy the fun visual effects— you can divert water from the Salt River to the canals and irrigation ditches that crisscross the landscape at the controls of a 40-foot model, for instance, or light up the city on a map that displays Tempe's growth, neighborhood by neighborhood. Displays and exhibits change, so visit online for updates. The museum is found on the southwest corner of Rural and Southern, at the Tempe Public Library campus.

Nightlife
The nightlife in Chandler's downtown and Mesa's Main Street seems to close up shop about 10 PM and relies heavily on the restaurants and shops to sustain evening happenings.

Tempe, however, is home to the Mill Avenue District, where students, locals, and tourists mingle among the 100-plus shops, restaurants, and entertainment hot spots until early morn. Along Mill Avenue and on nearby streets, from University north to Rio Salado Parkway, you will find laughter, lights, and hordes of people.

Take a stroll down the street-level staircase on the corner of 5th and Mill to **The Big Bang** (480-557-5595; 501 S. Mill) and its dueling pianos for a fun and raucous evening of music and laughter. **The Cherry Lounge and Pit** (480-966-3573; www.thecherryloungeaz .com; 411 S. Mill Ave.) attracts the young and single for dancing, drinking, and partying the night away. Studying is forbidden at **The Library Bar and Grill** (480-929-9002; www.the libraryusa.com; 501 S. Mill Ave., Suite 101), where the wait staff wear "uniforms"; pool players pack it in at the **Mill Cue Club** (480-966-0068; www.millcueclub.com; 607 S. Mill Ave.). Off Mill you'll find the Tempe **IMPROV** (480-921-9877; 930 E. University Drive, Suite D1): It's big, it's famous, and it serves a kind of dinner. Expect nationally known comics and a hilariously good time.

Stage

BROADWAY PALM DINNER THEATRE
480-325-6700 or 888-504-7256.
www.broadwaypalmwest.com.
5247 E. Brown Rd., Mesa.
Admission: $49 Sun.–Fri., $52 Sat., $43 matinees, $20 ages 12 and under.

Opened in 2001, this professional dinner theater at the southeast corner of Higley and Brown packages a full-length Broadway musical with a buffet meal to create a wonderful

The Mesa Arts Center.

dinner-and-a-show experience. The theater seats 500, including 75 seats available for those wishing to watch the show only. Located in Mesa, Broadway Palm Dinner Theatre is a favorite for local fund-raisers and events.

Evening performances take place Tue.–Sat. (except May–Oct., when there aren't any Tue. events). The dinner buffet starts at 6 PM, with showtime 8 PM. At matinees, the lunch buffet begins at 11:45 AM; showtime is 1:15 PM. The Sunday Twilights performance includes a 5:30 PM buffet; showtime is 7 PM. Tickets can be purchased online at www.broadwaypalmwest .com. Prices include dinner, show, and tax, but not gratuity. Show-only tickets are $25 each.

GAMMAGE AUDITORIUM
480-965-5062.
www.asugammage.com.
E. Apache Blvd. & S. Mill Ave., ASU campus, Tempe.

Gammage Auditorium, which seats more than 3,000 patrons, was the last design of internationally known architect Frank Lloyd Wright. The building, well known in the Tempe area for its resemblance to a tiered wedding cake, is acoustically sound and hosts concerts, theater, film, dance, and special events year-round.

Parking is free but limited. We suggest you arrive early. Fees vary by performance. Tickets can be ordered through the box office, which is open Mon.–Fri. 10 AM–6 PM (till 5 PM Mon.–Thu. in summer), as well as 2 hours prior to each event. Call 480-965-3434 or, for group services, 480-965 6678. Tickets can be ordered online at www.ticketmaster.com or www.asugammage.com. All major credit cards are accepted.

MESA ARTS CENTER
Box office 480-644-6500; administration 480-644-6501.
www.mesaartscenter.com.
1 E. Main St., PO Box 1466, Mesa 85211-1466.

The Mesa Arts Center boasts 212,755 square feet of space, making it the largest and most comprehensive arts center in Arizona. Home to visual and the performing arts as well as an educational venue, the center is located in the center of downtown Mesa at the southeast corner of Main and Center Sts. It utilizes four state-of-the-art and outdoor entertainment areas to bring a variety of live performances to the East Valley. Events range from country star Vince Gill to the world-renowned Vienna Choir Boys, hometown favorites like the Mesa Symphony Orchestra, off-Broadway shows including *Fully Committed*, the ballet, Shakespearean plays, and Broadway shows like *Cats*. Program schedules and tickets are available online. The box office is open Mon.–Sat. 10 AM–5 PM, Sun. noon–4 PM, and 2 hours prior to showtimes.

SHOPPING

Shopping Malls
Arizona Mills (480-491-9700; 5000 Arizona Mills Circle, Tempe). Located at I-10 and US 60, Arizona Mills is the state's largest value and entertainment mega mall. It features more than 175 manufacturers' outlets, restaurants, and entertainment venues. Outlets range from Ann Taylor Loft to Bebe's to Off Rodeo Drive and Virgin Records Megastore.

Restaurants include Garcia's Mexican, Rainforest Café, and a food court. Claim Jumper is located across the parking lot off Baseline, as is Joe's Crab Shack. The Harkins Cinema features 24 theaters with stadium seating; it includes an IMAX theater boasting eight-story, 120-foot-wide screens and an exciting viewing experience. GameWorks—a high-tech entertainment facility—has a variety of virtual-reality games and even vintage retro games like PacMan, Tetris, and Donkey Kong. It also serves a full menu of food.

Fiesta Mall (480-833-4121; www.shopfiesta.com; US 60 at the Alma School exit, Mesa). Standard mall shops including Victoria's Secret, and Bath and Body Works; department stores like Dillard's and JCPenney; and mall kiosks. There are several restaurants, including Mimi's, Red Lobster, and Chevy's Mexican Restaurant.

Chandler Fashion Center (480-812-8488; www.westcor.com; 3111 W. Chandler Blvd., Chandler). The southeast Valley's newest mall is still reeling from the convergence of locals starving for a shopping mecca close to home. You'll find a number of high-end stores, like Nordstrom, Williams-Sonoma, and Pottery Barn, as well as standard choices such as Gap and Baby Gap, a variety of popular chain restaurants like P. F. Chang's and The Cheesecake Factory, and a great theater. Still, it's often so crowded here on weekends that even valet parking can't keep up.

Superstition Springs Center (480-832-0212; www.superstitionsprings.com; 6555 E. Southern Ave., Mesa). Found on US 60 at Power Rd. Another Westcor shopping success in the Valley, this location features more than 130 restaurants and shops, including favorites like Macy's, Bath and Body Works, Spencers, JCPenney, and Super Saver Cinemas.

Shopping Districts

MILL AVENUE

The Mill Avenue District (www.downtowntempe.com) is located in downtown Tempe close to Tempe Town Lake and Arizona State University's Main Campus, and features more than 100 shops, restaurants, and bars. Favorites include **Bath and Body Works**, **Abercrombie and Fitch**, **Borders Books and Music**, **Chester's Harley-Davidson**, and **Z Gallerie** along with local favorites like **Yucatecan Imports** and **Lotions and Potions**. Restaurant experiences include local favorites **Monti's La Casa Vieja**; **Caffé Boa**; **House of Tricks**; **Rula Bula Irish Pub**; and national/regional chains like **Fatburger, the Last Great Hamburger Stand**, **Z'Tejas Southwestern Grill** (for the best frozen Chambord margaritas), and **Hooters**. You will also find a energetic nightlife teeming with all age groups at spots like The Cherry Pit, The Library, and the Mill Cue Club.

Parking is often troublesome on weekends, but try the CenterPoint parking lot, accessible from 6th St.

DOWNTOWN CHANDLER

With the Crowne Plaza San Marcos Resort and Spa as downtown Chandler's main focal point, the area has been restored to a vibrant shopping and dining district. You will find great restaurants including **La Stalla Cucina Rustica** (480-855-9990; 68 W. Buffalo St.), an Italian eatery located across from the historic San Marcos Resort, and **Serrano's Mexican Restaurant** (480-899-3318; 141 S. Arizona Ave.)—a local favorite that serves great Mexican food at a fair price; this is their original location. You will also find a variety of alluring shops ranging from **Naughty but Nice Lingerie Boutique** (480-917-0481; 1 E.

Boston St.) to one of the Valley's oldest western-wear retailers—**Saba's Western Wear** (480-963-4496; 67 W. Boston St.). Other great shops include **Urban Crib** (480-722-7573, 85 W. Boston Street), an eclectic mix of household decor; **Country Cottage Gift, Floral & Shoppe** (480-726-7673; 236 S. Wall St.); **The Vision Gallery** (480-917-6859; www.vision-gallery.org; 80 S. San Marcos Place), managed by the Chandler Cultural Foundation, featuring rotating exhibits of works on canvas, watercolors, glass, mixed media, and sculpture (all art is for sale); and **Mind Over Splatter** (480-899-1174; 64 S. San Marcos Place), where you can make your own artwork on pottery.

Specialty Shops

Changing Hands Bookstore (480-730-0205; www.changinghands.com; 6428 S. McClintock Dr., Tempe). New and gently used books populate the shelves of this Tempe shop. Located adjacent to Wildflower Bread Company, Changing Hands celebrates local and national authors with weekly and daily events as well as monthly book signings by some of today's most popular authors.

McFarlane Toys (480-785-2553; www.spawn.com/store/showroom; 8945 S. Harl Ave., Suite 112, Tempe). An award-winning toy store that's a short distance from downtown Phoenix and Sky Harbor International Airport.

Definitely Debra (480-491-0903; www.definitelydebra.com). Specializes in items for the blushing bride, including handmade cards, invitations, fine stationery, and home decor. This charming shop is located at McClintock and Warner in Tempe.

Other locally owned shops located in the East Valley include **Domestic Bliss** (480-733-0552; www.domesticblissdesign.com; 166 W. Main St., Suite 104) in Mesa, where they

Tempe.

Hohokam Stadium in Mesa, where the Chicago Cubs play in spring.

sell unique home decor; **Granny's Chocolate Creations** (480-926-2424 or 800-382-0066; www.grannyschocolate.com; 1035 N. McQueen Rd., #116) in Gilbert; and **The Orange Patch** (480-962-4490; 2717 E. Lehi Rd.) and **Orange Patch Too** (480-832-0230 or 888-832-0230; 3825 E. McKellips Rd.), both in Mesa.

The **Route 66 & Die Cast Car Store** (480-654-0815; www.theroute66store.net; 4815 E. Main St., Suite 24) is located in Mesa, where Route 66 is alive and well. This store celebrates the way it was when Route 66 passed through northern Arizona. A trip to **Wide World of Maps** (480-844-1134; www.maps4u.com; 1444 W. Southern Ave., Mesa) can set you up for your itinerary—they have a great collection of books and maps about the region, including some you might not find at other stores. The unique collection comprises geographic, topographic, and place and trail maps of the Valley and surrounding areas. Globes, GPS gadgets, and framing are available. It's found on the north side of Southern in a strip mall.

Bookmans Entertainment Exchange (480-835-0505; www.bookmans.com; 1056 S. Country Club Dr., Mesa) sells and exchanges used books, magazines, CDs, records, video games, and more. This has to be one of the largest used-book collections in the Valley. They have additional locations in Tucson and Flagstaff, and in 2005 opened another Valley location in central Phoenix (602-433-0255; 8034 N. 19th Ave., Phoenix).

Tour Arizona's own olive mill—the **Queen Creek Olive Mill** (480-888-9290; www.queen-creekolivemill.com; 25062 S. Meridian Rd., Queen Creek). This family-owned business grows and presses olives for the production of extra-virgin olive oil. Arizona's climate makes for ideal growing conditions and an extended season. Tours (including an opportunity to taste-test) are available Tue.–Sat. 10 AM–4 PM, Sun. 10 AM–2 PM, for $5 per person. Arrive early, as space is limited to 35 people. There's also a little shop where you can sample the olive oils and other treats.

SPECTATOR SPORTS

Cactus League Spring Training

ANAHEIM ANGELS

Recorded information 480-350-5205, 602-438-9300, or 888-994-2567.
www.angelsbaseball.com.
Tempe Diablo Stadium, 2200 W. Alameda Dr., Tempe.

Located off 1-10, the Tempe Diablo Stadium has hosted the Anaheim Angels for more than 16 years. Ticket prices start as low as $5, and are available on site or online. The complex includes six and a half practice fields in addition to the main stadium, which was dedicated as Gene Autry Field in 1999 in honor of the former Angels' owner who passed away after the 1998 season. Parking for the stadium features two parking lots (east and west) with 1,350 paved parking spaces, including two disabled entryways as well as field and service access. To reach the stadium, take the Broadway St. exit off I-10; travel west on Broadway to 48th St. and turn left. The stadium is 0.5 mile on the left; to enter the ballpark, turn left onto Alameda.

CHICAGO CUBS

Recorded information 480-964-4467 or 800-905-3315.
www.cubspringtraining.com.
HoHoKam Park, 1235 N. Center St., Mesa.

HoHoKam Stadium, in Mesa, hosts the Chicago Cubs. Ticket prices range $5–15 and can be purchased on site or online; wheelchair-accessible seating is available. Parking is found on site, and several local entrepreneurs open their parking lots for $3–8 per car. The stadium is conveniently located a short distance north of US 60 (Country Club or Mesa Dr. exits). The box office is at the front entrance.

6

GLENDALE AND THE WEST VALLEY

Surprise, Litchfield, Goodyear, Avondale, and the Sun Cities

The West Valley, which makes up the western portion of the Greater Phoenix metropolitan area or Valley of the Sun, comprises 13 communities: Avondale, Buckeye, El Mirage, Glendale, Goodyear, Litchfield Park, Peoria, Sun City, Sun City West, Surprise, Tolleson, Wickenburg, and Youngtown. It's considered one of the fastest-growing regions in Arizona.

Glendale

The largest of the West Valley cities is Glendale. It began in 1892 as a religious settlement, but its proximity to Phoenix and the Santa Fe Railroad inspired opportunity and growth. During World War II, Glendale became home to Luke Air Force Base, today the largest training base for the US Air Force; over the latter half of the 20th century, the city grew to more than 200,000 people. Today as the home of two professional sports teams—the Arizona Cardinals (NFL) and Phoenix Coyotes (NHL)—and host to the NCAA's Fiesta Bowl, Glendale is quickly becoming a sports lovers' paradise. The downtown historic districts attract more than a million visitors a year, and Glendale expect to see over 125,000 football fans just for Super Bowl XLII in 2008.

Despite all the changes, Glendale's heritage remains a big part of its charm. Visitors and residents can enjoy a weekly art walk through the historic downtown, sites like the Sahuaro and Manistee Ranches, browsing the city's 90 antiques and specialty shops, and touring the Cerreta Candy Company, a family-owned chocolate factory that has been around since the late 1970s. Country music and NASCAR fans might enjoy a visit and stay in the hometown of country music legend Marty Robbins. But while the past may be the foundation of Glendale's charm, the city has fast-forwarded into the 21st century with the recent addition of University of Phoenix Stadium—the most state-of-the-art football venue in the country—and Westgate City Center, a futuristic shopping experience straight out of *Back to the Future Part II*.

Peoria

Peoria cropped up along the Arizona Canal upon its completion in 1885 and has since grown to almost 150,000 people. It's home to the San Diego Padres' and Seattle Mariners'

Historic Downtown Glendale from Murphy Park.

spring training camps; a Smithsonian Institution affiliate, the Challenger Space Center of Arizona; and Lake Pleasant Regional Park, which offers myriad recreational opportunities, including camping, boating, hiking, and fishing. You can also enjoy a charming downtown area, dinner and a Broadway musical, hang gliding, and in-line, roller, and ice skating.

The 101, which travels through much of Peoria, provides easy access to the rest of the Valley, including North Phoenix, North Scottsdale, Carefree, and Cave Creek. It is adjacent to Glendale on the east and Sun City on the west; its southern border isn't far from University of Phoenix Stadium, home of the Arizona Cardinals and Super Bowl XLII.

LODGING

While lodging rates in the West Valley tend to be lower than in areas such as Scottsdale and parts of Phoenix, keep in mind that Super Bowl XLII in 2008 will put this part of the Valley on the map. Depending on the time of year you visit and the hotel you choose, prices might more than quadruple. Availability may be nonexistent as the big game draws closer, and even afterward.

Credit Cards

The following abbreviations are used for credit card information:

AE: American Express
CB: Carte Blanche
D: Discover Card
DC: Diner's Club
MC: MasterCard
V: Visa

GLENDALE

Due to the new development in Glendale and the West Valley, including the addition of University of Phoenix Stadium, several new hotels will have opened by late 2007, after this book goes to press. They include the **Renaissance Phoenix Glendale Hotel** (623-937-3700; www.renaissancephoenix

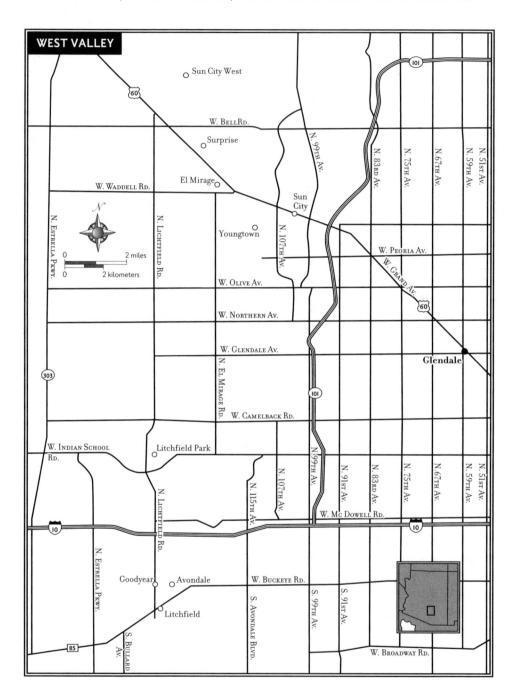

glendale.com; 9495 W. Coyotes Blvd., Glendale), located between Westgate City Center and University of Phoenix Stadium and adjacent to Jobing.com Arena, where the Phoenix Coyotes play. It will feature an on-site restaurant, pool, fitness center, full-service spa, and 320 brand-new rooms with wireless Internet access. Also opening is the **SpringHill Suites by Marriott Phoenix Glendale** (623-772-9200; 7370 N. Zanjero

Blvd., Glendale), just north of Westgate City Center and minutes from the Arizona Cardinals' new stadium and Jobing.com Arena.

GLENDALE GASLIGHT INN
623-934-9119.
www.GlendaleGaslightInn.com.
5747 W. Glendale Ave, Glendale.
Prices: $145–500.
Credit Cards: AE, D, MC, V.
Handicapped Access: 2 rooms.
Pets: Yes, with $20 deposit; pets are not allowed in food areas.

Self-described as "retro-chic," the Glendale Gaslight Inn offers an upscale experience in Historic Downtown Glendale. Uniquely decorated rooms, monogrammed bathrobes, 1,000-thread-count sheets, and wireless Internet are only some of the amenities you will find at this circa-1925 hotel. Enjoy the on-site coffee shop and piano wine bar or stroll the downtown area's 100 shops, restaurants, and sites. The downtown area is only minutes away from University of Phoenix Stadium and Peoria Sports Complex; it's 20 minutes from Phoenix Sky Harbor Airport. This quaint little inn offers an alternative to chain hotels.

HOLIDAY INN 51ST AVENUE
602-484-9009.
www.holiday-inn.com/phx-west.
1500 N. 51st Ave., Phoenix.
Prices: $127–275.
Credit Cards: AE, D, DC, MC, V.
Handicapped Access: 7 rooms.
Pets: Small dogs and cats allowed; nonrefundable $25 fee per pet.

You will find a full-service restaurant and bar, as well as room service, at this Holiday Inn where kids eat free. Amenities include complimentary high-speed wireless Internet in all guest rooms and public areas, an outdoor covered pool and Jacuzzi, and a mini exercise room. Ask about smoking

rooms; most rooms are nonsmoking.

QUALITY INN & SUITES AT TALAVI
602-896-8900 or 877-982-5284.
www.qisphoenix.com.
5511 W. Bell Rd., Glendale.
Prices: $90–130.
Credit Cards: AE, CD, D, DC, MC, V.
Handicapped Access: Yes.
Pets: No.

Guest privileges include access to LA Fitness clubs, wireless high-speed Internet access, a heated pool/spa, and a conference room for 50. Rooms offer coffeemaker, refrigerator, microwave, hair dryer, and iron with ironing board. This hotel is close to Arrowhead Town Center shopping and restaurants, Arrowhead Country Club, and the Peoria Sports Complex.

QUALITY INN—GLENDALE
623-939-9431 or 800-333-7172.
www.choicehotels.com.
7116 N. 59th Ave., Glendale.
Prices: $100.
Credit Cards; AE, D, MC, V.
Handicapped Access: Yes; rooms are being remodeled as of spring 2007.
Pets: No.

Located in Historic Downtown Glendale, this Quality Inn provides immediate access to more than 100 shops and restaurants. It is only 3 miles from University of Phoenix Stadium and just 7 miles from the Peoria Sports Complex, where the Seattle Mariners and San Diego Padres play. The courtyard rooms feature a refrigerator, free high-speed wireless Internet, and a complimentary deluxe continental breakfast.

SPRINGHILL SUITES BY MARRIOTT PHOENIX GLENDALE/PEORIA
623-878-6666.
7810 W. Bell Rd., Glendale 85308.
Prices: $99–219.
Credit Cards: AE, CB, D, DC, MC, V.

A guest room at the Glendale Gaslight Inn. Photo courtesy of the Glendale Gaslight Inn

Handicapped Access: Yes.
Pets: Service animals allowed for persons with disabilities.

Located just a mile from Peoria Sports Complex, where the Padres and the Mariners play their spring training games, this all-studio-suites hotel is a perfect place to stay if you plan on spending March watching your favorite pastime. The rooms are decked out with high-speed Internet access, microwave oven, and mini refrigerator. On-site amenities include a 24-hour fitness center, outdoor heated pool, and complimentary continental breakfast.

PEORIA
Cibola Vista Resort & Spa (602-889-4646; www.cibolavista.com; 27501 N. Lake Pleasant Rd.) and **Residence Inn by Marriott Phoenix NW/Glendale** (623-979-2074; 8435 W. Paradise Lane) will have opened in Peoria by late fall 2007.

COMFORT SUITES PEORIA SPORTS COMPLEX
623-334-3993.
8473 W. Paradise Lane, Peoria.
Prices: $119–129.
Credit Cards: AE, CB, D, DC, MC, V.
Handicapped Access: Yes.
Pets: 2 pets per room, under 35 pounds; $50 per stay

This hotel is only a short walk to the Peoria Sports Complex, and is an ideal choice for Padres and Mariners fans visiting the state for spring training games.

SURPRISE
HAMPTON INN & SUITES—SURPRISE
623-537-9122.
14783 W. Grand Ave., Surprise 85374.
Prices: $139.
Credit Cards: AE, CB, D, DC, MC, V.
Handicapped Access: Yes.
Pets: Up to 60 pounds, with a $25 deposit.

This Hampton Inn is situated on US 60/Grand Ave. near Surprise Stadium and Heard Museum West. Amenities include complimentary breakfast, pool, and exercise room.

QUALITY INN & SUITES OF THE SUN CITIES
623-583-3500.
16741 N. Greasewood St., Surprise.
Prices: $69–99.
Credit Cards: AE, CB, D, DC, MC, V.
Handicapped Access: Yes.
Pets: No.

This hotel is conveniently located near several West Valley recreational activities, including Surprise Stadium, the West Valley Art Center, several golf courses, Arrowhead Mall, and the Peoria Sports Complex. It features an indoor heated pool and whirlpool and a free full breakfast. In-room amenities include free high-speed wireless Internet.

WINDMILL SUITES AT SUN CITY WEST
623-583-0133 or 800-547-4747.
www.windmillinns.com.
12545 W. Bell Rd., Surprise.
Prices: $78–149.
Credit Cards: AE, D, DC, MC, V.
Handicapped Access: Yes.
Pets: Yes, no charge; learn more about their pets welcome policy online.

This hotel features a fitness room, heated pool and whirlpool, and 127 Southwest-style suites with wet bar and two televisions. It is located near Sun City West and Sun City Grand—two of Del Webb's active adult communities—and Luke Air Force Base. Enjoy the free continental breakfast or have their mini breakfast (hot beverage, muffin, juice, and newspaper) delivered to your room.

GOODYEAR
HAMPTON INN & SUITES
623-536-1313 or 800-HAMPTON.
www.hamptoninn.com.

2000 N. Litchfield Rd., Goodyear 85338.
Prices: $99–179.
Credit Cards: AE, CB, D, DC, MC, V.
Handicapped Access: 6 rooms.
Pets: Fee required.

You will find a jetted bathtub and wireless high speed Internet in each of the 110 guest rooms and suites. And the suites make you feel more at home with their separate living room, large-screen TV, and fully equipped kitchen. Located close to shopping and dining as well as Palm Valley Golf Course, Glendale Arena, and the Wildlife World Zoo, Hampton Inn & Suites provides a good place to stay while exploring the West Valley. Proximity to I-10 also makes it easy to access Phoenix and the rest of the area.

HOLIDAY INN EXPRESS GOODYEAR
623-535-1313 or 800-HOLIDAY.
1313 N. Litchfield Rd., Goodyear 85338.
Prices: $99–249.
Credit Cards: AE, CB, D, DC, MC, V.
Handicapped Access: 5 rooms.
Pets: $20 deposit due at check-in.

This hotel features guest rooms (some smoking; call for details) and suites and offers a complimentary buffet breakfast, free Internet access, whirlpool, and pool. The hotel is conveniently located near several restaurants and sites, including Wildlife World Zoo, Wigwam Resort, and Luke Air Force Base. It is mere minutes from I-10, providing easy access to Phoenix and the rest of the Valley.

RESIDENCE INN BY MARRIOTT PHOENIX GOODYEAR
623-866-1313.
2020 N. Litchfield Rd., Goodyear 85338.
Prices: $179–239.
Credit Cards: AE, CB, D, DC, MC, V.
Handicapped Access: Yes.
Pets: No.

This hotel sits on the beautiful Palm Valley

Golf Course and is located just off I-10, close to restaurants, shopping, and a movie theater. It features complimentary breakfast. In-room amenities vary by room, but suites include wireless Internet access and fully equipped kitchen. Ask about the suites with the jetted tub and fireplace or a golf course view.

LITCHFIELD PARK
WIGWAM GOLF RESORT & SPA, THE
623-935-3811 or 800-327-0396.
www.wigwamresort.com.
300 Wigwam Blvd., Litchfield Park 85340.
Prices: $165–365.
Credit Cards: AE, CB, D, DC, MC, V.
Handicapped Access: 7 rooms.
Pets: Small dogs; call for details.

This historic Four Diamond resort was built in 1918 and features beautiful rooms, lush landscaping, three 18-hole golf courses, nine tennis courts, a beauty salon, two pools, complimentary bike rental, a fitness center, and the Red Door Spa. Located off Litchfield Rd. in the charming town of Litchfield Park, it's a perfect escape from the bustling city. The award-winning Arizona Kitchen features weekly chef-created delicacies inspired by the Sonoran Desert and founded in classical French cuisine. Guests can also dine poolside at the Pool Cabana overlooking the Gold Course (one of the resort's three courses), at the Grille on the Greens, or at the recently opened Red's Steakhouse, which serves steaks and fresh fish.

AVONDALE
HILTON GARDEN INN PHOENIX/AVONDALE
623-882-3351.
www.hiltongardeninn.com.
11460 W. Hilton Way, Avondale 85323.
Prices: $119–249.
Credit Cards: MC, V.
Handicapped Access: 13 rooms.
Pets: No.

This hotel opened in early 2007 and features 123 guest rooms and suites, free Internet access, a 24-hour exercise room, a pool, and an on-site restaurant and bar. It's located conveniently close to restaurants, shopping, golf, and recreational activities such as horseback riding, bicycling, and hiking as well as key sites like Glendale (Jobing.com) Arena, University of Phoenix Stadium, and Phoenix International Raceway. A complimentary shuttle provides service within a 5-mile radius.

DINING

Credit Cards
The following abbreviations are used for credit card information:
AE: American Express
CB: Carte Blanche
D: Discover Card
DC: Diner's Club
MC: MasterCard
V: Visa

BUCKEYE
VERRADO GRILLE
623-388-3013.
www.ravenatverrado.com.
4242 N. Golf Dr., Buckeye.
Open: Daily for all 3 meals.
Prices: Moderate to expensive.
Cuisine: Eclectic.
Credit Cards: AE, D, MC, V.

Lunch and dinner menus feature an assortment of dishes including Thai chicken salad, barbecued pulled pork sandwich, and pan-roasted duck. Breakfast includes treats like banana walnut pancakes, biscuits and gravy, and the breakfast quesadilla. The golf course setting and patio seating options make this restaurant a relaxing morning or afternoon choice—and breathtaking at sunset.

GLENDALE
A TOUCH OF EUROPEAN CAFÉ
623-847-7119.
7146 N. 57th Dr., Glendale.

Open: Mon.–Wed. 10:30 AM–2:30 PM, Thu.–
Fri. 10:30 AM–7:30 PM, Sat. 2:30–4:30 PM.
Prices: Inexpensive to moderate.
Cuisine: Eastern European.
Credit Cards: AE, D, MC, V.

Located in the historic Caitlin Court District of downtown Glendale, this little café has been discovered by *The New Yorker*. The husband-and-wife team of Waldemor and Malgorzata Okula, originally from Poland, own and operate this café (just five tables!) out of a tiny cottage. Try the borscht, hunter's stew, and pierogi.

BIT-ZEE MAMA'S RESTAURANT

623-931-0562.
www.historic-glendale.net/bitzee_mama's
.htm.
7023 N. 58th Ave., Glendale.
Open: Daily for all 3 meals; closes Mon. at 3 PM, Sun. at 12:30 PM.
Prices: Inexpensive.
Cuisine: Mexican and American.
Credit Cards: AE, MC, V.

Deemed the "Best Mexican Food" by *Phoenix New Times*' Reader's Choice Awards in 2006, Bit-zee Mama's in Historic Downtown Glendale serves good Mexican American fare at affordable prices. Join them Friday and Sunday for live entertainment, and on the second Saturday of each month for Comedy Club. Die-hard breakfast fans have been known to traverse the Valley for their large and delicious breakfast menu.

CUCINA TAGLIANI ITALIAN KITCHEN

602-547-2782.
www.cucinatagliani.com.
17045 N. 59th Ave., #101, Glendale.
Open: Daily for lunch and dinner; closed July 4, Thanksgiving, Christmas Day, New Year's Day.
Prices: Moderate.
Cuisine: Italian American.
Credit Cards: AE, D, MC, V.
Special Features: Happy hour daily 3–7 PM

in the bar only; live music Fri. 7–10 PM on the patio, weather permitting.

This family-owned restaurant has been heralded locally as one of "the best Italian restaurants in the Valley." Tasty, traditional Italian dishes and enormous portions (even the half-sized pasta bowls are fit for two) make this a Valley favorite, and their dessert menu puts them over the top. The chocolate mascarpone cake is absolutely decadent and sized to serve at least three, so bring friends.

GLENDALE GASLIGHT INN

623-934-9119.
www.GlendaleGaslightInn.com.
5747 W. Glendale Ave, Glendale.
Open: Daily for breakfast, lunch, appetizers, and dessert.
Prices: Moderate.
Cuisine: American.
Credit Cards: AE, D, MC, V.
Special Features: Happy hour Mon.–Fri. 4–7 PM.

The Coffee House serves coffees, teas, salads, and sandwiches. Evenings the fare is light, including sandwiches, appetizers, and a full dessert menu. Wine & Jazz Bar features quality local talent Thu.–Sat. nights. Happy hour brings you half off house wines and all beers. Reservations are recommended for jazz events.

HAUS MURPHY'S

623-939-2480.
www.hausmurphys.com.
5739 W. Glendale Avenue, Glendale.
Open: Tue.–Sun. for lunch and dinner.
Prices: Moderate.
Cuisine: German.
Credit Cards: AE, D, MC, V.

Lovers of German fare will find this a restaurant after their own hearts. The schnitzel, sausage, sauerbraten, and German beers have Valley visitors coming back year after year. The beer garden offers a wonderful outdoor dining experience. Enjoy live entertainment Fri.–Sun. nights. And don't forget to try the apple strudel.

MAHARAJA PALACE

602-547-1000.
5775 W. Bell Rd., Glendale.
Open: Daily for lunch Mon.–Fri. 11:30 AM–2:30 PM, Sat. 11:30 AM–3 PM; dinner starting at 5 PM.
Prices: Inexpensive.
Cuisine: Indian.
Credit Cards: AE, D, DC, MC, V.

Friendly staff, great traditional Indian food, and a laid-back atmosphere make this restaurant a local favorite. If you haven't had tandoori cuisine before, try the lunch buffet; you can sample the fare and find your favorites. Weekends tend to get crowded.

PETE'S FISH & CHIPS

623-937-6001.
www.petesfishandchips.com.
5516 W. Glendale Ave., Glendale.
Open: Mon.–Sat. 10 AM–10:30 PM.
Prices: Inexpensive.
Cuisine: Fast food.
Credit Cards: No; cash only.

Pete's has been serving fried fish, shrimp, oysters, scallops, burgers, dogs, and more to the Valley since 1947. It's all tasty without being too greasy; portions are nicely sized, and prices are good. Pete's has been a local favorite for more than 60 years, so they must be doing something right! Well-kept property and friendly staff; drive through or sit on the patio. There are seven additional locations Valley-wide, including Phoenix, Tempe, and Mesa.

SEOUL JUNG RESTAURANT

623-842-0400.
10040 N. 43rd Ave., Glendale.
Open: Daily for lunch and dinner.
Prices: Moderate to expensive.
Cuisine: Korean.
Credit Cards: V, MC.

This restaurant may be hard to find—it's located off 43rd Ave. in a mini mall—but it's worth the search. Barbecue your meat on their tabletop grills or order a dish from the kitchen. The menu is extensive and the food well loved by those who know good Korean fare when they taste it.

SIAMESE KITCHEN

623-931-3229.
4352 W. Olive Ave., Glendale.
Open: Daily for lunch and dinner.
Prices: Inexpensive.
Cuisine: Thai.
Credit Cards: MC, V.

This storefront restaurant specializes in dishes spiced to your liking.

SPICERY, THE

623-937-6534.
7141 N. 59th Ave., Glendale.
Open: Mon.–Sat. for breakfast, lunch, and tea; Sunday brunch.
Cuisine: American.
Prices: Inexpensive.
Credit Cards: Call.

This converted Victorian home serves homemade soups, breads, and desserts.

THEE PITT'S AGAIN

602-996-7488.
www.theepittsagain.com.
5558 W. Bell Rd., Glendale.
Open: Daily for lunch and dinner.
Prices: Inexpensive to moderate.
Cuisine: American.
Credit Cards: AE, D, MC, V.

This 1950s-style restaurant specializes in barbecued meats and strange fried delicacies like fried pickles or rattlesnake, along with pulled pork and beef brisket. You can even get a fried Twinkie.

ZANG ASIAN BISTRO

623-847-8888.
6835 N. 58th Dr., Glendale.

Open: Lunch and dinner Sun.–Thu. 11 AM–9 PM, Fri.–Sat. 11 AM–9:50 PM; closed Mon.
Prices: Inexpensive to moderate.
Cuisine: Asian.
Credit Cards: AE, D, MC, V.

The Asian-influenced dishes here are inspired by the travels of owner David Chang and global experiences of executive chef Kim Ming Poon. Located in Historic Downtown Glendale, this restaurant features fine dining for a pleasant price. Dishes reflect the cuisines of China, Japan, Indonesia, Malaysia, Singapore, and Vietnam.

GOODYEAR
ARTURO'S MEXICAN FOOD RESTAURANT AND LOUNGE
623-932-0241.
13290 W. Van Buren, Goodyear.
Open: Mon.–Sat. for lunch and dinner.
Prices: Inexpensive.
Cuisine: Mexican.
Credit Cards: AE, MC, V.

This family-owned and -operated Mexican restaurant has served the West Valley Sonoran-style fare for 50 years.

LITCHFIELD PARK
ARIZONA KITCHEN (AT WIGWAM RESORT)
623-935-3811.
www.wigwamresort.com.
300 Wigwam Blvd., Litchfield Park.
Open: Tue.–Sat. for all 3 meals; Sun.–Mon., lunch and breakfast only.
Prices: Moderate to very expensive.
Cuisine: Southwestern.
Credit Cards: AE, D, MC, V.

This award-winning restaurant at the Wigwam Resort serves Sonoran-inspired dishes by chef de cuisine Patrick Gaudet. The incredibly flavorful menu includes entrées like king salmon, Kobe short ribs, and chile rubbed maple leaf duck. Staff are attentive, and the setting uniquely is Southwest, with an old adobe fireplace and Native American pottery.

PEORIA
DILLON'S
623-979-5353.
www.dillonsrestaurant.com.
8706 W. Thunderbird Rd., Peoria.
Open: Mon.–Fri. for lunch, daily for dinner.
Prices: Moderate.
Cuisine: Home-style.
Credit Cards: AE, D, MC, V.
Other Locations: Arrowhead Mall, Glendale; Dillon's Grand is located at Sun City Grand in Surprise.

Specializing in barbecued and smoked meats, Dillon's serves a home-style menu complete with homemade cobbler and award-winning onion rings. Locals love the food and the atmosphere.

MCDUFFY'S PEORIA
623-334-5000.
www.mcduffys.com/peoria.
15814 N. 83rd Ave., Peoria.
Open: Daily for lunch and dinner.
Prices: Inexpensive.
Cuisine: American.
Credit Cards: AE, MC, V.
Special Features: Wed.–Sat. nights McDuffy's turns into a club complete with DJ; dance till the cows come home (2 AM in the Valley).

This 18-year-old tradition, originally located off Tempe's Mill Ave., has moved to the West Valley. Off-track betting, 90-plus televisions and jumbo screens, and close proximity to the Peoria Sports Complex make this a favorite of sports lovers. Full menu of standard American food; check out their lunch specials.

PALO VERDE PIZZERIA
623-979-9696.
8350 W. Paradise Lane, Peoria.
Open: Tue.–Sun. for lunch and dinner.
Prices: Inexpensive to moderate.
Cuisine: Pizza.
Credit Cards: Major credit cards.

It's a pizza place that serves great pizza. Close proximity to the Peoria Sports Complex makes it a favorite before or after a spring training game or event.

Wine Bar

SWEET O WINE AND CHOCOLATE LOUNGE
623-877-3898
www.sweetlounge.com
9380 W. Westgate Blvd., Suite D101, Glendale

Located at the newly opened WestGate City Center in Glendale, this fun little wine bar hits all the sweet spots—chocolate, wine, panini...who needs dinner? And the location is perfect—catch a movie, a hockey or football game, or a concert, or just relax after a day of shopping.

Food Purveyors

AJ'S FINE FOODS
623-537-2300 or 888-510-0764.
www.ajsfinefoods.com.
20050 N. 67th Ave., Glendale.

AJ's is an upscale market selling gourmet products, including made-to-order sushi, high-quality meats, fish, cheeses, and ready-made meals. You will also find an extensive selection of fine wines and liquors. Staff are wonderfully helpful in picking the right items for a special meal or the perfect wine to complement dinner. AJ's also features a selection of some of the best desserts around. Stop by for a quick lunch or pick up a gourmet meal ready to go. Additional stores located throughout the Valley. Open daily.

Health Food Stores

HI-HEALTH
602-547-0954.
www.hihealth.com.
5890 West Bell, #108, Glendale.

Hi-Health features quality health foods and nutritional supplements. Stores are located throughout the Valley, including Peoria, Sun City, Goodyear, and Surprise.

SPROUTS FARMERS MARKET
623-487-0330.
www.sprouts.com.
5130 W. Peoria Ave., Glendale

Arizona is the home of Sprouts Farmers Markets. This quickly growing retailer features farm-fresh produce, often from local growers, natural meats, cheeses, vitamins, and supplements all at reasonable prices. In the West Valley, Sprouts can also be found in Surprise, Avondale, and Peoria: additional locations throughout the Valley. Open daily.

Bakeries

La Fama Mexican Bakery (623-931-1460; 5328 W. Glendale Ave., Glendale). Sweet breads and traditional Mexican pastries.

La Purisima Bakery (623-842-1400; 4533 W. Glendale Ave., Glendale). Voted Best Mexican Bakery by *Phoenix New Times'* readers in 2000, this shop features traditional goodies like *pan dulce* (sweet bread), *galletas* (cookies), and fruit-filled empanadas.

My Daddy's Bakery and Café (623-583-3677; 11677 W. Bell Road, #1, Surprise). With a name like this, you have to find out more! Locals love the sandwiches, cakes, and other treats.

New York West Pastry and Bake Shop (623-583-7620; 10101 Grand Ave., Sun City). The name says it all: New York–style pastries and baked goods here in the West. Even New York natives can't tell the difference. Well...

Panaderia El Ranchito (623-925-2906; 534 E. Western Ave., Avondale). Located in Old Town Avondale, this little Mexican bakery features cakes by the slice and cookies.

CULTURE

Cinema

Glendale Drive-In (623-939-9715; www.drive-ins.com/theater/aztglen; 5650 N. 55th Ave., Glendale). Call for showtimes.

Historic Places

PEORIA ARIZONA HISTORICAL SOCIETY

623-487-8030.
10304 N. 83rd Ave., PO Box 186, Peoria 85380.
Open: Tue. and Sun. 1–3 PM, Wed. 10 AM–noon, Thu.–Sat. 10 AM–2 PM; closed Mon.
Admission: Free, but donations accepted.

This museum—converted from a two-room school—preserves and shares the history of the area. Its exhibits include antique dolls, a doctor's buggy, old quilts, and a 1900 kitchen corner. Wander the blacksmith shop, dairy, and other exhibits as part of the agricultural museum while you await your scheduled tour of the 1939 jail—original cells and all.

SAHUARO RANCH

623-930-2820.
www.ci.glendale.az.us/ParksandRecreation/SahuaroRanchPark.cfm.
9802 N. 59th Ave., Glendale.

William Henry Bartlett homesteaded Sahuaro Ranch in 1886, following the completion of the Arizona Canal in 1885, which opened up 100,000 acres of desert land to irrigation and farming. By 1891 he controlled more than 2,000 acres and was considered one of the largest ranchers in the area. In its heyday Sahuaro Ranch was a beautiful, parklike estate with rosebushes, palm trees, and a pond with a bridge leading to an island gazebo. At one time or another alfalfa, fig trees, citrus trees, and cotton had been planted on the original 640-acre farm. In 1927 Richard W. Smith purchased the ranch and planted citrus, pecan, and date groves. When Smith died in 1944, he left the ranch to his son Richard S. Smith, and in 1966 the city of Glendale began the 11-year process of purchasing 80 of those original 640 acres. Today the city's holdings include 17 acres that have been placed on the National Register of Historic Places, including the ranch's first permanent dwelling—the Adobe House built in 1887, as well as the original fruit-packing shed, foreman's house, barnyard, and guest house, all built in the latter part of the 19th century. The ranch is located next to Glendale Community College and provides a softball field, volleyball courts, soccer fields, and a dog park to the surrounding community. For historical tours, call 623-930-4200.

Historic/Walking Tours

THAT THURSDAY THING IN GLENDALE

Glendale Visitor Center 623-930-4500
www.visitglendale.com
Open: 3rd Thu. of the month 6–9 PM.
Admission: Free.

Visit Historic Downtown Glendale on the third Thursday of the month and enjoy live entertainment, free horse-drawn carriage rides, art, and more. There is usually a theme and free trolley service. Area shops extend their hours, and live entertainment peppers the sidewalks.

Libraries

Glendale Public Library (623-930-3530; TDD/TTY 623-842-3760; www.ci.glendale.az.us/Library; 5959 W. Brown St., Glendale). Open Mon.–Thu. 9 AM–9 PM, Fri. 9 AM–6 PM, Sat. 9 AM–5 PM, Sun. 1–5 PM.

Peoria Public Library, Main Branch (623-773-7555; www.peoriaaz.com/library/library_main.asp; 8463 W. Monroe St., Peoria). Open Sun. 1–5 PM, Mon.–Thu. 9 AM–8 PM, Fri.–Sat. 9 AM–6 PM.

Surprise Regional Library (602-652-3000; 16089 N. Bullard Ave., Surprise). Open Mon.–Thu. 9 AM–9 PM, Fri.–Sat. 9 AM–5 PM, Sun. 1–5 PM. Free. Surprise Regional Library features a children's library, adult library, multimedia computer lab, and more than 40,000 items in a variety of formats.

Museums

BEAD MUSEUM, THE

623-931-2737; store 623-930-7395.
www.beadmuseumaz.org.
5754 W. Glenn Dr., Glendale.
Open: Mon.–Sat. 10 AM–5 PM, Thu. 10 AM–8 PM, Sun. 11 AM–4 PM.
Admission: $4 adults, $2 ages 4–12; members free. Free to all Thu. after 5 PM.

Located one block north of Glendale Ave. at 58th Ave. (next to the Glendale Civic Center) in Historic Downtown Glendale, the Bead Museum is home to an international collection of more than 100,000 beads and beaded artifacts. These are not your average beads—many items are handmade, ceremonial artifacts and representative of amazing talent and cultural traditions from all over the world. Guided tours, group tours, and workshops are available; call the museum educator to schedule tours and workshops in advance.

CHALLENGER SPACE CENTER

623-322-2001.
www.azchallenger.org.
21170 N. 83rd Ave., Peoria.
Open: Mon.–Fri. 9 AM–4 PM, Sat. 10 AM–4 PM; closed Sun. and major holidays.
Admission: $6 adults, $4 ages 6–18 and 55-plus; children 5 and under are free, as are Challenger members.

The Challenger Space Center features, among other exhibits, the Columbia Shuttle Memorial Display in honor of the crew members who perished February 1, 2003; a meteorite exhibit on loan from ASU's Center for Meteorite Study: and a display depicting the history of the space program, While they focus on educational programming, they also offer a variety of opportunities for the general public, including a simulated space mission, planetarium shows, and telescope classes and stargazing events for families at various times throughout the year. The center is a large white building located on 83rd Ave. adjacent to

Charming shops line the sidewalks in Historic Downtown Glendale.

Sunrise Mountain High School. To get there from the rest of the Valley, take the Loop 101 (which you can access in the East Valley from I-10 on the south or I-17 on the north) to the Union Hills exit, then go north on 83rd Ave. From Peoria, Glendale, or nearby Sun City, you can take surface streets to 83rd Ave. north.

DEER VALLEY ROCK ART CENTER
623-582-8007.
www.asu.edu/clas/shesc/dvrac.
3711 W. Deer Valley Rd., Glendale.
Open: Tue.–Fri. 8 AM–2 PM (May–Sep.); Tue.–Fri. 9 AM–5 PM (Oct.–Apr.); Sat. 9 AM–5 PM, Sun. noon–5 PM; closed Mon.
Admission: $5 adults, $3 seniors and students, $2 ages 6–12; under 5 free.

A part of Arizona State University's College of Liberal Arts and Sciences, the Deer Valley Rock Art Center is protector of the Valley's largest concentration of Native American rock art. It features an interpretive trail that will take you among hundreds of ancient drawings called petroglyphs; the 47-acre facility encompasses a museum, archaeological site, nature preserve, and research center. The museum provides historical information about the drawings and the area. The trail closes half an hour before the museum. Guided tours start at 10 AM on Saturday, Oct.–Apr.; free with museum admission; reservations not required.

WEST VALLEY ART MUSEUM
623-972-0635.
www.wvam.org.
17420 N. Ave. of the Arts (114th Ave. and Bell Rd.), Surprise.
Open: Tue.–Sun. 10 AM–4 PM; closed major holidays.
Admission: $7 adults, $2 students with ID; 5 and under free.

For more than 25 years the West Valley Art Museum has focused primarily on the visual works of Arizona artists and collections from all cultures.

WILDLIFE WORLD ZOO
623-935-WILD.
www.wildlifeworld.com.
16501 W. Northern Ave., Litchfield Park.
Open: Daily 9 AM–5 PM, including holidays.
Prices: $16.99 plus tax adults, $8.99 plus tax ages 3–12; under 2 free.

The Valley's largest collection of exotic animals represents more than 400 species, including white tigers, white rhinos, jaguars, giraffes, zebras, monkeys, and leopards. The zoo features three indoor exhibits for reptiles, small mammals, and aquariums, and three interactive shows. You can also enjoy the African Train Ride, Australian Boat Ride, Exotic Animal Carousel, and Wildlife Sky Ride. There is a café on site and free parking. The park's latest additions—Nash (yes . . . named after Phoenix Sun star Steve Nash) and Raja—are baby tigers; you may have seen Raja on *Good Morning America*. Note that no credit cards are accepted; there is an ATM on site.

Stage

ARIZONA BROADWAY THEATRE

623-776-8400.

www.azbroadwaytheatre.com.

7701 W. Paradise Lane, Peoria.

This new 400-seat dinner-theater auditorium (found just off Bell Rd. and the Loop 101, next to the Peoria Sports Complex) is the northwest Valley's answer to professional theater. Regaling patrons with classical Broadway musicals and an elegant dinner menu, Arizona Broadway Theatre is a popular and entertaining venue. Tue.–Sat., dinner begins at 6:15 PM, and shows at 8; Sat. matinee lunches begin at 12:15 PM, with shows at 2. Sunday brunch begins at 11:15 AM, with a 1 PM showtime, while Sunday Twilight dinners begin at 5:15 PM, shows at 7. Prices ($43–53) are per person and include dinner, show, and tax.

RECREATION

Maricopa County Parks System (602-506-2930; www.maricopa.gov/parks) includes 10 parks offering a variety of recreational activities and camping conditions. These range from the developed sites at Estrella Mountain and Lake Pleasant Regional Parks—which offer electrical/water hookups, dump stations, restrooms, picnic tables, and grills—to primitive sites at Buckeye Regional Park, with no amenities at all.

Before you go camping, it is important to familiarize yourself with the parks and their rules, especially those related to fire safety. Maricopa County limits stays to 14 consecutive days and often closes during the very hot summer months of June, July, and August. The parks are located far enough away from the city that you can enjoy the outdoors, and many offer beautiful examples of the Sonoran Desert, including the colorful sunrises and sunsets that are a must for any visitor. Camping fees are per day, nonrefundable, and must be paid in advance. Tent and RV rates are $18 for developed sites (electrical/water hookups, dump station, restrooms, picnic tables, and grills), $10 for semi-developed sites (restrooms, picnic tables, and grills—available at White Tank and Lake Pleasant only), and $5 for shoreline camping, which offers no amenities and is available at Lake Pleasant only. Sites are available on a first-come, first-served basis.

ESTRELLA MOUNTAIN REGIONAL PARK

623-932-3911.

www.maricopa.gov/parks/estrella.

14805 W. Vineyard Ave., Goodyear.

Open: Daily, Sun.–Thu. 6 AM–8 PM, Fri.–Sat. 6 AM–10 PM.

This regional park, located south of I-10 close to Phoenix International Raceway, covers almost 20,000 acres and provides space for camping, hiking, biking, running, horseback riding, fishing, golfing, and picnicking. Campsites are the developed kind, which means you'll find water and electrical hookups along with the typical picnic table and fire ring. The park features more than 30 trails that can accommodate hikers, mountain bikers, and horseback riders as well as a series of competitive tracks totaling 13 miles. The tracks are usually used by mountain bikers; however, horseback riders and runners have been known to use the trails for training purposes. The park recommends the technical loop (2.86

Outdoor shopping at Westgate City Center.

miles) for experts only. The park's web site provides an excellent set of trail maps that you can print.

Located at the confluence of the Gila and Agua Fria Rivers, the park features catch-and-release fishing along the banks of the Gila River. (See Fishing in the Phoenix chapter.) Renovated in 1998, the **Estrella Mountain Golf Course** features a traditional parkland-style par-71 course for golfers of all levels. For more information, visit www.estrella-golf.com or call 623-932-3714.

LAKE PLEASANT REGIONAL PARK
Contact station 928-501-1710; operations center 602-372-7460.
www.maricopa.gov/parks/lake_pleasant.
41835 N. Castle Hot Springs Rd., Morristown.

Lake Pleasant Regional Park, located in the northwest Valley approximately 15 miles north of Sun City, provides developed campsites with electrical and water hookups, dump station, restrooms, picnic tables, and grills. In addition to camping, the park offers boating, fishing, swimming, and hiking trails. Call for more information and to obtain permits. Lake Pleasant is a popular site during the hotter months and an excellent escape from urban life during the cooler part of the year.

Lake Pleasant provides the only shoreline camping experience (for $5) of the county parks. Boaters can enter this expansive body of water from one of two launching ramps. Both have restroom facilities and paved parking lots; they're functional to a water elevation of 1,600 feet. The 10-lane parking area allows for 480 vehicles, 355 vehicles with trailers, and 124 cars. The four-lane ramp is located at the north end of the lake; the parking area allows for 112 vehicles with boat trailers.

WHITE TANK MOUNTAIN REGIONAL PARK

623-935-2505.
www.maricopa.gov/parks/white_tank.
13025 N. White Tank Mountain Rd., Waddell.
Open: Daily, Sun.–Thu. 6 AM–8 PM, Fri.–Sat. 6 AM–10 PM.

At 30,000 acres, this regional park is Maricopa County's largest, and provides the mountainous backdrop on the Valley's west side. It features 25 miles of multiuse trails as well as a 10-mile competitive track designed for fast-paced mountain bikers, runners, and horseback riders at a trot/gallop. White Tank's 40 campsites are considered semi-primitive; there are no electrical or water hookups, but grills, picnic tables, and comfort stations with showers are available. See above for additional details about camping in Maricopa County's regional parks. Note that Olive Ave. becomes White Tank Mountain Rd., where the park is located.

White Tank Riding Stables offers guided riding tours Nov.–Apr. One-hour rides start at $33 per person; private rides are available for $60 per hour, and children 7 and under can ride a pony for 15 minutes ($15 per child). Moonlight rides and wagon rides are available. The stables are located at 20300 W. Olive Ave. in Waddell. Call 623-935-7455 or visit www.whitetanksriding.com for more information.

THUNDERBIRD CONSERVATION PARK

623-930-2820.
www.glendaleaz.com.
59th Avenue just south of Pinnacle Peak Rd., Glendale.
Open: Daily sunrise to sunset.

Once part of the Maricopa County Regional Parks System, Thunderbird Conservation Park is now owned and operated by the city of Glendale. This 1,100-plus-acre park features 20 miles of trails; activities include hiking, mountain biking, running, horseback riding, picnicking, and four viewing blinds—the better to catch a glimpse of desert fauna. Three of these blinds are accessible from trails, while a fourth is located off 59th Ave. and handicapped accessible.

XERISCAPE BOTANICAL GARDEN

623-930-3596.
www.glendaleaz.com/waterconservation.
5959 W. Brown, at the Glendale Main Library.
Open: Daily.

Since 1990, the award-winning garden has grown to 4 acres of 400 plant species.

SURPRISE AQUATIC CENTER

623-266-4644.

15831 N. Bullard, Surprise.

Open: Late May–early August, Mon.–Fri. noon–8 PM, Sat. 10 AM–6 PM, Sun. noon–6 PM.

The Surprise Aquatic Center features a zero-depth area with water play features, flume slide, tunnel slide, vortex whirlpool, eight-lane competition pool, and diving well with two 1-meter boards. Surprise residents pay 50 cents ages 17 and under, $1.50 adults; please provide proof of residency. The nonresident fee is $5 per person.

Golf

See chapter 9, Golf Courses & Spas.

SHOPPING

Shopping Malls

Westcor Arrowhead Towne Center (623-979-7777; www.westcor.com; 7700 W. Arrowhead Towne Center Dr., Glendale). Arrowhead Towne Center (at West Bell Rd. at the Loop 101) features more than 170 shops, dining options, and department stores including JCPenney, Mervyn's, and Dillard's; a 14-theater cinema; and comfortable bathrooms and nursing rooms for families. Check out the Peoria Nissan Town Center play area with your little ones.

Westgate City Center (off the Loop 101 on the west side of town, south of Glendale Rd.; www.westgateaz.com). Located adjacent to University of Phoenix Cardinal Stadium and Glendale Arena (Jobing.com Arena), this colorful, futuristic plaza features stories-high billboards, water and light shows, and an urban mix of retail, office, and living space.

Specialty Stores

HISTORIC DOWNTOWN GLENDALE

Bags & Beans (623-847-2423; bagsandbeans@hotmail.com; 7003 N. 58th Ave., at the rear). This chic boutique features clothing, purses, jewelry, and other accessories, not to mention a full-service coffee bar.

ZinGáro Home Accents (623-934-0999; www.shopzingaro.com; 5746 W. Glendale Ave.). Open Mon.–Sat. 10 AM–6 PM, Sun. 11 AM–5 PM; summer/holiday hours may vary. ZinGáro features artist works from 22 states (including Arizona) and 49 countries. These unique pieces cover a wide range of styles and media. Find art glass, sculptures, pottery, permanent botanicals, clocks, crystals, and Arizona's well-known Soleri wind bells. Shipping service and complimentary gift wrap are available.

A Mad Hatter's Antiques, Collectibles, Home Décor (623-931-1991 or 866-931-1991; www.amadhatters.com; 5734 W. Glendale Ave.). Open daily; online shopping. This center offers 20,000 square feet of antiques and collectibles, vintage and current. You'll find Christmas decor year-round; home decor styles include Classic Traditional, Victorian, French Country, Tuscan, Cottage, Retro, Primitive, Country, and Western Lodge. Also special details for baby's or children's rooms.

The Apple Tree (623-435-8486; www.appletreecountryshop.com; 5811 W. Glendale Ave.). Open daily. One of Historic Downtown Glendale's oldest and largest antiques and home decor stores, The Apple Tree features furniture, folk art, prints, rugs, lighting, linens, and a huge selection of gifts, candles, and collectibles. They specialize in country primitives and quality reproductions.

Cerreta Candy Co., Inc. (623-930-1000; 5345 W. Glendale Ave.). Handmade candies—see chapter 3 (p. 95) for information on tours.

Comforts of Home (623-435-6813; www.historic-glendale.net/comforts_of_home.htm; 7162 N. 57th Dr.). Open Mon.–Sat. 10 AM–5 PM; holiday/summer hours may vary. This charming cottage shop features unique gifts, baskets, and Arizona artists and products.

Glass Creations (623-939-5966, 7011 N. 58th Ave.). Open daily; extended holiday hours. This little shop across from Murphy Park specializes in American-made art glass and features the largest selection of Fenton Art Glass in Arizona. Find just the right curio or accent piece for your collection.

Sanctuary of Sacred Space (623-934-1324; 5807 W. Myrtle Ave.). Open Tue.–Fri. noon–5 PM, Sat.–Sun. 10 AM–5 PM. New Age gifts, supplies, services, classes, and presentations are offered in this charming home built in 1925.

SPECTATOR SPORTS

The West Valley is quickly becoming *the* place to be if you're a fan of professional sports. The Phoenix Coyotes (NHL), Arizona Cardinals (NFL), NASCAR's two annual events at Phoenix International Raceway, and the Tostitos Fiesta Bowl (NCAA football) have pushed the West Valley to the forefront of the Valley sports scene.

The **Arizona Cardinals** play Sep.–Dec. After sharing ASU's Sun Devil Stadium for years, the Cards have finally moved into University of Phoenix Stadium (1 Cardinals Dr., Glendale). For game schedules and ticket information, visit www.azcardinals.com or call 602-379-0102. The **Phoenix Coyotes** play at Jobing.com Arena (formerly Glendale Arena). For game dates and ticket information, contact 623-850-PUCK or www.phoenixcoyotes.com. Indy Racing League in March and NASCAR events in April and November take place at **Phoenix International Raceway** (602-252-2227; www.phoenixintlraceway.com). The **Tostitos Fiesta Bowl** (480-350-0911. www.tostitosfiestabowl.com)—now at University of Phoenix Stadium in Glendale—typically falls in late December or early January.

JOBING.COM ARENA

623-772-3200.
www.glendalearenaaz.com.
9400 W. Maryland Ave., Glendale.

Located between Glendale and Maryland Avenues, Jobing.com Arena (formerly the Glendale Arena) is east of the Loop 101 (or Agua Fria Freeway, as it's known in the West Valley). The arena is home to National Hockey League's Phoenix Coyotes and the National Lacrosse League's Arizona Sting. You will also find a variety of music and entertainment events throughout the year. Past events have included country music stars Tim McGraw and Faith Hill, pop vocalist John Mayer, and the amazing acrobatic and musical performances of Cirque du Soleil.

The ticket office is open Mon.–Fri. 10 AM–6 PM; it's open Sat. 10 AM–4 PM for on-sale or ticketed events only. Tickets can be purchased through Ticketmaster.com or Ticketmaster Charge-By-Phone at 480-784-4444 or directly through Jobing.com Arena: 623-772-3800.

The Home of the Arizona Cardinals

University of Phoenix Stadium in Glendale, Arizona—home of the Arizona Cardinals—opened in August 2006. This amazing feat of technology and horticulture was designed by internationally known architect Peter Eisenman in conjunction with HOK Sport, Hunt Construction Group, and Urban Earth Design. Intended to capture its desert home, the stadium's exterior skin represents a barrel cactus, while the alternating panels of metal reflect the ever-changing desert light.

Its 18.9-million-pound retractable field tray makes natural grass play possible, even in the desert. But this isn't the only thing that makes the new stadium the NFL's "most technologically advanced." Try the 650 high-definition televisions, two high-resolution video scoreboards, 88 luxury lofts, three party suites, 7,500 club seats, two 39,000-square-foot VIP Club Lounges, full air-conditioning, two *huge* noise "thermometers" that gauge how loud the crowd is, and, amazingly, a retractable translucent roof that brings the outdoors in without the full blast of the Phoenix sun. On top of it all, this $455 million stadium is protected by 1/16th inch of 'Bird-Air" fabric strong enough to withstand 11,000 pounds per square foot!

In addition to hosting crazy Cardinals' fans, it has also welcomed the Monster Truck Rally, Tostitos Fiesta Bowl, and BCS National Championship Game, among many other events, concerts, and trade shows. In February 2008 the University of Phoenix Stadium and Glendale will host Super Bowl XLII. Tours are available daily depending on event schedules; for more information, see Spectator Sports.

The Arizona Cardinals have moved into the University of Phoenix Stadium.

To order Coyotes tickets, call 480-563-PUCK or order through Ticketmaster. Arizona Sting tickets can be purchased via Ticketmaster or the arena.

UNIVERSITY OF PHOENIX STADIUM

623-433-7100; tour hotline 623-433-7165.
www.azcardinalsstadium.com.
1 Cardinals Dr., Glendale.
Hours: Mon.–Fri. 10 AM–6 PM, Sat. 9 AM–2:30 PM on non-event days; on event days, hours vary by event.
Admission: Event tickets vary by event; tour tickets are $7 adults, $5 ages 4–12, 65-plus, and military with ID; children 3 and under are free.

University of Phoenix Stadium—the latest and greatest football stadium in the National Football League—is home to the Arizona Cardinals and will host the Super Bowl in 2008. In addition to football, you'll find such events here as the Phoenix Bridal Show, the Monster Truck Rally, and the Tostitos Fiesta Bowl.

To tour this state-of-the-art facility, purchase tickets via Ticketmaster (480-784-4444) or at the University of Phoenix Stadium box office (602-379-0102). Tours run about 1½ hours and require about a mile of walking, so wear comfortable shoes. Tours are wheelchair accessible, and begin at 12:30 and 2:30 PM Thu.–Fri. and 12:30 and 2:30 PM on Sat., schedule permitting.

Cactus League Spring Training

The West Valley is home to 4 of the 12 MLB teams during the season of spring training. The Kansas City Royals and Texas Rangers train at Surprise Stadium, while the San Diego Padres and Seattle Mariners make the Peoria Sports Complex home for the month of March. For more information, visit www.cactus-league.com or teams' individual sites. Tickets start at $5 and are available online on the web, on site, or by phone. Please note that most stadiums do not allow food and beverage, large bags, or coolers.

KANSAS CITY ROYALS

623-594-5600 or 480-784-4444.
www.kcroyals.com.

TEXAS RANGERS

texas.rangers.mlb.com.
Surprise Stadium, 15960 N. Bullard Ave., Surprise.

Built in 2002, Surprise Stadium hosts the Kansas City Royals and the Texas Rangers; each team has its own clubhouse. The stadium is located 1.5 miles west of the intersection of Bell Rd. and Grand Ave. (US 60). Bullard Ave. is located off Bell Rd., 1.5 miles west of Grand Ave., or 2.5 miles east of the Loop 303.

SEATTLE MARINERS

www.mariners.org.

SAN DIEGO PADRES

www.padres.com.
Peoria Sports Complex, 16101 N. 83rd Ave., Peoria.
623-878-4337 or 800-409-1511.

The Peoria Sports Complex hosts both the San Diego Padres and the Seattle Mariners. From I-17 north (Black Canyon Freeway), exit at Bell Rd.; go west and turn left onto 83rd Ave. The complex is 0.5 mile ahead on the left.

7

SEDONA

The Red Rock Vortex

About 115 miles north of Phoenix along I-17—tucked among towering monoliths, sandwiched between the Prescott and Coconino National Forests, and straddling the lush greenery of Oak Creek—is Sedona. Named after the wife of T. C. Schnebly, in collaboration with the US Postal Service, the city has become synonymous with the rich hues and breathtaking scenery of redrock country. Like the rest of the state, Sedona is a unique combination of mountainous terrain, beautiful weather, and incredible scenery. But the vibrant contrast of fire-red rocks, lush green vegetation, and sapphire-blue skies make for an awe-inspiring experience unlike anything you've ever seen. Take one look and you'll stop wondering why *USA Weekend* named Sedona the most beautiful place in the United States.

Once an economic and agricultural center, Sedona and surrounding areas supplied produce to the mining town of Jerome, the military site at Camp Verde, and Flagstaff, less than 30 miles north. The area was first settled by the Sinagua and later the Yavapai and Apache. Between 1876 and 1901, as people moved west, individuals and families settled among the towering red rocks and forests of piñon, juniper, and cypress trees along Oak Creek, building irrigation ditches, planting crops and orchards, and establishing the trails and dirt paths that later become the roads into and around the red rocks.

In 1901 T. C. Schnebly and his wife, Sedona—lured by enchanting tales of this place—built a home and settled close to where present-day Los Abrigados Resort is located. In 1902, as numerous complaints about slow mail delivery service reached T. C., he decided to establish a post office. Stories hold that he battled with the USPS over names—Schnebly Station, Red Rock Crossing, and Oak Creek Station are said to be among his choices—before, at the suggestion of his brother, submitting his wife Sedona's name. The postal service must have liked the idea, too.

Today Sedona annually welcomes four million visitors who want to experience the area's incredible beauty firsthand. Yet visual pleasure is not all that the area has to offer—though it's more than enough. You'll also find an endless number of hiking trails, jeep tours, art galleries, shops, restaurants, golf courses, and spas, as well as plenty of places to take in the view.

Many who visit, however, wonder if there's even more. Simultaneously a place of activity and calm, Sedona seems to infuse visitors with a peaceful tranquility. Amid all the strolling tourists and bustle of activity, you can find pockets of quietude; moments to pause, look up at the surrounding buttes and mesas, and know that you are somewhere special. Explana-

Bell Rock at Sedona.

tions abound as to what makes Sedona unique—the metaphysical power of its vortexes, the intense electromagnetic energy given off by all that oxidized iron (the red in the rocks), or simply the clean air and beautiful views. Wherever the power originates, visitors seem to agree that Sedona is an uplifting experience.

TRANSPORTATION

Phoenix to Sedona

Option 1: Sedona is a mere 2-hour, 113-mile drive from the Valley. For the most straight-forward route, take I-17 north to exit 298. Pick up AZ 179 and continue for about 14 miles, then turn right onto AZ 89A into Sedona.

Option 2: Take I-17 north to exit 289; turn left onto AZ 260, and continue west to AZ 89A. Turn right onto 89A and proceed to Sedona. This alternate route, which will take you just east of the towns of Cottonwood and Clarkdale, offers an expansive view of the red rocks as they come into view on the horizon. It also takes you through the more residential part of Sedona. (See if you can find the not-so-golden arches as you head through town. A city ordinance requires that businesses color-coordinate with the scenery—even McDonald's!)

Option 3: For the most roundabout and scenic route, turn off I-17 at exit 262; take AZ 69 west (toward Cordes Junction Rd./Prescott) all the way to Fain Rd. Turn right onto Fain and continue to AZ 89A. The road is winding with steep sides as you climb through the Prescott

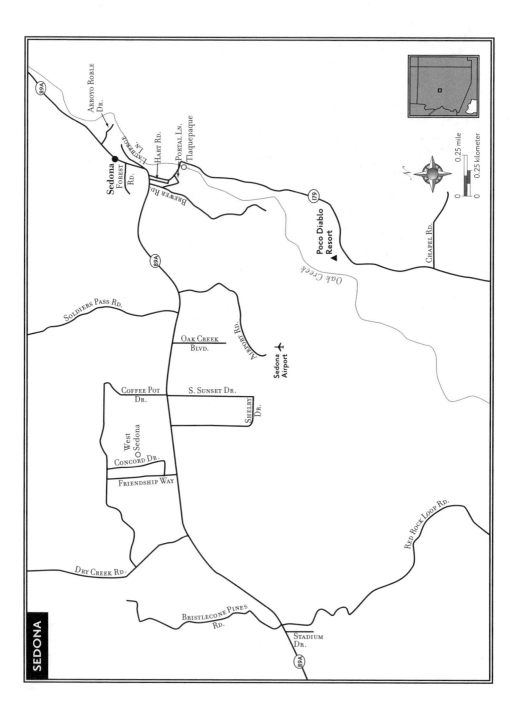

SEDONA

National Forest. You'll leave behind the plains and ascend into ponderosa pines. The area was mined in the early part of the last century—a careful eye (not the driver's) can find tell-tale signs of abandoned mining, including holes in the cliffs, wooden trestles, and even equipment. The views are incredible, with the San Francisco Peaks in the distance and the red rocks of Sedona in the foreground. This route will take you through the old mining town of Jerome (see chapter 8, Side Trips, for more about a visit to Jerome), as well as Clarkdale and Cottonwood, as you descend again. Stay on 89A the rest of the way, the red rocks of Sedona before you.

Option 4: Not interested in driving to Sedona, or not sure what to see when you're there? Consider a guided tour. **Detours of Arizona** offers a wonderful experience complete with historical and geological tidbits. The tours are customizable—if you and your group prefer to shop or visit the various rock formations, for instance, guides can accommodate your needs. They can even drop the shoppers off at one location and take the hikers up to Cathedral Rock, Red Rock Crossing, or Oak Creek Canyon. For more information about Detours and their tour options, see chapter 3.

Getting Around Sedona

Two main highways run through redrock country. AZ 179 diverges from I-17 and heads in a more or less north–south direction from I-17 through the Village of Oak Creek, then past Bell Rock, where it winds its way to the second highway, AZ 89A. AZ89A bisects Sedona on an east–west course from Cottonwood/Clarkdale through West Sedona and Uptown, where it heads north through Slide Rock National Park to Flagstaff. Sedona itself can be divided into three main regions: the Village of Oak Creek south of town on 179; Uptown Sedona, the Main St. shopping area along 89A headed north of the Y; and West Sedona on 89A south of the Y, where you'll find the library, the hospital, grocery shopping, and the Sedona–Oak Creek Airport. *The Y* is what locals call the juncture of AZ 179 and 89A.

By Car

Driving around Sedona is fairly easy—although the roads are windy and the scenery is incredible (distractingly so). A tour company can help you find and access the best places. There are three visitor centers that all feature walls of pamphlets on all of the things to see and do here: off 179 as you head into town off I-17; in Uptown on 89A, south of Forest Ave.; and off 89A just as you head into town from Jerome/Cottonwood/Clarkdale.

By Shuttle

In late 2006 **Sedona RoadRunner** transit service began operating as a free shuttle between the Hillside Galleries on AZ 179 and the city parking lot one block east of Jordan Rd. on the northern end of Uptown (Main St.). Two shuttles provide nonstop service 9 AM–6:30 PM every day except Thanksgiving, Christmas, and New Year's. The shuttles complete alternating 20-minute loops along AZ 179 and AZ 89A and the city parking lot in Uptown. You can catch one at the city parking lot, at several stops along AZ 89A, at Hillside Galleries, or at Tlaquepaque. The last pickup begins Uptown at 6:10 PM, Tlaquepaque at 6:15, and the Hillside Galleries at 6:20; it ends at the city parking lot at 6:30.

LODGING

Sedona offers the weary traveler everything from cabins to bed & breakfasts to upscale resorts. Depending upon how you want to experience the area, you might be interested in some of the top choices available.

Staying in the Village of Oak Creek puts you on the south end of the Sedona area and close to Bell Rock vortex, Northern Bell, and Courthouse Butte, as well as the Staudes Chapel of the Holy Cross off Chapel Road on the east side of AZ 179. To the west of AZ 179, you'll find Castle Rock, the Cathedral Rock vortex, and the Crescent Moon Recreation Center. There are a number of trailheads to pick up in this area as well as shopping centers, golf courses, and an outlet center. Lodging options include the Hilton Sedona Resort & Spa.

In the southern part of Sedona you will find the Poco Diablo Resort, with its golf and spa treatments, in a mostly residential neighborhood. While it's located between the Village of Oak Creek and the shopping of Uptown Sedona and Tlaquepaque Village (just south of the Y on AZ 179), it's a short drive from any of these locales. Farther north on AZ 179 are Los Abrigados; the Hillside, with a number of art galleries and shops; and Tlaquepaque Village, an arts, crafts, and shopping experience. A few trailheads are close by, as are Camel Head and Snoopy Rock; you can pick up Schnebly Hill Rod just east of 179.

Take a right onto AZ 89A at the Y and you'll head into Uptown Sedona, with hundreds of shops, restaurants, art galleries, and attractions. Hotels and resorts include Best Western Arroyo Roble Hotel & Creekside Villas, Amara Creekside Resort, and L'Auberge. There are several trailheads north of Uptown off 89A.

If you turn left at the Y, you will head into West Sedona and its many trailheads; in fact, quite a few of the roads off 89A lead to trailheads. Also look for the famous Sphinx, Capitol Butte, Coffee Pot Rock, and Chimney Rock formations. Hotels in this area include Best Western Inn of Sedona, Hampton Inn Sedona, and Kokopelli Suites.

Credit Cards

The following abbreviations are used for credit card information:

AE: American Express
CB: Carte Blanche
D: Discover Card
DC: Diner's Club
MC: MasterCard
V: Visa

Bed & Breakfasts

There are more than 20 bed & breakfasts in Sedona and surrounding areas. The **Bed & Breakfast Guild of Sedona** (800-915-4442; www.bbsedona.net) is an excellent place to find the best one for you. Each offers a unique experience influenced by its particular location and the personality of its owners; you'll find B&Bs that cater to couples, hiking or golf enthusiasts, nature lovers, or those looking to escape the urban rush. They range in size from 2-bedroom cottages to 16-room inns. Prices can run from $125 a night to almost $1,500, though most fall within the $150–250 range. Amenities vary from site to site, but all B&B members of Premier provide a full breakfast and private bath. Several sites are child-friendly; two welcome pets (the Lodge at Sedona and Grace's Secret Garden); and several feature swimming pools, rooms with two beds, Internet access, and/or outdoor hot tubs.

Hotels

There are number of hotel and resort options available in Sedona and the Village of Oak Creek, ranging from no-frills establishments to luxury resorts complete with golf course and spa. Prices range from less than $100 to $2,000 and depend upon the time of year. Most rooms seem to hover around $200–350.

BEST WESTERN ARROYO ROBLE HOTEL & CREEKSIDE VILLAS

928-282-4001 or 800-773-3662.
www.bestwesternsedona.com.
400 N. AZ 89A, PO Box NN, Sedona 86336.
Prices: $89–350.
Credit Cards: AE, CB, DC, D, MC, V.
Handicapped Access: 1 room.
Pets: No.

Located in Uptown Sedona overlooking Oak Creek Canyon, this five-story Best Western features king and double-queen rooms with a private patio or balcony to enjoy the amazing views. Amenities include private Oak Creek access, indoor–outdoor pools and whirlpools, a weight room, tennis and racquetball courts, and a steam room/sauna.

BEST WESTERN INN OF SEDONA

928-282-3072 or 800-292-6344.
www.innofsedona.com.
1200 W. AZ 89A, Sedona 86336.
Prices: $119–155.
Credit Cards: AE, D, MC, V.
Handicapped Access: 1 room.
Pets: Pet rooms available.

Located in West Sedona, this award-winning hotel offers incredible views of Sedona's red rocks from its outdoor pool and spa. It features recently upgraded two-bed queen and king rooms, some with fireplace. Amenities include free Internet access and continental breakfast; vacation packages are available.

HAMPTON INN—SEDONA

928-282-4700.
www.hamptoninn.com.
1800 W. AZ 89A, Sedona 86336.
Prices: $149–159.
Credit Cards: AE, CB, DC, D, MC, V.
Handicapped Access: Yes.
Pets: No.

This 56-room hotel in West Sedona features an outdoor heated pool and whirlpool. The rooms have microwave and refrigerator; complimentary high-speed Internet access is available, and a free deluxe continental buffet is offered daily.

KOKOPELLI SUITES

800-789-7393; reservations 928-204-1146.
www.kokopellisuites.com.
3119 W. AZ 89A, Sedona 86336.
Prices: $79–239.
Credit Cards: AE, D, MC, V.
Handicapped Access: Call.
Pets: No.

This all-suites hotel opened in 1996 and offers large one-room suites with separate sitting areas. The Cocksomb Suite has two large rooms and includes a kitchen and dining area. Heated pool and spa; deluxe continental breakfast.

Resorts

AMARA RESORT AND SPA

928-282-4828 or 866-455-6610.
www.amararesort.com.
310 N. AZ 89A, Sedona 86336.
Prices: $158–508.
Credit Cards: AE, DC, D, MC, V.
Handicapped Access: 4 rooms.
Pets: No.

This 100-room luxury resort located in Uptown Sedona overlooks Oak Creek Canyon and offers the tranquility of a creekside resort as well as easy access to the Uptown shops and restaurants. The outdoor heated saltwater pool and hot tub are in a courtyard setting with amazing views of the canyon and the red rocks beyond. Three restaurants offer distinct dining experiences. Amara Spa offers a full complement of services and treatments, including massages, facials, nail care, and body wraps.

ENCHANTMENT RESORT

800-826-4180.
www.enchantmentresort.com.

525 Boynton Canyon Rd., Sedona 86336.
Prices: $350–1,650.
Credit Cards: AE, CB, DC, D, MC, V.
Handicapped Access: 4 rooms.
Pets: No.

Northwest of Sedona, you will find a variety of activities available at Enchantment, including swimming, croquet, tennis, hiking, and the Camp Coyote children's program. The resort features six pools, three 18-hole championship golf courses close by, and three restaurants: Yavapai (fine dining), Tii Gavo (casual dining), and Mii amo Café (healthful dining). The award-winning Mii amo spa (928-203-8500 or 888-749-2137; www.miiamo.com) is 24,000-square-foot facility; all-inclusive spa packages and a full menu of treatments and services are available.

HILTON SEDONA RESORT & SPA
928-284-4040 or 877-2-REDROCK.
www.hiltonsedona.com.
90 Ridge Trail Dr., Sedona 86351.
Prices: $139–299.
Credit Cards: AE, CB, DC, D, MC, V.
Handicapped Access: 3 rooms.
Pets: Yes, up to 50 pounds; deposit required.

This 219-suite resort on the Sedona Resort Golf Course features an on-site restaurant and bar, three pools, children's programs, and a fitness center. Room amenities include fireplace, wet bar with microwave, and private balcony or patio. Hilton Sedona Resort & Spa has both a championship golf course and a full-service spa offering body wraps, massages, and facials; for more information, visit www.hiltonsedonaspa.com.

L'AUBERGE DE SEDONA RESORT
928-282-1661 or 800-272-6777.
www.lauberge.com.
301 L'Auberge Lane, Sedona 86336.
Prices: $175–2,000.

Credit Cards: AE, DC, MC, V.
Handicapped Access: Yes.
Pets: See the web site for the resort's pet program.

This beautiful European-style resort features cottages and a lodge; a restaurant that serves French cuisine; and a spa with body wraps, facials, and massages. Try their Signature Seasonal Massage, which incorporates jojoba and essential oils and hydrates and rejuvenates the body (90 minutes, $175). Choose a one- or two-bedroom cottage situated along the creek or in the garden, stay in a guest room or junior suite at the Lodge with a private patio or balcony, or rent the entire Creek House for a family reunion. Stargaze Friday night with the resort's professional astronomer, or dine at the award-winning restaurant.

LOS ABRIGADOS RESORT & SPA
928-282-1777 or 800-521-3131.
www.ilxresorts.com.
160 Portal Lane, Sedona 86336.
Prices: $225–1,750.
Credit Cards: AE, CB, DC, D, MC, V.
Handicapped Access: Call.
Pets: No.

This Sedona resort is located on 22 acres on the banks of the Oak Creek, and features three award-winning restaurants, two pools, and the Sedona Spa. Additional amenities include on-site miniature golf, pool, and fitness center. Chef Gino Di Fabio, who trained in Rome, plans the delicious menu choices for both Joey Bistro (an Italian bistro named after the 40 Joes that adorn the walls—these Joes are of literary, sports, and entertainment fame) and Steaks & Sticks (a sports bar and grill serving steaks, chops, and seafood, all while guests enjoy horse racing simulcast live from the tracks, as well as three large-screen projection televisions broadcasting the games of the day).

RADISSON POCO DIABLO RESORT

928-282-7333 or 800-333-3333.
www.radisson.com/sedonaaz.
1752 S. AZ 179, Sedona 86336.
Prices: $129–299.
Credit Cards: AE, DC, D, MC, V.
Handicapped Access: 4 rooms.
Pets: No.

The newly renovated Radisson Poco Diablo
Resort—located on 22 acres—features patio
and garden rooms, massage therapy, a
nine-hole golf course, and a heated pool
and spa. It's found in a residential neighborhood off AZ 179 and equidistant between
the Village of Oak Creek and the attractions
of Tlaquepaque Arts & Crafts Village, Hillside Sedona, and Uptown Sedona.

SEDONA ROUGE HOTEL & SPA

928-203-4111 or 866-312-4111.
www.sedonarouge.com.
2250 W. AZ 89A, Sedona, AZ 86336.
Prices: $149–324.
Credit Cards: AE, D, MC, V.
Handicapped Access: 3 rooms.
Pets: Yes, with $50 nonrefundable deposit.

This 77-room boutique hotel is a new addition to Sedona's choice accommodations.
The hotel features a full-service spa, lush
gardens, a courtyard, a swimming pool, and
Nautilus equipment. The spa offers massages, facials, body treatments, and spa
packages. Richly appointed rooms favor
exotic decor (bath towels from Turkey,
Moroccan end tables, and Syrian chests);
amenities include complimentary wireless
Internet access and a nightly turndown
service. Sedona Rouge is also home to Reds,
a bistro-style restaurant serving American
favorites infused with flavors from around
the world.

DINING

The demands of Sedona's millions of visitors, many from other countries, have kept
local restaurants on their toes. Offering
unique, world-class culinary experiences,
small-town Sedona has a big-city menu.

Credit Cards

The following abbreviations are used for
credit card information:
AE: American Express
CB: Carte Blanche
D: Discover Card
DC: Diner's Club
MC: MasterCard
V: Visa

ENCHANTMENT'S YAVAPAI RESTAURANT

928-282-2900.
www.enchantmentresort.com.
525 Boynton Canyon Rd., Sedona.
Open: Daily for all 3 meals; Sunday brunch
10:30 AM–2:30 PM.
Prices: Expensive to very expensive.
Cuisine: American.
Credit Cards: AE, D, MC, V.

Awarded the Best of Award of Excellence by
Wine Spectator magazine in 2006, the Yavapai Restaurant at Enchantment Resort features 180-degree views of beautiful
Boynton Canyon. Outdoor and indoor seating is available; floor-to-ceiling windows
span the dining room, inviting the best of
redrock country into your dining experience. Jazz brunch on Sundays; reservations
required; no jeans or athletic shoes.

GALLERY ON OAK CREEK RESTAURANT

928-340-8900 or 866-455-6610.
www.amararesort.com.
310 N. AZ 89A, Sedona.
Open: Daily for all 3 meals, 7 AM–10 PM.
Prices: Expensive.
Cuisine: New American.
Credit Cards: AE, D, MC, V.

Art and food come together at the Gallery on
Oak Creek Restaurant, located at Amara
Creekside Resort in Uptown Sedona. Enjoy

the delicious food and warm, inviting service at this award-winning restaurant; dine alfresco beneath the stars or take an indoor table among the sculptures and art with views of redrock country. Stop by the bar for a martini or browse the art on display. You'll find works of art for sale from eight different galleries in town.

KEN'S CREEKSIDE RESTAURANT

928-282-1705.
www.kenscreekside.com.
251 AZ 179, Creekside Plaza, Sedona.
Open: Daily, lunch 11:30 AM–4 PM, dinner 5 PM–close.
Prices: Expensive.
Cuisine: Continental.
Credit Cards: AE, D, MC, V.

Dine overlooking Oak Creek at this romantic restaurant offering Continental cuisine. Enjoy patio seating or sit inside beside one of several picture windows. This charming local favorite offers the some of the best views (catch Snoopy taking a nap!) of the surrounding redrock formations as well as a casual fine-dining experience. Check out the southwestern art by Ken's wife, well-known artist Marilyn Erickson, or listen for Ken singing show tunes for his guests!

L'AUBERGE RESTAURANT ON OAK CREEK

928-282-1661 or 800-272-6777.
www.lauberge.com.
301 L'Auberge Lane, Sedona.
Open: Mon.–Sat., breakfast 7–10:30 AM, lunch 11:30 AM–2:30 PM, dinner 5:30–9 PM; Sunday, champagne brunch 9 AM–2 PM, hors d'oeuvres 2:30–5:30 PM, dinner 5:30–9:30 PM.
Prices: Expensive to very expensive.
Cuisine: New American.
Credit Cards: AE, DC, MC, V.

Located at the L'Auberge de Sedona resort, this award-winning restaurant serves French-infused American cuisine creek-side—on the terrace or in the window-lined dining room. The seasonally influenced menu changes daily, and the six-course dinner tasting menu is worth consideration. Wine lovers rejoice, as the restaurant is a 14-time winner of *Wine Spectator* magazine's coveted Best of Award of Excellence.

RENÉ AT TLAQUEPAQUE

928-282-9225.
www.rene-sedona.com.
336 AZ 179, Suite 118, Sedona.
Open: Daily, lunch Mon.–Fri. 11:30 AM–2 PM, Sat.–Sun. 11:30 AM–2:30 PM; dinner Sun.–Thu. 5:30–8:30 PM, Fri.–Sat. 5:30–9 PM.
Prices: Expensive.
Cuisine: Classic French.
Credit Cards: MC, V, AE.

Nestled in a quiet corner of Tlaquepaque Arts and Crafts Village, René's has been serving locals and tourists alike since 1977. Designed by executive chef Ruben Sandoval, the restaurant's signature dishes incorporate flavors of the Southwest with French, American, and Continental cuisine. Enjoy the award-winning wine list, alfresco dining, and charming ambience.

Bar & Grills

COWBOY CLUB GRILLE AND SPIRITS

928-282-4200.
www.cowboyclub.com.
241 N. AZ 89A, Sedona.
Open: Lunch and dinner, 11 AM–4 PM and 5–10 PM.
Prices: Expensive.
Cuisine: Steak house.
Credit Cards: AE, CB, DC, D, MC, V.

Also home of the Silver Saddle Room, this circa-1946 building was originally the Oak Creek Tavern. One of only three main buildings in Sedona at the time, it served as combination saloon, pool hall, grocery store, and meeting place. In the 1950s it

A scenic shot of Sedona.

became a different kind of meeting place—one for some of the era's biggest Hollywood stars as they stopped in for a cold one after filming for the day. With more than 50 movies filmed in Sedona through the years, the tavern saw the likes of Burt Lancaster, John Wayne, Jane Wyman, Rock Hudson, Jimmy Stewart, and Donna Reed, to name only a few. In the mid-1960s—June 23, 1965, to be exact—several cowboy artists sat around the fireplace and organized the well-known Cowboy Artists of America (CAA). Today the Cowboy Club features works by CAA artists, original wooden walls, and some of the best buffalo and Angus steaks around, as well as delicious poultry and seafood. The menu changes seasonally, but you'll find cactus fries and grilled rattlesnake year-round.

You'll find an upscale dining experience in the rustic elegance of the Silver Saddle Room (no kids' menu here), as well as the same great choices of steak, seafood, and poultry complete with all the bells and whistles, including appetizer, dessert, and sorbet intermezzo. "Dressy casual" and reservations are recommended for the Silver Saddle Room, where dinner is served 5–10 PM daily.

CUCINA RUSTICA

928-284-3010.
www.cucinarustica.com.
7000 AZ 179, Suite 126-A, Sedona.
Open: Daily for dinner 5 PM–close.
Prices: Moderate to expensive.
Cuisine: Italian.
Credit Cards: AE, MC, V.

Located at Tequa Festival Marketplace in the Village of Oak Creek, this local favorite serves Old World Italian and Mediterranean cuisine. Dine alfresco on the shaded patio, where you can enjoy the cascading waterfall and the panoramic view, or indoors where the rich rustic decor and friendly service invite you to stay. The food has received rave reviews and the wine list is extensive, with a healthy selection of wines by the glass.

OAXACA RESTAURANT & ROOFTOP CANTINA

928-282-4179.
www.oaxacarestaurant.com.
321 N. AZ 89A, Sedona.
Open: Daily for all 3 meals, 8 AM–9 PM.
Prices: Inexpensive.
Cuisine: Mexican.
Credit Cards: AE, D, MC, V.

Oaxaca (pronounced *wa-HA-ka*), a Sonoran–Mexican restaurant, features rooftop dining with breathtaking views and south-of-the-border decor. Enjoy vegetarian and heart-healthy choices at this 35-year-old restaurant located in Uptown Sedona, as well as traditional Mexican fare that you may not find on other menus, including cactus (yes, the kind you see on the side of the road)—these nopalitos cactus pads are marinated, grilled, and served with a saucy mixture of roasted tomato, red peppers, chile peppers, and almonds; and *coronados*—corn fries in a cone, served with guacamole and salsa.

ORCHARDS BAR AND GRILL

928-282-1661 or 877-700-2944.
254 N. AZ 89A, Sedona.
Open: Daily for all 3 meals, 7 AM–9 PM (opening at 8 AM in winter months).
Prices: Inexpensive to moderate.
Cuisine: American.
Credit Cards: AE, D, MC, V.

Located at the juncture of Jordan Rd. and AZ 89A, this charming local favorite serves traditional American fare—sandwiches, homemade soups, hand-tossed pizzas, pastas, and salads—in a relaxing and inviting atmosphere. You'll also find seafood, steak, and barbecued ribs. Finish off your meal with one of several delectable desserts, including choices from nearby Cold Stone Creamery and Black Cow Café. Espresso, coffee, and pastries round out a full breakfast menu.

SZECHUAN RESTAURANT & MARTINI BAR

928-282-9288.
www.szechuan-restaurants.com.
1350 W. AZ 89A, #21, Sedona.
Open: Daily for lunch and dinner, Sun.–Thu. 11 AM–9:30 PM, Fri.–Sat. 11 AM–10 PM.
Prices: Inexpensive to moderate.
Cuisine: Chinese and Japanese.
Credit Cards: AE, D, MC, V.

Located in West Sedona but with roots stretching to the province of Guangxi, China, this restaurant features traditional Chinese cuisine and a Japanese-style sushi bar. The full-service martini bar is open 3 PM–midnight daily.

Cafés

Sedona may be a tourist town, but it hasn't wandered too far from its high-desert beginnings. Thus it's no surprise to find a number of café-style eateries serving up hearty, all-American fare. Sprinkled throughout town, along AZ 179 and 89A both north and south of the Y, are choices like the **Blue Moon Café** (928-284-1831; www.bluemooncafe.us; 6101 AZ 179, Suite B), where they serve breakfast all day as well as everyday café fare such as burgers, sandwiches, pizza, and home-style dinners; they serve beer and wine and boast the best Phillys in town. The **Coffee Pot Restaurant** (928-282-6626; 2050 W. AZ 89A) has *too* many choices, what with 101 omelets and breakfast served all day; you'll also find Mexican and American dishes and, some say, the best breakfast (and coffee) in Sedona.

Other not-so-traditional but very popular café choices include **Sedona Raw Gourmet Café** (928-282-2997; www.sedonarawcafe.com; 1595 W. AZ 89A)—a vegetarian's dream come true, with vegetarian soups, salads, and entrées for lunch and dinner, as well as chocolate treats crafted by Kelly Johnson, who uses only the best raw chocolate and low-glycemic agave. And look for the ever-delicious but decadent **Black Cow Café** (928-203-9868; 229 N. AZ 89A), where they serve baked goods, coffee, and homemade ice cream daily 10:30 AM–9 PM.

SURROUNDING AREAS

The Ranch House (928-567-4492; www .beavercreekgolfsedona.com; 4250 N Montezuma Ave., Lake Montezuma), originally operated as a dude ranch by the Bell family (of phone fame), was a Verde Valley highlight in its heyday, with visitors like Clark Gable and Bette Davis. Today it's the home of Beaver Creek Golf Club and the newly revived historic Ranch House Restaurant and Lounge. The restaurant offers all-you-can-eat pork ribs on Monday and a fish fry on Friday, with live music on weekends. You may also want to look into chapter 8, Side Trips, for additional places to visit in the vicinity of Sedona, including Flagstaff and Jerome.

CULTURE

Sedona has a rich artistic community. Numerous art studios and galleries dot the hillsides; major events include the annual 3-day Sedona International Film Festival along with Chamber Music Sedona, which recently staged its 20th anniversary music festival—a glorious weeklong affair.

CHAMBER MUSIC SEDONA

928-204-2415.
www.chambermusicsedona.org.
3100 W. AZ 89A, Suite B, Sedona.

Chamber Music Sedona offers residencies to world-class musicians and performs Sep.–May; guests can enjoy musical renditions by such performers as violinist Hilary Hahn, the Emerson String Quartet, and Opus One at St. John Vianney Church.

GALLERY OF MODERN MASTERS

928-282-3313 or 888-282-3313.
www.galleryofmodernmasters.com.
671 AZ 179, Suite AST-3 & 4, Hillside Sedona.
Open: Daily Mon.–Thu. 10 AM–6 PM, Fri.–Sat. 10 AM–8 PM.

Located in Hillside Sedona off AZ 179, the Gallery of Modern Masters features one of the largest collections of 20th-century modern masters' work in Arizona, including sculptures, hand-blown glass, photography, oils, and ceramics. You will find works by masters Salvador Dalí, Henry Moore, and Pablo Picasso, as well contemporary pieces by ceramist Michel Gustavson, photographers Keoki Flagg and Ian Whitehead, and mixed media artist Dominique Caron, among others. The gallery also hosts events such as Art, Wine and Talk Receptions.

SEDONA ARTS CENTER

928-282-3809 or 888-954-4442.
www.sedonaartscenter.com.
15 Art Barn Rd., Sedona.

Founded in 1957, Sedona Arts Center is the oldest arts organization in northern Arizona. It supports the arts in Sedona through education, development, and appreciation. SAC offers more than 250 classes and workshops, and hosts revolving art exhibits as well as special events throughout the year.

SEDONA HERITAGE MUSEUM

928-282-7038.
www.sedonamuseum.org.
735 Jordan Rd., Sedona.
Open: Daily 11 AM–3 PM.
Admission: $3.

Established in the late 1920s, the Jordan farmstead is an old apple orchard once operated by Walter and Ruth Jordan. The property, listed on the National Register of Historic Places, features a 1929 tractor shed, a 1931 redrock cabin, and a fruit-packing warehouse built in 1947. In 1991 Sedona purchased the last of the land that made up the original farmstead and established the Jordan Historical Park in conjunction with the Sedona Historical Society. The city leases the property to the historical society and the Sedona Heritage Museum, which highlights pioneer history, movies made in Sedona, and cowboy life, and preserves vintage machinery, the original orchard, and a nature trail.

SEDONA VISUAL ARTISTS COALITION

928-204-2963.
www.sedonaartistscoalition.org.
55 N. Slopes Dr., Sedona.

Founded in 1996 by Nancy Robb Dunst, the coalition has grown from a gathering of 8 to more than 200 professional artists. The coalition supports the arts in Sedona by sharing techniques and opportunities, planning visits to and exhibitions in various galleries, and collaborating on efforts to design and create art for the city of Sedona. Media represented include photography, oil and acrylics, mixed media, watercolor, fiber, wood, glass, ceramics, metal, and film.

Events

PLEIN AIR FESTIVAL

928-282-3809 or 888-954-4442.
www.sedonapleinairfestival.com.
15 Art Barn Rd., Sedona Arts Center, Sedona.

Plein Air Festival—the name means "in the open air"—celebrates the works created by 30 of the country's finest artists during this weeklong tribute to Sedona each October. Artists with their paints and easels can be found on street corners, at trailheads, and at resorts, painting their surroundings. Paintings created throughout the week are available at the public art sale held the last day of the event.

RAW SPIRIT FESTIVAL

928-776-1497.
www.rawspiritfest.com.

This annual October event, held at the Radisson Poco Diablo Resort, celebrates the joys of vegetarianism with gourmet raw vegan meals, music, and fun.

SEDONA ARTS FESTIVAL

928-204-9456.
www.sedonaartsfestival.org.
PO Box 2729, Sedona 86339.
Admission: $8 adults (good for both days); kids under 12 free.

This fall celebration typically arrives in early October. Over 100 artists, live entertainers, raffles, and more make this a great 2-day event. Free parking and complimentary shuttle service.

SEDONA INTERNATIONAL FILM FESTIVAL

928-282-1177.
www.sedonafilmfestival.com.
PO Box 162, Sedona 86339.

This weeklong annual event—typically held at the end of February or beginning of March—shows award-winning feature, documentary, short, and animated films from around the world.

SEDONA JAZZ ON THE ROCKS INC.

928-282-1985.
www.sedonajazz.com.
1487 W. AZ 89A, Suite 9, Sedona.

For almost 30 years this 5-day annual jazz festival has graced the September air with delightful sounds of some of the best musicians anywhere. Held at the Radisson Poco Diablo Resort and other area resorts and locales, the event brings together legendary performers and emerging talent, including up-and-comers from high schools around the state. Free events can be enjoyed around town; main events cost anywhere from $10 for the film screening, to $20 for a single-evening jam session, to $65 for lawn seats at the all-day jazz-fest, to $80 and up for jazz and food pairings like the Jazz Circle Party (wine tasting, hors d'oeuvres, and jazz at a private home; $100 per ticket). Package pricing is available for multiple events. For more information and to obtain a complete schedule of events, check out the comprehensive web site.

RECREATION

Hiking

Located in the heart of the Coconino National Forest and bordered on the east and north by Munds Mountain Wilderness Area and Red Rock–Secret Mountain Wilderness Area, respectively, the Sedona area is crisscrossed with more than 100 trails of varying degrees of difficulty. There are also several parks and recreational areas including Red Rock State Park, Crescent Moon Recreation Park, Posse Grounds Park, and Slide Rock State Park.

For the best information on directions to trailheads, trail length, and difficulty, consult the Coconino National Forest web site at www.redrockcountry.org; click on Maps &

Brochures. The available PDF map offers complete listing of trailheads and trails within the Coconino National Forest; for specific information about trails, click on Recreational Activities (Red Rock District) and scroll down for a complete list, including distance, difficulty, elevation, and uses. Popular routes include the easy **Bell Rock Pathway** (3 miles one way). Both bikers and hikers are welcome on this smooth, wide trail that parallels AZ 179; you can pick up two trailheads, Bell Rock Vista and Little Horse, at mileposts 307.5 and 309.4, respectively. **Baldwin/Templeton/Cathedral Rock** (2 miles one way) allows you to catch views of Cathedral Rock and Wilson Mountain along a trail that also accesses Oak Creek. Pick up the trailhead at the end of Verde Valley School Rd. off 179. **Jim Thompson Trail** (2.4 miles one way) is easily accessible from Park Ridge Rd., which starts off as Jordan Rd. in Uptown Sedona.

Moderate trails like **Devils Bridge** (0.9 mile one way)—which climbs 400 feet to a natural rock arch—offer a steeper climb with great views. The Devils Bridge Trailhead is accessible 1.5 miles down FR 152. Similarly, the **Jordan Trail** (off Park Ridge Rd.) is a 2-mile loop with a 200-foot climb. This trail leads to a huge sinkhole called Devil's Kitchen in the Soldier Pass area. For an almost 4-mile loop, try **Courthouse Butte Loop**. This 250-climb is a gentle one as the trail sweeps around Bell Rock and Courthouse Butte at the edge of the Munds Mountain Wilderness Area. Catch the trailhead off 179 in the Village of Oak Creek at the Bell Rock Pathway kiosk. The **Brins Mesa Trail**, which may still be suffering damage from a 2005 fire, is a 3-mile (one-way) trail with a 600-foot change in elevation. The climb is worth it—you end up on a flat mesa with panoramic views of Sedona and the awe-inspiring 2,000-foot-high Mogollon Rim; hikers share this path with horseback riders. The trail is accessible from Park Ridge/Jordan Rd. in Uptown and is intersected by the Soldier Pass Trail.

For a difficult hike and a 2,300-foot climb, conquer the **Wilson Mountain Trail** (5.6 miles one way). This all-day trek can be started at Midgely Bridge off AZ 89A. As with all physical activity in Arizona, it's important to stay hydrated. Bring plenty of water, and let someone know where you're going and when you plan to return. Be aware: the trail may still be closed due to the Brins Fire in 2006.

Keep in mind that a Red Rock Pass is necessary when parking on Forest Service land. You can pick up one of these passes at either of the two sporting outfitters in town, as well as many of the resorts, hotels, grocery stores, and visitor centers in the area; you can also purchase passes online at www.publiclands.org or via telephone (with Visa or MasterCard) by calling one of the following offices: South Gateway (928-284-5324 or 928-284-5322); Verde Ranger District (928-567-4121); Peaks Ranger District (928-526-0866); or the Coconino National Forest Supervisor's Office (928-527-3600). For more information about where to pick up a Red Rock Pass, visit www.redrockcountry.org.

NATIONAL FOREST SERVICE
Red Rock Ranger District, Coconino National Forest.
928-203-7500 or 928-282-4119.
www.redrockcountry.org.
PO Box 20429, Sedona 86341-0429.
New temporary physical address: 7780 E. Beaver Creek Ranger Station Rd. (FR 618, 2 miles east of I-17 at exit 298), Rimrock 86335.
Open: Mon.–Fri. 8 AM–4:30 PM.

SOUTH GATEWAY VISITOR CENTER

928-284-5323.
7000 AZ 179, Suite 101 (in the Tequa Plaza Center), Village of Oak Creek 86351.
Open: Daily 8:30 AM–5 PM.

Biking & ATVing

While mountain bikes and ATVs are allowed in some areas, be aware that bikes are not allowed in specially designated wilderness areas (Munds Mountain Wilderness Area and Red Rock Secret Wilderness Area)—only in the national forest proper. Also, keep in mind that a Red Rock Pass is required for parking on national forest land. See Hiking, above, for more information about passes and trails.

Camping & Picnicking

A number of popular camping sites in the area allow for a combination of hiking, biking, fishing, climbing, horseback riding, swimming, wading, birding, photography, wildlife-watching, picnicking, tent camping, and camp trailers and recreational vehicles. Red Rock Passes are necessary for parking on national forest lands; the cost for a campsite ranges $15–20 per night, and fees apply for any additional vehicles. Only cash and Arizona checks are accepted. Some sites tend to get quite crowded on weekends, and only about half of the sites take reservations, including Manzanita, Chavez Crossing Group Site, Pine Flat, and Cave Springs Campgrounds. Other, nonreservation sites include Bootlegger, Beaver Creek, and Clear Creek Camp and Group Site Campgrounds. Most sites do not have utility hookups and have a maximum stay of 7 days. To be safe, always keep your pets leashed and restrained; do not carry glass containers onto Forest Service land; and as always, bring plenty of water. For more information about camping in the region, visit www.redrock country.org and click on Recreational Activities (Red Rock District).

State Parks

RED ROCK STATE PARK

928-282-6907
www.azparks.gov/Parks/parkhtml/redrock.html

This park features several trail options that parallel Oak Creek and link to the national forest. Access it off Red Rock Loop Rd. from AZ 89A; it's about 7 miles north of Sedona. There is a $5-per-car fee year-round. Red Rock State Park offers opportunities for recreational and educational experiences; call 928-282-6907 for details. Summer hours are 8 AM–7 PM; winter, 8 AM–5 PM; fall and spring, 8 AM–6 PM.

SLIDE ROCK STATE PARK

928-282-3034.
www.pr.state.az.us/Parks/parkhtml/sliderock.html.
6871 N. AZ 89A, Sedona.

Slide Rock State Park in the heart of Oak Creek Canyon is a favorite spot on hot summer days; it features a natural waterslide that kids (and adults) can't get enough of. Originally part of the 43-acre Pendley homestead and apple farm, today the park is on the National Register of Historic Places and features wading, fishing, hiking, swimming, and bird-watching. There's a $10 fee per vehicle (one to four adults) and a $2 charge per individual from Memorial Day weekend through Labor Day weekend.

Tours & Excursions

PINK JEEP TOURS
800-873-3662.
www.pinkjeeptours.com.

Serving Sedona visitors since 1960, Pink Jeep Tours provides more than 10 off-road adventures through the surrounding wilderness areas. Experience the geological, historical, and archaeological treasures that Sedona has to share with these award-winning excursions. Their most popular trips are Broken Arrow, a 2-hour, 100 percent off-road trip that explores Submarine Rock and Chicken Point in Munds Mountain Wilderness Area; the Ancient Ruin tour, which explores the 700-year-old Sinaguan cliff dwelling; and Diamondback Gulch, a 2½-hour off-road ride that takes in the well-known rock formations visible from West Sedona—Capitol Butte, Chimney Rock, Lizard Head, and Doe Mesa. Other trips include the Scenic Rim Tour, 2,000 feet in the air along the Mogollon Rim; the Coyote Canyons tour; the Rock Art Expedition to some of the best petroglyph sites in the state; and various hiking and Grand Canyon tours. Prices range from $45 (Coyote Canyons) to $102 (Ancient Ruin/Diamondback Gulch Combo) for adults, to $33.75 and $76.50, respectively, for ages 12 and under. For tour guides a 15 percent gratuity is recommended; they require a two-person minimum per trip. Reservations are recommended, and 24-hour cancellations are required. Be sure to wear lots of sunscreen (bring extra), a hat, sunglasses, and comfortable shoes.

MAVERICK HELICOPTER TOURS
702-261-0007.
www.maverickhelicopter.com.

For the best views of redrock country, consider a helicopter tour. Named one of Travel Channel's "Ten Best Helicopter Thrills" twice, Maverick Helicopter provides a comfortable, safe, state-of-the-art experience. Fees start at $89 for a 10-minute tour of Bell and Cathedral Rocks, and range up to $599 for a 3-hour tour of Sedona sites and a 45-minute tour of the Grand Canyon. You can also get a DVD recording of your experience.

Wildlife

Birding. According to the Northern Arizona Audubon Society (www.nazas.org), Sedona's elevation, changing seasons, and rich riparian areas support a varied population of birds—and thus good birding year-round. Depending on the season, you may find neotropical birds or waterfowl as they migrate through the area to more comfortable climes. Top birding spots in the Sedona area include Red Rock State Park and Oak Creek Canyon. Additional information is available at the District Ranger Station in Sedona.

OUT OF AFRICA WILDLIFE PARK
928-567-2842.
www.outofafricapark.com.
Off Verde Valley Justice Center Rd., at AZ 260, Camp Verde.

Out of Africa, originally sited in the Phoenix metropolitan area, relocated several years ago to the Verde Valley. Get up close and personal with some of Africa's people-friendly animals, and watch from behind fences as brave trainers work with the more dangerous predators. This park offers a unique and informative animal encounter. Tiger Splash is quite an experience—watch as trainers and tigers play in the water.

Shopping

There are several main shopping districts/areas in Sedona, including Tlaquepaque on AZ 179 just south of the Y, Uptown Sedona (turn right at the Y off 179), Hillside on AZ 179 south of Tlaquepaque Village, and the shops in West Sedona (turn left onto 89A from AZ 179).

Shopping Districts

HILLSIDE SEDONA
928-282-4500.
www.hillsidesedona.net.
671 AZ 179, Sedona.

Hillside Sedona is well known for its collection of art galleries, restaurants, and specialty shops. Galleries include the Gallery of Modern Masters (see Culture, above). Restaurants, specialty shops, wine tasting, and home decor shops round out this experience of some of Sedona's finest.

TLAQUEPAQUE
928-282-4838.
www.tlaq.com.
336 AZ 179, Sedona.
Open: Daily except for Christmas Day and Thanksgiving.

Built in the mid-1970s, this Spanish-style arts village hosts a variety of boutiques, galleries, and specialty shops, as well as five restaurants. The vision of Abe Miller, Tlaquepaque (pronounced *TLA-keh-PAH-keh*) was designed in the tradition of Mexican artisans and builders, incorporating plazas, fountains and verandas, ironwork, hand-painted tiles, and plenty of shady spaces beneath a thick canopy of cottonwood and sycamore trees. The village, named after a suburb of Guadalajara, Mexico, features western, traditional, and contemporary art and sculpture, including works in bronze, clay, paper, wood, and stone as well as Southwest photography; also look for decorative rugs, handmade Andean arts and crafts, clothing, paintings, quilts, decorative glass and jewelry, bath products, candles, seasonal decor, and pottery.

Restaurants include **El Rincon Restaurante Mexicano** (928-282-4648; www.elrincon-restaurant.com), serving Arizona-style Mexican cuisine; **How Sweet It Is Chocolate Shoppe** (928-282-5455); **Oak Creek Brewery and Grill** (928-282-3300; www.oakcreek pub.com), with American grill fare and beers brewed on site; and **Secret Garden Café** (928-203-9564), which serves gourmet soups, salads, and coffees.

At **Center for the New Age Inc.** (928-282-2085; www.sedonanewagecenter.com; 341 AZ 179), you can immerse yourself in the New Age experience. Harnessing the spiritual magnetism of Sedona, the center features aura readings and photography, vortex tours and

Uptown.

information, as well as astrology and numerology reports and New Age music and jewelry. The **Gold Door Gallery** (928-282-6629; www.golddoorgallery.com; 2155 W. AZ 89A, Suite 106) has been located in the Tlaquepaque Artisan Center since 1972 and features unique jewelry designed by some of Arizona's best artists, specializing in Arizona gemstones; their on-staff gemologists can assist in choosing the highest-quality pieces. For leather goods, including jackets, purses, wallets, and belts, visit **The Hyde-Out** (928-282-1292; 336 AZ 179, Suite B-102) next to the Tlaquepaque Chapel. The first store to open at Tlaquepaque in 1973 was **Ninibah** (928-282-4256; www.houseoftheshalako.com). Located next to the creek, Ninibah features Hopi kachina dolls, collectible Pueblo pottery, Native American jewelry, and Navajo sand paintings.

UPTOWN SEDONA
SEDONA CENTER
928-282-4527.
www.sedona-center.com.
310 N. AZ 89A, Sedona.

Set against an enchanting redrock backdrop, Sedona Center will meet your shopping, hiking, dining, and even lodging needs (the Amara Creekside Resort is located here). You will find more than 30 boutique-style shops offering an array of items, including jewelry, art, and home decor. There are three restaurants, including the Gallery at Amara Resort and Spa (see Dining, above); the Canyon Breeze Restaurant and Bar serves coffee, smoothies, pizza, sandwiches, and salads. Grab a table beside one of the picture windows for a relaxing and warmer (during winter) experience of the surrounding beauty; on balmier days, sit on the outdoor patio. Or stop in at the Amara Cantina and Bar, which features Sonoran-style Mexican fare and a sports bar.

SHOPS AT HYATT PIÑON POINTE
928-282-8884.
www.theshopsathyattpinonpointe.com.
101 N. AZ 89A, Suite E-23, Sedona.

The Shops at Hyatt Piñon Pointe comprises 18 stores, galleries, restaurants, and a spa, all just north of the Y in Uptown Sedona. The open courtyard setting and patio seating offer spectacular views of the surrounding redrock formations. You'll find galleries such as Visions Fine Art and the Turquoise Tortoise; wine tasting at The Art of Wine; shopping at Chico's, Zivney Collection, and Marchesa's; and body treatments at Breathe Spa. Restaurants include Arizona favorite Wildflower Bread Company (for wonderful soups, salads, and sandwiches), the Italian-style Bistro Bella Terra, Starbucks, and Arizona's own Cold Stone Creamery.

THE COTTAGE GALLERY GIFTS & GARDEN
928-282-4304 or 888-382-4304.
www.cottagegallerysedona.com.
325 Jordan Rd., Sedona.

Take a load off and relax after an afternoon of shopping at this cozy cottage, where the bistro tables and garden setting invite you in. Browse the one-of-a-kind garden accents, hand-painted silk scarves, colorful glass pieces, waterfall pottery, watercolors, and other works created by local artists.

Marketplaces
There are a variety of marketplaces in Sedona, including **Tequa Festival Marketplace** (805-496-4336, 7000 AZ 179), an upscale retail center located at the entrance to the Sedona Golf Resort in the Village of Oak Creek, featuring live performances weekly in the Kiva Courtyard, including live jazz; four-star dining such as Cucina Rustica (see Dining); and galleries and boutiques. You'll find Indian jewelry, rugs, pottery, and baskets at **Hoel's Indian Shop** (928-282-3925; www.hoelsindianshop.com; 9589 N. AZ 89A), located 10 miles north of Sedona on AZ 89A. The **Sedona Trading Post** (928-284-2555; 10 Bell Rock Plaza, Suite A) features more than more than 50 arts and crafts dealers under one roof.

New Age
New Age shops are plentiful throughout Sedona. In Uptown you'll find **Body Bliss Factory Direct** (928-282-1599; www.bodyblissfactorydirect.com; 320 N. AZ 89A, Suite Q, Sinagua Plaza), where you can indulge your New Age senses with gemstones and crystals, as well as spa, bath, and body products made in Sedona. Schedule a body treatment, get a gemstone oracle reading, or find feng shui products to balance your chi at home. You'll also find **Sedona Crystal Vortex** (928-282-3543; www.sedonacrystalvortex.com; 271 N. AZ 89A) and a plethora of New Age experiences, including psychic readers and massage therapists specializing in relationships, health, and money; aura photography, astrology, palmistry, and past-life readings, as well as exclusive gifts, handcrafted jewelry, crystals, and feng shui products. To take a little bit of Sedona home with you, visit **Candle, Bath & Body** (928-203-

0764, 320 N. AZ 89A, #14) for Sedona Spa products (www.sedonaworldwide.com) in addition to candles, gifts, incense, and readings by well-known Sedona psychic Nirup (www.psychicnirup.com).

Jewelry

There are a number of jewelry shops in Uptown Sedona featuring designer and traditional, Native American, and custom pieces. **George Kelly Jewelers** (928-282-8884; 101 N. AZ 89A, Suite E-23, Shops at Hyatt Pinon Pointe) offers designer and traditional fine jewelry, European leather handbags, and accessories. You can get custom jewelry at **Randy Polk Designs** (928-203-1126 or 480-445-0345; 301 N. AZ 89A, Suite A). **Wayne B. Light Custom Jewelry** (928-282-2131 or 800-894-2131; www.wayneblight.com; 3000 W. AZ 89A) offers a large selection of custom jewelry, fine jewelry, and diamonds. **Garland's Indian Jewelry** (928-282-6632; www.garlandsjewelry.com; 3953 N. AZ 89A) features Native American jewelry as well as new and antique art, kachinas, pottery and baskets, books, and sand paintings.

Native American

Uptown Sedona hosts its share of shops specializing in Native American goods. **Blue Eyed Bear** (928-282-1158 or 800-378-6510; 299 N. AZ 89A) sells the original contemporary Native American and Southwest jewelry designed by well-known artisans Robert Taylor and Don Lucas. You'll find Native American gifts at **The Naja Inc.** (928-282-4755 or 888-494-8900; 235 N. AZ 89A, Oak Creek Market Place). For Navajo rugs and Indian art, try **Garland's Navajo Rugs** (928-282-4070; 411 AZ 179); for Indian jewelry, alabaster, bronze and glass sculptures, pottery, and paintings, check out the **Turquoise Buffalo** (928-282-2994 or 888-282-2994; www.turquoisebuffalo.com; 252 N. AZ 89A). In addition to the Native American jewelry, arts, and crafts at **Joe Wilcox Indian Den** (928-282-2661 or 866-274-5008; www.joewilcoxsedona.com; 320 N. AZ 89A, Suite J), you'll also discover moccasins, home decor, and Southwest-style gifts.

Specialty Shops

SEDONA SPORTS
928-282-1317 or 866-204-2377.
www.sedonasports.com.
251 AZ 179 Suite A-4, Creekside Plaza, Sedona.

Sedona Sports features supplies for fishing, camping, swimming, and mountain biking, including the rental of bikes, GPS, jogging strollers, baby carriers, binoculars, and fishing poles. Located across from Tlaquepaque, they have served visitors and locals for more than 35 years. Mountain bike rentals are reasonably priced—$25–40 for a half day, $35–50 for a full—and include bike, helmet, and fanny pack with tools, tubes, map, and a liter of water. You can also rent bikes on a weekly basis. Fishing licenses and Red Rock Passes (necessary for parking on national forest land), maps, and books on the area are also available.

CHEERS
928-282-1193 or 800-658-5742.
www.dirtstore.com.
201 N. AZ 89A, Sedona.

Dirt don't hurt! Especially when it's the red dirt Sedona is so famous for. Take home an authentic red shirt, dyed in 100 percent Sedona clay from these T-shirt and souvenir shops scattered throughout town. You'll find baseball hats and clothing with other pithy sayings, like LIFE'S SHORT PLAY DIRTY and OLDER THAN DIRT.

West Sedona

In West Sedona, perhaps the least touristy area of Sedona, you'll find shops and plazas interspersed with fast-food restaurants, government buildings, and residential neighbor-hoods. Shops to check out include **Mystical Bazaar** (928-204-5615; www.mysticalbazaar.com; 1449 W. AZ 89A, Suite 3) featuring aura photography, psychic readings, angel channeling, vortex tours, original jewelry, gifts, clothing, gemstones, Tarot cards, books, and music. Arizona's largest distributor of Native American art and artifacts is **Kachina House** (928-204-9750 or 866-587-0547; www.kachinahouse.com; 2920 Hopi Dr.), which houses Native American pottery, Indian artifacts and jewelry, Hopi and Navajo katsinas, sand paintings, and original art in its 5,000-square-foot showroom and warehouse in West Sedona. **Canyon Outfitters** (928-282-5293; 2701 W. AZ 89A) is Sedona's largest outdoor store for hiking, camping, rock climbing, clothing, and accessories. **Saddlerock Barn Consignments** (928-282-8518; www.saddlerockbarn.com; 164 Coffee Pot Dr., Suite J) is the place to go for antiques, used furniture, collectibles, artwork, and estate and moving sales.

SPAS

Also see Lodging—Resorts (above).

SEDONA'S NEW DAY SPA
928-282-7502.
www.sedonanewdayspa.com.
1449 W. AZ 89A, Suite 1, Sedona.

In addition to traditional services such as massages, body treatments, hot stones, Sedona clay wrap, facials, waxing, and nails, the Sedona New Day Spa features intuitive readings and energy-balancing massages as well as a Men's Spa with services designed especially for men. Check their web site for various packages and discounts.

RETREAT AND HEAL
928-282-5237.
www.retreatandheal.com.
460 Harmony Dr., Sedona.

Harnessing the healing power of Sedona, Retreat and Heal is a spiritual and wellness retreat offering spiritual vortex tours, health spa services, intuitive readings, and hyp-notherapy for women and couples. Find the tools to live a healthy and balanced existence. Day packages plus weekend and weekly rates.

FANGO HAIR & DAY SPA SALON
928-204-9880 or 888-419-0312.

www.fangodayspa.com.
2681 W. AZ 89A, Sedona.

The Fango Day Spa is a traditional salon and spa offering a warm and inviting experience with a European flavor. Enjoy manicures, pedicures, facials, and massages, as well as salon services.

GOLF

KRAZY KYOTE ACTIVITIES & TOURS
928-204-9481; fax 928-204-9460.
401A Jordan Rd., Sedona.

Not sure where to golf? Contact Krazy Kyote golf reservation service to book a golf experience for you. They have relationships with several Sedona courses and can create an outing suited to your level of experience.

IMPORTANT INFORMATION

Police
Emergency: 911.
Non-emergency: 928-282-3100

Fire
Emergency: 911.
Non-emergency: 928-282-6800.

Hospitals and Medical Services
Emergency: 911.
Non-emergency: **Sedona Urgent Care** (928-203-4813; 2530 W. AZ 89A, Bldg. A, Sedona). Minor illness or accident care on a nonappointment basis.

Area Codes
The area code in Sedona is 928.

Banks
As a tourist town, Sedona offers its share of the ATMs and branches of many major banks. Find ATM machines in Uptown and Tlaquepaque shopping districts.

Climate, Weather, What to Wear
Located in Arizona's high desert, the city of Sedona enjoys four mild seasons; temperatures range 46–75 degrees Fahrenheit. Winter is cold—it's been known to snow—but somehow this is a beautiful and enjoyable cold. Keep in mind that even on cooler days, you're still in the desert. Sweat evaporates before you even notice it. Drink plenty of water.

ADA Accessibility

For more information, download Amenities for Persons with Disabilities, www.sedonaaz
.gov/documents/view.aspx?PK=6861; or contact the city at 928-282-3113; TDD 928-204-
7102.

Local Governments

City of Sedona (928-204-7127; www.sedonaaz.gov; 102 Roadrunner Dr., Sedona, AZ
86336). The city manager is Eric Levitt (928-204-7186).

Tourist Information

800-288-7336 or 928-282-7722.
info@sedonachamber.com.
www.visitsedona.com.
Visitor centers are located at 331 Forest Rd., Uptown Sedona, and the Tequa Plaza, Village of
Oak Creek. Hours are Mon.–Sat. 8.30 AM–5 PM, Sun. and holidays 9 AM–3 PM; closed
Christmas, Thanksgiving, and New Year's.

8

Side Trips

Roaming the Desert

AZ 88 from Tortilla Flat to Roosevelt Dam

The Apache Trail—used as early as AD 900 by the Salado Indians as a footpath through the mountains, and later expanded to facilitate the building of the Roosevelt Dam in the early 20th century—wanders through some of the state's most beautiful desert terrain. It is best seen from a tour van with a knowledgeable guide pointing out exactly where to feast your eyes. A novice tourist can get lost in the breathtaking beauty along the trail. This narrow dirt road hugs the mountain walls as it dips and spirals through lush canyons, above sparkling blue lakes, and amid saguaro forests from Roosevelt Lake in the Mazatzal Mountains through the Superstition Wilderness to AZ 88 at Tortilla Flat. The view is awe inspiring, and some of the hairpin turns are downright spine tingling—a disastrous combination for a curious driver. So leave the driving to a tour company (see the sidebar for a suggestion) and gorge yourself on one stunning view after another. Not only will they keep you safely on the road, but they'll point out the various desert floras both native and transplant, recite the local lore, and tell you where to point and when to click the camera. Ask in advance where the best seat is to take pictures out your window—it will be worth it!

Tortilla Flat

Located about 18 miles northeast of Apache Junction on AZ 88, Tortilla Flat was built in 1904 as a rest stop along the Apache Trail and now has a total population of about three. But this little one-horse town knows how to serve up a good time. The walls of its only restaurant and bar are covered in dollar bills from visitors. Grab a saddle (the seat of the bar stools), order a cold draft and a juicy burger, and listen to the live entertainment out on the patio. Wander next door to the ice cream and candy shop for dessert. The town sits above Canyon Lake on the Apache Trail.

SUPERSTITION MOUNTAIN MUSEUM
480-983-4888.
www.superstitionmountainmuseum.org.
4087 N. Apache Trail, Apache Junction.

Since 1979 the Superstition Mountain Historical Society has amassed literally tons of historic artifacts and memorabilia significant to the region, including about 60 tons of mining equipment from Phelps Dodge—the largest mining conglomerate in the state. The Superstition Mountains—aptly named—comprise 160,000 acres cloaked in 9,000 years of mystery. Archaeological studies indicate that the area was inhabited some 7,000 years BC; more

Roosevelt Lake.

recent inhabitants have included the Salado and Hohokam, who lived here until the mid–15th century when they mysteriously abandoned the area, and the Apache, who arrived about the same time the other peoples disappeared. More recent mysteries include the legend of the Lost Dutchman Mine. Legend holds that a miner named Jacob Waltz, known locally as the Dutchman, discovered a gold mine in the mid– to late 19th century; he never told anyone where it was, however, and his partner met with an untimely death. So the secret went with Jacob to his grave in 1891. And though many treasurer hunters have searched—and some have even died trying—not a single person has ever found the lost mine or the gold. The museum and its exhibits provide a feel for the mining life and share the legends that locals love to retell. The museum is located 3.5 miles northeast of Apache Junction on the Apache Trail.

SUPERSTITION WILDERNESS AREA
Mesa Ranger District
480-610-3300
26 N. MacDonald, Room 120, Mesa

You will find lakes, canyons, trails, and solitude (if you visit during the week) among the 160,000 acres of rocky buttes, saguaro cacti, and mountainous terrain here. Trails and paths lead off the graded dirt Apache Trail into the desert wilderness, allowing you to enjoy hiking, fishing, boating, and camping. The area is full of wildlife, some species poisonous, as well as steep canyons, sudden drop-offs, and crumbling rock. Be sure to stick to designated trails, bring plenty of water, and wear sunscreen. Be prepared for significant temperature changes even in warmer months; the days may be hot, but evenings can cool quickly once the sun sets. Tell someone where you're going and when you expect to return.

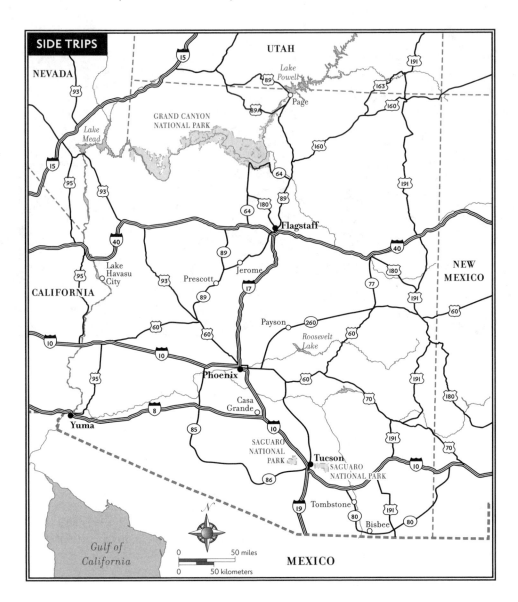

CASA GRANDE

The city of Casa Grande is located almost equidistant between Phoenix and Tucson. Founded in 1879, it is home to about 30,000 people, and features seven hotel/motels, including the Francisco Grande Hotel and Golf Resort (480-237-4238; www.franciscogrande.com; 26000 W. Gila Bend Hwy.). You'll find 15 RV parks, too.

CASA GRANDE VALLEY HISTORICAL SOCIETY & MUSEUM

520-836-2223.
www.cgvhs.org.
110 W. Florence Blvd., Casa Grande.
Open: Sep. 15–May 15, Mon.–Sat. 1–5 PM.; closed major holidays.

Take a Detour

Not sure where you want to go in Arizona? Consider hiring one of the Valley's tour companies for a one-of-a-kind adventure that hits all the hot spots. Several companies in the area specialize in single- and multiday tours. One of the best—for their creative tours, excellent guides, and flexibility—is Detours of Arizona.

Owned by partners Jeff Slade and Jeff Haflett, Detours features trips "off the beaten path." These adventures range from the breathtaking Apache Trail day tour to the 5-day, 4-night Tony Hillerman Tour (which takes avid readers of Hillerman's mystery novels to the very people and places they've read about!). Additional day trips are offered to Greater Phoenix, the Grand Canyon, Sedona, and Tombstone. Multiday tours include a 3-day, 2-night visit to Monument Valley and Canyon de Chelly; a 4-day, 3-night Apache Pass trip that takes you to seven historical locales throughout southeast Arizona; and a 5-day, 4-night yoga trip that lets you perfect your poses at some of northern Arizona's most visually energizing sites.

Detours guide Bluebird demonstrates how Native American tribes made rope out of agave plants.

The Detours tour van.

The wonderful thing about Detours is their willingness to customize their trips for you and your traveling companions. Guides are passionate about Arizona and about sharing what they know; they're full of facts, anecdotes, and legends. Whether your group fills the van or you're joining the trip by yourself, these engaging guides are do a fine job of making sure everyone has a wonderful time. To book a trip or request more information, contact www.detouraz.com or 866-438-6877. If you don't see what you're looking for, give them a call and they'll create a tour just for you, from single-day events to 10-day trips.

Once known as Terminus, the city of Casa Grande has since been named after the Casa Grande Indian Ruins—which in turn received their name in 1694, from the Spanish Jesuit priest Francisco Eusebio Kino. This little museum depicts the cultural and agricultural history of the city and its people. Tours, lecture series, workshops, and programs are offered.

CASA GRANDE RUINS NATIONAL MONUMENT

520-723-3172.
www.nps.gov/cagr.
1100 Ruins Dr., Coolidge.
Open: Daily 8 AM–5 PM; closed December 25.
Admission: $5 adults; ages 15 and younger are free; tickets are good for 7 days from purchase.

The Apache Trail winds through the Superstition Mountains.

Made with an estimated 6 million pounds of caliche (a mixture of clay, sand, and calcium carbonate found in the Desert Southwest), the Casa Grande or "Big House" is a four-story structure dating to about AD 1300–1400 and considered one of the largest ancient structures in North America. It is also considered one of the most mysterious. Constructed by the same Hohokam people who built the irrigation ditches in the Salt River Valley, Casa Grande was abandoned sometime during the early part of the 15th century. It was rediscovered by many passers-through before it was renamed by Father Kino in 1694, and has been studied by numerous archaeologists. Some contend that the house was used to chart the stars; others believe it was the home of the tribe's most revered elders. Take a self-guided tour around Casa Grande; you can follow the signs. Guided tours are available Dec.–Apr. Call for their tour schedule. At the visitor center you can view a 15-minute video, purchase your tickets, and browse the bookstore and museum. You will also find bathrooms here.

To reach the ruins from I-10, take the exit to AZ 87/287; the paved entrance road leads 0.75 mile to the parking lot and visitor center.

BISBEE

The once booming mining town of Bisbee (www.discoverbisbee.com or www.cityofbisbee .com) is now a quiet little artists' colony ensconced in its past. Established in 1880 to support the Copper Queen Mine and named after one of the mine's financial backers—Judge Dewitt Bisbee—this town, in its heyday, provided the infrastructure for 20,000 people.

COPPER QUEEN MINE TOURS

520-432-2071 or 866-432-2071.
www.queenminetour.com.
Open: Daily; tours start at 9 AM, 10:30 AM, noon, 2 PM, and 3:30 PM and last about 1½ hours.
Reservations are recommended, not required.
Admission: $12 plus tax adults, $5 plus tax ages 4–15; children under 4 are free.

The Copper Queen produced almost 3 million ounces of gold and more than 8 billion pounds of copper in almost 100 years of operation. In that time its miners scraped, shoveled, drilled, and hauled more than $6 billion worth of ore from its depths. Closed in the mid-1970s when it began losing its profitability, the mine reopened in 1976 as a tour. Don a hard hat, lantern, and yellow slicker, hop on the mine train, and head 1,500 feet underground where it's 47 degrees Fahrenheit year-round.

VAN TOURS OF HISTORIC BISBEE & SURFACE MINES

520-432-2071 or 866-432-207.
Open: Daily tours at 10:30 AM, noon, 2 PM, and 3:30 PM.
Admission: $10 plus tax adults; children under 4 are free.

This 1½-hour tour focuses on the tales of old Bisbee. Guides point out top spots like the mining mansions, the Lavender Pit (it swallowed a neighborhood whole about 50 years ago), and the historic district, including such famous haunts as the Copper Queen Hotel.

TUCSON

With a population topping one million in 2007, Tucson is our state's second largest city and home to ASU's archrival University of Arizona. (It's a friendly competition that may have started when Phoenix won the bid to serve as state capital.) While both cities embody the informality of the Old West, Tucson may be more relaxed and content with its origins. Nicknamed the Old Pueblo for the presidio that marks its place in territorial and border history, Tucson—rich with Native American, Spanish, and Mexican influences—was founded a good 100 years before Phoenix. It's bordered by four mountain ranges: the Tucson Mountains to the west, Rincon on the south, Santa Catalina on the north, and Santa Rita to the east. Stunning views abound from mountaintop vistas as well as street corners and highways. This southern city's desert beauty is perhaps the greatest part of its charm.

Tucson Visitor Center (888-2-TUCSON.; www.visittucson.org.; 100 S. Church Ave., Tucson, in La Placita Village).

ARIZONA STATE MUSEUM

520-621-6302.
www.statemuseum.arizona.edu.
1013 E. University Blvd., Tucson.
Open: Mon.–Sat. 10 AM–5 PM, Sun. noon–5 PM.
Admission: Suggested donation of $3 per person.

The Arizona State Museum, a Smithsonian Institution affiliate, was founded in 1893. As the oldest and largest anthropology museum in the Southwest, it is home to the largest whole-vessel collection of Southwest Indian pottery in the world. Upcoming exhibits include Set in Stone: 2000 Years of Gem and Mineral Trade in the Southwest. This exhibit, running Dec. 2007–Feb. 2009, highlights Native American jewelry then and now as well as the prominence of turquoise—Arizona's state gem.

The museum's library is open to the public Mon.–Fri. 9:30 AM–4:30 PM on a noncirculating basis; it's closed state and national holidays. Note also that the museum store is closed 12:30–1 PM.

To reach the museum from I-10, take Speedway Blvd. east to Euclid Ave. Turn south onto Euclid and proceed to the parking facilities. You can use the uncovered lot at Tyndall and 2nd only a block away, but there is a fee on weekdays. Parking is free on weekends.

PIMA AIR AND SPACE MUSEUM
520-618-4815.
www.pimaair.org.
6000 E. Valencia Rd., Tucson.
Open: Daily 9 AM–5 PM; last admission at 4 PM.
Closed: Thanksgiving and Christmas.
Admission: June–Oct., $11.75 adults; $9.75 seniors, AAA members, and military; $8 ages 7–12; children 6 and under are free. Nov.–May, $13.50 adults; $10.75 seniors, AAA members, and military; $9 ages 7–12; children 6 and under are free. Admission to the AMARC (the "boneyard"), combination tickets, group discounts, and 2-day passes are available; call for details.

The Pima Air and Space Museum is the largest aircraft museum in the West. More than 250 aircraft including bombers, fighter planes, transports, and civil and NASA vessels call the PASM home. You'll find exhibits following the history of air travel from the Wright brothers to NASA, as well as the historical significance of aircraft and their personnel.

Hour-and-a-half docent-led walking tours will take you through exhibits in Hangars 1, 3, and 4. These tours are free with admission; call for times. You can also take a 1-hour tram tour ($5 fee) narrated by a docent—many of whom have experience with the planes you'll see. On this ride among the museum's outdoor 160-plus aircraft display, you'll see three huge B-52 bombers, an SR-71 Blackbird, and much more.

The Aerospace Maintenance and Regeneration Center (AMARC) or "boneyard" is located on the Davis-Monthan Air Force Base. To tour this facility (for an additional $6 fee), contact 520-574-0462 and ask for the reservation desk; reservations are strongly recommended.

The museum also includes a gift shop selling aircraft-themed merchandise. An on-site café, located on the north side of Hangar 1, serves hamburgers, hot dogs, and beverages 9:30 AM–4 PM. Wheelchairs, wagons, and strollers—located at the museum entrance inside Hangar 1—are available free to visitors. Smoking is permitted outside in designated areas only. Food and beverage are not allowed in any of the museum hangars.

To reach the museum from I-10, take the Valencia Rd. exit (on the south end of Tucson) and continue about 2 miles to the entrance.

TITAN MISSILE MUSEUM
520-625-7736.
www.pimaair.org.

1580 W. Duval Mine Rd., Sahuarita.
Open: Daily 9 AM–5 PM; closed Thanksgiving and Christmas.
Admission: $8.50 adults; $7.50 seniors, groups of 20 or more, and military; $5 ages 7–12; children 6 and under are free. If you're planning to visit the Pima Air and Space Museum, too, there is a combined price of $18.

Located 25 miles south of Tucson, the Titan Missile Museum is the last of the 54 Titan II Intercontinental Ballistic Missile (ICBM) complexes that were "on alert" during the height of the Cold War. In 1982, a year after President Ronald Reagan announced the disassembly of the missiles, this particular site was ready for deactivation and destruction. A group of volunteers and the US Air Force collaborated to deactivate the missile and preserve the site as a museum, which opened to the public in 1986. In 1994 the site was named a National Historic Landmark; in 2003 the museum opened the Count Ferdinand von Galen Education and Research Center to preserve missile program artifacts and develop and facilitate the museum's educational mission. The tour includes a six-story view of the Titan II missile in its silo, a visit to the underground launch control center, and a simulated missile launch.

Note that no commercial photography is permitted without written permission. Walking shoes are required (the museum requests no heels; there's a flight of 55 steps to access the underground part of the tour); all food and beverage (except bottled water) are prohibited, and smoking is not permitted inside or on the tour. Despite those 55 steps, the facility is ADA compliant, and an elevator is available for those in need. A museum store sells great toys and gifts; sales support the museum.

To reach the museum from Tucson, take I-19 south toward Green Valley and Nogales; exit at Duval Mine Road (exit 69), turn west, and follow the signs. The entrance is on the north side of the road approximately 0.1 mile past the intersection of La Canada and Duval Mine Rd.

DEGRAZIA GALLERY IN THE SUN

520-299-9191 or 800-545-2185.
www.degrazia.org.
6300 N. Swan, Tucson.
Open: Daily 10 AM–4 PM; closed Thanksgiving, Christmas, New Year's Day, and Easter.
Admission: Free.

Ettore "Ted" DeGrazia, born in 1909 in the small mining camp of Morenci in eastern Arizona, was the son of a miner who went on to become one of the Southwest's best-known and most beloved artists. After his works appeared in *Arizona Highways* in 1941, and inspired by the praise of Diego Rivera and José Clemente, with whom he'd worked in Mexico, DeGrazia earned three degrees, including a master of arts from University of Arizona. His bright, whimsical paintings and sketches of children, angels, and southwestern figures have been reproduced throughout the world on greeting cards, calendars, ornaments, and prints.

In the 1950s the Gallery of the Sun was designed by DeGrazia and built with the help of Native American friends proficient at making adobe brick. The 10-acre spot is nestled in the foothills of the Catalina Mountains on Swan Rd. north of Sunrise Dr., and includes the artist's home and studio as well as a small gallery and a larger gallery built a decade and a half later in 1965. Today a collection of 15,000 original works, including oils, watercolors, sketches, and sculptures, revolves around a permanent exhibit of six paintings depicting

The Apache Trail is tight in spots as it wends through the mountains.

Native cultures and historical events of the Southwest. For some, DeGrazia is synonymous with Tucson and even the Southwest; and in 2006 the Gallery of the Sun Historic District was added to the National Register. The gallery and site are preserved and managed by the DeGrazia Foundation, established by the artist. You will find an array of DeGrazia reproductions and even originals on consignment for sale in the gallery gift shop. Free parking and space for RVs and buses.

DESERT MUSEUM

520-883-2702.
www.desertmuseum.org.
2021 N. Kinney Rd., Tucson.
Open: Daily Mar.–Sep. 7:30 AM–5 PM and Oct.–Feb. 8:30 AM–5 PM; no entry permitted after 4:15. Jun.–Aug., the museum is open Sat. till 10 PM.
Admission: June–Aug., $9 adults, $2 ages 6–12; Sep.–May, $12 adults, $4 ages 6–12; children 5 and under are free.

The Arizona–Sonora Desert Museum is 2 miles of paths across 21 acres of the Sonoran Desert. You will find mountain lions, prairie dogs, gila monsters, javelina, and rattlesnakes among the 300 animal species that call this combination zoo, natural history museum, and botanical garden home. More than 1,000 kinds of desert flora will expand your sense of the desert, which is greener and prettier than you might expect.

To reach the museum from I-10, exit at Prince Rd. (note that the Speedway Blvd. exit is closed April 2007–spring 2010); travel south along the frontage road for 3 miles, then turn west onto Speedway Blvd. into the Tucson Mountains. Turn right onto Kinney Rd,; after about 2.5 miles the Desert Museum will be on your left.

SAGUARO NATIONAL PARK

Rincon Mountain District Visitor Center 520-733-5153.
www.nps.gov/sagu.
Open: Daily 7 AM–sunset; visitor centers 9 AM–5 PM. Closed December 25.
Admission: $10 per vehicle/motorcycle; $5 per individual on foot/bicycle; receipt is valid for 7 days.

Saguaro National Park straddles Tucson, with the Rincon Mountain District to the east, the Tucson Mountain District to the west. The park is excellent for biking. Try the paved, 8-mile Cactus Forest Loop Drive in the Rincon, or the gravel, 6-mile Bajada Loop Drive through the Tucson Mountains. Bring plenty of water; you can fill up at either of the visitor centers. Pit toilets are available at all picnic areas. Bring ID and emergency contact information. Helmets are required for anyone bicycling (passengers, too) under the age of 18; however, they are recommended for all bicyclists. After dark you must have a rear reflector and a headlight. Bicyclists are required to obey all traffic laws and signals.

To reach the Rincon Mountain District, take I-10 to exit 275 (Houghton Rd.); drive 9.5 miles north to Old Spanish Trail and turn right. Continue 3 miles southeast to the park entrance on the left side of the road.

For the Tucson Mountain District, take I-10 to exit 242 (Avra Valley Rd.), drive 5 miles west to Sandario Rd., and turn left. Proceed 9 miles south to Kinney Rd.; turn left. After 2 more miles the visitor center is on your left.

Spring Training in Tucson

Teams training in Tucson include the Arizona Diamondbacks, Chicago White Sox, and the Colorado Rockies. At Tucson Electric Park (520-434-1111 or 866-672-1343; 2500 E. Ajo Way, Tucson) you'll find the Arizona Diamondbacks (www.azdiamondbacks.com) and the Chicago White Sox (www.whitesox.com). The Colorado Rockies (www.coloradorockies .com) play at Hi Corbett Field (520-327-9467 or 800-388-ROCK; 3400 E. Camino Campestre, Tucson).

Events

World Famous Tucson Rodeo (520-741-2233; www.tucsonrodeo.com; Tucson Rodeo Grounds). Considered one of the top 20 professional rodeos in all of North America, the Tucson Rodeo is an 8-day celebration, including a parade, held in mid- to late February.

International Gem & Mineral Show (Tucson Gem & Mineral Society; 520-322-5773; www.tgms.org). This showcase, held in early to mid-February, is touted as "the world's largest marketplace of its kind." Almost 50 locations throughout Tucson participate in this once-a-year event where you can browse and buy precious gems, minerals, fossils, jewelry, beads, and more from international dealers.

PAYSON

Enjoy cooler weather and ponderosa pines just 90 minutes from the Valley: At 5,000 feet, Payson (www.ci.payson.az.us) is a year-round retreat for Valley residents. The town celebrates its western heritage with events like "the World's Oldest Continuous Rodeo," the Old-Time Fiddlers' State Championship, and the Bluegrass Festival. Natural attractions include Tonto Natural Bridge and the Mogollon Rim.

TONTO NATURAL BRIDGE STATE PARK

520-476-4202.
PO Box 1245, Payson 85547.

Tonto Natural Bridge is 13 miles northwest of Payson off AZ 87. This 400-foot-wide natural travertine bridge is considered the world's largest of its kind. It spans Pine Creek 183 feet above the water; trails and paths offer various scenic views of the bridge.

JEROME

Clinging to the side of Cleopatra Hill in the Prescott National Forest is the city of Jerome (www.jeromechamber.com)—a town that, in its heyday, was the toast of investors. Today it is a crumbling, though charming, artists' retreat—a ghost town clinging to its mortal body. You will find shops, galleries, and restaurants interspersed with condemned structures, empty basements where buildings once stood, and a jailhouse that slid down the side of the mountain. While the miners pulled billions of dollars' of copper, gold, and silver out of the hundreds of miles of tunnels beneath Jerome, the land above hiccupped and rocked, shattering windows, shifting foundations, and moving the town down the mountainside inches at a time. After 75 years of mining, operations ceased in 1953, and the population dropped from 15,000 at its peak in the 1920s to 50 people. In 1976 Jerome became a National Historic Landmark. Among the ruins and shops and bed & breakfasts, you will find plaques relating the history of the city, Douglas Mansion State Park, and a thriving artists' community. Check out the **English Restaurant**—a holdover from earlier mining days. The **Jerome Grand Hote**l was once the town hospital and is now a charming hotel with unbelievable views of the Verde Valley and Sedona; its restaurant, the **Asylum**, is one of only 2,800 restaurants worldwide to be given the Wine Spectator Award of Excellence. The menu is first class and on par with some of the top restaurants in the Valley of the Sun. Don't forget **Way West**, a gift store with all sorts of great books about Jerome and Central Arizona that you might not find anywhere else. For dinner and a movie the old-fashioned way— a chuckwagon meal and stage show on the Verde River—try **Blazin' M Ranch Western Dinner Theater** (928-634-0334 or 800-937-8643; www.blazinm.com; 1875 Mabery Ranch Rd.) just down the mountain in Cottonwood. Or try a wine tasting. In Cornville—a short jaunt from Jerome and Cottonwood—you'll find both the **Oak Creek Vineyards & Winery** (928-649-0290, 1555 N. Page Springs Rd.) and **Page Springs Vineyard & Cellars** (928-639-3004, www.pagespringscellars.com, 1500 N. Page Springs Rd.).

Flagstaff

Home to Northern Arizona University and a number of museums, attractions, restaurants, and B&Bs, Flagstaff is worth a visit. From here, you can visit the Grand Canyon, Lake Powell, Sedona, the Navajo and Hopi Reservations, and Monument Valley. In town, take time for the Lowell Observatory, Museum of Northern Arizona, the Grand Canyon Railway, Meteor Crater, Riordan Mansion, or the Flagstaff Arizona Snowbowl.

   Flagstaff Visitor Center (928-774-9541 or 800-842-7293; www.ci.flagstaff.az.us or www.flagstaffarizona.org; 1 E. Route 66, Flagstaff 86001).

Attractions

The Arboretum at Flagstaff (928-774-1442; www.thearb.org; 4001 S. Woody Mountain Rd.). From April through October you can hike through this 200-acre wildflower meadow at 7,000 feet—considered one of the country's largest collection of high-country wildflowers. **The Arizona Historical Society–Pioneer Museum** (928-774-6272; www.arizonahistorical society.org; 2340 N. Fort Valley Rd.) has captured and preserved Flagstaff and northern

Arizona's dynamic past. At an elevation of 7,000 feet and with an average snowfall of 260 inches, the **Arizona Snowbowl** (928-779-1951; snow report 928-779-4577; www.arizonas-nowbowl.com; off US 180, north on Snowbowl Rd.) makes winter sports a distinct possibility. Ski mid-Dec.–mid-Apr. 9 AM–4 PM; summertime (Memorial Day–mid-Oct.) means a scenic sky ride to 11,500 feet 10 AM–4 PM. Enjoy the quietude of the world's largest contiguous ponderosa pine forest at **Coconino National Forest** (928-527-3600; www.fs.fed.us/r3/coconino; 1824 S. Thompson St.). The ecology changes from desert cactus at 2,600 feet to alpine tundra at more than 12,600 feet.

MONTEZUMA CASTLE NATIONAL MONUMENT
602-567-5276.
PO Box 219, 527 Main St., Camp Verde 86322.

In the Verde Valley about 50 miles south of Flagstaff, high above the floodplain of Beaver Creek, lies one of the best-preserved cliff dwellings in North America. This five-story, 20-room dwelling was built by the Sinagua Indians more than 600 years ago. Assuming the prehistoric ruins were built by the Aztec emperor Montezuma (who never even visited the structure), early settlers named it Montezuma Castle. The national monument has a museum displaying artifacts found at the site, a short hiking and biking trail, and self-guided tour signs describing the cultural and natural significance of the area. Dogs are allowed on the trail, but must be on a leash no longer than 6 feet. Montezuma Castle is located in the Tonto National Forest.

Restaurants and Bed & Breakfasts
If you're planning to spend the night in Flag (as Arizonans like to call it), stay at one of the town's B&Bs—charming alternatives to brand hotels. Consider **The Inn at 410 Bed and**

Shops in Jerome.

Breakfast (928-774-0088 or 800-774-2008; www.inn410.com; 410 N. Leroux St.), deemed Arizona's best by the *Arizona Republic*; or **Starlight Pines Bed and Breakfast** (928-527-1912 or 800-752-1912; www.starlightpinesbb.com; 3380 E. Lockett Rd.)—considered Flagstaff's most romantic.

Restaurants include **Brix** (928-213-1021; www.brixflagstaff.com; 413 N. San Francisco), a charming eatery that serves a wonderful lunch and dinner menu; the extensive wine list offers an array of by-the-glass choices. **Cottage Place** (928-774-8431; www.cottageplace .com; 126 W. Cottage Ave.) is an award-winning establishment of 25 years serving amazing entrées like scallop sauté en croute, Gorgonzola encrusted filet, and grilled duck breast.

Events

Events in Flagstaff include the **Northern Arizona Book Festival** (928-380-8682, www.nazbookfestival.org) held each spring. **Movies in the Square** (928-607-2347, www.flagdba.com) are shown Friday nights in Flagstaff's downtown Heritage Square May–mid-September. There's also the Museum of Northern Arizona Heritage Program's (928-774-5213, www.musnaz.org) **Hopi and Navajo Festivals of Arts and Culture** in July and **Celebraciones de la Gente** in October. **Route 66 Days** (928-607-2347, www.flagstaff route66days.com), a celebration of the "Mother Road" with live music, a vintage and hot-rod car show, and a parade, is held the second weekend in September. And at the end of the year, check out Flagstaff's **New Year's Eve Pinecone Drop** (928-779-1919, ext. 430, www.weatherfordhotel.com). Leave the fancy ball in Times Square; in the ponderosa pine forest, the giant pinecone holds the honors.

GRAND CANYON

520-638-7875.
www.nps.gov/grca.
Backcountry office: Grand Canyon National Park, PO Box 12, Grand Canyon 86023.

Arizona is the Grand Canyon state, and Grand Canyon National Park is a World Heritage Site—a magnificent place that defies all attempts to describe it, one that draws people from all over the world to gawk at, helicopter over, climb into, and raft down. Thus, a trip to the big hole in the ground is strongly recommended; it is something you simply have to see for yourself.

The Grand Canyon—carved by millennia of exposure to the Colorado River and the natural erosion of weather, rain, wind, and time—is the main focus of the park, which encompasses 277 miles of river and adjacent uplands from the southern point of Glen Canyon National Recreation Area to the eastern border of Lake Mead National Recreation Area. Visitors come to take pictures, hike, bike, wander the numerous paths, and browse the exhibits and displays. The South Rim is more accessible to visitors from the Phoenix area; the North Rim is only open mid-May through late October.

PRESCOTT

The first capital of the Arizona Territory, Prescott (www.visit-prescott.com), pronounced *PRESS-kit*, remains steeped in its frontier heritage. Bordered by the Prescott National Forest, "Everybody's Hometown" enjoys four mild seasons and cooler temperatures than the

Valley. Its elevation and proximity to the national forest make it an ideal spot for hiking, mountain biking, and horseback riding. You'll also find historical sites, shops featuring local artists, and the infamous Whiskey Row's numerous saloons, including cinematic superstar **The Palace Restaurant and Saloon** (928-541-1996; www.historicpalace.com; 120 S. Montezuma,), established in 1877 and featured in the film *Junior Bonner* with Steve McQueen, among others. The saloon still has the same 1880s Brunswick Bar that some of the frontier's toughest customers rubbed elbows with.

Attractions

Paolo Soleri's **Arcosanti** (928-632-7135; www.arcosanti.org; 2 miles east of Cordes Junction)—a practice in arcology (architecture and ecology)—is still under construction; guests can tour the compound or even stay the night. Catch the horses at **Yavapai Downs** (928-775-8000; 10401 AZ 89A, Prescott Valley), northern Arizona's newest live horse racing venue. Or gamble your coins away at the slot machines at **Bucky's Casino** (928-541-0453; www.buckyscasino.com; 1500 E. AZ 69, Prescott) or **Yavapai Casino** (928-778-9219; www.buckyscasino.com; 1505 E. AZ 69, Prescott).

Culture

Discover art at one of Prescott's cultural institutions. **Phippen Art Museum** (928-778-1385; www.phippenartmuseum.org; 4701 AZ 89 N.) features contemporary and historic art of the American West. **Sharlot Hall Museum** (928-445-3122; www.sharlot.org; 415 W. Gurley St.) hosts exhibits and artifacts that reveal the stories of Arizona's settlers and supports the Blue Rose Theater, which presents historical dramas. **Smoki Museum** (928-445-1230; www.smokimuseum.org; 147 N. Arizona St.) has promoted appreciation for Native American culture since 1935 and houses the largest collection of Kate Cory oil paintings in the country. **Yavapai College Gallery and Sculpture Garden** (928-776-2031; www.yc.edu; 1100 E. Sheldon St.) features changing exhibits of local, regional, and national artists; the Sculpture Garden (www.friendsofyca.org) accommodates some interesting contemporary pieces, including a leaping frog, a hammered copper fountain, and a welded family. Enjoy a private tour of 40 years' worth of cinema technology and Arizona film history at **Professor Hall's Cinema Museum** (928-777-9134; www.silentmovies.com), open by appointment only.

Several entities in town support theater and fine arts, including the **Prescott Fine Arts Association** (928-445-3286; www.pfaa.net; 208 N. Marina St.), which features theatrical performances, concerts, and art shows by local artists; and the **Yavapai College Performance Hall and Arts Gallery** (928-776-2033; 1100 E. Sheldon St.), which plays host to world-famous performing artists like the Vienna Boys Choir as well as state and local groups such as the Phoenix Symphony Orchestra.

Events

At the **Thursday Night Street Fair** (928-443-0067; www.theprescottgatewaymall.com; Prescott Gateway Mall), enjoy live music and food every Thursday 5–8:30 PM in June and July. Attend **Roughstock Rodeo** (928-445-3103; www.worldsoldestrodeo.com) at the Prescott Rodeo Grounds—home of the World's Oldest Rodeo. Browse artwork by 200 of the best western artists in the country at the **Annual Phippen Museum of Western Art Show & Sale** (928-778-1385; www.phippenartmuseum.org; Prescott Courthouse Plaza), or enjoy the traditional crafts and skills of central Arizonans at the **Annual Folk Arts Fair** (928-

445-3122; Sharlot Hall Museum): horseshoeing, weaving, blacksmithing, quilting, and more. Listen to bluegrass musicians during the **Annual Prescott Bluegrass Festival** (928-771-9827; Prescott Courthouse Plaza).

Best known of all, every year in late June and early July residents and visitors alike flock to the Prescott Rodeo Grounds to partake in **Prescott Frontier Days & the World's Oldest Rodeo** (call 866-407-6336 for tickets; www.worldsoldestrodeo.com). This 120-year-old tradition includes a parade, arts and crafts, rodeo dances, and, of course, rodeo performances.

Lining up a putt at the San Marcos. Photo provided courtesy of San Marcos

9

Golf Courses & Spas

Relax and Play in the Desert

The Phoenix area's 300-plus days a year of sun and incredible scenery make it a top choice for vacationers of all backgrounds and activity levels. And many visitors (serious enthusiasts and dabblers alike) agree that a game of golf and a bit of pampering are essential parts of any vacation in the Valley—especially when the neighbors back home are shivering under a foot of snow!

GOLF

From municipal facilities to championship layouts designed by some of golf's greatest players, any of the Valley's 200 courses—with their blue skies and mountain backdrops—are worthy of a game. Whether golf is an obsession or an occasional indulgence, you will find a range of course styles, prices, and locations that challenge your skills and provide ample enjoyment until you can return for another round.

The San Marcos Golf Resort in Chandler opened in 1913, and with it Arizona's oldest grass golf course was born. This 18-hole golf course has challenged presidents, dignitaries, and celebrities; it now operates as the Crowne Plaza San Marcos Golf Resort. The rich golf tradition started by the San Marcos echoes in many of the Valley's golf courses, including the Wigwam Golf Resort and Spa in Litchfield; the Arizona Biltmore Golf Club, adjacent to Arizona Biltmore Resort; the Phoenix Country Club—original home of the Phoenix Open (now the FBR Open); and The Players' Club (TPC) Scottsdale, the current home of the FBR Open.

Rentals

Most Valley golf courses offer you the option of renting clubs and carts. Cart fees range from complimentary to about $25; many fall between $5 and $10.

What to Wear

Arizona may be fairly informal—after all, there isn't a dress code for Phoenix Symphony Hall—but most of the Valley's golf courses still hold with more traditional golf attire. At the Raven Golf Club at South Mountain, for instance, a collared shirt and Bermuda shorts are required, and denim is not allowed. Arizona Biltmore Golf Club and ASU Karsten Golf Course are more lenient, requiring only a collared shirt (denim remains out of bounds). At

Grayhawk Golf Club a collared shirt is required and denim is okay, but cutoffs are a no-no, whereas at Gainey Ranch Golf Club you can only go wrong with cutoffs and a tank top. If you're unable to determine the dress code, a quick call or visit to the course's web site should set you straight. If you prefer to wing it, a collared shirt and no denim should keep you safe on all but the most stringent courses.

Tee Times

Making reservations for your tee time is generally necessary at the Valley's more popular courses. This is especially the case during peak golf season, which in Phoenix and Scottsdale is anytime except the hottest of summer months—July and August. Still, even in summer, mornings can fill quickly. Some area golf courses offer online tee times, and as of spring 2007 the Arizona Golf Association (www.azgolf.org) offers online tee times for members. The traditional method of calling to set your tee time works, too.

The Weather

Phoenix, Scottsdale, and neighboring cities all offer variations on perfect golf weather. Indeed, depending on what *perfect golf weather* means to you, you might find that peak season is any day the sun is shining, which opens up the whole year for you.

SPRING (mid-Feb.–May 1). Warm sunny days make this the perfect time of year to golf. Temperatures are ideal, ranging from about 50 degrees on the low end to about 75 on the high. Do note, however, that Phoenix topped out at almost 100 degrees in mid-March 2007, and temperatures commonly get up over 80. The great thing about Arizona's "dry heat" is that 80 degrees isn't all that hot.

SUMMER (May 1–mid-Sep.). Summer in the Valley tends to have two mini seasons—dry and rainy—and both seem to have too many days that reach more than 100 degrees. During the dry summer, little or no rainfall hampers golf time; however, the rainy season makes up for this with wild thunderstorms that arrive with little or no warning. At the first hint of dark skies, high winds, and thunder, consider hightailing it back to the clubhouse, as these monsoon storms are known for their electrifying light shows. If you're a golf fanatic, the summer heat won't stop you; your tee times will simply be in early morning, when the sun hasn't risen high enough in the sky to cook everything in its rays. Even better, prices tend to be a lot lower than the cooler months—you can golf some of the Valley's top courses for half the price. Many resorts entice brave visitors with vacation packages.

FALL (mid-Sep.–late Nov.). Depending on how long the summer weather lingers, golfing in September and October can still be a bit warm. Courses tend to overseed this time of year, but the weather is definitely on its way to inviting more folks to come out and play.

WINTER (Dec.–mid-Feb.). Winter play is somewhat cooler than spring. Temperatures hover around 60; 80-plus-degree days are very unlikely. Prices begin creeping back up again as the Valley's part-time residents and early visitors drift into town to catch the FBR Open at TPC of Scottsdale. However, since so many golf lovers are in town, the Valley's resorts like to offer fun vacation packages this time of year.

Water

Drink lots of water. And just when you think you've had enough, drink some more. The dry weather and beautiful sun conspire to wring every last bit of moisture out of you—and all while you enjoy your favorite game. This is especially troublesome during the cooler months when you don't even feel hot on the course.

Sun Protection

Keep in mind that even in cooler months the sun is bright, and sunscreen, hats, and sunglasses are useful in preventing sunburn and headaches—which could potentially ruin the rest of your vacation. Reapply as directed; sunscreen seems to evaporate out here.

VALLEY GOLF COURSES

$: $30–60
$$: $60–90
$$$: $90–120
$$$$: $120–150
$$$$$: $150+

PHOENIX

ARIZONA BILTMORE GOLF CLUB

602-955-9655.
2400 E. Missouri, Phoenix.
Resort, 36 holes, $$$$$.
Greens Grass Type: Bermuda.
Fairways Grass Type: Bermuda.
Accepts Tee Times: Yes.
Earliest Call for Tee Time: 7 AM.
Driving Range: Yes.
Dress Code: Collared shirt; no denim.
Spikes: No metal spikes.
Rental Clubs: Yes.
Carts: Yes.

Set in the heart of the Biltmore District adjacent to the Arizona Biltmore, this country club is a local favorite featuring incredible views and two championship courses. The Adobe course was designed by William Bell back in 1929, when the resort was first built.

DOVE VALLEY RANCH GOLF CLUB

480-473-1444.
33244 N. Black Mountain Pkwy., Phoenix.
Public, 18 holes, $$$.
Greens Grass Type: Winter rye.
Fairways Grass Type: Winter rye.
Accepts Tee Times: Yes.
Earliest Call for Tee Time: 6 AM.

Driving Range: Yes.
Dress Code: No tank tops or cutoffs.
Spikes: No.
Rental Clubs: Yes.
Carts: Electric, path access.

Located in North Phoenix, this desert course, designed by Trent Jones Jr. and built in 1998, offers challenging play—more so on the back nine, where the fairways are narrower than the front nine.

FOOTHILLS GOLF CLUB, THE

480-460-4653.
2201 E. Clubhouse Dr., Phoenix.
Public, 18 holes, $$$.
Greens Grass Type: Bermuda.
Fairways Grass Type: Bermuda.
Accepts Tee Times: Yes.
Earliest Call for Tee Time: 6:30 AM.
Driving Range: Yes.
Dress Code: No denim; collared shirt and Bermuda shorts required.
Spikes: No.
Rental Clubs: Yes.
Carts: Electric, course access.

This desert links-style course, designed by Tom Weiskopf and Jay Morrish, isn't quite a target course.

MARYVALE MUNICIPAL GOLF COURSE

623-846-4022.
5902 W. Indian School Rd., Phoenix.
Public, 18 holes, $.
Greens Grass Type: Bermuda.
Fairways Grass Type: Bermuda.
Accepts Tee Times: Yes.

Earliest Call for Tee Time: 6:30 AM.
Driving Range: Yes.
Dress Code: Casual—jeans and tank tops are okay.
Spikes: No.
Rental Clubs: Yes.
Carts: Electric, course access.

Built in Maryvale in 1961, this fairly straightforward course is well shaded by mature trees.

RAVEN GOLF CLUB AT SOUTH MOUNTAIN, THE

602-243-3636.
3636 E. Baseline Rd., Phoenix.
Public, 18 holes, $$$$$.
Greens Grass Type: Tifdwarf.
Fairways Grass Type: Bermuda.
Accepts Tee Times: Yes.
Earliest Call for Tee Time: 7 AM.
Driving Range: Yes.
Dress Code: Collared shirt; no denim.
Spikes: Yes.
Rental Clubs: Yes.
Carts: Electric, course access.

This pine-tree-lined golf course is reminiscent of a midwestern-style course. It has been ranked as one of the best in Arizona by *Golf Digest*.

EAST VALLEY
ASU KARSTEN GOLF COURSE

480-921-8070.
1125 E. Rio Salado Pkwy., Tempe.
Public, 18 holes, $$$.
Greens Grass Type: Tifdwarf.
Fairways Grass Type: Bermuda.
Accepts Tee Times: Yes.
Earliest Call for Tee Time: 7 AM.
Driving Range: Yes.
Dress Code: No T-shirts or denim.
Spikes: Yes.
Rental Clubs: Yes.
Carts: Electric, course access.

Named after Karsten Solheim, the founder of the Ping Golf Company, ASU Karsten is located close to Arizona State University's Main Campus in Tempe. *Golf for Women* considered this course one of the most "women-friendly" golf courses in the United States.

AUGUSTA RANCH GOLF CLUB

480-354-1234.
2401 S. Lansing, Mesa.
Public, 18 holes, $.
Greens Grass Type: Tifdwarf.
Fairways Grass Type: Bermuda.
Accepts Tee Times: Yes.
Earliest Call for Tee Time: 7 AM.
Driving Range: No.
Dress Code: Collared shirt; no denim.
Spikes: Yes.
Rental Clubs: Yes.
Carts: Electric, path access.

Considered a good choice for beginners, this desert-style course is fairly new.

CROWNE PLAZA SAN MARCOS COUNTRY CLUB

480-963-3358.
100 N. Dakota St., Chandler.
Resort, 18 holes, $$$.
Greens Grass Type: Bermuda.
Fairways Grass Type: Bermuda.
Accepts Tee Times: Yes.
Earliest Call for Tee Time: 7 AM.
Driving Range: Yes.
Dress Code: Collared shirt; no denim.
Spikes: Yes.
Rental Clubs: Yes.
Carts: Electric, path access.

The first grass golf course in Arizona, San Marcos offers a mature landscape with more than 300 palm trees lining the fairways; it hosts the Senior State Tournament each year.

DOBSON RANCH GOLF COURSE

480-644-2291.
2155 S. Dobson Rd., Mesa.
Public, 18 holes, $.

Golf on the Cutting Edge
by Cori Brett

Golfers fortunate enough to live and vacation in the Valley of the Sun are surrounded by the best that the game has to offer, from high tech to high fashion. Just watch players at Kierland Golf Club navigate the hilly course on trendy Segways with golf bags strapped to the side. Coolwell air-conditioned golf carts mock the summer sun, directing cool, dry air to each player. Want some exercise? Walk the new Saguaro Course at We-Ko-Pa Golf Club with the Sun Mountain Sports "Speed E" battery-powered cart. It carries a full-sized golf bag and moves as much as 90 yards at a time on its own when directed, leaving golfers to stride the fairways unencumbered.

Of course walking 18 holes and playing well demand strength and endurance. Famed golf instructor Jim McLean just opened his first Arizona golf school, at the Wigwam Golf Resort and Spa, where innovative teachers integrate physical fitness routines with traditional golf swing mechanics for ultimate performance. The right equipment also makes a big difference. That's why Hot Stix is booked up weeks in advance. Custom club fitting at its best, Hot Stix evaluates your swing and recommends the best clubs among top-ranked lines, then allows you to take them out on the course to demo. The only way to go.

In my view, the Valley is one of the most progressive golf destinations around. You can always find the latest and greatest in new trends that are here to stay.

Cori Brett is a Scottsdale-based golf travel writer and author whose articles have appeared in Travel + Leisure Golf, Fortune, SPA, Private Clubs, and other national publications.

Greens Grass Type: Bermuda.
Fairways Grass Type: Bermuda.
Accepts Tee Times: Yes.
Earliest Call for Tee Time: 5 AM.
Driving Range: Yes.
Dress Code: No.
Spikes: Yes.
Rental Clubs: Yes.
Carts: Gas, Course access.

This 18-hole championship course offers an inexpensive golf experience, along with a lighted driving range and putting green.

GOLD CANYON GOLF RESORT
480-982-9449.
6100 S. Kings Ranch Rd., Gold Canyon.
Public, 36 holes, $$.
Greens Grass Type: Bermuda.
Fairways Grass Type: Bermuda.
Accepts Tee Times: Yes.
Earliest Call for Tee Time: 6 AM.

Driving Range: Yes.
Dress Code: No.
Spikes: No.
Rental Clubs: Yes.
Carts: Electric, path access.

This very popular golf resort offers two 18-hole championship courses to choose from. Avid golfers prefer the more challenging target-style Dinosaur Mountain Course. One of *GOLF Magazine*'s Top 100 Teachers, Scott Sackett, offers instruction through Resort Golf Schools, located on site. For more information, call 800-541-7707.

KOKOPELLI GOLF COURSE
480-926-3589.
1800 W. Guadalupe Rd., Gilbert.
Public, 18 holes, $$$.
Greens Grass Type: Bermuda.
Fairways Grass Type: Bermuda.
Accepts Tee Times: Yes.

Earliest Call for Tee Time: 7 AM; call 480-962-GOLF.
Driving Range: Yes.
Dress Code: Collared shirt.
Spikes: Yes.
Rental Clubs: Yes.
Carts: Electric, course access.

Designed by John Allen, this course features plenty of challenging shots, seven lakes, and beautiful views.

LAS SENDAS GOLF CLUB

480-396-4000.
7555 E. Eagle Crest Dr., Mesa.
Public, 18 holes, $$$$$.
Greens Grass Type: Bent.
Fairways Grass Type: Bermuda.
Accepts Tee Times: Yes.
Earliest Call for Tee Time: 7 AM.
Driving Range: Yes.
Dress Code: Collared shirt; no denim.
Spikes: No.
Rental Clubs: Yes.
Carts: Electric, course access.

Designed by Robert Trent Jones Jr. and built in 1995, this high-desert course was the first for Jones in the Phoenix area. Las Sendas was ranked by *Golf Digest* as one of the state's best.

LEISURE WORLD COUNTRY CLUB

480-832-0003.
908 S. Power Rd., Mesa.
Private, 36 holes, $$.
Greens Grass Type: Bermuda grass.
Fairways Grass Type: Bermuda grass.
Accepts Tee Times: No.
Earliest Call for Tee Time: 7AM.
Driving Range: Yes.
Dress Code: Collared shirt; no cutoffs.
Spikes: No.
Rental Clubs: Yes.
Carts: Electric, course access.

Built in 1979, Leisure World Country Club offers both a regulation 18-hole course and an executive 18-hole course. While the course is set in an active adult golf community, nonmembers can enjoy golf at member rates.

LONGBOW GOLF CLUB

480-807-5400.
5400 E. McDowell Rd., Mesa.
Public, 18 holes, $$$.
Greens Grass Type: Bermuda.
Fairways Grass Type: Winter rye.
Accepts Tee Times: Yes.
Earliest Call for Tee Time: 7 AM.
Driving Range: Yes.
Dress Code: Collared shirt; no denim.
Spikes: No.
Rental Clubs: Yes.
Carts: Electric, course access.

Located across the street from Boeing, Longbow was named after one of Boeing's helicopters, the Apache Longbow.

OCOTILLO GOLF COURSE

480-917-6660.
3751 S. Clubhouse Dr., Chandler.
Public, 54 holes, $$$$.
Greens Grass Type: Bermuda grass.
Fairways Grass Type: Bermuda grass.
Accepts Tee Times: Yes.
Earliest Call for Tee Time: 6 AM.
Driving Range: Yes.
Dress Code: Collared shirt; no denim.
Spikes: Yes.
Rental Clubs: Yes.
Carts: Electric, path access.

This golf course is very popular with the locals and well known for its water features. Three 9-hole courses can be combined to create three separate 18-hole courses.

PAINTED MOUNTAIN GOLF CLUB

480-832-0156.
6210 E. McKellips Rd., Mesa.
Public, 27 holes, $$.
Greens Grass Type: Tifdwarf.
Fairways Grass Type: Bermuda.

Accepts Tee Times: Yes.
Earliest Call for Tee Time: 6 AM.
Driving Range: No.
Dress Code: Collared shirt; no denim.
Spikes: No.
Rental Clubs: Yes.

Painted Mountain offers golfers an 18-hole desert course and a 9-hole executive course.

TOKA STICKS GOLF COURSE

480-988-9405.
6910 E. Williamsfield Rd., Mesa.
Public, 18 holes, $$.
Greens Grass Type: Bermuda.
Fairways Grass Type: Bermuda.
Accepts Tee Times: Yes.
Earliest Call for Tee Time: 6:30 AM.
Driving Range: Yes.
Dress Code: Collared shirt; denim is okay.
Spikes: No.
Rental Clubs: Yes.
Carts: Electric, Course access.

Built in 1945 and designed by the US Army Corp of Engineers, this was originally called Williams Golf Course due to its close proximity to the Air Force base of the same name. It was redesigned in 1997. The landscaping is mature, with two lakes that come into play at several points along the course.

TRILOGY GOLF COURSE

480-988-0004.
4415 E. Village Pkwy., Gilbert.
Public, 18 holes, $$.
Greens Grass Type: Winter rye.
Fairways Grass Type: Winter rye.
Accepts Tee Times: Yes.
Earliest Call for Tee Time: 7 AM.
Driving Range: Yes.
Dress Code: Collared shirt; no denim.
Spikes: No metal spikes.
Rental Clubs: Yes.
Carts: Electric, course access.

Built as part of Trilogy's active adult com-

munity, this desert-style course offers a series of challenges to both new and avid players.

SCOTTSDALE
BOULDERS GOLF CLUB & RESORT

480-488-9028.
34636 N. Tom Darlington, Carefree.
Resort, 36 holes, $$$$$.
Greens Grass Type: Bent.
Fairways Grass Type: Winter rye.
Accepts Tee Times: Yes.
Earliest Call for Tee Time: 7 AM.
Driving Range: Yes.
Dress Code: Collared shirt; no denim.
Spikes: No.
Rental Clubs: Yes.
Carts: Electric, path access.

These two 18-hole golf courses are respectively private and public, and have been named as top courses by *GOLF Magazine*.

DESERT CANYON GOLF CLUB

480-837-1173.
www.desertcanyongolf.com.
10440 N. Indian Wells Dr., Fountain Hills.
Public, 18 holes, $$$$$.
Greens Grass Type: Bermuda.
Fairways Grass Type: Bermuda.
Accepts Tee Times: Yes.
Earliest Call for Tee Time: 6:30 AM.
Driving Range: Yes.
Dress Code: Collared shirt; no cutoffs.
Spikes: No.
Rental Clubs: Yes.
Carts: Gas, course access.

Desert Canyon is home of the famous Fountain—the tallest in the world—and plays host to the Southwest Pro-Am. There's a putting green.

GAINEY RANCH GOLF CLUB

480-483-2582.
7600 Gainey Club Dr., Scottsdale.
Private/Resort, 54 holes, $$$$$.
Greens Grass Type: Bermuda.

Golfers in spring. Photo provided courtesy of Camelback Inn

Fairways Grass Type: Bermuda.
Accepts Tee Times: Yes.
Earliest Call for Tee Time: 7 AM.
Driving Range: No.
Dress Code: Collared shirt, no cutoffs;
denim is okay.
Spikes: No.
Rental Clubs: No.
Carts: Electric, course access.

Three very different 9-hole courses can be combined to create three 18-hole games with a wide variety of terrain. Guests of the adjacent hotel can play at this private club.

GOLF CLUB AT EAGLE MOUNTAIN, THE

480-816-1234.
www.eaglemtn.com.

14915 E. Eagle Mountain Pkwy., Fountain Hills.
Public, 18 holes, $$$$$.
Greens Grass Type: Tifdwarf.
Fairways Grass Type: Bermuda.
Accepts Tee Times: Yes.
Earliest Call for Tee Time: 7 AM.
Driving Range: Yes.
Dress Code: Shirt and shoes required.
Spikes: No.
Rental Clubs: Yes.
Carts: Electric, course access.

Awarded accolades and praise from various golf publications since it opened in 1996, The Golf Club at Eagle Mountain has hosted several charity tournaments and events. It features magnificent views of the McDowell Mountains and challenging golf.

LEGEND TRAIL GOLF CLUB

480-488-7434.
9462 Legendary Lane, Scottsdale.
Public, 18 holes, $$$$$.
Greens Grass Type: Bent.
Fairways Grass Type: Bermuda.
Accepts Tee Times: Yes.
Earliest Call for Tee Time: 7 AM.
Driving Range: Yes.
Dress Code: No denim or T-shirts.
Spikes: Yes.
Rental Clubs: Yes.
Carts: Electric, path access.

Named one of the top 100 courses in the country by *GOLF Magazine*, Legend Trail is located in North Scottsdale and features panoramic views of some of the city's most prominent natural landmarks, including Pinnacle Peak, Camelback, and Mummy Mountain. You will find sweeping views of the Valley, too.

MCCORMICK RANCH GOLF CLUB

480-948-0260.
7505 E. McCormick Pkwy., Scottsdale.
Public, 36 holes, $$$$$.
Greens Grass Type: Winter rye.
Fairways Grass Type: Bermuda.
Earliest Call for Tee Time: 7 AM.
Driving Range: Yes.
Dress Code: Sleeves; no denim.
Spikes: No.
Rental Clubs: Yes.
Carts: Electric, course access.

This golf club, set in front of the McDowell Mountains, features two championship courses for public use. The Palm course sports a recently redesigned front 9 as well as 10 water holes.

GRAYHAWK GOLF CLUB

480-502-1800.
8620 E. Thompson Peak Pkwy., Scottsdale.
Public, 36 holes, $$$$$.
Greens Grass Type: Bent.
Fairways Grass Type: Tifdwarf.

Accepts Tee Times: Yes.
Earliest Call for Tee Time: 8 AM.
Driving Range: Yes.
Dress Code: Proper golf attire.
Spikes: Yes.
Rental Clubs: Yes.
Carts: Electric, Path access.

Both 18-hole golf courses have been named among the top 100 by *GOLF Magazine*. Breathtaking views of the McDowell Mountains and the Valley round out this golfing experience. The club has hosted several tournaments, including the Anderson Consulting World Match Championship—considered the "world's richest"—as well as the first World Championship of Golf and the Williams World Challenge.

ORANGE TREE
GOLF & CONFERENCE RESORT

480-948-3730.
10601 N. 56th St., Scottsdale.
Resort, 18 holes, $$$$.
Greens Grass Type: Tifdwarf.
Fairways Grass Type: Bermuda.
Accepts Tee Times: Yes.
Earliest Call for Tee Time: 7 AM.
Driving Range: Yes.
Dress Code: Collared shirt; no denim.
Spikes: Yes.
Rental Clubs: Yes.
Carts: Electric, course access.

Originally built in 1957 as a private club, this fairly flat course offers four lakes and mature vegetation.

PHOENICIAN, THE

480-423-2449.
6000 E. Camelback Rd., Scottsdale.
Resort, 54 holes, $$$$$.
Greens Grass Type: Bent.
Fairways Grass Type: Bermuda.
Accepts Tee Times: Yes.
Earliest Call for Tee Time: 7 AM.
Driving Range: Yes; available to playing golfers.

Dress Code: Collared shirt; no denim.
Spikes: No.
Rental Clubs: Yes.
Carts: Electric, path access.

This resort features three 9-hole courses that can be combined into three separate 18-hole options. Named by *GOLF Magazine* to their 1998 list of Silver Medal Resorts, the Phoenician is set in the mountains and provides incredible views as you golf.

RANCHO MANANA GOLF CLUB

480-488-0398.
5734 E. Rancho Manana Blvd., Cave Creek.
Semiprivate, 18 holes, $$$$.
Greens Grass Type: Bent.
Fairways Grass Type: Winter rye.
Accepts Tee Times: Yes.
Earliest Call for Tee Time: 7 AM.
Driving Range: Yes.
Dress Code: Collared shirt; no denim.
Spikes: Yes.
Rental Clubs: Yes.
Carts: Electric, path access.

Considered one of the most scenic courses in Arizona, Rancho Manana is located in Cave Creek and features challenging play as well as views of the Black and Superstition Mountains.

TALKING STICK GOLF CLUB

480-860-2221.
9998 E. Indian Bend Rd., Scottsdale.
Public, 36 holes, $$$$.
Greens Grass Type: Tifdwarf.
Fairways Grass Type: Bermuda.
Accepts Tee Times: Yes.
Earliest Call for Tee Time: 6:30 AM.
Driving Range: Yes.
Dress Code: No denim; collared shirt and Bermuda shorts required.
Spikes: Yes.
Rental Clubs: Yes.
Carts: Electric, course access.

This East Valley golf club features the tree-less link-style North Course, which was named one of the top modern courses in the nation by *Golfweek*; however, recreational golfers prefer the South Course.

TPC SCOTTSDALE

480-585-4334.
17020 N. Hayden Rd., Scottsdale.
Resort, 36 holes, $$$$$.
Greens Grass Type: Bermuda Grass.
Fairways Grass Type: Bermuda Grass.
Accepts Tee Times: Yes.
Earliest Call for Tee Time: 6 AM; call 480-585-4334.
Driving Range: Yes.
Dress Code: Collared shirt; no denim.
Spikes: Yes.
Rental Clubs: Yes.
Carts: Electric, course access.

The famous TPC Scottsdale features the Stadium Course, which hosts the PGA Tour's FBR Open in late January every year. This resort facility, named by *GOLF Magazine* to its 1998 list of Silver Medal Resorts, also offers the target-style Desert Course. Practice where the pros do—TPC's practice facility is used by more than 25 PGA Tour professionals.

TROON NORTH GOLF CLUB

480-585-5300.
10320 E. Dynamite Blvd., Scottsdale.
Semiprivate, 36 holes, $$$$$.
Greens Grass Type: Bent.
Fairways Grass Type: Bermuda.
Accepts Tee Times: Yes.
Earliest Call for Tee Time: 7 AM; call 480-585-7700.
Driving Range: Yes.
Dress Code: No denim.
Spikes: Yes.
Rental Clubs: Yes.
Carts: Electric, path access.

Designed by Tom Weiskopf and Jay Morrish, Troon North features two 18-hole courses:

The Monument Course and The Pinnacle Course. Both have been listed in *GOLF Magazine* among the Top 100 Courses You Can Play in the US. Troon North offers some of the most beautiful golf course views in the Valley.

WESTIN KIERLAND RESORT & SPA, THE

480-922-9283.
15636 Clubgate Dr., Scottsdale.
Public, 54 holes, $$$$$.
Greens Grass Type: Bent.
Fairways Grass Type: Winter rye.
Accepts Tee Times: Yes.
Earliest Call for Tee Time: 6:30 AM.
Driving Range: Yes; $35 fee.
Dress Code: Collared shirt; no denim.
Spikes: Yes.
Rental Clubs: Yes.
Carts: Electric, path access.

Located in North Phoenix as part of the Westin Kierland Resort and Spa, this 27-hole facility provides three combinations of an 18-hole game and stunning views. The course is meticulously manicured and features desert fauna.

WEST VALLEY

EAGLE'S NEST COUNTRY CLUB
AT PEBBLE CREEK RESORT

623-935-6750.
3645 Clubhouse Dr., Goodyear.
Semiprivate, 18 holes, $.
Greens Grass Type: Bermuda.
Fairways Grass Type: Bermuda.
Accepts Tee Times: Yes.
Earliest Call for Tee Time: 6:30 AM.
Driving Range: Yes.
Dress Code: Collared shirt; no denim.
Spikes: Yes.
Rental Clubs: Yes.
Carts: Gas, path access.

Set in Goodyear, west of Phoenix, this championship course is fairly straightforward.

GLENDALE

DESERT MIRAGE GOLF COURSE

623-772-0110.
8710 W. Maryland, Glendale.
Public, 9 holes, $.
Greens Grass Type: Bermuda.
Fairways Grass Type: Bermudas.
Accepts Tee Times: Yes.
Earliest Call for Tee Time: 7 AM.
Driving Range: Yes.
Dress Code: No.
Spikes: No.
Rental Clubs: Yes.
Carts: Electric, Course access.

This nine-hole course is user-friendly with wide-open fairways and undulating hills.

GLEN LAKES GOLF COURSE

623-939-7541.
5450 W. Northern Ave., Glendale.
Public, 9 holes, $.
Greens Grass Type: Bermuda Grass.
Fairways Grass Type: Bermuda Grass.
Accepts Tee Times: Yes.
Earliest Call for Tee Time: 6 AM.
Driving Range: Yes.
Dress Code: No.
Spikes: Yes.
Rental Clubs: Yes.
Carts: Gas, course access.

This affordable nine-hole executive course is great for a practice session or short game. It features a misted and lighted driving range.

HILLCREST GOLF CLUB
AT SUN CITY WEST

623-584-1500.
20002 N. Star Ridge Dr., Sun City West.
Public, 18 holes, $$.
Greens Grass Type: Bermuda.
Fairways Grass Type: Bermuda.
Accepts Tee Times: Yes.
Earliest Call for Tee Time: 7 AM.
Driving Range: Yes.
Dress Code: Collared shirt; no denim.

Spikes: No.
Rental Clubs: Yes.
Carts: Electric, course access.

Set in the West Valley, this 18-hole course features 25 acres of beautiful blue water. It's designed to accommodate all skill levels.

LEGEND AT ARROWHEAD, THE
623-561-1902.
21025 N. 67th Ave., Glendale.
Semiprivate, 18, $$$$.
Greens Grass Type: Bermuda.
Fairways Grass Type: Bermuda.
Accepts Tee Times: Yes.
Earliest Call for Tee Time: 6 AM.
Driving Range: Yes.
Dress Code: Collared shirt; no denim.
Spikes: Yes.
Rental Clubs: Yes.
Carts: Electric, course access.

This challenging course, designed by Arnold Palmer and Ed Seay and built in 1998, is in excellent condition.

PALM VALLEY GOLF CLUB
623-935-2500.
2211 N. Litchfield Rd., Goodyear.
Public, $$$.
Greens Grass Type: Bermuda.
Fairways Grass Type: Bermuda.

Accepts Tee Times: Yes.
Earliest Call for Tee Time: 6 AM.
Driving Range: Yes.
Dress Code: No T-shirts.
Spikes: No steel spikes.
Rental Clubs: Yes.
Carts: Electric, Course access.

This golf club features two 18-hole courses, including the link-style Palms Course.

PEBBLEBROOK GOLF COURSE AT SUN CITY WEST
623-584-3100.
18836 N. 128th Ave., Sun City West.
Private, 18 holes, $$.
Greens Grass Type: Bermuda.
Fairways Grass Type: Bermudas.
Accepts Tee Times: Yes.
Earliest Call for Tee Time: 6:30 AM.
Driving Range: Yes.
Dress Code: Collared shirt; no denim.
Spikes: Yes.
Rental Clubs: Yes.
Carts: Electric, course access.

Located in the active adult community of Sun City West, Pebblebrook was one of the first golf courses in this area. It features a challenging course for all levels of play; the landscape is mature, with lakes and creeks meandering through.

Special Golf Services

Arizona Golf Association (602-944-3035; www.azgolf.org; 7226 N. 16th St., Suite 200, Phoenix). This association offers excellent information about the state's many golf courses, including dress codes, pricing, and tournament information. In spring 2007 members will be able to book tee times online.

Golf Couriers (602-405-5105; 1820 E. Frier Dr., Phoenix). Golf reservation services.

In Celebration of Golf (480-951-4444; www.celebrategolf.com; 7001 N. Scottsdale Rd., Suite 172, Scottsdale). Celebrate the golfing life at this unique emporium dedicated to everything golf. You'll find golf gifts ranging from a few dollars to over $3,500. Memorabilia offered ranges from autographed biographies and autobiographies of famous golfers; hickory-shafted clubs and autographed golf balls; hundreds of books—some rare—on the game, the players, the courses, and their designers; artwork depicting the sport; and furniture and furnishings that embody the golfing spirit. The 15,000-square-foot facility also has men's and ladies' pro shops, and the Spike Shop for comfortable golf shoes and socks. Additional locales at Terminals 2 and 4 at Phoenix Sky Harbor International Airport.

Private Preserve Golf Inc. (480-609-1547; 8912 E. Pinnacle Peak Rd., Suite 461, Scottsdale). Get tee times at some of the Valley's top "members only" courses. Private Preserve Golf offers its VIP clients half- and full-day golf outings for up to three players.

JDR Tours (800-759-8747 or 602-264-2833; fax 602-264-3500; 5125 N. 16th St., Suite A-121, Phoenix). Golf reservation services.

Katherine Roberts Yoga for Golfers (888-313-9642; www.krtotalfitness.com; 6143 E. Lowden Rd., Cave Creek). Featured in *GOLF Magazine*, *USA Today*, and *Golf for Women*. Katherine Roberts has designed yoga techniques to increase range of motion and "mind–body performance" for golfers both on and off the course. Choose from hands-on golf fitness workshops taught by instructors trained and certified in Yoga for Golfers.

SPAS

As early as the late 19th century, Phoenix beckoned to those from wetter climates with promises of a healthier existence. People arrived here in droves. The dry climate and warm sun have revitalized the health of thousands of the Valley's residents both past and present.

Today the Valley's promises are more extravagant than the warm sun and dry climate—you will find some of the top spas in the country here. The Arizona sun and the area's world-class facilities join efforts to pamper your body and spirit into restorative peace. Inspired by some of the globe's oldest traditions and most exotic therapies, the Valley's spas have incorporated practices from the Sonoran Desert, Asia, and Europe to bring a rejuvenating experience in a variety of settings.

Photo provided courtesy of Camelback Inn

Reservations

Booking your spa treatment(s) 4–6 weeks in advance affords you the greatest number of choices for services and time frames. However, that doesn't mean you can't call that week or ask your hotel concierge to secure services for you. You will be asked for a credit card number to reserve services, and be sure to double-check the spa's cancellation policies. Most spas require a 4- to 24-hour notice to cancel any treatments; many will charge your card the full amount if you don't cancel within the specified time frame.

Check-In

Your trip to the spa should be a relaxing and invigorating experience, so plan to arrive at least 30 minutes in advance. Some spas require that you check in at least 15 minutes prior to your first appointment. This ensures that you will be ready to begin on time; it also provides ample time to shower or use the whirlpool or sauna first. Prompt arrival is important, as spa appointments begin and end at the specified hour. Late arrival means less time for your treatment.

Attire

Since you will be changing into a robe prior to your treatment, it is recommended that you not bring your jewelry or valuables with you. In keeping with the tranquil environment, spas request that all pagers and cell phones be turned off.

Gratuities

Many spas add an 18–20 percent gratuity to your bill, while others provide a tip envelope. Prices listed in this book do not include gratuities, and are subject to change.

Age

Most Valley spas require that their guests be at least 16 years old; however, some do allow for younger guests as long as they are accompanied by an adult. Please check with your spa choice prior to making arrangements for younger guests.

Expectant Mothers

Several of the Valley's spas offer massages and treatments just for moms-to-be; ask if these options are available.

Tips and Suggestions

Drink plenty of water before and after your spa appointment—the dry desert air coupled with your treatment can drain your water reserves.

Body Treatments and Services

The Valley's spas offer a combination of treatments and services, including the following:

FACIALS. A deep cleansing of the face via a variety of methods including steam, exfoliation, extraction, creams, masks, peels, and massages.

MASSAGE. Manual manipulation of the body or parts of the body to relieve tension and improve circulation.

HOT STONE MASSAGE. This Native American tradition uses heated stones placed strategically on the body to relax muscles.

BODY WRAPS. A combination of oils, herbs, and minerals is applied to the body and used to drain toxins, relieve stress, and rejuvenate.

AROMATHERAPY. The use of liquid plant oils or essential oils to effect positive changes in mood and health.

WATSU. A derivative of Zen shiatsu, this massage is performed in warm water, about 95 degrees; a therapist fully supports the individual while gently rocking and stretching the body, relieving stress and muscle tension; the water allows for manipulation and movement that wouldn't be possible on a massage table.

The Valley offers a variety of day and destination spas. Day spas are frequented for one or more treatments in a single day; destination spas, on the other hand, are typically located in a resort setting, and guests may enjoy treatments throughout their stay.

Day Spas

BOXERS MEN'S SALON, LTD.
602-340-8052.
7 W. Monroe St., Phoenix.

Boxer's is a full-service salon and spa just for men. Services include haircuts, manicures, pedicures, teeth whitening, straight-razor shaves, facials, massages, personal fitness training, and shoe shine.

FUCHSIA
480-813-7465.
www.fuchsiaspa.com.
1854 S. Val Vista Dr., Mesa.

Fuchsia is not your traditional spa; in fact, they strive to be anything but. Fun, spirited, and pink—it might just be the spa for women of the new millennium. The spa offers chemical peels, massages, aromatherapy, reflexology, and facials. Fuchsia offers monthly memberships for $59, and discounts to members. All massages and facials are offered at fixed prices, so there are no surprises when you get ready to pay. It's located on the east side of Mesa.

HEALING ARTS DAY SPA, THE
480-897-2146.
www.thehealingartsdayspa.com.
1845 S. Dobson Rd., Suite 110, Mesa.
Other Locations: 5055 W. Ray Road, Suite 12, Chandler (480-893-2826).

With sites in Mesa and Chandler, the Healing Arts Day Spa offers a variety of products and services designed to rejuvenate the body, mind, and soul, including massage services, body wraps, skin care, and body exfoliation. After an afternoon in the Arizona sun, try an aloe vera rehydrating wrap—a 30-minute session is $40. This soothing wrap is perfect for restoring moisture to your body. Men can try the gentleman's organic spa facial—a deep-cleansing facial and facial masque followed by a pressure-point massage. The popular La Stone

Therapy, based on the Native American belief in the power of healing stones, starts at $70 for a 60-minute session. Ask about introductory prices.

J'S INTEGRATIVE THERAPIES
480-961-7751.
www.jsmindbodyandsoul.com.
By appointment only.

J's offers a wonderfully rejuvenating experience from the moment you arrive for your appointment. Their goal is to make your experience as stress-free and relaxing as possible. The space is designed for privacy, quietude, and personalized service. Choose from an array of treatments including facials, massages, anti-aging therapies, and body treatments. Try a quick-fix mini facial ($45)—this 45-minute treatment is just enough to set your spirits right again. Or flush toxins from your body with a 90-minute light touch lymphatic massage ($95). You might also choose to take your body in an inch or two with J's 60-minute Body Inch Loss and Contouring body wrap ($90).

LAMAR EVERYDAY SPA, THE
480-945-7066.
www.thelamar.com.
5115 N. Scottsdale Rd., Scottsdale.

Off Scottsdale Rd. north of Chaparral in Scottsdale, the Lamar Everyday Spa is a Phoenix favorite. Its island-inspired theme brings a little bit of the oceanside to the Sonoran Desert. Lamar offers nicely priced massages, manicures, pedicures, body wraps, and scrubs. Take a relaxing dip in the pool or unwind in the private Oasis Courtyard. Swedish relaxation massages start at $50 for 25 minutes; manicures are $25.

LIQUID ENERGY DAY SPA
480-892-1960.
www.adayawayspaonline.com.
835 E. Southern Ave., Suite 5, Mesa.

Liquid Energy is located inside the Painted Mountain Golf Resort in Mesa, and offers body polishes, massages, wellness therapy, and body sugaring.

MANDALA TEAROOM & APOTHECARY

480-423-8828.
www.mandalaapothecary.com.
7027 E. 5th Ave., Scottsdale.

Mandala Apothecary is an organic beauty boutique offering organic beauty products and holistic body treatments, including acupuncture, organic facials, nutrition counseling, yoga therapy, and massages. They offer prenatal massages as well. Located on 5th Ave. in Old Town Scottsdale, Mandala creates a tranquil and relaxing experience designed to help you get in touch with your own well-being.

RED DOOR SPA AT WIGWAM RESORT

623-535-4967.
www.reddoorspas.com.
195 Old Litchfield Rd., Litchfield.

This 26,000-square-foot facility opened in late December 2005 to provide guests of the Wigwam Resort Elizabeth Arden—inspired services and treatments. The spa features 16,000 square feet of indoor-outdoor space and 16 treatment rooms, some with outdoor patios.

SKIN CARE BY KLARA

480-247-8240.
www.skincarebyklara.com.
16447 N. Scottsdale Rd., Suite 105, Scottsdale.

A European day spa for both men and women, Skin Care by Klara offers more than skin care. Several types of massage therapies, including aromatherapy, deep tissue, and hot stone, as well as body wraps, facial treatments, and hair removal.

SPA AT GAINEY VILLAGE, THE

480-609-6980.
www.villageclubs.com.
7477 E. Doubletree Ranch Rd., Scottsdale.

One of the Village Clubs and Spas located throughout North Scottsdale, this 80,000-square-foot health club includes a resort pool, café, and day care. The 25-room spa offers a variety of treatments inspired by the Sonoran Desert, including massages like the LaStone Therapy (a therapist uses heated basalt stones from the Salt River Valley); the Sonoran Aloe Facial, which incorporates ingredients like aloe vera, honey, sage, lavender, and citrus fruit found in the desert; manicures and pedicures; and body treatments like the Rosemary Mint Awakening Body Wrap or the Desert Clay Body Masque. Salon and hair care, too.

SPA DU SOLEIL

480-994-5400.
www.spadusoleil.com.
7040 E. 3rd Ave., Scottsdale.

Voted Scottsdale's best day spa, SPA du Soleil is located in the Scottsdale arts district in Old Town and offers a variety of treatments including massage therapy, body sculpting, facials, manicures, and pedicures, as well as a number of packages designed to pamper you from head to toe.

STEVEN PAUL SALON & SPA

480-603-1000.
www.stevenpaulsalon.com.
7045 E. 3rd Ave., Scottsdale.

The Steven Paul Salon is located in the arts district in Old Town Scottsdale. This charming salon offers an array of services including facials, massage therapy, nail care, and hair care for you and your pooch. Check out Stephen Paws, the exclusive, on-site dog grooming service. A trendy boutique and a full-menu café can make this salon and spa an all-day stop.

VH SPA AT HOTEL VALLEY HO

480-248-2000 or 866-882-4484.
www.hotelvalleyho.com.
6850 E. Main St., Scottsdale.

VH (Vitality + Health) Spa is found in Scottsdale's newly refurbished Hotel Valley Ho. Eight private treatment rooms, steam baths, and individual showers make for a private, relaxing affair. Enjoy various body treatments, manicures, pedicures, facials, and massages—perhaps a red flower Hammam full-body massage imported from Turkish Hammam bathhouses. Moroccan mint tea, coffee, olives, fresh lemons, jasmine, amber, and cloves combine to electrify your senses and detoxify and replenish your body. Ninety-minute sessions run $185; or try the scrub and moisture only without the finishing massage at $95 for 45 minutes. They have a number of poolside massages, including the OH! So Cool Foot Refresher—30 minutes (at $65) will leave your sandaled feet feeling soft and happy. Travelers can also work out in the open-air fitness studio overlooking the pool; yoga and Pilates classes are available throughout the week.

Destination Spas

AGAVE, THE ARIZONA SPA, AT THE WESTIN KIERLAND RESORT

480-624-1500.
www.kierlandresort.com.
902 E. Greenway Pkwy., The Westin Kierland Resort & Spa, Scottsdale 85254.

Agave is a full-service spa specializing in treatments inspired by the agave—a moisture-rich plant native to the Sonoran Desert. The spa offers several exclusive treatments, some developed by their own therapist, including the Agave Body Glow, an exfoliating treatment that begins with a full salt scrub with grapefruit essential oils and agave to rid the body of dry skin; an application of warm shea butter restores

moisture. Fifty-minute sessions range $135–155. Agave, the Arizona Spa, offers treatments for men. Golfers can request the Golfer's Massage, designed to release toxins and tension, after a long day on one of Kierland's two 18-hole courses. Fifty- and 80-minute sessions are available for $135–220. Also available are spa packages to pamper guests from top to bottom, facials, body treatments, massages, health and fitness services, and mind and body wellness. Pamper the teenager in your family with a facial, manicure, or pedicure; Agave's "family-focused treatments" are designed just for teens.

AJI SPA

602-225-0100; 520-796-8416; fax 520-796-8334.
www.wildhorsepassresort.com.
5594 W. Wild Horse Pass Blvd., Chandler 85226.

Aji is the Pima word for "sanctuary," and Aji Spa infuses its treatments and therapies with the traditions and ingredients of the Pima and Maricopa cultures of Central Arizona. Located at Sheraton Wild Horse Pass within the Gila River Indian Community, Aji Spa features more than 17,000 square foot of space and includes 17 treatment rooms, a fitness center, salon, Watsu pool, and traditional roundhouse. The treatments are steeped in the traditions and legends of the Maricopa and Pima Indians and utilize local plants and minerals. Not surprisingly, water is considered one of the most important elements of their desert existence. The Shuhthagi or Watsu massage is performed in the Watsu pool; a therapist fully supports the individual while gently rocking and stretching the body, relieving stress and muscle tension. The signature Bahn or Blue Coyote Wrap is based on the Pima legend of the Bluebird and the Coyote. This treatment incorporates Azulene mud, which is applied to the body. Upon removal of the blue mud, a full-body massage with cedar/sage oil follows. The Ho'dai or Gila River Rock Massage incorporates the Pima and Maricopa tradition of using hot rocks to relieve pain and comfort the spirit—strategically placed hot and cold stones soothe your muscles, release toxins from your body, and restore balance. Try the Kahagam or Bluebird Facial. This signature treatment incorporates jasmine to oxygenate and hydrate your skin.

ALVADORA SPA

602-977-6400.
www.royalpalmshotel.com.
5200 E. Camelback Rd., Royal Palms Resort and Spa, Phoenix 85018.

The Alvadora Spa is a favorite of locals and visitors alike. Tucked in the lush folds of the Royal Palms Resort at the base of Camelback Mountain, this two-level open-air space features nine treatment rooms and incorporates the plants, oils, and minerals of the Mediterranean region. The spa offers day packages ranging about $162–487 (depending on the combination of treatments you choose), as well as individual services. A variety of 60- and 90-minute massages are on offer, like an aromatherapy massage with essential oils ($125–195); a luxurious 30-minute herbal Botanica Bath ($65); or a 60-minute detoxifying Frango Mud Wrap ($125–135). Other services include facials, body scrubs and wraps, manicures, and pedicures.

ARIZONA BILTMORE SPA

602-381-7632 or 800-950-0086.
www.arizonabiltmore.com/spa.
2400 E. Missouri Ave., Arizona Biltmore Resort, Phoenix 85016.

The Arizona Biltmore Spa combines the practices of medieval China and Native Americans of the Sonoran Desert to bring a variety of services and body treatments to its guests. The 22,000-square-foot facility includes several outdoor retreat areas and a cascading whirlpool; men's and women's private locker rooms have amenities such as a dry sauna, wet steam, Jacuzzi whirlpool, and power shower. In your locker you will find a robe, slippers, and a towel for your stay. The spa's signature treatment—the Dream Catcher—is a Native American–inspired massage that incorporates essential oils and heated stones strategically placed along your spine while you receive a delightful foot massage. This 80-minute treatment ends with a full-body massage ($210). The spa also provides a full complement of 50- and 80-minute massages, body scrubs (the 50-minute Gentle Jojoba Body Glow incorporates native plants like jojoba and sage for $135), body wraps (during the 80-minute, $195 Desert Heat Therapy Wrap, warm Arizona desert mud revives and energizes your skin), facials, a variety of manicures and pedicures, and a full-service salon. Ask about special holiday treatments like the $85 Chocolate Peppermint Pedicure (Dec.) or Pumpkin Enzyme Peel (Nov.–Jan.). Day packages range $205–775 depending on the combination of treatments.

CENTRE FOR WELL-BEING AT THE PHOENICIAN, THE

480-941-8200.
6000 E. Camelback Rd., Scottsdale 85251.
www.thephoenician.com.

Located at The Phoenician, the Centre for Well-Being has been recognized as a premier facility. Spa guests indulging in massages, consultations, and body or skin care treatments have full-day complimentary access to all amenities within the 22,000-square-foot spa, including a fitness studio, private lockers, robe and slippers, whirlpools, steam rooms, saunas, Swiss showers, Mediation Atrium, and complimentary refreshments at Waters Bar. There are 24 private treatment rooms and a full-service salon; signature services include

Alvadora Spa at Royal Palms Resort and Spa. Photo provided courtesy of Royal Palms Resort and Spa

Table Thai Massage, a traditional Thai technique adapted to the massage table that uses gentle stretching and rocking motions to relieve stress in the body ($220 for 85 minutes). The Myoxy Caviar Granite Stone Face Massage is an 80-minute anti-aging treatment that incorporates caviar, Escutox, pearl extract, and facial stone massage ($250). In addition to the traditional spa services like body scrubs and wraps, facials, manicures, and pedicures, the Centre for Well-Being's unique options include meditation, astrology, hypnotherapy sessions, belly dancing lessons, private hikes, and Reiki Chakra Balancing treatment.

GOLDEN DOOR SPA
AT THE BOULDERS RESORT, THE
480-595-3500.

www.goldendoorspa.com.
34631 N. Tom Darlington Dr., Carefree 85377.

The Golden Door Spa at The Boulders offers a variety of treatments, including several imbued with Native American traditions. Try LaStone (heated stones), Watsu (body manipulation in a warm pool), or Turquoise Wrap, which incorporates the positive energy, protection, and self-confidence Native Americans believe the color turquoise embodies ($170 for 50 minutes). The spa features 33,000 square feet of relaxation. Traditional spa services, combined with a variety of unique services like a 50-minute numerology session ($85) or a Chocolate Champagne Wrap ($190 for 80 minutes), combine to make this an unusual spa experience.

Evening at the Sanctuary on Camelback. Photo provided courtesy of Sanctuary on Camelback

REVIVE SPA
AT THE JW MARRIOTT RESORT

480-293-5000 or 800-835-6206.
www.jwdesertridgeresort.com.
5350 E. Marriott Dr., Phoenix 85054.

Set in the Sonoran Desert landscape in North Phoenix, the JW Marriott's 28,000-square-foot Revive Spa incorporates desert elements into a variety of traditional spa treatments—facials, massages, body wraps, and scrubs. Enjoy unique treatments like the 50-minute Prickly Pear Cleansing Buff—a mild prickly pear scrub followed by a shallow oil soak and massage ($155); or

the 80-minute foot treatment called the Desert Ridge, which incorporates eucalyptus and aromatherapy oil, leaving your sandaled feet baby soft ($190).

SANCTUARY SPA, THE

480-607-2330.
www.sanctuaryoncamelback.com.
5700 E. McDonald Dr., Paradise Valley 85253.

The Asian-inspired Sanctuary Spa at Sanctuary on Camelback Mountain features 14 indoor and outdoor treatment rooms. Modern architecture and desert mountain settings, combined with a meditation garden, reflecting pond, and Watsu pool, make this urban retreat a relaxing experience. The spa offers guests a fitness center and movement studio with Pilates, meditation, and yoga classes available. Unique treatments include Luk Pra Kope, a 2-hour massage from Thailand that uses medicinal herbs to massage away stress and tension while your dry, desert feet are soaked in fresh lime and essential oils; and the seasonal Winter Candlelight Watsu (60 or 90 minutes), which brings the elements of fire and water together beneath the night sky in this unique twist on the traditional Watsu treatment ($140–200).

SPA AT CAMELBACK INN, A JW MARRIOTT RESORT & SPA

480-596-7040.
www.camelbackspa.com.
5402 E. Lincoln Dr., Scottsdale 85253.

This award-winning spa is consistently voted one of the best in Phoenix and has been ranked as among the finest in the world. The 32,000-square-foot facility features 32 treatment rooms, a fitness studio, an Olympic-sized lap pool, and Sprouts, Scottsdale's only spa restaurant. Guests can enjoy a variety of massages, facials, and body treatments, a full complement of salon services, and fitness training sessions. Try the Camelback Signature Massage Treatment—a combination of hot and cold stones, aromatherapy, reflexology, detoxification, and scalp and facial massages stuffed into a 60-minute session that will leave you feeling balanced and stress-free ($135). The 60-minute Camelback Signature Facial combines grapefruit, mandarin orange, cranberry, and pomegranate into an aromatherapy extravaganza; enjoy a hot stone hand and foot massage while your skin is detoxified ($145). The 60-minute Camelback Signature Body Wrap incorporates vitamin C, citrus, and scented oils to

hydrate and rejuvenate your body ($155). Guests can enjoy a tasty and healthy menu at Sprouts.

SPA AT FOUR SEASONS RESORT SCOTTSDALE

480-515-5700.
www.fourseasons.com.
10600 E. Crescent Moon Dr., Scottsdale 85262.

Nestled in the desert around Pinnacle Peak Mountain, the Four Seasons Spa sits high above the Valley and offers stunning views of the Sonoran Desert. The full-service facility incorporates elements of the four seasons and Native American traditions to bring you a variety of skin and body treatments, scrubs, wraps, facials, and massages, such as the truncated two-in-one Head Over Heels treatment—where not one, but two therapists conspire to leave you feeling twice as good in half the time. Enjoy reflexology and a foot massage while simultaneously receiving a facial of your choice. Or try the 50-minute Jojoba and Prickly Pear Polish—a prickly pear sugar scrub is topped off by a prickly pear/jojoba body butter polish, leaving you relaxed and feeling yummy.

WILLOW STREAM, THE SPA AT THE FAIRMONT SCOTTSDALE PRINCESS

480-585-2732.
www.willowstream.com.
7575 E. Princess Dr., Scottsdale 85255.

At 44,000 square feet, this is the largest spa in the Valley. Amenities such as a eucalyptus steam room, cold plunge pool, and Swiss shower make The Willow Stream Spa a luxuriating choice. Guests can enjoy a variety of treatments infused with native Arizona plants and minerals, all unique to the Willow Stream experience. A high protein, low-carb menu offers healthy and tasty food and beverage options.

10

INFORMATION

Where, Why, When, What, and How

AMBULANCE/FIRE/POLICE

For emergency help in the Valley, dial 911 or 0 for an operator.
Poison Control: 602-253-3334.
Center for Prevention of Abuse and Violence (CASA): 602-254-6400.
National Sexual Assault Hotline: 800-656-HOPE.
Arizona Department of Public Safety: PO Box 6638, Phoenix 85005; www.azdps.gov.
Highway Patrol: main switchboard 602-223-2000; road conditions 888-411-7623.
Arizona Counter Terrorism Information Center (ACTIC): 602-644-5805 or 877-2-SAVEAZ.
Maricopa County Sheriff's Office: Sheriff Joe Arpaio 602-876-1801; Chiefs and Commanders 602-876-1801; www.mcso.org; 100 W. Washington, Suite 1900, Phoenix 85033.
Phoenix Police Department Information Desk: 602-262-7626; no reports or dispatch.

Non-Emergency Police Numbers

Phoenix	602-262-6151
Scottsdale	480-312-5000
Tempe	480-350-8311
Mesa	480-644-2211
Gilbert	480-503-6500
Chandler	480-782-4132
Glendale	623-930-3000
Surprise	623-583-1085
Peoria	623-773-8311
Sun City and Sun City West	623-972-2555

As an unincorporated part of Maricopa County, the Sun Cities are protected by the Maricopa County Sheriff's Office; a volunteer Sheriff's Posse handles non-emergency calls.

EMERGENCY MANAGEMENT

Arizona Department of Emergency Management (602-244-0504 or 877-240-9735; www.dem.state.az.us).

Gabby, a Copper Square ambassador.

Maricopa County—Emergency Management (602-273-1411;
    www.maricopa.gov/emerg_mgt; 2035 N. 52nd St., Phoenix).
City of Phoenix Emergency Management Program (602-495-2077;
    www.ci.phoenix.az.us/EMERGENCYMGMT/index.html).

AREA CODES

Until the late 1990s the Valley had one area code; however, with the rapid growth of Phoenix
and its surrounding cities came two new ones. The original 602 area code covers most of
the city of Phoenix. Generally, the East Valley—including Tempe, Scottsdale, Mesa, Gilbert,
Chandler, Fountain Hills, and Paradise Valley—uses 480. And the West Valley including
Glendale, Peoria, Surprise, and the Sun Cities (Sun City and Sun City West) is serviced by
area code 623.

TOWN GOVERNMENTS

City of Phoenix, Phoenix City Hall (city operator 602-262-6011; www.phoenix.gov; 200 W.
    Washington St., Phoenix 85003).
Scottsdale, city manager (480-312-2800; general city information 480-312-6500;
    www.scottsdaleaz.gov; 3939 N. Drinkwater Blvd., Scottsdale 85251).
City of Tempe (city operator 480-967-2001; www.tempe.gov; 31 E. 5th S., Tempe 85281).
City of Mesa (480-644-2011; www.cityofmesa.org; PO Box 1466, Mesa 85211).

Gilbert (480-503-6871; TDD 480-503-6080; www.ci.gilbert.az.us; 50 E. Civic Center Dr., Gilbert 85296).

Chandler, city manager (480-782-2210; www.chandleraz.gov; 55 N. Arizona Place, Suite 301, Chandler 85225).

City of Glendale (main switchboard 623-930-2000; www.glendaleaz.com; 5850 W. Glendale Ave., Glendale 85301).

Surprise (623-583-1000; TTY 623-875-4208; www.surpriseaz.com; 12425 W. Bell Rd., Surprise 85374).

Peoria, City of Peoria Municipal Complex (623-773-7000; www.peoriaaz.com; 8401 W. Monroe St., Peoria 85345).

BANKS AND AUTOMATED TELLER MACHINES (ATMs)

As a major metropolitan city, Greater Phoenix supports major banking institutions including Chase Bank, Bank of America, and Wells Fargo. Finding an ATM machine is as easy as heading to the local 7 Eleven, Circle K, or gas station; most have ATM machines inside.

RECOMMENDED READING

Apache Junction and the Superstition Mountains highlights the mysterious Superstition Mountains and the city at its feet, including the legend of the Lost Dutchman Mine; it's by award-winning author Jane Eppinga, who has written multiple books about Arizona and its sometimes shady past. Other Eppinga books include *Arizona Sheriffs: Badges and Bad Men* (a historical look at the precarious balance of good and evil in the Wild West) and *Arizona Twilight Tales* (spook stories and haunting tales about our state).

Arizona's son and state historian Marshall Trimble takes readers through the history of Arizona from prehistoric tribes to statehood in *Arizona: A Cavalcade of History*. Other Trimble books include *Arizona Trivia* (tidbits about history, entertainment, geography, and sports) and *Arizoniana* (the history of "old Arizona").

The good, the bad, and the ugly are represented in *Arizona Politicians* by James W. Johnson and David Fitzsimmons, published in 2002. For a nonfiction murder mystery, check out *Trunk Murderess: Winnie Ruth Judd* by Phoenix journalist and author Jana Bommersbach, which recounts one of the most legendary crime sagas in Arizona history: Did Judd really murder her three friends and ship them off to California in a trunk?

As the fourth largest city in the state in one of the fastest-growing areas of the Valley, Glendale has risen to the challenge of becoming a mover and shaker—now home of the Phoenix Coyotes (NHL) and the Arizona Cardinals (NFL), Glendale will host the Super Bowl in 2008. Find out more about how this little city grew up in the historic account *Glendale* by Carol J. Coffelt St. Clair and Charles S. St. Clair.

Phoenix Then and Now by Paul Scharbach and John H. Akers is an amazing photographic journey through the yesteryears of Phoenix. Side by side sit then-and-now photos of some of the city's most famous sites, such as the San Carlos Hotel, the Heard Building, and the Orpheum Theatre.

Take the time to wander through the desert with *50 Hikes in Arizona*. Martin Tessmer presents a variety hikes, from the urban trails of Phoenix and Tucson to hikes through the Grand Canyon and everywhere in between. With an elevation range of 70 to 12,700 feet, the state has a lot to offer—pine forests, waterfalls, canyons, cacti, and snow!

Find the best fishing spots in the state, including highlights of Arizona's urban lakes, in G. J. Sagi's *Fishing Arizona*. You can also check out the *Game and Fish Water Maps*, which maps more than 700 sites including the Arizona Game & Fish Department's game water catchments, springs, potholes, seeps, and habitat enclosures.

Experience the essence of Arizona's past in the ghost towns and historical haunts that are quickly fading in the desert sun—*Ghost Towns and Historical Haunts of Arizona* by Thelma Heatwole can guide you. Or wander Arizona's hidden highways through the small towns, ghost towns, and the other spaces of the forgotten past along with *Hidden Highways in Arizona* by Richard Harris.

Take to the mountains on your bike. *Mountain Biking Phoenix* by Bruce Grubbs presents 35 of the area's best rides.

Arizona Curiosities (Quirky Characters, Roadside Oddities & Other Offbeat Stuff) is a recently updated book presenting the quirkier side of the Valentine State. Find silly facts and weird stuff in this funny look at Arizona by author Sam Lowe.

Arizona is considered one of the most pet-friendly states. Find out where to stay and what to do with your best friends in *Doin' Arizona with Your Pooch!* by Eileen Barish.

If you're moving to the Valley, consider the *Phoenix Relocation Guide*, published by the Phoenix Convention and Visitor's Bureau, or the *Insider's Guide to Phoenix*, 5th edition, written by Catherine Reynolds, Mary Paganelli Votto, and Sean McLachlan.

BEST BETS

If your time here is limited, don't miss out on these great places.

When in Phoenix, any of the area resorts will provide excellent accommodations, but those located in the Biltmore District stand out above the rest for their first-class service, elegant style, and individuality in making the desert part of their resort experience—specifically **Sanctuary on Camelback** (480-948-2100 or 800-245-2051; 5700 E. McDonald Dr., Paradise Valley) for its Asian-inspired tranquility; the **Royal Palms Resort and Spa** (602-840-3610 or 800-672-6011; www.royalpalmshotel.com; 5200 E. Camelback Rd., Phoenix) for its Old World ambience; the **Hermosa Inn** (602-955-8614 or 800-241-1210; www.hermosainn.com; 5532 N. Palo Cristi Rd., Scottsdale) for its cowboy charm; **Arizona Biltmore** (602-955-6600 or 800-950-2575; www.arizonabiltmore.com; 2400 E. Missouri Ave., Phoenix) for its historic glamour; and the **Camelback Inn** (480-948-1700 or 800-582-2169; www.camelbackspa.com; 5402 E. Lincoln Dr., Scottsdale) for its sophistication and class.

A delicious breakfast spread can be had at any of the five resorts listed above, but **La Grande Orange** serves breakfast desert-style, with the doors wide open, or on the patio beneath the mesquite and palo verde trees, with Camelback Mountain challenging you to an early-morning climb. Or you could breakfast at **My Florist Café**, followed by a leisurely drive through the surrounding historic districts—a Sunday-morning treat. For lunch, try the **Fry Bread House** (602-351-2345, 4140 N. 7th Ave., Phoenix) with its Native American fare, or the **Duck and Decanter** (602-266-6637; www.duckanddecanter.com; 1 N. Central Ave., Phoenix) for gourmet sandwiches. Dinnertime can mean Mexican cuisine at **Barrio Café** (602-636-0240; www.barriocafe.com; 2814 N. 16th St., Phoenix), or a taste of 1950s Phoenix at **Durant's** (602-264-5967; www.durantsfinefoods.com; 2611 N. Central Ave.,

Phoenix). There's also **Pizzeria Bianco** (602-258-8300; www.pizzeriabianco.com; 623 E. Adams St., Phoenix)—because you can't pass up world-renowned pizza made by a James Beard Best Chef: Southwest award winner!

As far as attractions go, don't miss the **Heard Museum** (602-252-8848; www.heard.org; 2301 N. Central Ave., Phoenix), a spectacular display of Native American arts and crafts; a stroll through the **Desert Botanical Garden** (480-941-1225; www.dbg.org; 1201 N. Galvin Pkwy., Phoenix); the **Phoenix Art Museum** (602-257-1222; www.phxart.org; 1625 N. Central Ave., Phoenix); or shoe shopping at **Biltmore Fashion Square** (602-955-8400; www.shopbiltmore.com; 2502 E. Camelback Rd., Phoenix). Since this is the desert, if you're here during winter months, a swim in one of the heated resort pools is very much in order. Don't miss a climb to the crest of Camelback Mountain or Squaw Peak, or a hike on one of the many paths through the South Mountain Preserve; the views are spectacular, and the relaxing feeling you get is invaluable.

A stay in the West Valley means a night at the **Glendale Gaslight Inn** (623-934-9119; www.glendalegaslightinn.com; 5747 W. Glendale Ave., Glendale) for its charm and proximity to all that Historic Old Town Glendale has to offer. Breakfast at **Bitzee-Mama's** (623-931-0562; www.historic-glendale.net/bitzee_mama's.htm; 7023 N. 58th Ave., Glendale) will make you feel like a native, as will lunch or dinner at **Pete's Fish & Chips** (623-937-6001; www.petesfishandchips.com; 5516 W. Glendale Ave., Glendale) or **Haus Murphy's** (623-939-2480; www.hausmurphys.com; 5739 W. Glendale Avenue, Glendale) for good German fare. For dinner, try **Arturo's Mexican Food Restaurant and Lounge** (623-932-0241; 13290 W. Van Buren, Goodyear) or the **Arizona Kitchen** at the Wigwam Resort (623-935-3811; www.wigwamresort.com; 300 Wigwam Blvd., Litchfield Park) for true southwestern-style cuisine. To cap off the night, have a glass of wine and an exquisite dessert at **Sweet O Wine and Chocolate Lounge** (623-877-3898; www.sweetlounge.com; 9380 W. Westgate Blvd., Suite D101, Glendale).

Don't miss a tour (or better yet, a game) at **University of Phoenix Stadium** (623-433-7165; www.azcardinalsstadium.com; 1 Cardinals Dr., Glendale); a simulated space mission at the **Challenger Space Center** (623-322-2001; www.azchallenger.org; 21170 N. 83rd Ave., Peoria); or tigers Raja and Nash at the **Wildlife World Zoo** (623-935-WILD; www.wildlifeworld.com; 16501 W. Northern Ave., Litchfield Park).

Scottsdale and East Valley visitors can stay at Camelback Inn bordering the Biltmore District; **Westin Kierland** (480-624-1000 or 800-WESTIN-1; www.kierlandresort.com; 6902 E. Greenway Pkwy., Scottsdale); or the Boulders Resort and Spa (480-488-9009 or 800-553-1717; www.theboulders.com; 34631 N. Tom Darlington Dr., Carefree) in Carefree. In Tempe look for **The Buttes** (602-225-9000 or 888-867-7492; www.marriott.com; 2000 Westcourt Way), which features spectacular views of the Valley, or **Tempe Mission Palms** (480-894-1400 or 800-547-8705; www.missionpalms.com; 60 E. 5th St.) located in the heart of Tempe's Mill Avenue District. The historic **Crowne Plaza San Marcos Golf Resort** (480-812-0900 or 800-528-8071; www.sanmarcosresort.com; 1 San Marcos Place) is on Chandler's town square.

Enjoy a hearty breakfast at **Crackers and Co. Café** (480-898-1717; www.crackersandcompanycafe.com; 535 W. Iron Ave., Mesa); a cup of coffee and live jazz at the **Gold Bar** 480-839-3082; www.goldbarespresso.com.; 3141 S. McClintock Dr.) in Tempe; or a gourmet omelet from **The Breakfast Club** in Scottsdale (480-222-2582; www.breakfastbar.com; 4400 N. Scottsdale Rd.). Lunch might be tacos at **Frank and Lupe's** (480-990-9844; 4121 N. Marshall Way, Scottsdale), or a burger at the **Blu Burger Grille** (480-948-3443;

Presidential Suite at Royal Palms Resort and Spa. Photo provided courtesy of Royal Palms Resort and Spa

www.bluburger.com; 15425 N. Scottsdale Rd.). Dinner options include an evening under twinkle lights at **House of Tricks** (480-968-1114; www.houseoftricks.com; 114 E. 7th St.) in Tempe; the landmark **Pink Pony Steakhouse** (480-945-6697; 3831 N. Scottsdale Rd.) in Scottsdale; and a delightful culinary experience infused with Native American flavors and desert foods at **Kai Restaurant** in Chandler (602-225-0100 or 888-218-8989; www.wild-horsepassresort.com; 5549 W. Wild Horse Pass Blvd.).

Don't miss browsing the shopping districts of downtown Scottsdale, or wandering through the Mill Avenue District in Tempe, down Main Street in Mesa, or around Chandler's town square. Catch a Broadway play at **Gammage Auditorium** (480-965-5062; www.asugammage.com; E. Apache Blvd. & S. Mill Ave., ASU campus, Tempe) and art at the **Mesa Arts Center** (480-644-6501; www.mesaartscenter.com; 1 E. Main St., Mesa) or the **Scottsdale Museum of Contemporary Art** (480-874-4666; www.smoca.org; 7380 E. 2nd St., Scottsdale).

Keep in mind that outdoor activities are don't-miss opportunities while in the Valley. Any number of executive courses can get you a quick game of golf before you jet off to your next engagement; relaxing beside a heated pool in February or hiking Camelback Mountain in December can rejuvenate your spirit before you head home. And spa treatments can fit neatly into any 2-hour slot.

CLIMATE, WEATHER, WHAT TO WEAR

The average temperature in the Valley of the Sun is about 85 degrees Fahrenheit, with the sun shining 300-plus days a year and rainfall averaging little more than 7.5 inches. Depending on the season, temperatures can range from 90 degrees during the day to 60 in the evenings. If you're planning activities that will have you outdoors a good part of the day, it is best to dress in layers. You'll find that you may need a sweatshirt during the cooler morning or evening, while shorts and a T-shirt may suffice during the hottest hours. If you're planning activities that will take you between indoors and outdoors, consider a light jacket or sweater that you can easily put on or take off and carry with you—even during the hottest months. The Valley may be one of the few places in the nation where you go *outside* to warm up; buildings keep the air-conditioning fairly high to combat the heat and the sun, so you may find yourself chilled indoors even if the temperature is over 100 outside.

The Valley has four seasons: spring (mid-Feb.–May 1); summer (May 1–mid-Sep.); fall (mid-Sep.–late Nov.); and winter (Dec.–mid-Feb.). Spring temperatures range from about 50 to 75 degrees—but it's been known to reach the high 80s and 90s here the closer it gets to May. The wonderful part is that once the sun sets, the temperatures drop to a more comfortable level and light jackets and slacks are often necessary. Summer in the Valley is broken into two mini seasons—dry and rainy. Both are hot, with temperatures over 100 most days and sometimes as high as 110 to 113. May and June tend to be drier, while July, August, and even September are muggier and wetter as thunderstorms sweep through the Valley. Sleeveless shirts, shorts, sandals, and lots of sunscreen are recommended, as are hats and sunglasses during the summer months (sunscreen, hats, and sunglasses are useful in warding off sunburn and headaches all year). Find a pool and get in, but remember to drink lots of water at this time of year—you may not notice that you're sweating, but you are. Temperatures start dropping in late September when the nights begin to cool off; as October approaches, the days do, too. Much of September has temperatures close to 100 degrees; in October, however, you'll find them closer to 80 and 90, with the evenings dropping to around 60 or 70. November drops to the 70s during the day and the 50s in the evenings. Winter is by far the coolest time of the year; though temperatures rarely drop below freezing even at night; still, it can and does happen. January and February tend to be rainy and cool. However, the days are often pleasant with temperatures hovering in the 60s; evenings can fall to as low as the low 40s.

But It's a Dry Heat

The "dry heat" people think about when they think *Phoenix* is not altogether a myth. Low humidity make higher temperatures more comfortable; 80-degree weather here may not even be noticeably warm. The mugginess often associated with summers in the Midwest and Southeast only arises during the wet months of July and August, when torrential rains can drench the Valley on a moment's notice. Temperatures in June, July, August, and even

September are still very hot; it is not uncommon for the Valley to experience an average of almost 90 days of 100-plus-degree temperatures each summer.

Water

Common signs that your body may be overheating include nausea, vomiting, headaches, fatigue, weakness, and mental fuzziness. The best way to combat heat illness is to proactively drink lots of water. And just when you think you've had enough, drink some more. It is not uncommon to see locals carrying water bottles wherever they go. Even during the cooler months, you will need to drink more water than usual—especially if you're exercising. It bears repeating: You may not notice that you're sweating, but you are. That gritty feeling on your skin after prolonged exposure to the heat is the salt left over after your sweat has evaporated. Paying attention to your body and its warning signs is key to enjoying your stay in the desert.

Sun Protection

Keep in mind that even in cooler months the sun is bright, and sunscreen, hats, and sunglasses are useful in preventing sunburn and headaches, which can ruin the rest of your vacation. Reapply sunscreen as directed.

For more information about the weather in the Valley, call the National Weather Service forecast office at 602-275-0073 or visit www.wrh.noaa.gov/Phoenix.

TOURIST INFORMATION & ONLINE ADDRESSES BY CITY

Arizona Office of Tourism (602-364-3700; www.azot.com; 1110 W. Washington, Suite 155, Phoenix 85007).

PHOENIX

Downtown Phoenix Visitor Information Center (602-254-6500 or 877-CALL-PHX; www.visitphoenix.com; 50 N. 2nd S., Phoenix 85004). At 2nd and Adams Sts. Open Mon.–Fri. 8 AM–5 PM.

Biltmore Visitor Information Center (www.visitphoenix.com; 2404 E. Camelback Rd., #100E, Phoenix 85016). Located between Macy's and MAC at the northeast corner of 24th St. and Camelback Rd.

SCOTTSDALE

Scottsdale Convention and Visitors Bureau (480-421-1004; www.scottsdalecvb.com; 4343 N. Scottsdale Rd., Suite 170, Scottsdale 85251).

Concierge Desk at Scottsdale Fashion Square, Information Center (480-941-2140; 7014 E. Camelback Rd., Scottsdale 85251-1234).

FOUNTAIN HILLS

Fountain Hills Chamber of Commerce (480-837-1654; www.fountainhillschamber.com; 16837 E. Palisades Blvd., Fountain Hills 85268).

CAREFREE & CAVE CREEK

Carefree/Cave Creek Chamber of Commerce (480-488-3381; www.carefreecavecreek.org; 748 Easy St., Suite 9, Carefree 85377).

Tempe

Tempe Convention & Visitors Bureau (480-894-8158; www.tempecvb.com; 51 W. 3rd St., Suite 105, Tempe 85281).

Arizona Mills Mall (480-491-7300; 5000 Arizona Mills Circle, Tempe).

Tempe Chamber of Commerce, Information Center (480-967-7891; www.tempechamber .org; 909 E. Apache Blvd., Tempe 85285-8500).

ASU Visitor Center, Information Center (480-965-0100; www.asu.edu/ia/visitor; 826 E. Apache Blvd., Tempe 85285).

Mesa

Mesa Convention and Visitors Bureau (480-827-4700; www.mesacvb.com; 120 N. Center, Mesa 85201).

Chandler

Chandler Office of Tourism (480-782-3037; www.visitchandler.com; 215 E. Buffalo St., Chandler 85225).

Chandler Fashion Center, a division of Chandler Visitors Center (480-857-8609; 3111 W. Chandler Blvd., Chandler 85226).

Chandler Chamber of Commerce, Information Center (480-963-4571; www.chandler chamber.com; 25 S. Arizona Place, Suite 201, Chandler 85225).

Gilbert

Gilbert Chamber of Commerce (480-892-0056; www.gilbertaz.com; 119 N. Gilbert Rd., Suite 101, Gilbert 85299-0527).

Apache Junction

Apache Junction Chamber of Commerce (480-982-3141; www.apachejunctioncoc.com; 567 W. Apache Trail, Apache Junction 85220).

Northwest Valley Chamber of Commerce (623-583-0692; www.northwestvalley.com; 12801 W. Bell Rd., Suite 14, Surprise 85374).

Glendale

Glendale Office of Tourism & Visitor Center (623-930-4500; www.visitglendale.com; 5800 W. Glenn Dr., Suite 140, Glendale 85301).

Glendale Chamber of Commerce, Information Center (623-937-4754; www.glendaleaz chamber.org; 7105 N. 59th Ave., Glendale 85311).

Peoria

Peoria Chamber of Commerce (623-979-3601; www.peoriachamber.com; 1061 N. 83rd Dr., Peoria 85345).

Sun City

Sun City Visitor Center (623-997-5000; www.suncityaz.org; 16824 N. 99th Ave., Sun City 85351).

Seasonal Events

For more events, visit the Side Trips chapter for central and southern Arizona. You will also find events listed and mentioned in the regional chapters.

January

WORLD'S GREATEST COLLECTOR CAR AUCTION

480-421-6694.
www.barrett-jackson.com.
Mid-January, Scottsdale.

Barrett-Jackson—provider of products and services to classic and collector car owners and enthusiasts around the world—hosts the 9-day "World's Greatest Collector Car Auction." Going on almost 40 years, this auction has drawn bidders from all 50 states and across the globe; more than 250,000 people show up annually to catch the latest trends in collector cars and to see what's on the block. Top sellers have included "Carroll Shelby's Personal Supersnake"—a 1966 Shelby Cobra 427—for $5.5 million, and a 1954 Dodge Firearrow II Convertible Concept Car for $1.1 million. In 2008 the auction will take place January 12–20 at WestWorld of Scottsdale.

FBR OPEN

602-870-0163.
www.fbropen.com.
Late January–early February, Scottsdale.

"The Greatest Show on Grass," also known as the FBR Open and previously known as the Phoenix Open, may be one of the best-loved and rowdiest PGA events around. Held on TPC's stadium golf course in Scottsdale, the weeklong Open draws more than half a million visitors and some of the sport's greatest golfers. Event dates in 2008 are January 28–February 3.

MUSIC IN THE GARDEN WINTER CONCERT SERIES

480-941-1225.
www.dbg.org.
January–early March, Phoenix.
Admission: $10 members, $16 nonmembers, $8 ages 3–12; free for ages 2 and under.

Local jazz favorites play Sunday noon–2 PM at Desert Botanical Garden January through early March. The fee includes admission to the garden, but food, cash bar, and wine tasting are additional. Food orders must be placed in advance with Fabulous Food Catering (www.fabulousfood.net). It is recommended that you order tickets in advance. There is also a spring concert series mid-March through June on Friday evenings 7 PM–9 PM (March–May) and 7:30 PM–9:30 PM (June).

February

SUPER BOWL XLII, 2008

www.azsuperbowl.com.
February 3, 2008, Glendale.

In 2008 Glendale—new home of the Arizona Cardinals and University of Phoenix Stadium—will host the XLII Super Bowl. Expected to draw an additional 120,000 people to the Valley the same weekend as the FBR Open, the Super Bowl will shine the spotlight on Glendale and the West Valley.

ARIZONA RENAISSANCE FESTIVAL & ARTISAN MARKETPLACE

520-463-2700.
www.royalfaires.com/Arizona.
Early February–early April, Apache Junction.
Admission: About $20 adults, $18 seniors, $8 ages 5–12.

The Arizona Renaissance Festival, one of the country's largest Renaissance events, is a 2-month celebration of the Renaissance period with jousting, an outdoor circus, arts and crafts, and period dress, games, and food. Open daily 10 AM–6 PM.

ANNUAL WORLD CHAMPIONSHIP HOOP DANCE CONTEST

Heard Museum 602-252-8848.
www.heard.org.

Early February, Phoenix.
Admission: $10 adults, $9 seniors 65-plus, $3 ages 4–12; children under 4 are free.

This 2-day event celebrates the precision and grace of Native American hoop dancers from the United States and Canada. The World Championship Hoop Dance Contest is held on the grounds of the Heard Museum's Phoenix location; ticket prices include museum admission, and visitors can sample Native American foods and watch the dancers perform. Dates for 2008 are February 9–10, 10 AM–5 PM.

March

ARIZONA RENAISSANCE FESTIVAL & ARTISAN MARKETPLACE
This festival continues through March (see February, above).

THE ANNUAL HEARD MUSEUM GUILD INDIAN FAIR & MARKET
Heard Museum 602-252-8848.
www.heard.org.
March, Phoenix.

This fair, which will celebrate its 50th year in 2008, brings together more than 600 of the best American Indian artists and their works, including jewelry, sculptures, pottery, beadwork, baskets, paintings, and more. Visitors can also enjoy music, performances, and food. Admission prices include entrance to the museum.

ANNUAL SPRING PAINT OUT
480-941-1225.
www.dbg.org.
March, Phoenix.

Watch as some of the Valley's best landscape artists secure their niche on site at the Desert Botanical Garden every Saturday in March and paint the desert in full spring regalia. The Annual Spring Paint Out is followed by an art show and sale the last weekend of the month.

SPRING BUTTERFLY EXHIBIT
480-941-1225 or visit online at www.dbg.org.
Early March–mid-May, Phoenix

The butterfly exhibit at the Marshall Butterfly Pavilion, Desert Botanical Garden, is a magnificent display of nature's splendor that extends more than 2 months.

TEMPE SPRING FESTIVAL OF THE ARTS
480-967-4877.
www.tempefestivalofthearts.com.
Late March–early April, Tempe.
Admission: Free.

This annual festival, held in conjunction with the Circle K Tempe Music Festival (the largest music festival in Arizona), draws a quarter of a million people over the course of 3 days. Held Friday, Saturday, and Sunday on Mill Avenue in Tempe, more than 350 fine artists and craftspeople host stalls featuring original works of pottery, paintings, sculptures, apparel, home decor, soaps, candles, and more; recent additions include an appearance by Arizona wineries. Guests can enjoy music, street entertainers or "buskers," and food.

CIRCLE K TEMPE MUSIC FESTIVAL
480-663-0700.
www.tempemusicfestival.com.
Late March–early April, Tempe.
Admission: $25–125.

Held in conjunction with the Spring Festival of Arts on Saturday and Sunday, the largest music festival in Arizona features music from national, regional, and local talent and draws better than 25,000 people. National talent has included the Fray, Gin Blossoms, and Cowboy Mouth; local bands have included favorites such as the James Kole Band.

LITCHFIELD PARK ART & CULINARY FESTIVAL
623-935-9040.

www.litchfield-park.org.
Late March or early April, Litchfield Park.
Admission: Free.

This annual event is one of the largest festivals in the West Valley, with over 140 booths featuring original works of arts and crafts. The festival also highlights wine tastings and culinary demonstrations from some of the Valley's best chefs. Admission is free, but there is a small fee for entry into the Wine Garden and Culinary Tent. The event typically runs Saturday and Sunday 10 AM–5 PM.

JAZZ IN THE GARDEN
SPRING CONCERT SERIES
480-941-1225.
www.dbg.org.
March–June, Phoenix.
Admission: $14 members, $20 nonmembers.

Enjoy the music of local favorites each Friday night March through June at Desert Botanical Garden. Guests can simply enjoy the music or have dinner, too (provided by Fabulous Food Catering—additional charges apply, and ordering must be done in advance at www.fabulousfood.net). Guests must be 21 or older to attend. Tickets tend to go fast; for more information or to order tickets in advance, contact the Desert Botanical Garden. In March, April, and May the concerts run 7–9 PM; in June, 7:30–9:30 PM. There is also a Winter Concert Series January through early March, Sunday noon–2 PM.

April

SPRING BUTTERFLY EXHIBIT
The exhibit continues at the Desert Botanical Garden (see March, above).

FORKS AND CORKS
Arizona Hotel & Lodging Association 602-604-0729.

www.forksandcorks.org.
Early April, Phoenix.

This 21-years-and-over annual event features some of the state's top chefs from Arizona's finest restaurants; it's hosted jointly by the Arizona Hotel & Lodging Association and the Restaurant Education Foundation.

SCOTTSDALE CULINARY FESTIVAL
480-945-7193.
www.scottsdaleculinaryfestival.org.
Mid-April, Scottsdale.

Founded in 1992 by the Scottsdale League of the Arts, this annual event has contributed more than $2 million to art and art education throughout the Valley. It lasts a week, usually in mid-April, and offers the best of the best in food, drink, and entertainment. There's a culinary student and hall of fame awards dinner, a black-tie progressive dinner, a reserve wine tasting, cooking demonstrations by nationally recognized chefs, and a 2-day picnic hosted by some of the best restaurants and entertainers in the Valley. It draws over 40,000 visitors a year.

MARICOPA COUNTY FAIR
602-252-0717.
www.maricopacountyfair.org.
Phoenix.

Five days of cotton candy, treacherous carnival rides, and great country music are found annually at the county fairgrounds in central Phoenix.

GLENDALE JAZZ & BLUES FESTIVAL
Office of Special Events 623-930-2299.
www.glendaleaz.org
Glendale.
Admission: Free.

A free 2-day annual celebration of jazz and blues in Historic Downtown Glendale.

NASCAR-BUSCH SERIES
www.phoenixraceway.com.

This race is held annually at Phoenix International Raceway; more information is available online.

May

QUEEN CREEK PEACH FESTIVAL

www.schnepffarms.com.
Queen Creek.

The annual 2-week-long Queen Creek Peach Festival held at Schnepf Farm features train rides, carousel rides, farm games, peach picking, and a country store with delicious homemade goods like peach pie and peach syrup. The peach festival always depends on the heartiness of the crop.

WYATT EARP DAYS

Tombstone Chamber of Commerce, 888-457-3291.
www.tombstone.org.
Late May, Tombstone.

In late May, Tombstone—"the town too tough to die"—celebrates the Old West. Costumed entertainers regale guests with tales and reenactments of a bygone era.

June

KIDSFAIRE

866-283-8600
www.thekidsfaire.com.
Early June, Glendale.

Held in early June at Cardinals Stadium, Kidsfaire celebrates children with fun activities, family booths, and entertainment.

July

GLENDALE'S HOMETOWN FOURTH OF JULY CELEBRATION

623-930-2299.
www.ci.glendale.az.us.

Bring your blankets and lawn chairs out to Glendale Community College for Glendale's Hometown Fourth of July. Cool off under the stars and the magnificent fireworks display; enjoy live music, kids' activities, and food and beverages.

October

RAINBOWS FESTIVAL

602-770-8241 or 602-770-8241.

Schnepf Farms—home of the peach festival.

Phoenix.
Admission: Free.

The Rainbows Festival, held annually in downtown Phoenix in Heritage Square Park, highlights the diversity of Phoenix. The 2-day event is free.

THE BEST OF THE WEST COWBOY ARTISTS OF AMERICA EXHIBITION AND SALE
Phoenix Art Museum 602-257-1222. www.phxart.org.

Held annually at the Phoenix Art Museum, this exhibition celebrates art and the cowboy life.

ANNUAL SCOTTSDALE INTERNATIONAL FILM FESTIVAL
www.scottsdalefilmfestival.com. Scottsdale.

The Annual Scottsdale International Film Festival held at Harkins Camelview 5 and Fashion Square 7 showcases great cinema and facilitates postfilm discussions with filmmakers and costume designers. The opportunity to roll out well-known films such as *Babel* (starring Brad Pitt) and *The Queen* (starring Helen Mirren) in 2006 prior to their release to the general public has put SIFF on the list of reputable film festivals.

WAY OUT WEST OKTOBERFEST
www.wowoktoberfest.com. Early October, Tempe Town Lake. Admission: Free.

The annual Way Out West October Fest is a family event started by the Tempe Sister City (TSC) organization in 1973 to honor Tempe's relationship with new sister city Regensberg, Germany (one of seven) in the style of the Old West. Jeans, cowboy boots, lederhosen, and flip-flops are welcome. Admission, kids' activities, and entertainment are all free. You can purchase tickets

for food and beer on site. Enjoy a tour of world beers, brats, and hot dogs, live music, performances from each of the sister cities, and arts and crafts. Funds raised from this event send teachers and high school students abroad each year.

ARIZONA STATE FAIR
www.azstatefair.com. Mid-October–early November (closed Monday).

The Arizona State Fair is more than 120 years old. Having started in 1884 as a small territorial event, it has since grown to attract hundreds of thousands of statewide visitors each year. Where else can you find a deep-fried Twinkie, rides that make your head spin, and great country music?

November

ARIZONA STATE FAIR
The state fair continues (see October, above).

NASCAR–CHECKER AUTO PARTS 500 WEEKEND
623-463-5400. www.phoenixraceway.com. Early November, Phoenix.

The NASCAR–Checker Auto Parts 500 Weekend is held annually at Phoenix International Raceway.

GLENDALE GLITTERS
623-930-2960. www.ci.glendale.az.us/events. November–early January, Historic Downtown Glendale.

The 2-day Glendale Glitters Spectacular Opening Weekend event kicks off the spectacular Glendale Glitters Holiday Light Display, which runs through the holiday season until early January, when it culminates with the Glendale Glitter and Glow event. Enjoy arts and crafts, food and festivities, horse-drawn carriage rides, and a visit with Santa, and see the one million multicolored lights that illuminate Glendale's 12-block historic downtown district. In early January the Glendale Glitter and Glow takes place at 59th and Glendale Aves. 5–10 PM. In addition to the all those lights, three dozen hot-air balloons illuminate the area for the last night of Glendale Glitters Holiday Light Display.

PHOENIX ZOOLIGHTS
www.phoenixzoo.org.
Thanksgiving–mid-January, Phoenix.

Named one of the top five kids' zoos in the country, Phoenix Zoo outdoes itself year after year with its holiday lights, music, and animals. Phoenix Zoolights—held from Thanksgiving until the Rock and Roll Marathon in mid-January—is an incredible display that overwhelms the senses and awes the imagination. For children of all ages.

ARTFEST OF SCOTTSDALE
www.888artfest.com.
480-968-5353.
Mid-November, Scottsdale.
Admission: Free.

The free annual ArtFest of Scottsdale on the Civic Center Plaza features more than 200 artists, musicians, restaurants, writers, and kids' crafts.

TEMPE FALL FESTIVAL OF THE ARTS
480-967-4877
www.tempefestivalofthearts.com.

Late November or early December, Tempe. Admission: Free.

This weekend-long fall festival is held Friday, Saturday, and Sunday on Mill Avenue. More than 350 fine artists and craftspeople host stalls featuring original works of pottery, paintings, sculptures, apparel, home decor, soaps, candles and more; recent additions include an appearance by Arizona wineries. Guests can enjoy music, street entertainers or "buskers," and food.

APS FANTASY OF LIGHTS OPENING NIGHT & PARADE
www.downtowntempe.com/fantasy-of-lights.asp
Saturday after Thanksgiving, Tempe. Admission: Free.

Enjoy the APS Fantasy of Lights Opening Night & Parade on Mill Avenue each year. The event starts the holiday season off with a tree-lighting ceremony, fireworks, and a visit from Santa Claus. The parade includes floats, marching bands, and decorated cars; afterward, guests can enjoy live entertainment throughout the Mill Avenue District.

December

GLENDALE GLITTERS
The holiday light display continues (see November, above).

PHOENIX ZOOLIGHTS
Phoenix Zoolights continues (see November, above).

General Index

A

A Touch of European Café, 174–75
AAA Cab, 35
Actors Theatre of Phoenix at Herberger
    Theater, 85
Adventures Out West, 90
Agave, the Arizona Spa, at the Westin Kier-
    land Resort, 247
airlines/airports, 32–34
Airport Ramada Limited, 58
Airport Sleep Inn by Choice Hotels, 58
AJI Spa, 247–48
Aj's, 149
AJ's Fine Foods: Glendale, 178; Phoenix,
    73–74
Alice Cooperstown, 61
Alltel Ice Den, 97
Alpha Cab, 35
Alvadora Spa, 248
Amara Resort and Spa, 195
Amazing Jake's, 98
Amtrak, 32
Anaheim Angels, 167
AndyFood, 128
Annual Folk Arts Fair, 228–29
Annual Heard Museum Guild Indian Fair &
    Market, The, 262
Annual Phippen Museum of Western Art
    Show & Sale, 228
Annual Prescott Bluegrass Festival, 229
Annual Scottsdale International Film Festi-
    val, 265
Annual Spring Paint Out, 262
Annual World Championship Hoop Dance
    Contest, 261–62
AOA Adventures, 92
Apache Lake Marina, 96
Apache Palms RV Park, 148
Apache Trail, 214

APS Fantasy of Lights Opening Night &
    Parade, 266
Arboretum at Flagstaff, The, 225
Arcadia Farms, 120–21
Arcadia Ice, 97
Arcosanti, 228
area codes, 253
Arizona Biltmore Golf Club, 233
Arizona Biltmore Resort & Spa, 55–56
Arizona Biltmore Spa, 248
Arizona Broadway Theatre, 183
Arizona Canal, 18, 91
Arizona Cardinals, 107, 187, 188
Arizona Center, 105–6
Arizona Climbing and Adventure School,
    101, 102
Arizona Diamondbacks, 22, 107, 224
Arizona Doll & Toy Museum, 78
Arizona Golf Association, 242
Arizona Golf Resort and Conference Center,
    143
Arizona Highways, 42
Arizona Historical Society-Pioneer
    Museum, 225–26
Arizona Kitchen (at Wigwam Resort),
    177
Arizona Limousines, 36
Arizona Opera Company, 85–86
Arizona Railway Museum, 99–100
Arizona Renaissance Festival & Artisan
    Marketplace, 261, 262
Arizona Science Center, 82–83
Arizona Shuttle, 30, 33
Arizona Snowbowl, 226
Arizona State Fair, 265
Arizona State Museum, 219–20
Arizona State University, 157–58
Arizona State University Art Museum at
    Nelson Fine Arts Center, 158–59

Arizona State University's Virginia G. Piper Center for Creative Writing, 157–58
Arizona Theatre Company, 86
Arizona Wing Commemorative Air Force Museum, 159
Art Studios at Mesa Arts Center, 158
Artfest of Scottsdale, 266
Artisan Hotel, 50
Arturo's Mexican Food Restaurant and Lounge, 177
ASU Athletics, 107
ASU Karsten Golf Course, 234
Asylum, 225
ATMs, 254
ATVing, 205
Augusta Ranch Golf Club, 234
Awesome Atom's Science Store, 100
Axis/Radius, 132
AZ on the Rocks, 97
AZ 88 from Tortilla Flat To Roosevelt Dam, 214
Aztec RV Resort, 148

B
Baldwin/Templeton/Cathedral Rock, 204
Ballet Arizona, 86–87
ballooning, 90
banks, 254
Bar Bianco, 64, 85
Barcelona North Scottsdale, 132
Barrio Café, 65
Bead Museum, The, 180
Bed & Breakfast Guild of Sedona, 194
Bell Rock Pathway, 204
best bets, 255–58
Best of the West Cowboy Artists of America Exhibition and Sale, The, 265
Best Western Arroyo Roble Hotel & Creekside Villas, 195
Best Western Bell Hotel, 52
Best Western Central Phoenix Inn, 50
Best Western Dobson Ranch Inn & Resort, 143
Best Western Inn of Sedona, 195
Best Western InnSuites Hotel Phoenix, 52
Best Western Mezona Inn, 144

Best Western Superstition Springs Inn & Suites, 144
Best Western Tempe by the Mall, 141
Big Bang, The, 162
Big Surf, 103
biking, 40, 92–93, 205
Biltmore District/Camelback Corridor, 45
Biltmore Fashion Park, 103–4
Bisbee, 218–19
Bison Witches, 149–50
Bistro @ Kokopelli Winery, 149
Bistro 24 (at the Ritz-Carlton), 67–68
Bit-Zee Mama's Restaurant, 175
Black Cow Café, 201
Blazin' M Ranch Western Dinner Theater, 225
Blu Burger Grille, 128
Blue Moon Café, 200
Blue Wasabi-DC Ranch, 132
boating, 95
Bommersbach, Jana, 23
Boulders Golf Club & Resort, 237
Boulders Resort & Golden Door Spa, The, 119
Boxers Men's Salon, LTD., 245
Breakfast Club, The, 128
Brett, Cori, 235
Brins Mesa Trail, 204
Brix, 227
Broadway Palm Dinner Theatre, 162–63
Bucky's Casino, 228
Budget Inn Motel, 48
buses: around the Valley, 34–35; to Phoenix, 30–32
Buttes, A Marriott Resort, 141
Byblos Restaurant, 150

C
Cactus League, 108–9, 137, 167, 189
Café Carumba, 121–23
Cafe Lalibela, 150–51
Caffe Boa, 151
Camelback Colonnade, 104
Camelback Inn, A JW Marriott Resort and Spa, 115
Camelback Mountain, 94
camping, 95–96, 205

canals, 91
canoeing, 103
Canyon Lake Marina and Campground, 96
Canyon Vistas RV Resort, 148
car rentals, 33, 39–40
Carefree, 113
Carefree Resort & Villas, 119–20
Carlsbad Tavern & Restaurant, 123
Carriage Manor RV Resort, 148
Casa Grande, 216–18
Casa Grande Ruins National Monument,
    217–18
Casa Grande Valley Historical Society &
    Museum, 216–17
Casino Arizona, 96
casinos, 96
Cattletrack Studios and Stables Galleria, 130
Cave Creek, 113
Cave Creek Regional Park, 96
Cave Creek Trailrides, 100
Celebraciones de la Gente, 227
Celebrity Theatre, 87
Centre for Well-Being at the Phoenician,
    The, 248–49
Cerreta Candy Company, 97–98
Challenger Space Center, 180–82
Chamber Music Sedona, 201
Chandler Municipal Airport, 34
Chandler Museum, 159–60
Chandler Public Library, 158
Chaparral Suites Resort Scottsdale, 115
Chase Field, 21
Checker Cab, 36
Cherry Lounge and Pit, The, 162
Chester's Harley Davidson, 40
Cheuvront Wine and Cheese Café, 72–73
Chicago Cubs, 167
Chicago White Sox, 224
Chop Shop, 84
Chuck E. Cheese, 98
Cibola Vista Resort & Spa, 172
Cinema Latino de Phoenix, 76
cinemas, 76, 129, 157, 179
Circle K Tempe Music Festival, 262
City Bakery at Bentley Projects, 61–62
Coach and Willie's, 62
Coconino National Forest, 226

Cofco Chinese Cultural Center, 104
Coffee Pot Restaurant, 200
Colangelo, Jerry, 22
Colorado Rockies, 224
Comedy Spot, The, 132
Comfort Inn: Chandler, 146; Fountain Hills,
    114
Comfort Inn & Suites at ASU, 141
Comfort Inn North, 52–53
Comfort Suites Airport, 143
Comfort Suites of Old Town Scottsdale, 115
Comfort Suites Peoria Sports Complex, 172
Compass Restaurant, The, 62
Consolidated Canal, 91
Copper Queen Mine Tours, 219
Copperwynd Resort and Club, 114–15
Coronado Café, 65–66
Cottage Place, 227
cotton, 20, 21–22
Coup des Tartes, 66–67
Courthouse Butte Loop, 204
Courtyard by Marriott Phoenix Mesa, 144
Courtyard by Marriott Scottsdale Mayo
    Clinic, 116
Courtyard Phoenix Airport, 58–59
Courtyard Phoenix Camelback, 56
Courtyard Phoenix North, 53
Courtyard Tempe Downtown, 141
Cowbow Ciao, 123
Cowboy Club Grille and Spirits, 198–99
Cracker Jax, 98
Crackers & Co. Café, 151
credit cards, 48, 61
Cricket Pavilion, 83–84
Crosscut Canal, 91
Crown Room, 132
Crowne Plaza Phoenix, 53
Crowne Plaza Phoenix-Airport, 59
Crowne Plaza San Marcos Country Club, 234
Crowne Plaza San Marcos Resort and Con-
    ference Center, 146–47
Cucina Rustica, 199
Cucina Tagliani Italian Kitchen, 175

D

Days Inn Scottsdale, 116
Days Inn-East Mesa, 144

Deer Valley Rock Art Center, 182
DeGrazia Gallery in the Sun, 221–23
Desert Botanical Garden, 76–77
Desert Breeze Park, 103
Desert Canyon Golf Club, 237
Desert Mirage Golf Course, 241
Desert Museum, 223
Desert Ridge Marketplace, 105
Desert Rose Limousine Service, 36
Desert Vista RV Resort, 148
Desert Voyagers Guided Raft Trips, 103
Detours of Arizona, 193, 217
Detours-Off the Beaten Path, 101–2
Devils Bridge, 204
Dillon's, 177
Discount Cab, 36
Dobson Ranch Golf Course, 234–35
Dodge Theatre, 87
Don & Charlie's Restaurant, 123
Donovan's Steak and Chop House, 68
Doubletree Guest Suites Phoenix-Gateway
    Center, 59
Doubletree Paradise Valley Resort, 116
Dove Valley Ranch Golf Club, 233
Downtown Phoenix Public Market, 73
Driver Provider, 36
driving: around Sedona, 193; around the
    Valley, 36–40, 41; HOV lanes, 39;
    mileage chart to Phoenix, 30; to
    Phoenix, 25–30
Duck and Decanter, 70–71
Durant's, 67
D'Vine Wine Bar & Bistro, 151–52

E

Eagle Rider Motorcycle Rentals, 40
Eagle View RV Resort, 148
Eagle's Nest Country Club at Pebble Creek
    Resort, 241
Eastern Canal, 91
Econo Lodge at AZ State University, 141–42
Eddie V's Edgewater Grille, 123–24
e4, 131
El Chorro Restaurant and Lodge, 68
El Zocalo Mexican Grille, 152
Embassy Suites Hotel, Phoenix-Scottsdale,
    A Golf Resort, 53–54

Embassy Suites Phoenix Airport-44th
    Street, 59
Embassy Suites Phoenix Biltmore, 56
Embassy Suites Phoenix/Tempe, 142
emergency phone numbers and contacts,
    252–53
Encanto Palmcroft Home Tour, 79
Enchantment Resort, 195–96
Enchantment's Yavapai Restaurant, 197
English Restaurant, 225
Epicurean Palette, The, 128
Espinel, Louisa Ronstadt, 23
Estrella Mountain Regional Park, 183–84
events, 202–3, 224, 227, 228–29, 260–66
ExecuCar/SuperShuttle, 36
Extended Stay America Phoenix-Midtown,
    50–51
Extended Stay Deluxe Phoenix-Scottsdale,
    116

F

Fairfield Inn, 147
Fairmont Scottsdale Princess, 116
Fango Hair & Day Spa Salon, 211–12
Farm at South Mountain, The, 69
Farm House Restaurant, 152
Farm Kitchen, The, 70
Farrelli's Cinema Supper Club, 129
FBR Open, 108, 261
Fiddlesticks, 99
Fiesta Inn Resort, 142
56 East Bar & Kitchen, 149
Firebird International Raceway, 17
fishing, 100–101
fitness centers/indoor gyms, 96–97
Fitness Works, 97
Flagstaff, 225–27
Foothills Golf Club, The, 233
Forks and Corks, 263
Fort McDowell, 18, 96
Fountain Hills, 113
Four Peaks Brewing Company, 152
Four Points Sheraton Phoenix Metrocenter,
    54
Four Seasons Resort Scottsdale at Troon
    North, 116–17
Frank and Lupe's, 124

Frank Lloyd Wright's Taliesin West, 130
Friday's Front Row Sports Grill, 62–63
Fry Bread House, 67
Fuchsia, 245
Furio, 133
Fusion Restaurant & Lounge, 124

G

Gainey Ranch Golf Club, 237–38
Gallery of Modern Masters, 201
Gallery on Oak Creek Restaurant, 197–98
Gammage Auditorium, 163
Garcia's Las Avenidas, 71–72
Gila River Indian Community, 17
Glen Lakes Golf Course, 241
Glendale and the West Valley: bakeries, 178;
    culture, 179–83; dining, 174–78; food
    purveyors, 178; golf, 241–42; health food
    stores, 178; lodging, 169–74; map, 170;
    overview, 168–69; recreation, 183–86;
    shopping, 186–87; spectator sports,
    187–89; wine bars, 178
Glendale Drive-In, 179
Glendale Gaslight Inn, 171, 175
Glendale Glitters, 265–66
Glendale Jazz & Blues Festival, 263
Glendale Municipal Airport, 34
Glendale Public Library, 180
Glendale's Hometown Fourth of July Cele-
    bration, 264
Gold Bar Espresso, 152–53
Gold Canyon Golf Resort, 143, 235
Gold Canyon RV & Golf Resort, 148
Golden Door Spa at the Boulders Resort,
    The, 249
golf: attire, 231–32; courses, 233–42;
    drinking water, 232–33; rentals, 231;
    special golf services, 242–43; sun pro-
    tection, 233; tee times, 232; weather, 232
Golf Club at Eagle Mountain, The, 238
Golf Couriers, 242
Golfland, 98–99
Grace Inn at Ahwatukee, 51
Grand Canal, 91
Grand Canyon, 227
Grayhawk Golf Club, 239
Greater Phoenix, 23

Greyhound Lines, Inc., 30–32
Grimaldi's Coal Brick-Oven Pizzeria,
    150
Guedo's Taco Shop, 152
guides and outfitters, 101–2

H

Haflett, Jeff, 217
Hall, Sharlot, 23
Hampton Inn & Suites, Goodyear, 173
Hampton Inn & Suites-Surprise, 172–73
Hampton Inn Phoenix Airport North, 59
Hampton Inn Phoenix/Midtown, 51
Hampton Inn-Sedona, 195
HandlebarJ Restaurant & Saloon, 124–25
Hard Rock Cafe, 63
Harrah's Ak-Chin Casino Resort, 96
Hart, Pearl, 23
Haus Murphy's, 175–76
Havana Café, 68
Hawthorn Suites, 147
Healing Arts Day Spa, The, 245
Heard Museum, Phoenix, 81
Heard Museum North Scottsdale, 131
Herberger Theater Center, 87–88
Hermosa Inn, 120
Hi-Health, 74, 178
hiking, 93–95, 203–4
Hillcrest Golf Club at Sun City West, 241–42
Hilton Garden Inn Phoenix Airport, 59
Hilton Garden Inn Phoenix/Avondale, 174
Hilton Garden Inn Phoenix/Midtown, 51
Hilton Phoenix Airport, 59–60
Hilton Phoenix East/Mesa, 144
Hilton Sedona Resort & Spa, 196
Hilton Suites Phoenix, 51
Historic Heritage Square/Heritage & Sci-
    ence Park, 77
Historic Old Town Scottsdale, 129–30
historic places and tours, 77–80, 179
history: the early people, 15–16; the land,
    14–15; modern Native Americans, 16–17;
    social history, 17–23
Holiday Inn at Ocotillo, 147–48
Holiday Inn Express Goodyear, 173
Holiday Inn Express Hotel & Suites Down-
    town Phoenix, 48

Holiday Inn Express Hotel & Suites Phoenix Airport, 60
Holiday Inn Hotel & Suites at Fountain Hills, 115
Holiday Inn Hotel and Suites, 144–45
Holiday Inn 51st Avenue, 171
Homewood Suites Hotel-Highland, 56
Hopi and Navajo Festivals of Arts and Culture, 227
horse racing, 107–8
horseback riding, 100
Hotel Valley HO, 117
House of Tricks Restaurant, 153–54
hunting, 100–101
Hyatt Regency Phoenix, 48–49
Hyatt Regency Scottsdale Resort & Spa at Gainey Ranch, 117–18

I

IMPROV, 162
In Celebration of Golf, 242–43
Indian Bend Wash, 19, 92
Indy Racing League, 107
Inn at Eagle Mountain, 115
Inn at 410 Bed and Breakfast, The, 226–27
InnSuites Hotel Tempe/Phoenix Airport, 142
Intercontinental Montelucia Resort & Spa, 55
International Gem & Mineral Show, 224

J

Jackson's on Third, 84–85
Jazz in the Garden Spring Concert Series, 263
JDR Tours, 243
Jeepers, 98
Jerome, 224–25
Jerome Grand Hotel, 225
Jim Thompson Trail, 204
Jobing.com Arena, 187–88
Joe's Real BBQ, 154
Johnny's Uptown Restaurant & Music Club, 85
Jordan Trail, 204
J's Integrative Therapies, 245
JW Marriott Desert Ridge Resort & Spa, Phoenix, 54

K

Kai Restaurant, 154–55
Kansas City Royals, 189
Katherine Roberts Yoga for Golfers, 243
kayaking, 103
Kazimierz World Wine Bar, 128
Ken's Creekside Restaurant, 198
kids' activities, 97–100
Kidsfaire, 264
Kiwanis Park Recreation Center, 98
Kokopelli Golf Course, 235–36
Kokopelli Suites, 195
Krazy Kyote Activities Tours, 212
Kyoto Japanese Restaurant, 125

L

La Fama Mexican Bakery, 178
LA Fitness, 97
La Grande Orange, 71
La Purisima Bakery, 178
La Quinta Inn & Suites Phoenix Mesa East, 145
La Quinta Inn & Suites Phoenix Mesa West, 145
Lake Pleasant Regional Park, 96, 184–85
Lamar Everyday Spa, The, 245
Las Sendas Golf Club, 236
L'Auberge de Sedona Resort, 196
L'Auberge Restaurant on Oak Creek, 198
Legacy Golf Resort, The, 51–52
Legend at Arrowhead, The, 242
Legend Trail Golf Club, 239
Leisure World Country Club, 236
libraries: Chandler, 158; Glendale, 180; Mesa, 158; Peoria, 180; Phoenix, 80–81; Scottsdale, 130; Surprise, 180; Tempe, 158
Library Bar and Grill, The, 162
Lifetime Fitness, 97
limo services, around the Valley, 36
Lindley Stadium, 20
Liquid Energy Day Spa, 245–46
Litchfield Park Art & Culinary Festival, 262–63
Longbow Golf Club, 236
Lon's at the Hermosa, 125–26
Los Abrigados Resort & Spa, 196

Lost Dutchman State Park, 96
Lozen (Apache warrior), 23
Luke Air Force Base, 21, 34
Luke Days Air Show, 34

M

Macalpine's Soda Fountain, 71
Maharaja Palace, 176
Majerle's Sports Grill, 84
Makutu's Island, 98
Malee's on Main Thai Bistro, 126
Mandala Tearoom & Apothecary, 246
Marcello's Pasta Grill, 155
Maricopa, 18
Maricopa County Fair, 263
Maricopa County Parks System, 95–96,
    100, 183
Maryvale Municipal Golf Course, 233–34
Maverick Helicopter Tours, 206
McCormick Ranch Golf Club, 239
McCormick-Stillman Railroad Park, 99
McDowell Mountain Regional Park, 96
McDuffy's Peoria, 177
MCTours LLC, 40
Mesa Arts Center, 163
Mesa Contemporary Arts at Mesa Arts Cen-
    ter, 160
Mesa Falcon Field, 34
Mesa Public Library, 158
Mesa Southwest Museum, 160
Metro Light Rail, 35
Mi Catering, 73
Mi Cocina, Mi Pais, 72
Mill Cue Club, 162
Millennium Resort-Scottsdale McCormick
    Ranch, 118
Milwaukee Brewers, 109
Mint Thai Café, 155
Montezuma Castle National Monument, 226
Monti's La Casa Vieja, 155
Morning Glory Café, 70
motorcycling, around the Valley, 40
Mountain Standard Time, 25
Movies in the Square, 227
museums: Apache Junction, 214–15; Casa
    Grande, 216–17; Chandler, 99–100,
    159–60; Flagstaff, 225–26; Glendale,
180, 182; Mesa, 159, 160; Peoria, 180–82;
    Phoenix, 81–83; Prescott, 228; Scotts-
    dale, 130–31; Sedona, 202; Surprise, 182;
    Tempe, 158–59, 160–61; Tuscon, 219–23
Music in the Garden Winter Concert Series,
    261
My Daddy's Bakery and Café, 178
My Florist Café, 71
Myst and the Ballroom, 131–32
Mystery Castle, 99

N

NASCAR, 107
NASCAR-Busch Series, 263–64
NASCAR-Checker Auto Parts 500 Weekend,
    265
National Forest Service, 204
National Trail, 93
Nello's, 150
New Year's Eve Pinecone Drop, 227
New York West Pastry and Bake Shop, 178
98 South Wine Bar & Kitchen, 149
Northern Arizona Book Festival, 227

O

Oak Creek Vineyards & Winery, 225
Oakland A's, 109
Oaxaca Restaurant & Rooftop Cantina, 200
Oceanside Ice Arena, 97
Ocotillo Golf Course, 236
Old Town Scottsdale, 46, 134–36
Open Road Tours, 101–2
Orange Table Café, 128
Orange Tree Golf & Conference Resort, 239
Orchards Bar and Grill, 200
Oregano's Pizza Bistro, 151
Organ Stop Pizza, 150
Orpheum Theatre, 78, 88
Out of Africa Wildlife Park, 206–7
outfitters, 101–2
Over the Rainbow, 90

P

Pacific Standard Time, 25
Page Springs Vineyard & Cellars, 225
Painted Mountain Golf Club, 236–37

Palace Restaurant and Saloon, The, 228
Palm Valley Golf Club, 242
Palo Verde Pizzeria, 177–78
Panaderia El Ranchito, 178
Pane Bianco, 67
Papago Park, 93
Paparazzini's, 155–56
Park Plaza Hotel, 54
Pasta Brioni's, 126–27
Paws Concierge, The, 61
Payson, 224
Pebblebrook Golf Course at Sun City West,
    242
Peoria Arizona Historical Society, 179
Peoria Public Library, 180
Peter Piper Pizza, 98
Peterson House Museum, 160–61
Pete's Fish & Chips, 176
Phippen Art Museum, 228
Phoenicia Grill, 156
Phoenician, The, 118, 239–40
Phoenix: caterers, 73; culture, 74–90;
    deli/gourmet shops, 73–74; dining,
    61–73; farmers markets, 73; golf,
    233–34; health food stores, 74; history,
    18–23; lodging, 48–61; map, 44; mileage
    chart, 30; nightlife, 84–85; overview,
    42–48; pets, 61; recreation, 90–103;
    shopping, 103–7; spas, 245, 248, 250–51;
    transportation to, 25–34; wine bars,
    72–73; wines & liquors, 74
Phoenix Airport Marriott, 60
Phoenix Art Museum, 81–82
Phoenix Coyotes, 107, 187
Phoenix Deer Valley Airport, 34
Phoenix First Friday Art Walk Downtown,
    80
Phoenix Goodyear Airport, 34
Phoenix History Museum, 82
Phoenix International Raceway, 187
Phoenix Marriott Mesa, 145–46
Phoenix Mercury, 107
Phoenix Public Library, 80–81
Phoenix Rock Gym, 97
Phoenix Sky Harbor International Airport,
    20, 32–33
Phoenix South Mountain Preserve, 93

Phoenix Suns, 107
Phoenix Symphony, The, 89
Phoenix Theatre, 89
Phoenix Zoo, 90
Phoenix Zoolights, 266
Piestewa Peak Park, 95
Pima Air and Space Museum, 220
Pink Jeep Tours, 206
Pink Pony Steakhouse, 127
Pinnacle Peak Park, 102
Pizzeria Bianco, 63–64, 150–51
Plein Air Festival, 202
Pointe Hilton Squaw Peak Resort, 54
Pointe Hilton Tapatio Cliffs Resort, 55
Pointe South Mountain Resort, 52
Pollack Tempe Cinemas, 157
Ponderosa Stables, 100
Praying Monk, 102
Prescott, 18, 227–29
Prescott Fine Arts Association, 228
Prescott Frontier Days & the World's Oldest
    Rodeo, 229
Private Preserve Golf Inc., 243
Professor Hall's Cinema Museum, 228
Pueblo Grande Museum, 82
Pure Fitness, 97

Q
Quality Inn & Suites at Talavi, 171
Quality Inn & Suites of the Sun Cities, 173
Quality Inn Airport, 143
Quality Inn-Glendale, 171
Queen Creek Peach Festival, 264
Quiessence, 69–70
Qwik Chinese, 128

R
Radisson Fort McDowell Resort & Casino,
    118
Radisson Hotel Phoenix Airport North,
    60–61
Radisson Hotel Phoenix/Chandler, 148
Radisson Poco Diablo Resort, 197
rafting, 103
Rainbows Festival, 264–65
Ranch House, The, 201
Rancho Manana Golf Club, 240

Raven Golf Club at South Mountain, The, 234
Raw Spirit Festival, 202–3
Rawhide Western Town, 17, 99
Reata Pass Steakhouse/Greasewood Flat, 127
recommended readings, 254–55
Red Door Spa at Wigwam Resort, 246
Red Rock State Park, 205
Renaissance Phoenix Glendale Hotel, 169–70
René at Tlaquepaque, 198
Residence Inn by Marriott, Mesa, 146
Residence Inn by Marriott Phoenix
    Goodyear, 173–74
Residence Inn by Marriott Phoenix
    NW/Glendale, 172
Residence Inn Phoenix Airport, 61
Retreat and Heal, 211
Revive Spa at the JW Marriott Resort, 250
Riazzi's Italian Garden, 156
Rinaldi's on Third, 156
Ritz-Carlton Phoenix, 56
Robert's Catering, 73
rock climbing, 102
Romeo's Euro Café, 156
Roosevelt Dam, 19–20
Rosati's, 150
Rosson House Museum, 77–78
Roughstock Rodeo, 228
Route 66 Days, 227
Royal Palms Resort and Spa, 56–57
Rula Bula Irish Pub & Restaurant, 156–57
RVs, 120, 148

S

Saguaro Lake Ranch, Inc., 96, 100
Saguaro National Park, 223
Sahuaro Ranch, 179
Salt Cellar, 127
Salt River Pima-Maricopa Indian Commu-
    nity, 17
Salt River Tubing & Recreation, Inc., 103
Sam's Café, 64–65
San Carlos Hotel, 49
San Diego Padres, 189
San Francisco Giants, 137
Sanctuary on Camelback Mountain Resort
    and Spa, 57
Sanctuary Spa, The, 250–51

Sandy's Dream Dolls, 100
Scottsdale: cooking schools, 128; culture,
    129–34; dining, 120–28; golf, 237–41;
    lodging, 114–20; map, 112; nightlife,
    131–34; overview, 111–13; shopping,
    134–37; spas, 245, 246–47, 248–49, 251;
    spectator sports, 137; wine bars and
    wineries, 128
Scottsdale Airport, 33–34
Scottsdale Artwalk, 129
Scottsdale Center for the Arts, 133
Scottsdale Culinary Festival, 263
Scottsdale Desert Stages Theatre, 134
Scottsdale Gallery Association, 131
Scottsdale Historical Society, 131
Scottsdale Limousine, 36
Scottsdale Museum of Contemporary Art, 131
Scottsdale Plaza Resort, 119
Scottsdale Public Library, 130
Scottsdale Resort & Conference Center, 119
Scottsdale Trailer Corral, 120
Scottsdale 6 Drive-In, 129
Seattle Mariners, 189
Sedona: culture, 201–3; dining, 197–201;
    golf, 212; important information,
    212–13; lodging, 194–97; map, 192;
    overview, 190–91; recreation, 203–7,
    212; shopping, 207–11; spas, 211–12;
    transportation around, 193; transporta-
    tion to, 191–93
Sedona Arts Center, 201–2
Sedona Arts Festival, 203
Sedona Heritage Museum, 202
Sedona International Film Festival, 203
Sedona Jazz on the Rocks Inc., 203
Sedona Phoenix Shuttle, 31
Sedona Raw Gourmet Café, 200–201
Sedona Road Runner, 193
Sedona Rouge Hotel & Spa, 197
Sedona Urgent Care, 212
Sedona Visual Artists Coalition, 202
Sedona's New Day Spa, 211
Seoul Jung Restaurant, 176
Sharlot Hall Museum, 228
Sheraton Crescent Hotel, 55
Sheraton Phoenix Downtown Hotel, 49
Sheraton Wild Horse Pass Resort & Spa, 148

shopping: antiques, 106–7; bookstores, 136; marketplaces, 209; New Age, 209–10; outlets, 106; shopping centers, malls and districts, 103–6, 134–35, 164–65, 186, 207–9; specialty stores, 106, 107, 136–37, 165–67, 186–87
shuttles, 193
Siamese Kitchen, 176
Siegel, Suzy R., 113
Skin Care by Klara, 246
Sky Mountain Limousine, 36
Slade, Jeff, 217
Slide Rock State Park, 205–6
Smoki Museum, 228
Snedigar Sportsplex, 102
Sonoran Motorcycle Rentals, Sales & Service, 40
South Canal, 91
South Gateway Visitor Center, 205
Southwest Chief, 32
Spa at Camelback Inn, A JW Marriott Resort & Spa, 251
Spa at Four Seasons Resort Scottsdale, 251
Spa at Gainey Village, The, 246
Spa du Soleil, 246
spas: age restrictions, 244; attire, 244; body treatments and services, 244; check-in, 243–44; day spas, 245–47; destination spas, 247–51; expectant mothers, 244; gratuities, 244; reservations, 243; tips and suggestions, 244
spectator sports, 107–9
Spicery, The, 176
sporting events, 107
sports complexes, 102–3
Sportsman's Fine Wine & Spirits, 74
Spring Butterfly Exhibit, 262, 263
Springhill Suites by Marriott Phoenix Glendale, 170–71
Springhill Suites by Marriott Phoenix Glendale/Peoria, 171–72
Springhill Suites Phoenix Downtown, 50
Sprouts Farmers Market, 74, 178
Starlight Limousines, 36
Starlight Pines Bed and Breakfast, 227
Steven Paul Salon & Spa, 246
Stockyards Restaurant & 1889 Saloon, 69

Stoudemire's Downtown, 65
Su Vino Winery, 128
Suede Euro-Asian Restaurant & Lounge, 133
Sugar Bowl Ice Cream Parlor & Restaurant, 128
Sugar Daddy's Blues, 133
sun protection, 259
Super Bowl XLII, 2008, 261
Super Shuttle, 33
Superstition Mountain Museum, 214–15
Superstition Wilderness Area, 215
Surprise Aquatic Center, 103, 186
Surprise Regional Library, 180
Sweet Basil Gourmetware & Cooking School, 128
Sweet O Wine and Chocolate Lounge, 178
Swilling Irrigation and Canal Company, 18
Szechuan Restaurant & Martini Bar, 200

T

Talking Stick Golf Club, 240
Tapino Kitchen & Wine Bar, 128
taxis, around the Valley, 35–36
Tempe and the East Valley: culture, 157–63; dining, 149–57; golf, 234–37; lodging, 139–48; map, 140; nightlife, 161–63; overview, 139; shopping, 163–67; spectator sports, 167
Tempe Beach Park, 92, 98
Tempe Bicycle, 93
Tempe Canal, 91
Tempe Fall Festival of the Arts, 266
Tempe Historical Museum, 161
Tempe Mission Palms Hotel & Conference Center, 142
Tempe Public Library, 158
Tempe Spring Festival of the Arts, 262
Tempe Town Lake, 103
Tender Loving Care Taxi, 36
Texas Eagle, 32
Texas Rangers, 189
That Thursday Thing in Glendale, 179–80
theater and stage, 85–90, 133–34, 162–63, 183
Thee Pitt's Again, 176
360 Adventures, 101, 102
Thunderbird Conservation Park, 185

Thursday Night Street Fair, 228
Titan Missile Museum, 220–21
Toka Sticks Golf Course, 237
Tonto Natural Bridge State Park, 224
Tony Hillerman Tour, 217
Tortilla Flat, 214
Tostitos Fiesta Bowl, 187
tourist information, 259–60
town governments, 253–54
TPC Scottsdale, 240
trails, multiuse, 91–92
trains, to Phoenix, 32
transportation: around Sedona, 193; around
    the Valley, 34–41; to Phoenix, 25–34; to
    Sedona, 191–93
Travelodge Suites, 146
Trilogy Golf Course, 237
Troon North Golf Club, 240–41
Tucson, 219–24
Tumbleweed Tennis Complex, 102
Turf Paradise, 107–8
24 Hour Fitness, 97
Twin Palms Hotel, 142–43

U
Uncorked! The Unpretentious Wine Bar,
    128
University of Phoenix Stadium, 188–89
Ussery Mountain Recreation Area, 96

V
Valley Limousine, 36
Valley Metro, 34–35
Valley of the Sun, 20, 22–23
Valley Youth Theatre, 89–90
Van Tours of Historic Bisbee & Surface
    Mines, 219
Verrado Grille, 174
VH Spa at Hotel Valley Ho, 247
Volume/Club 245, 84

W
walking tours, 41, 129, 179–80
water, drinking, 259
water parks, 103
Way Out West Oktoberfest, 265

Way West, 225
weather, 258–59
Weaver's Needle Travel Trailer Resort, 148
weddings, 113
West Canal, 91
West Valley Art Museum, 182
Westin Kierland Resort & Spa, 119, 241
White Tank Mountain Regional Park, 96, 185
White Tank Riding Stables, 100
Whiteman Hall at the Phoenix Art Museum,
    76
Wigwam Golf Resort & Spa, The, 174
Wild Horse Pass Resort and Spa, 17
Wildlife World Zoo, 182
Williams Air Force Base, 21, 34
Williams Gateway Airport, 34
Willo Home Tour, 79–80
Willow Stream, The Spa at the Fairmont
    Scottsdale Princess, 251
Wilson Mountain Trail, 204
Windemere Hotel and Conference Center,
    146
Windmill Inn Suites, 148
Windmill Suites at Sun City West, 173
Wingate Inn Phoenix, 50
World Famous Tucson Rodeo, 224
World's Greatest Collector Car Auction, 261
Wrigley Mansion Club, The, 78–79
Wyatt Earp Days, 264
Wyndham Phoenix Hotel, 50

X/Y/Z
Xeriscape Botanical Garden, 185

Yavapai Casino, 228
Yavapai College Gallery and Sculpture Gar-
    den, 228
Yavapai College Performance Hall and Arts
    Gallery, 228
Yavapai Downs, 228
Yellow Cab, 36

Zang Asian Bistro, 176–77
Zephyr Balloon, 90
zoos and wildlife, 90, 182, 206–7, 215

Lodging by Price and Location

Avondale
Starting at.........................$100-plus
Hilton Garden Inn Phoenix/Avondale, 174

Carefree
Starting at.........................$40-plus
Carefree Resort & Villas, 119–20
Starting at.........................$250-plus
Boulders Resort & Golden Door Spa,
The, 119

Chandler
Starting at.........................$40-plus
Comfort Inn, 146
Radisson Hotel Phoenix/Chandler, 148
Sheraton Wild Horse Pass Resort & Spa,
148
Starting at.........................$100-plus
Hawthorn Suites, 147
Holiday Inn at Ocotillo, 147–48
Starting at.........................$150-plus
Windmill Inn Suites, 148
Starting at.........................$200-plus
Crowne Plaza San Marcos Resort and
Conference Center, 146–47
Fairfield Inn, 147

Fountain Hills
Starting at.........................$100-plus
Holiday Inn & Suites at Fountain Hills, 115
Starting at.........................$200-plus
Inn at Eagle Mountain, 115
Starting at.........................$300-plus
Comfort Inn, 114
Call for rates
Copperwynd Resort and Club, 114–15

Glendale
Starting at.........................$40-plus

Quality Inn & Suites at Talavi, 171
Springhill Suites by Marriott Phoenix
Glendale/Peoria, 171–72
Starting at.........................$100-plus
Glendale Gaslight Inn, 171
Holiday Inn 51st Avenue, 171
Quality Inn-Glendale, 171

Gold Canyon
Starting at.........................$40-plus
Gold Canyon Golf Resort, 143

Goodyear
Starting at.........................$40-plus
Hampton Inn & Suites, 173
Holiday Inn Express Goodyear, 173
Starting at.........................$150-plus
Residence Inn by Marriott Phoenix
Goodyear, 173–74

Litchfield Park
Starting at.........................$150-plus
The Wigwam Golf Resort & Spa, 173–74

Mesa
Starting at.........................$40-plus
Arizona Golf Resort and Conference
Center, 143
Best Western Dobson Ranch Inn &
Resort, 143
Days Inn-East Mesa, 144
Holiday Inn Hotel and Suites, 144–45
Windemere Hotel and Conference Center, 146
Starting at.........................$100-plus
Best Western Mezona Inn, 144
Best Western Superstition Springs Inn &
Suites, 144
La Quinta Inn & Suites Phoenix Mesa

West, 145
Travelodge Suites, 146
Starting at.............................$150-plus
Hilton Phoenix East/Mesa, 144
La Quinta Inn & Suites Phoenix Mesa
   East, 145
Residence Inn by Marriott, 146
Starting at.............................$200-plus
Courtyard by Marriott Phoenix Mesa,
   144
Starting at..........................$250-plus
Phoenix Marriott Mesa, 145–46

Peoria
Starting at..........................$100-plus
Comfort Suites Peoria Sports Complex,
   172

Phoenix
Starting at..........................$40-plus
Airport Ramada Limited, 58
Airport Sleep Inn by Choice Hotels, 58
Best Western Central Phoenix Inn, 50
Best Western InnSuites Hotel Phoenix,
   52
Budget Inn Motel, 48
Comfort Inn North, 52–53
Courtyard Phoenix Camelback, 56
Crowne Plaza Phoenix, 53
Crowne Plaza Phoenix-Airport, 59
Embassy Suites Hotel, Phoenix-Scotts-
   dale, A Golf Resort, 53–54
Embassy Suites Phoenix Airport-44th
   Street, 59
Extended Stay America Phoenix-Mid-
   town, 50–51
Four Points Sheraton Phoenix Metro-
   center, 54
Grace Inn at Ahwatukee, 51
Hampton Inn Phoenix Airport North, 59
Hamton Inn Phoenix/Midtown, 51
Hilton Garden Inn Phoenix Airport, 59
Hilton Garden Inn Phoenix/Midtown, 51
Hilton Phoenix Airport, 59–60
Holiday Inn Express Hotel & Suites
   Phoenix Airport, 60

Homewood Suites Hotel-Highland, 56
Park Plaza Hotel, 54
Pointe Hilton Squaw Peak Resort, 54
Pointe Hilton Tapatio Cliffs Resort, 55
Radisson Hotel Phoenix Airport North,
   60–61
San Carlos Hotel, 49
Springhill Suites Phoenix Downtown, 50
Wingate Inn Phoenix, 50
Starting at..........................$100-plus
Artisan Hotel, 50
Best Western Bell Hotel, 52
Embassy Suites Phoenix Biltmore, 56
Hilton Suites Phoenix, 51
Holiday Inn Express Hotel & Suites
   Downtown Phoenix, 48
Phoenix Airport Marriott, 60
Residence Inn Phoenix Airport, 61
Sheraton Crescent Hotel, 55
Starting at..........................$150-plus
Doubletree Guest Suites Phoenix-Gate-
   way Center, 59
Hyatt Regency Phoenix, 48–49
Intercontinental Montelucia Resort &
   Spa, 55
JW Marriott Desert Ridge Resort & Spa,
   Phoenix, 54
Pointe South Mountain Resort, 52
Ritz-Carlton Phoenix, 56
Wyndham Phoenix Hotel, 50
Starting at..........................$200-plus
Courtyard Phoenix North, 53
Legacy Golf Resort, The, 51–52
Sanctuary on Camelback Mountain
   Resort and Spa, 57
Starting at..........................$250-plus
Arizona Biltmore Resort & Spa, 55–56
Courtyard Phoenix Airport, 58–59
Starting at..........................$350-plus
Royal Palms Resort and Spa, 56–57
Prices have not been set at this time
Sheraton Phoenix Downtown Hotel, 49

Scottsdale
Starting at..........................$40-plus
Scottsdale Plaza Resort, 119

Scottsdale Resort & Conference Center, 119

Starting at............................$100-plus
Extended Stay Deluxe Phoenix-Scotts-dale, 116
Millennium Resort-Scottsdale McCormick Ranch, 118

Starting at..........................$150-plus
Camelback Inn, A JW Marriott Resort and Spa, 115
Days Inn Scottsdale, 116
Hyatt Regency Scottsdale Resort & Spa at Gainey Ranch, 117–18
Phoenician, The, 118

Starting at..........................$200-plus
Courtyard by Marriott Scottsdale Mayo Clinic, 116

Starting at..........................$250-plus
Comfort Suites of Old Town Scottsdale, 115
Radisson Fort McDowell Resort & Casino, 118
Westin Kierland Resort & Spa, 119

Starting at..........................$300-plus
Doubletree Paradise Valley Resort, 116

Starting at..........................$500-plus
Fairmont Scottsdale Princess, 116
Four Seasons Resort Scottsdale at Troon North, 116–17
Hermosa Inn, 120

Call for rates
Chaparral Suites Resort Scottsdale, 115
Hotel Valley Ho, 117

Sedona
Starting at..........................$40-plus
Best Western Arroyo Roble Hotel & Creekside Villas, 195
Kokopelli Suites, 195

Starting at..........................$100-plus
Best Western Inn of Sedona, 195
Hampton Inn-Sedona, 195
Hilton Sedona Resort & Spa, 196
Radisson Poco Diablo Resort, 197
Sedona Rouge Hotel & Spa, 197

Starting at..........................$150-plus
Amara Resort & Spa, 195
L'Auberge Sedona Resort, 196

Starting at..........................$200-plus
Los Abrigados Resort & Spa, 196

Starting at..........................$350-plus
Enchantment Resort, 195–96

Surprise
Starting at..........................$40-plus
Quality Inn & Suites of the Sun Cities, 173
Windmill Suites at Sun City West, 173

Starting at..........................$100-plus
Hampton Inn & Suites-Surprise, 172–73

Tempe
Starting at..........................$40-plus
Econo Lodge at AZ State University, 141–42
Embassy Suites Phoenix/Tempe, 142
Fiesta Inn Resort, 142
InnSuites Hotel Tempe/Phoenix Airport, 142

Starting at..........................$100-plus
Best Western Tempe by the Mall, 141
Comfort Suites Airport, 143
Quality Inn Airport, 143

Starting at..........................$150-plus
Buttes, A Marriott Resort, 141
Comfort Inn & Suites at ASU, 141
Tempe Mission Palms Hotel & Conference Center, 142

Starting at..........................$250-plus
Courtyard Tempe Downtown, 141

Call for rates
Twin Palms Hotel, 142–43

Dining by Price and Location

Buckeye
Moderate-Expensive
Verrado Grille, 174

Chandler
Inexpensive
Guedo's Taco Shop, 152
Inexpensive-Moderate
El Zocalo Mexican Grille, 152
Moderate
Bistro @ Kokopelli Winery, 149
Moderate-Expensive
56 East Bar & Kitchen, 149
98 South Wine Bar & Kitchen, 149
Expensive
AJ's, 149
Very Expensive
Kai Restaurant, 154–55

Gilbert
Inexpensive
Farm House Restaurant, 152
Joe's Real BBQ, 154
Mint Thai Café, 155
Moderate
Romeo's Euro Café, 156

Glendale
Inexpensive
Bit-Zee Mama's Restaurant, 175
Maharaja Palace, 176
Pete's Fish & Chips, 176
Siamese Kitchen, 176
Spicery, The, 176
Inexpensive-Moderate
A Touch of European Café, 174–75
Thee Pitt's Again, 176
Zang Asian Bistro, 176–77

Moderate
Cucina Tagliani Italian Kitchen, 175
Glendale Gaslight Inn, 175
Haus Murphy's, 175–76
Moderate-Expensive
Seoul Jung Restaurant, 176

Goodyear
Inexpensive
Arturo's Mexican Food Restaurant and
Lounge, 177

Litchfield Park
Moderate-Very Expensive
Arizona Kitchen (at Wigwam Resort), 177

Mesa
Inexpensive
Crackers & Co. Café, 151
Moderate
D'Vine Wine Bar & Bistro, 151–52

Peoria
Inexpensive
McDuffy's Peoria, 177
Inexpensive-Moderate
Palo Verde Pizzeria, 177–78
Moderate
Dillon's, 177

Phoenix
Inexpensive
City Bakery at Bentley Projects, 61–62
Duck and Decanter, 70–71
Farm Kitchen, The, 70
Fry Bread House, 67
Mi Cocina, Mi Pais, 72
Pane Bianco, 67

Inexpensive-Moderate
La Grande Orange, 71
My Florist Café, 71
Inexpensive-Expensive
Coronado Café, 65–66
Moderate
Alice Cooperstown, 61
Bar Bianco, 64
Coach and Willie's, 62
Friday's Front Row Sports Grill, 62–63
Garcia's Las Avenidas, 71–72
Hard Rock Cafe, 63
Morning Glory Café, 70
Pizzeria Bianco, 63–64
Moderate-Expensive
Durant's, 67
Havana Café, 68
Sam's Café, 64–65
Stoudemire's Downtown, 65
Expensive
Barrio Café, 65
Bistro 24 (At the Ritz-Carlton), 67–68
Cheuvront Wine and Cheese Café, 72–73
Compass Restaurant, The, 62
Coup des Tartes, 66–67
Stockyards Restaurant & 1889 Saloon, 69
Expensive-Very Expensive
Donovan's Steak and Chop House, 68
El Chorro Restaurant and Lodge, 68
Quiessence, 69–70

Scottsdale
Inexpensive-Moderate
Frank and Lupe's, 124
Moderate
Arcadia Farms, 120–21
Café Carumba, 121–23
Carlsbad Tavern & Restaurant, 123
Malee's on Main Thai Bistro, 126
Pasta Brioni's, 126–27
Reata Pass Steakhouse/Greasewood Flat,
127

Moderate-Expensive
Fusion Restaurant & Lounge, 124
HandlebarJ Restaurant & Saloon, 124–25
Kyoto Japanese Restaurant, 125
Expensive
Don & Charlie's Restaurant, 123
Pink Pony Steakhouse, 127
Salt Cellar, 127
Expensive-Very Expensive
Cowbow Ciao, 123
Lon's at the Hermosa, 125–26
Very Expensive
Eddie V's Edgewater Grille, 123–24

Sedona
Inexpensive
Oaxaca Restaurant & Rooftop Cantina,
200
Inexpensive-Moderate
Orchards Bar and Grill, 200
Szechuan Restaurant & Martini Bar, 200
Moderate-Expensive
Cucina Rustica, 199
Expensive
Cowboy Club Grille and Spirirts, 198–99
Gallery on Oak Creek Restaurant,
197–98
Ken's Creekside Restaurant, 198
René at Tlaquepaque, 198
Expensive-Very Expensive
Enchantment's Yavapai Restaurant, 197
L'Auberge Restaurant on Oak Creek, 198

Tempe
Inexpensive
Bison Witches, 149–50
Four Peaks Brewing Company, 152
Gold Bar Espresso, 152–53
Phoenicia Grill, 156
Rinaldi's on Third, 156

Inexpensive-Moderate
Byblos Restaurant, 150
Cafe Lalibela, 150–51
Paparazzini's, 155–56
Riazzi's Italian Garden, 156
Rula Bula Irish Pub & Restaurant, 156–57
Moderate
Marcello's Pasta Grill, 155
Moderate-Expensive
Caffe Boa, 151
Monti's La Casa Vieja, 155
Expensive
House of Tricks Restaurant, 153–54

Dining by Cuisine

Buckeye
Eclectic
Verrado Grille, 174

Chandler
American/New American
56 East Bar & Kitchen, 149
98 South Wine Bar & Kitchen, 149
AJ's, 149
Kai Restaurant, 154–55
European
Bistro @ Kokopelli Winery, 149
Mexican
El Zocalo Mexican Grille, 152
Guedo's Taco Shop, 152
Native American
Kai Restaurant, 154–55

Gilbert
American/New American
Farm House Restaurant, 152
Mint Thai Café, 155
BBQ
Joe's Real BBQ, 154
Mediterranean
Romeo's Euro Café, 156

Glendale
American/New American
Bit-Zee Mama's Restaurant, 175
Glendale Gaslight Inn, 175
Spicery, The, 176
Thee Pitt's Again, 176
Asian
Zang Asian Bistro, 176–77
Eastern European
A Touch of European Café, 174–75
Fast Food
Pete's Fish & Chips, 176

German
Haus Murphy's, 175–76
Indian
Maharaja Palace, 176
Italian
Cucina Tagliani Italian Kitchen, 175
Korean
Seoul Jung Restaurant, 176
Mexican
Bit-Zee Mama's Restaurant, 175
Thai
Siamese Kitchen, 176

Goodyear
Mexican
Arturo's Mexican Food Restaurant and
Lounge, 177

Litchfield Park
Southwestern
Arizona Kitchen (at Wigwam Resort),
177

Mesa
American/New American
Crackers & Co. Café, 151
D'Vine Wine Bar & Bistro, 151–52
Italian and Pizza
Organ Stop Pizza, 150

Peoria
American/New American
McDuffy's Peoria, 177
Home-style
Dillon's, 177
Italian and Pizza
Palo Verde Pizzeria, 177–78

Phoenix

American/New American
Compass Restaurant, The, 62
Durant's, 67
El Chorro Restaurant and Lodge, 68
Farm Kitchen, The, 70
Friday's Front Row Sports Grill, 62–63
Hard Rock Cafe, 63
La Grande Orange, 71
Morning Glory Café, 70
My Florist Café, 71
Quiessence, 69–70
Stoudemire's Downtown, 65

Appetizers
Bar Bianco, 64

BBQ
Alice Cooperstown, 61

Cuban
Havana Café, 68

Deli
Duck and Decanter, 70–71

Eclectic
Cheuvront Wine and Cheese Café, 72–73

French
Bistro 24 (at the Ritz-Carlton), 67–68
Coup des Tartes, 66–67

Gourmet Comfort Food
Coronado Café, 65–66

Home-Style
Alice Cooperstown, 61

Italian and Pizza
Coach and Willie's, 62
Pizzeria Bianco, 63–64, 150

Latin American
Mi Cocina, Mi Pais, 72

Mexican
Barrio Café, 65
Garcia's Las Avenidas, 71–72

Native American
Fry Bread House, 67

Sandwiches and Salads
City Bakery at Bentley Projects, 61–62
Pane Bianco, 67

Soda Fountains
MacAlpine's Soda Fountain, 71

Southwestern
Sam's Café, 64–65

Steakhouses
Donovan's Steak and Chop House, 68
Stockyards Restaurant & 1889 Saloon, 69

Scottsdale

American Southwest
Arcadia Farms, 120–21
Café Carumba, 121–23

American/ New American
Cowboy Ciao, 123
Fusion Restaurant & Lounge, 124
Lon's at the Hermosa, 125–26

Italian and Pizza
Grimaldi's Coal Brick-Oven Pizzeria, 150
Pasta Brioni's, 126–27

Japanese
Kyoto Japanese Restaurant, 125

Mexican
Frank and Lupe's, 124

New Mexican
Carlsbad Tavern & Restaurant, 123

Seafood
Eddie V's Edgewater Grille, 123–24
Salt Cellar, 127

Steakhouses
Don & Charlie's Restaurant, 123
HandlebarJ Restaurant & Saloon, 124–25
Pink Pony Steakhouse, 127
Reata Pass Steakhouse/Greasewood Flat, 127

Thai
Malee's on Main Thai Bistro, 126

Sedona

American/New American
Enchantment's Yavapai Restaurant, 197
Gallery on Oak Creek Restaurant, 197–98
L'Auberge Restaurant on Oak Creek, 198
Orchards Bar and Grill, 200

Chinese/Japanese
Szechuan Restaurant & Martini Bar, 200

Continental
Ken's Creekside Restaurant, 198

French
René at Tlaquepaque, 198
Italian
Cucina Rustica, 199
Mexican
Oaxaca Restaurant & Rooftop Cantina,
200
Steakhouses
Cowboy Club Grille and Spirits, 198–99

Tempe
American/New American
Four Peaks Brewing Company, 152
House of Tricks Restaurant, 153–54
Coffee Bar
Gold Bar Espresso, 152–53
Deli
Bison Witches, 149–50
Rinaldi's on Third, 156
Ethiopian
Cafe Lalibela, 150–51
Greek
Phoenicia Grill, 156
Irish
Rula Bula Irish Pub & Restaurant,
156–57
Italian and Pizza
Caffe Boa, 151
Marcello's Pasta Grill, 155
Paparazzini's, 155–56
Riazzi's Italian Garden, 156
Rosati's, 150
Mediterranean
Byblos Restaurant, 150
Phoenicia Grill, 156
Middle Eastern
Byblos Restaurant, 150
Southwestern
House of Tricks Restaurant, 153–54
Steakhouses
Monti's La Casa Vieja, 155